MANUSCRIPTS

MANUSCRIPTS
The First Twenty Years

Priscilla S. Taylor, *Editor*

Herbert E. Klingelhofer,
Kenneth W. Rendell,
and John M. Taylor, *Coeditors*

Sponsored by The Manuscript Society

Greenwood Press
Westport, Connecticut • London, England

Library of Congress Cataloging in Publication Data

Main entry under title:

Manuscripts: the first twenty years.

1. Manuscripts—Collectors and collecting—United States—Addresses, essays, lectures. 2. Autographs—Collectors and collecting—United States—Addresses, essays, lectures. 3. United States—History—Manuscripts—Addresses, essays, lectures. I. Taylor, Priscilla S. II. Manuscript Society (U.S.)
Z109.M35 1984   091'.075   84-3846
ISBN 0-313-24281-X (lib. bdg.)

Library of Congress Catalog Card Number: 84-3846
ISBN: 0-313-24281-X

First published in 1984

Greenwood Press
A division of Congressional Information Service, Inc.
88 Post Road West, Westport, Connecticut 06881

Printed in the United States of America

10 9 8 7 6 5 4 3 2 1

Contents

Introduction

"A handful of sand," it has been said, "is an anthology of the universe." Conversely, however, no anthology--whether of the universe or of any part thereof--is a handful of sand. An anthology that is a collection of carefully selected articles and essays relating to the field of autographs and manuscripts is surely **multum in parvo,** for, like the library of Lucullus, it opens freely to the world the best that has been thought, said, and written on the subject.

The periodical from which the selections for **Manuscripts: The First Twenty Years** have been culled is the quarterly journal **Manuscripts,** organ of the Manuscript Society. The Manuscript Society was founded in 1948 as the National Society of Autograph Collectors; the periodical made its bow the same year as **The Autograph Collector's Journal.** Both the association and its quarterly are directed to a national audience--a varied membership united by an abiding interest in manuscripts. Collectors, dealers, librarians, archivists, and institutions are represented in a Society that "encourages the use of manuscripts for research," "facilitates the exchange of information and knowledge about manuscripts," and "fosters the preservation of manuscript material."

Those purposes the Society carries out in many ways: through annual meetings and auctions, television shows, newsletters, a research library, and the sponsorship of an extremely useful guidebook entitled **Autographs and Manuscripts: A Collector's Manual,** edited by Edmund Berkeley, Jr., with Herbert E. Klingelhofer and Kenneth W. Rendell (New York: Charles Scribner's Sons, 1978). Nowhere, however, are the Society's aims more effectively achieved than through its quarterly journal. There, for three and a half decades, have been recorded the adventures of collectors, the techniques of manuscript librarians, the philosophy and excitement of manuscript collecting, and the revealing place of the written word in history and in literature.

Now, from the first twenty years of that cornucopia has been selected a generous sampling of thought on the search for and amassing of manuscripts and autograph letters, and their role in the history of ideas. Here, in short, are the rich varieties of manuscript experience.

There is extraordinary topical variety in this anthology. The subjects range from the fellowship among collectors to methods of buying manuscripts at auction. Great collectors are covered, as well as the mysteries of price and the history of franking. From authenticating signatures to disposing of a collection at death, from the means of completing sets to the preservation of manuscripts, the selections run a wide gamut. The reader is even invited into that "vast terra incognita" where handwriting is shown to reflect character.

The delights of ephemera--from colonial currency to lottery tickets--are adumbrated. Calligraphy and writing systems are explored--the handwriting of Franklin, Washington, Lincoln. The stories of Robert E. Lee's Farewell Order and of the five manuscript copies of the Gettysburg Address are skillfully recounted. The exhilaration that accompanies the detective work involved in differentiating signatures or in searching out missing records, and the fascinations of code and cipher are zestfully conveyed.

Here too the collector is warned of the pitfalls of the adventure, including confused and mistaken identities as well as forgeries. And here for the scholar-collector are enormously useful lists, ranging from medieval monarchs and their autographs to a census of Arthur Middleton documents.

In the collecting areas discussed the variety is almost comparable, although, to be sure, the volume is weighted more heavily in history than in literature. In the field of American political history, contributors discuss colonial and Revolutionary rarities and books collected by presidents. From cabinet officers to Speakers of the House, from Signers of the Declaration of Independence to presidents themselves, American history has provided some of the most attractive and popular fields for manuscript collecting.

European political history is only slightly less popular, and the articles here that discuss the autographs of medieval kings, popes, and Holy Roman Emperors and the letters of signers of Israel's Declaration of Independence are sure to lure new collectors. Literature is not neglected. The signed literary editions of Rudyard Kipling are surveyed, and Swinburne and Melville are the subjects of fresh and informative investigation. The collecting of Gilbert and Sullivan autograph materials is described, and the letters of numerous composers are shown to reflect their hopes and despairs, their foibles and frailties.

Variety extends not only to subject and collecting area, but to attitude and approach. The **Manuscripts** anthology offers Gerald Carson's short and delicious advice on the etiquette of soliciting and supplying autograph signatures, and Lawrence S. Thompson's varied techniques for collecting source materials for a research library. Sharing the excitement of acquiring and working with holograph manuscripts, Lawrence Clark Powell transmits "the evocative power of handwriting." Personal anecdotes convey the thrill of the hunt; dispassionate scholarship assesses the find.

In a section of the anthology devoted to "Manuscripts as a Key to Biography and History," Broadus Mitchell asks: "How resurrect the dead?" In answer, he suggests: "The manuscript often offers what would seem to be beyond the possibility of recapture, the instant process of mind and purpose." Here are the instruments that dispel myths, necessitate new biographies, and cause episodes of our history to be rewritten. Opening windows upon the people who have guided or shaped our destinies, these essays sharpen our understanding of those who penned letters about themselves, their experiences, and their country. They demonstrate that personal papers may indeed offer clues to character, that contradictions exist between the public and the private man, that leaders and generals are but human beings, and that the testimony of a scrap of paper may be more revealing than the manifold evidence of a weighty tome.

And so, if the reader would know, for example, how a "diary-logbook" opened "an unknown chapter in our Civil War," where John Brown's letters may be found, or the identity of "the oldest genuine writing of a person of note," the answers lie within these pages. For the novice or expert collector, for the librarian and preserver, for the dealer in autograph materials, for scholar and historian, there are answers to many questions: What was the form of Napoleon's signatures? What were the fate and the significance of George Washington's discarded inaugural address? What signings had a bearing on Yorktown's "shining date with history"? What are the distinctions between signature and signum, sign manual and monogram?

The contributors to **Manuscripts: An Anthology** include some charter members of the Society whose names read like a rollcall of pioneers: Gordon T. Banks, Joseph E. Fields, Victor Hugo Paltsits, Forest H. Sweet, Justin G. Turner. The writers are as varied as their subjects. Like the Society of which they form a microcosm, they embrace collectors, dealers, and librarians, each group providing an expertise that informs and animates the whole. The articles were selected by Herbert E. Klingelhofer, Kenneth W. Rendell, and John M. Taylor.

The **Manuscripts** anthology has been skillfully edited by Priscilla Taylor, who has arranged, condensed, and, where possible, updated the articles, polishing their facets to attract the interest of a varied readership. The work reflects the productivity of a periodical's first two decades, and, with its apt illustrations, it does indeed recapture "the instant process of mind and purpose." No handful of sand, this compilation, but an anthology of the whole manuscripts universe whose fascinations abide here.

--Madeleine B. Stern
New York, September 1983

Glossary

AD   Autograph Document
ADS   Autograph Document Signed
AL   Autograph Letter
ALS   Autograph Letter Signed
AMs   Autograph Manuscript
AMsS   Autograph Manuscript Signed
AN   Autograph Note
ANS   Autograph Note Signed

DAB   Dictionary of American Biography
DNB   Dictionary of National Biography
DS   Document Signed

LS   Letter Signed

TLS   Typed Letter Signed

folio   A printer's sheet of paper folded once to make two leaves, double
            quarto size or larger

octavo (8vo)   A manuscript page about six by nine inches (originally
               determined by folding a printer's sheet of paper to form eight
               leaves)

quarto (4to)   A manuscript page of about nine and one-half by twelve inches
               (originally determined by folding a printer's sheet of paper
               twice to form four leaves)

Part 1.

POINTERS FOR THE COLLECTOR

The Proper Way*

Gerald Carson

Some modern autograph collectors may be surprised to learn that, in the opinion of past arbiters of **politesse**, their specialty has a definite affinity with such matters as how to bow to a lady whom you may know only slightly or only too well, how to drop a card upon a Washington hostess, or how to converse in a republican country. ("Never talk of ropes to a man whose father was hanged.") Nevertheless, the subject of gathering autographs from distinguished living persons does turn up in two manuals of decorum published nearly one hundred years ago. The inclusion of the topic suggests that the practice was widespread and that it had its problems.

In putting together a small collection of old etiquette books recently, I came first upon Florence Hartley's **The Ladies' Book of Etiquette and Manual of Politeness** (Boston, 1860). This is the short title. In the fashion of the time, the title page is practically a table of contents.

"Autograph letters," says Mrs. Hartley, meaning letters responding to a request, "should be very short; merely acknowledging the compliment paid by the request for the signature, and a few words expressing the pleasure you feel in granting the favor." The advice to the autograph seeker is as follows: "If you write to ask for an autograph, always inclose a postage stamp for the answer. Date every letter . . . and avoid postscripts."

Cecil B. Hartley--both the Hartleys were authors--wrote **The Gentleman's Book of Etiquette and Manual of Politeness** (Boston, 1860). He offers similar advice, spelling it out in somewhat more detail and starting with the letter of request. "Always enclose a postage stamp," he says first, and continues, "In such a letter some . . . compliment, expressive of the value of the name for which you ask, is in good taste. You may refer to the deeds or celebrity which have made the name so desirable, and also express your sense of the greatness of the favor, and the obligation the granting of it will confer."

Now, suppose you are a celebrity who has been asked politely for your signature. You feel moved to comply. Here is the way to go at the matter.

---

*Originally published in 1957.

"Autograph letters should be short," Cecil Hartley says in his book. The Hartleys see eye to eye on this and, indeed, express themselves in strikingly similar language.   Letters of response need contain "merely a few lines, thanking the person addressed for the compliment paid in requesting the signature, and expressive of the pleasure it gives you to comply with the request."

But what if you desire to refuse? Though Hartley will call you a "churl" for doing so, do not at least "fall into the error of an eccentric American whose high position in the army tempted a collector of autographs to request his signature." It seems the general wrote in reply:

Sir,

I'll be hanged if I send my autograph to anybody.

Yours,

_____ .

The Incurable Mania*

Lawrence S. Thompson

More than three-quarters of my life has been devoted off and on (mostly on) to collecting manuscripts and books. I must confess to some procedures that are not altogether scrupulous, but the final objectives are honorable ones.

My career as a collector had a shady origin. In the mid-1920s I had the dubious privilege of witnessing a grandiose Ku Klux Klan parade in Atlanta. The Imperial Wizard, a dentist known as Dr. Hiram Evans, was among the few unmasked representatives of Georgia aristocracy. I tore away from my adult escort and secured an autograph that I still preserve in the **enfer** of Biblioteca Thompsoniana: "Hiram Evans. To a son of our beloved Protestant South."

Two or three years later, the special campaign train of Alfred E. Smith pulled into the Union Depot of Raleigh, North Carolina, a sleepy southern community where I spent my first sixteen years. It was rumored that one car, to which there was no admittance for the public (undoubtedly Governor Smith's personal quarters), housed the staff of a special emissary from the Holy See, who was setting up a master plan to make a future satrapy of Dixie. But the "son of our beloved Protestant South" was undaunted and managed to secure Mr. Smith's signature on a bit of literature propagandizing the repeal of the Eighteenth Amendment. And a year or so later, the same little renegade Democrat, on a high school trip to Washington, stood upon the White House lawn for a group picture with Herbert Hoover.

The scope of my collecting has changed over the years, but not the basic logistics. Since 1954 I have made a strong effort to build a collection on integration and civil rights issues at the University of Kentucky, a most appropriate home for such a collection, since we did not secede until after Reconstruction was well under way. I am on the mailing list of every state sovereignty commission and every local citizens' council, and I have also managed to impress the NAACP and CORE that I must have their ephemera. I have arranged to secure clippings on our race problems from the major newspapers of Prague, Vienna, Moscow, Stockholm, and some other European capitals. Today, Kentucky holds a stately archive on the most inflammatory social issue of our day, an archive providing a perspective unknown to the agency in Nashville that is supported by millions from a foundation.

---

*Originally published in 1966.

Strict objectivity, total indifference to partisan issues on the site of collecting, and an unmitigated passion for identifying the truth are the hallmarks of the collector's trade. Like the Pythian Apollo at Delphi, the collector must endear himself and his purposes to the "haves," but he must also have the sympathy, the common sense, and the fundamental intellectual curiosity to identify the permanently valuable source materials.

In this short paper I propose to discuss a few devices I have used over the years for collecting source material, a handful of caveats for the embryonic institutional collector, and what I hope may be accepted as commonsense recommendations on interinstitutional relationships in the broad area of preserving source materials, especially manuscripts. I cannot emphasize too strongly that the activities from which this experience was gained were over and above a sixty- to eighty-hour week, that the main cost to the University of Kentucky was a little postage and Greyhound bus fare, and that any impecunious but aspiring research library can develop significant manuscript holdings in the same way.

Clues in the Library

Reading bibliographies and bibliographical literature should be the delicious vice of all scholarly librarians. Newsletters of research libraries are particularly rich guides to the acquisition of unusual and significant source material. In 1957 I noted a report from the Deutsche Staatsbibliothek (the modern torso of the old Royal Prussian Library) that it had received a dozen or so Tibetan xylographs from the Gosudarstvennaia Publichnaia Biblioteka M.N.R. (quondam im. I. V. Stalina). I decided that anything that could be acquired by the Royal Prussian Library--or whatever it is called now--should also be available to the University of Kentucky Library, and I promptly dispatched an airmail letter to Ulan Bator. I hardly expected a reply, certainly not within four or five months; but three weeks later I discovered I had broken the yurt curtain. Alert colleagues in rapidly developing Mongolia saw an opportunity to acquire Mongolica published in the West (periodical articles, newspaper clippings, and other ephemera dealing with Mongolia) and basic serials such as the Journal of the Royal Central Asian Society, the **Journal Asiatique,** and the **Zeitschrift der Deutschen Morgenländischen Gesellschaft,** all of which were generally unavailable to them.

Since 1957 there has been a steady flow of Mongolica from Lexington to Ulan Bator, and, vastly more important, the rise of a substantial collection of Tibetan xylographs and manuscripts in Lexington. Nobody in Fayette County, nor indeed in the wide expanse of Kentucky, can read the degenerate Devanagari chicken tracks on these xylographs. Fortunately, the University of Washington in Seattle produced a cataloguer in the person of a curious young graduate student, and his catalogue of the collection is forthcoming. Perhaps it will inspire the trustees of the University of Kentucky to establish an Institute of Tibetan Studies, much more urgently needed than the miscellaneous vocational schools with which nearly all tax-supported institutions burden themselves today.

Collections grow geometrically in an institution with imaginative leadership. The cataloguer who descended on us from the developing lands of the Pacific littoral provided a desiderata list for rounding out the little group of xylographs. Happily, an able geographer on the University of Kentucky staff was in Nepal and Bhutan at the time. In perfectly legal defiance of miscellaneous regulations of the Indian Ministry of Finance and the U.S. Commerce Department, the University of Kentucky managed to acquire at least two Tibetan texts unavailable outside Central Asia. Others will come later.

The history of religion in Kentucky is an essential element of the western tradition. Calvinists, Catholics, Campbellites, and others, even the Baptists and the Methodists, have had a basic role in the history of Kentucky. Over the past two decades I have made a strong effort to bring together in Lexington the key documents on the history of religion in Kentucky. We had a superlative start in the Samuel M. Wilson Library, which is one of the three best collections of books and manuscripts on the history of the Presbyterian Church in the United States (as well as of splinter groups north of the **belle rivière**). In the early 1950s we were able to photograph additional Presbyterian source materials, Shaker records from all over the Ohio Valley, and miscellaneous local records, from those of Reformed Jewish temples to Hardshell and Duck River Baptists and back again to Unitarians. Particularly fruitful in this area has been cooperation with the Genealogical Society of the Church of Jesus Christ of Latter Day Saints. This most comprehensive and perhaps most distinguished of all genealogical societies has undertaken the microfilm copying of all Kentucky public records (deed books, will books, order books, marriage bonds) through 1865, and has been generous enough to deposit a print in the University of Kentucky Library for our cooperation in establishing liaison with county authorities.

Honorary Degrees a Potent Incentive

A potent weapon in the hands of the academic collector is the honorary degree. It is not an honor to be given to every local tycoon who wants to set up a hundred-thousand-dollar foundation as a legal gimmick in his tax program. However, the honorary degree is a legitimate and proper honor for scholarly collectors (whether or not they have published original research), public figures whose official and private records contain significant material, and other persons of sufficient dignity and public prestige who can be benefactors. A college or university with a sound and consistent honorary degree policy need never fear accusations that it has prostituted itself in this area.

I must say that on the four occasions when I have been successful in proposing candidates for honorary degrees at the University of Kentucky, the institution has honored itself as well as the recipient by these awards, and the library has benefited substantially. Further, I have managed to restrict my formal proposals for honorary degrees to persons of unquestioned integrity.

Theft: The Ever-Present Threat

I must preface my discussion of the next channel of acquisition of research materials with a quotation from Catullus (**Carm.**, 68, 141): "Nec divis homines componier aequum est" (Nor is it fair to compare men with gods). Theft has been an eminently effective means of acquisition since the days of the earliest Alexandrians, but we are compelled to observe extreme discretion when we penetrate this delicate area. Even this author is not totally pure in heart in this respect, and he might be compelled to use a constitutional umbrella if he is questioned too closely.

Theft occurs mainly when the opportunity is thrust upon the potential biblio- or diplomaklept. The openings left by careless librarians and archivists are appalling. Some dozen years ago I was in a Kentucky county courthouse and happened to notice a perfect imprint of my Cat's Paw heel on a frayed and folded slip of paper on the floor. I picked it up, opened it, and beheld an autograph identical with one on a similar document that sold for $850 recently. To be quite certain that this precious document would be abused no further, I agreed with myself that the only honest decision would be to deposit it in the University of Kentucky Library for safekeeping. When and if there is proper archival management in the county concerned, this $850 document will be returned to the competent custodian.

But there are conscious and premeditated thefts from public archives. I could recite dozens of cases, but no specifics will pass my lips without a summons. Suffice it to say, our county archives in particular are chaotically organized, preserved, and serviced. There were records in Lincoln County-- one of the three original counties--which were filmed almost two decades ago by the University of Kentucky Library on a selective basis but which can no longer be located in the courthouse in Stanton. There is something rotten in Kentucky, at least as far as local archival management is concerned in most communities--and the same may be said of the vast majority of local jurisdictions in the other forty-nine states.

Solicitation

The conscientious collector of manuscripts for a research library must be prepared to bark up many a tree without squirrels. I have been summoned from one end of Kentucky to the other to pick up books and documents, sight unseen, and I have found it is always the best policy to go when called and to take everything to which no strings are attached and which is not nailed to the floor. On one occasion I was called to Bell County to pick up a "batch of family papers." I abandoned home and hearth and even a three-year-old daughter's birthday party to get myself thence, for the furniture was to be moved out the same day. I arrived as the Mayflower truck edged up to the back. It was the first time in my life I had ever been in a dead heat with a corpse. There were a couple of family Bibles (always instructive) and a handsome run of early Kentucky session laws useful for trading.

Once I was called to Harlan to pick up the original newspapers reporting the death of George Washington and the assassination of Abraham Lincoln "and other newspapers." The last three words saved me from the sassy reply no courteous bookman should give to the loving soul who has preserved the ubiquitous facsimiles. I filled the tank of my wheezing 1938 Chevrolet and started for the Cumberlands in a day long before our noble Eastern Kentucky Parkway had been built. After an exhausting fourteen-hour round trip through the most impressive hill country in America, I arrived back in Lexington with the two facsimiles plus some five hundred issues of otherwise unknown and unrecorded eastern Kentucky newspapers. That squirrelless tree can have some other varmints in its branches.

For fifteen years I roved Kentucky in search of manuscripts and printed books relating to our history, but it was a sideshow to the grueling routine of administration. Today the University of Kentucky has a full-time, energetic, imaginative, and extraordinarily effective field representative to follow up leads and develop new ones. It would be a reasonable policy for every research library with state or regional responsibilities to have a similar position. Far-sighted antiquarian booksellers have always had their book scouts, and there is every reason for research libraries to take many of their leaves from the books of the dealers. We must encourage imaginative bibliophilic nosiness if we are to support our researchers in the humanities and the social sciences in the manner to which they should be accustomed.

For almost two decades I tried to develop a collection of source materials and a research library of which our basketball team could be proud. Almost anyone with a little book-sense can purchase original collections or even order photographic copies if he is a little less particular. However, coherent, meaningful collections of regional historical and literary manuscripts can best be assembled by the old formulas prescribed by Lyman Draper over a century ago.

The same basic **modus operandi** applies to almost any area in the broad field of the humanities and social studies, but common sense must temper every project. Several years ago I conceived the notion of exhibiting sample manuscripts of modern poets along with their printed work as a suggestion to our readers that there was something to contemporary poetry after all. I selected more than a hundred poets who write in English and sent them letters (1) requesting them to give or lend us a manuscript appropriate for the show and (2) reminding them of the importance of selecting a depository for their correspondence and manuscripts, not necessarily in Lexington.

The results were singularly gratifying and instructive, and, **mutatis mutandis,** might be followed by other libraries. We acquired a representative selection of single manuscripts from most of the best poets of our day, along with a number of dedication copies (unsolicited, but welcome), all admirably suited for a continuing exhibit over a period of three years in a case set aside for this purpose. We uncovered five poets with affiliations to Kentucky and no other special loyalties, and their papers are now in Lexington or destined to come to us; we also discovered three poets with no institutional or regional loyalties whatsoever who have deposited or will deposit their papers in the

University of Kentucky. Perhaps most important of all, I was able to direct some thirty poets to deposit or plan to deposit their manuscripts and correspondence in an appropriate institution, either their alma mater or some other library or archive to which they had some allegiance. I assured them that if they were Kansans or Virginians their papers would be equally well cared for and perhaps better appreciated in Lawrence or Charlottesville than in Lexington. These chickens will come back to roost in a Kentucky bibliothecal barnyard some day, perhaps five, ten, or even twenty years from now, in the form of reciprocal courtesies from some other member of the great brotherhood of librarians. Common sense and a generous attitude toward other institutions should be ingrained in the collector. Both will pay off over the long haul.

One library with which Kentucky has had singularly cordial relations was able to direct to us the papers of a post-Civil War Kentucky governor. Another library that has swapped favors of all varieties with us placed on indefinite deposit in Lexington a handsome collection of papers on the textile industry in nineteenth-century Kentucky. Despite individual cases to the contrary, cutthroat rivalry has no place in the world of collecting. The world of the bookman must be one of mutual self-respect up and down the line-- among collectors, dealers, and librarians, and especially within each category. No collector should hesitate to use any reasonable device for acquisition--a little flattery, a little theft, and a little pandering with academic titles--if the final objectives of learning are thereby served. But there are limits beyond which no collector may go, and there are bonds of mutual interests which he must constantly strengthen. Those of us who are initiated have one purpose only beyond the material necessity of earning daily bread: dedicated service to learning. Without genuine devotion to this ideal we are only proud possessors.

The Power to Evoke*

Lawrence Clark Powell

"The power to evoke." What does it mean? In choosing this title I had in mind something quite personal, namely, that I find myself increasingly susceptible to the evocative power of handwriting, as compared with the power of print. For me, autograph manuscripts possess a power to evoke their authors and their times in a measure unmatched by any other form of communication. This paper is based on my experience as a bookman. As my life with books and manuscripts and their writers has widened and deepened, I have become increasingly watchful for and sensitive to signatures and annotations in books, to holograph letters and manuscript works, because of their power to summon images and memories, the very ambience of a time and a place.

I must confess to a prejudice against autograph collectors. The term evokes for me the image of a foxy fellow snipping the signatures from letters and throwing the rest away. Or of rampant bobby-soxers, rushing a crooner into a corner, in order to get his signature in their autograph albums. Or of myself as a boy, going with my father into the Chicago Cubs' dugout, accompanied by their owner, Albert Lasker, and emerging with an autograph baseball, signed by the entire team, including the famed Grover Cleveland Alexander! For months that ball stayed immaculate. Then I tentatively played a little catch with it, albeit with clean hands and gloves, until finally I could stand it no longer, and the once precious ball was batted into oblivion on the neighborhood sandlot. I have little patience with either collectors or libraries who look upon autograph manuscripts merely as museum pieces, to be stared at under glass and not actively used for study and research. Not that I believe in wearing our manuscripts to shreds! Controlled use, but use, is what I advocate.

That baseball was my first and only autograph signature collection. As one grows up, one puts away childish things--or should: cigar bands, bottle tops, matchbooks, stamps, and autograph signatures. I recognize a rising scale of values in collecting, from the primitive to the civilized, starting with shells and beads and culminating in manuscripts and books. And as people become more civilized, they seek more comprehensive and subtle manifestations of the creative impulse--books that reveal the vast range of human experience and manuscripts that are the earlier flower, books being the fruit.

---

*Originally published in 1953.

I was prejudiced at first against this society because of its misleading name, "National Society of Autograph Collectors," which evoked for me the vision of a band of adolescent vandals or worse. And then I met Justin Turner, our dynamic president, to whom manuscripts are what they are to me: the most basic, pristine, and vivid evidences of the creative spirit. Let us say, for example, that a manuscript of a poem, play, essay, novel, or letter is like the unclothed body of a person. All is revealed and made clear to the eye. The printed book, however, is the clothed person; often more attractive, it is true, but no longer completely revelatory and evocative.

As I learned from Justin Turner the purpose and scope of this society--to collect, preserve, and study manuscripts of all times and places, languages and forms--I found myself increasingly sympathetic with these aims and purposes.

Writing Is Basic

I am not a graphologist, and yet I find myself fascinated by the infinite variations in human handwriting. I have a feeling of reverence before manuscripts. I loathe typescripts, except as a means of getting a manuscript translated into print. I see no point in preserving an author's uncorrected typescript, although I must confess to harboring more than one in my library, for want of better representation of an author.

As for myself, I would no more think of composing any kind of writing directly on the typewriter than I would of kissing a girl through plate glass. I cannot come to grips with our muscular and evasive English language without forming the letters and the words and the sentences with pencil on paper, directly shaping the language, as rivers write their signature on the land.

In the past twenty years I have handled manuscripts of many periods and languages, and always with delight in their variety and differences. I have sat drinking red wine with John Steinbeck and marveled at the way he penned the manuscript of his ribald **Tortilla Flat** in his minuscular hand in the ruled ledger books that had belonged to the treasurer of Salinas County, California--his father.

I have worked every day for a month in a Los Angeles bank vault, cataloguing the manuscripts of D. H. Lawrence. Most of them were written outdoors in a notebook held on his lap, and the Lawrentian script is as serenely regular as his books are not! I have had the thrill of discovering and transcribing the first manuscript newspaper on the Pacific Coast--the eccentric **Flumgudgeon Gazette and Bumble Bee Budget**, written in Oregon in 1845 by the Curltail Coon, a pseudonym I subsequently revealed as that of the Virginia emigrant Charles E. Pickett, better known as Philosopher Pickett.

I have traveled down the California coast, from Carmel to Big Sur, with a U.S. Topographic Survey map lent to me by the poet Robinson Jeffers; and when I turned it over and looked at the back I was amazed to find a jungle of penciled manuscript notes, which I finally deciphered as the working draft of a narrative poem by Jeffers.

And I have handled hundreds of autograph letters and manuscripts of Oscar Wilde, all written rhythmically in one of the loveliest scripts ever penned, so characteristic of the wit, music, and high style of the Irish master at his peak.

I am a great collector, reader, and lover of printed books, but I believe that no creation of man has the evocative power of his holograph manuscripts. I want now to recall a few of my experiences with manuscripts, to share some of the excitement I have known in collecting and working with them.

A Calligrapher?

I am no calligrapher and doubt that I am capable of mastering any careful hand. Certainly I am not patient. When my little prose stream begins to flow, my cursive hand leans heavily to the right, and I have as difficult a time keeping up with it as my secretary does in deciphering it!

Besides, who wants to have a hand that resembles that of a thousand others? If it is mere legibility that is sought, then to the typewriter, my hearties! I suppose this merely shows my ignorance of the aims of modern calligraphy. The joy of forming beautiful handwritten letters I can understand and approve--perhaps envy. The fact is, I was conditioned early to hate calligraphers. When I was in the third or fifth grade, Miss Angevine came once a week to teach arm-movement writing in the Spencerian mode. Those endless ink ovals! Those forests of push-pull, push-pull! "Lawrence, don't cramp your fingers so! Hold your pen loosely, and write with your whole arm from the elbow down!" I could not do it then, and I can not do it now. Since then I have written millions of words, with my fingers squeezing the lead out of a Scripto pencil; and I have yet to suffer the writer's cramp Miss Angevine threatened would be our fate if we did not learn "arm movement."

But I can forgive her everything now, for having smelled so sweetly of hair and skin, chalk dust, and newly sharpened cedarwood pencils. In the course of some half-hearted research in preparation for this paper, I read that "the degree to which a person conforms to the instruction and drills of his penmanship teachers is an indication of his character." So what!

Let us turn back to that remarkable English calligrapher who will have been dead 250 years on May 26. Samuel Pepys was a great man in his age, the latter seventeenth century, the age of Dryden. If he is the author of the raciest diary ever published, he was also secretary of the Admiralty and "father of the Royal Navy," and as president of the Royal Society his name is the imprimatur on the title page of Newton's monumental **Principia.** He was a man of endless curiosity--and very good glands!

A highlight of my stay in England year before last was a trip to Cambridge to see the library Pepys left to his alma mater, Magdalene College. The great moment of that visit was my first sight of the immortal diary itself. Composed fastidiously in shorthand, each page's entry islanded in a sea of margins, the diary manuscript puzzled me, disappointed me. It was **not** evocative of the popular Pepys. All the rich raciness of the diary, its life-packed, swarming, sensual, indiscriminate abundance, was here reduced to copperplate cypher. Did Pepys compose it pell-mell in longhand and later transcribe it into shorthand?

He kept it less than a decade and then, faced by blindness, he put it aside forever. It must have taken long nocturnal hours to compose, by candlelight, and he guarded the diary, along with his moneybags, as his most precious possession.

Evocative or not of this or that aspect of Pepys's character, sight of the six stately quarto volumes of the diary, running to 3,012 pages in all, was one of the great manuscript experiences of my life. And that night, before going to sleep, I walked in the twilight on the great green stretch behind the University Arms Hotel known as Parker's Piece, and saw five simultaneous games of cricket being played. I was thankful for the fate that had spared Pepys's manuscripts from destruction.

A passage written by Pepys's friend Evelyn was in my mind as I moved about Europe year before last, hunting treasure with my trusty biblio-Geiger counter:

> For it would grieve one's heart to make any farther Inquirie, were it not to stir one up with the greater zeale to endeavor the finding out of such of them as may yet possibly lie hid and undiscovered, notwithstanding all the diligent searches which from time to time have been made. And therefore nothing ought to discourage the Learned and Curious, especially such as amongst them are Travellars abroad, who have the greatest and most rightly advantages of any other, for the finding out these straid pieces, and reduce the scatter'd limbs of **Hippolytus,** as the most inestimable Treasure they can bring home, or oblige the world, and celebrate their names to posterity: Nor are such to disdaine the rum'aging sometimes of the most neglected corners of Shops, and other obscure places, however cover'd with dust and cobwebs, wherever one may heare or suspect some old Parchments may have been cast; and to enquire what Trades and other Crafts (besides the Leafe Gold beaters, Book-binders, past-board, and the makers of Musical Instruments, who use it about the ribbs of Lutes, and other occasions) employ them in their works, and are us'd to buy, and have brought to them to sell, from Upholsters and Brokers, and from Country and illiterate people and servants, who now and then light upon old and neglected Manuscripts cast behind the doore, or other blind corner of the house; and to procure amongst those sort of people that whatever old writings and parchments of that nature come to their hands, they be encourag'd to bring them to you, or give you notice; since by this meanes you may possibly happen upon that which may be a thousand times worth your paines and expense.

Striking It Rich

Probably the biggest manuscript strike I made was by a purchase at auction. I am not one of those self-sufficient librarians who does his own bidding at auction. I lean heavily on my bookseller friends. And so when I saw a notice of a forthcoming sale of seventeenth- and eighteenth-century newsletters, partly printed and partly manuscript--720 of them in all, dated from 1682 to 1710--I knew in a flash that I had to have them. And so I did something I have never done before or since--gave my agent absolute discretion to bid as high as necessary to get them.

This was in November 1950. Before I could view the sale, I was called away from London on a trip to France, and on the actual day of the sale I was in Nice. I was at breakfast the next morning, savoring a meal of freshly baked croissants, sweet butter, and café au lait--the English may have the books, but the French have the food!--when a cable was handed me. The cable had just two words: "GOT 'EM!"

The following morning brought **The Times,** with an account of the sale and of the amount I owed my successful agent. It might have been worse! The collection of 720 letters cost only a little more than a dollar apiece. Yale and the Bodleian were the underbidders.

It was not until I had returned to London and examined the big bundle that I fully realized the richness of this haul. The letters were all sent by a London correspondent to a noble family in Derbyshire--a sort of Kiplinger news service it was--giving news and gossip in great abundance. The printed letters all included a blank page on which the correspondent had added last-minute, stop-press news in manuscript.

I found the letters powerfully evocative of the London of Pepys's time. They also made me long (momentarily) for a life of retirement and seclusion, such as that lived three hundred years ago by another London diarist who was also a great collector and annotator of his books. I refer to Narcissus Luttrell (1657-1732), who, in the laconic words of the DNB, "for many years lived in complete seclusion at Chelsea, studied much, chronicled the stirring events of his time, and collected an extensive library, including some valuable manuscripts." His political diary was published a century ago, but a personal diary has never seen print. This latter is preserved in the British Museum, and with great expectations I obtained a microfilm of it. What a disappointment! It was bad enough to find it written in Greek characters in the English language, but far worse to discover that it told hardly more than his hour of rising and who preached the day's sermon!

Infinitely more exciting is a bound volume in the Clark Library of poetical broadsides collected by Luttrell in 1683-84, which bears the wonderful binder's title "Poetry Long Waies." On each broadside Luttrell wrote the date he bought it and the price paid, together with sharp comments on the character of the pieces.

The Personal Side

One of the great joys of collecting is the fellowship it engenders. The best things are always happening to collectors. For example, last year in a London dealer's catalogue I saw itemized a seventeenth-century indenture, bearing as one of the signatures that of John Dryden. At the Clark Library we are definitely "crackers," as the English would say, about two authors, John Dryden and Oscar Wilde, of whose books and manuscripts we have unrivaled collections. We are now reediting Dryden's complete works for the first time since Sir Walter Scott's edition of 1808, and many a scrap is caught by our fine-toothed comb. My first thought in seeing the Dryden-signed indenture was of vexation at the dealer's not having sent it to us with a bill, without even bothering to catalogue it. Somehow she did not--all of us have our lapses--and so I promptly cabled for it.

Vexation turned to something just short of rage when the reply came back that the indenture had been sold. I ground my teeth and thought uncharitably of Huntington, Yale, Harvard, Folger, Newberry, any one of which might have done this to Clark!

But no, it had been bought by an English writer, a Londoner who lived around the corner, figuratively speaking, from the shop in New Bond Street. He was interested in Dryden, the wretch! And no, he would not give anyone a photostat. He was ill and cranky.

And so I settled back and waited for him to get better, or better yet, get worse--even die! He did! My eye lit up one morning last winter in Los Angeles, when I saw a four-line dispatch from London of this writer's demise.

I cabled Miss Myers--why go on pretending to conceal her identity, the good Winnie Myers, the former pooh-bah of the Antiquarian Booksellers Association, great friend to manuscript collectors--and asked her to close in, not for "the kill" but for the post mortem.

More trouble! The deceased writer's entire library of books and manuscripts, she reported, was to be sold at Sotheby's. Very well, I replied, bid on the indenture for Clark. Gladly, replied Miss Myers, but Professor Osborn of Yale wants me to do the same for him! He, too, had ordered the indenture from her catalogue, and had later been rebuffed by the successful buyer.

I sat down and wrote the following letter:

Dear Jim: As you doubtless know, I have been after that Dryden document ever since Winnie Myers sold it to Meyerstein. Now I learn that it is coming up at Sotheby's on December 15. I am asking Miss Myers to bid for us. Are you determined to bid on this or would you be so kind as to yield to our pre-eminence in the Dryden field? I should be glad of course to give you a photostat, if we succeed in getting the piece. It would seem to be most unfortunate if our competitive bidding ran the price way up.

I received the following reply:

> Dear Larry: Your letter about the Dryden document in the Meyerstein sale is welcome, and not unexpected. I shall be glad to withdraw my bid, of course, knowing that the document will find such an appropriate home.

The rest of this story is even happier. It has to do with money. The indenture was originally sold by Myers for 18 pounds, and so at the Sotheby sale I gave Winnie a top of 25 pounds. It was knocked down to us for 3 pounds 10 shillings!

Material "Comes Home"

Well known is the worldwide Walpole monopoly exercised by Wilmarth S. Lewis of Farmington, Connecticut--the fabulous "Lefty" Lewis, whose Yale Walpole edition is one of the noblest literary monuments of all time. Those who read the profile of him in **The New Yorker**, the pictorial spread on him in **Life**, and his own wise and witty book called **Collector's Progress** know that Lewis has an undisputed claim on Walpoleana whenever it appears on the market. His magnetic charm has even extracted Walpole items from libraries that hitherto thought their treasures had come to stay.

All of this is common knowledge among bookmen. Less well known is the fact that Lewis, even as Jim Osborn, recognizes similar claims in other areas. Let me illustrate what I mean.

When Lewis visited the Clark Library last year, he was impressed by the breadth and depth of our Oscar Wilde collection. It contains nearly four thousand items of print, manuscript, and picture, and I hope it will serve eventually as the basis for the first critical edition of Wilde's works, even as our Dryden collection is doing for the earlier century. When Lewis returned to Farmington, he wrote me a letter in which he confessed to having recently bought Oscar Wilde's seventy-five pages of unpublished manuscript notes for a lecture on Chatterton and Horace Walpole. He went on to say,

> It is hard to determine the relative claims in such a case: Wilde versus Walpole-Chatterton, but I have tried to do so, and I think the Wilde interest of this manuscript is perhaps the greater. So--at the risk of appearing quixotically generous--I'll offer it to you for what I paid for it.

It would have been churlish to refuse such an offer. Need I say that I acted promptly on behalf of the University of California at Los Angeles!

Although I am not a graphologist or a handwriting psychologist, I do believe that the study of handwriting and character is a vast terra incognita. Even when a man forsakes his natural hand for the anonymous chancery script of the modern calligraphers, does that not tell us something of his character?

I often think of handwriting as a kind of musical symbolism that begins to vibrate and sing and communicate only when the eye of man sets it free. No two natural hands are identical, any more than two people, even twins, are identical. What makes people write as they do?

Last winter I visited Wilmarth Lewis at Farmington, and we talked about handwriting and character, with particular reference to Walpole. Nothing occurs at Farmington, even breakfast, without reference to Walpole!

Later I asked Lewis to recall this conversation, and he wrote me as follows:

> In my opinion the study of handwriting is the most promising unexplored area left. Were I in your shoes I would build up as fine a library as I could on calligraphy. The significance of a man's handwriting as a key to his character and personality seems to me obvious. Unfortunately, it is a subject that is still not quite reputable. I told you how surprised I was when a great English historian (in a whisper) confessed that he employed a "psychographologist." Handwriting has been held in somewhat the same repute as phrenology and reading tea leaves, but there is no question whatever in my mind of its immense value to scholars. I hope you will go briskly ahead and become the greatest library in the world on it.

From Manuscript to Vote

My final story concerns how a manuscript letter determined my vote in the 1952 presidential election. Until summer I had not decided how I was going to vote. I was reared a rock-ribbed Republican by a father who was an associate of Hoover, and over my boyhood bed there hung a cherished picture bearing the autographed inscription, "To Lawrence Powell from his friend Herbert Hoover."

And then the Depression ruined my family and made a Democrat of me, after a brief and barren sojourn in the desert of the Far Left. The years passed, and by the summer of 1952, it was a tossup as to how I would vote. Although still a Democrat, I was skeptical of Adlai Stevenson, inclined to the suspicion that he might be the creation of an advertising agency. It has been done before!

Then I had lunch with Justin Turner a few days before the Demoratic convention, and he showed me a letter he had just received from Governor Stevenson. It was a holograph letter--a long letter, not a note--and it was **not** a political letter in any sense. It was rather a letter of thanks for a gift of Lincoln autograph material which Turner had made to the Illinois Historical Society. It was a wonderful letter, revealing a profound devotion to Lincoln, and it evoked for me all the pageant of American history--the Pilgrims and the rockbound coast, the forest and prairie, the muddy rivers, mountains and desert, the seacoast of California, and the great Americans who are somehow always there when they are most needed, to rally us and to lead us, to speak for us in the tragic drama of history--and finally to go offstage and yield their places to others.

All this was both explicit and interlinear in Stevenson's handwritten letter, with an overpowering immediacy alien to the printed page.

I voted for Adlai Stevenson because of that manuscript letter. It spoke to me of sincerity, integrity, and culture, in the American tradition. And if he had to lose, I am glad it was to another great American who is our president now.

And that is what I mean by "the power to evoke."

The Morgans as Autograph Collectors*

Frederick B. Adams, Jr.

While the autograph collections of the Pierpont Morgan Library are not its chief claim to honor, those who have read about or seen our recent exhibition of letters know that we have several items of interest in that department. Furthermore, the autographs hold a position of sentimental importance in the library, because they were the cornerstones on which the collections were built.

It is clear that the founder, J. Pierpont Morgan, was born with the collector's instinct. His father, Junius, was a collector before him, and we may judge Junius Morgan's reputation from a letter addressed to him in 1881: "Understanding that you are interested in rare autographs, manuscripts and memorials of eminent men of both hemispheres, I send you herewith two that you will, I think, find difficult to match or duplicate." The enclosures turned out to be two letters written by his son Pierpont Morgan, at the age of twelve, to a spinster school teacher complaining of unfair grading in--of all things--arithmetic.

It was this first Junius Morgan who, some time in the early 1880s, gave his son Pierpont a valuable manuscript from his own collection. This was the work of a favorite author, Sir Walter Scott, and was the complete holograph manuscript in three volumes of **Guy Mannering.** The first volume contains Junius Morgan's handsome armorial bookplate and a note that he had purchased the manuscript at the earl of Clare's sale in London in January 1881. This is believed to be the first author's manuscript (as distinct from letters) to come into the Pierpont Morgan collection, and it was the basis of a great Walter Scott corpus that ultimately grew to include the original manuscripts of no fewer than fifteen of his major works. Scholars continue to study and edit our Scott manuscripts, and we continue to add to them. Just three months ago we were able to purchase from a member of this society the final agreement between J. G. Lockhart, Scott's son-in-law and biographer, and the publisher Robert Cadell, in which Lockhart transfers the entire remaining copyright of Scott's works to Cadell in return for the latter's canceling Scott's indebtedness and paying off the heavy mortgage of 8,500 pounds on Abbotsford.

---

*Originally published in 1950.

Young Pierpont Morgan's first enthusiasm was autographs. The earliest evidence of his prowess that I have discovered was revealed by an entry in his line-a-day diary under the date of August 4, 1851: "Received letter from Pres. Fillmore." The "letter" was a little orange card inscribed with the signature of Millard Fillmore and enclosed in an envelope personally franked by Fillmore. Thus, a collector of fourteen was fortunate enough to get two presidential signatures in response to his request for one. Today we have them in the library.

It was also in the summer of 1851 that Pierpont (living in Boston) formed a partnership with his Hartford cousin Jim Goodwin. In deference to Jim's seniority, the "firm" was called Goodwin, Morgan & Co. They did errands for each other in Boston and Hartford, exchanged letters in a formal businesslike manner, and seem to have engaged in the buying, selling, and exchanging of autographs. Fortunately, Pierpont never felt like trading either of his Millard Fillmores for anything else.

The stimulation of living in the city that was at the intellectual center of the United States and of being able to ride out on horseback on occasional afternoons to visit his famous grandfather, John Pierpont, who had retired to Medford, Massachusetts, undoubtedly helped to make the young Morgan an autograph collector. He records in his diary for October 3, for instance, "Received some letters from distinguished men for autographs." And on the next day he records, "In afternoon went out to Cambridge and got Mr. Everett and [Mr.] Sparks autographs." Edward Everett had been president of Harvard College from 1846 to 1849 and Jared Sparks succeeded him, serving until early 1853. Therefore, in one afternoon Pierpont tackled two presidents of Harvard. The visit to Sparks must have been particularly interesting for him because Pierpont had in his library the historian's **Life of Washington** in two volumes, which he had received as a Christmas gift from his mother in 1845. Pierpont's interest in American historical documents of the Revolutionary period was to last throughout his life, and the Morgan Library is today well supplied with materials of this time in our country's history.

Early in 1852 we find Pierpont writing to Jim Goodwin about autographs of Dr. Holmes and Henry Clay and expressing his delight that he was on the track of an autograph signature of Prince Albert.

Episcopal Autographs

Parallel with this interest in the important figures of literature and politics was an equally great concern for the leaders in the Protestant Episcopal Church. Very few boys have set out to collect the autographs of Episcopal bishops, but Pierpont did, and the Morgan Library contains six of the many Episcopal autographs which Pierpont was able to acquire between August 1851 and the spring of 1852, when illness seems to have interrupted his labors. But in later years he returned to the pursuit, and the bishops' autographs, which he continued to collect even in his seventies, now occupy twelve imposing folio volumes in the library. Of the 172 bishops of the American church up to the year 1900, Mr. Morgan eventually acquired autograph letters and documents of all but four. Dr. Richard G. Salomon, a noted scholar who was consulting these papers last summer, told me that this is one of the really important collections of original historical material on the Episcopal Church. His article about the bishops' autographs appeared in the March 1950 issue of the **Historical Magazine** of the Protestant Episcopal Church, and almost simultaneously I received a letter from the Reverend Du Bose Murphy of Tuscaloosa, Alabama, enclosing as his gift to the library a fine ALS of Bishop G. H. Kinsolving, one of the four who had been missing from our collection. So now we have only three to go.

The last years of Pierpont Morgan's education were spent abroad, first at school in Vevey, Switzerland, then at the University of Gottingen in Germany. During this period he picked up much of the stained glass that now adorns the windows of the rooms in the main building of the library. Apparently, he took a great many of his autographs with him on his travels, and this practice was responsible for a sad occurrence that might have discouraged a lesser man. He related the story in a letter to Jim Goodwin dated November 4, 1856:

> I don't think I have told you of an accident which happened [to] some of my property during the vacation. When I was going away for the vacation, not wishing to carry so much luggage about with me, I packed up one trunk to leave here. I filled it with all kinds of knick-knacks of no value to anybody but myself, among other things my collection of autographs, daguerreotypes and photographs of my friends in Vevey and Gottingen, and various papers, all my letters received from January to July 1856, bills, etc., etc. When I got to the depot I found that by mistake the porter had brought it down with the others, and I told him to carry it back when he went. I then went onto the platform, and whilst the rest of the Americans were there to see us off a rascal seized the opportunity to make way with the trunk, and it was only found in the field several days after cut open, with a photograph of Mother I had lying by the side of it. The thieves were discovered and several articles of no particular value were found in their possession. But my autographs and letters had been burnt up, and the likenesses which I can never replace, were destroyed. I was called up the other day into court and had to testify, and the rascals were sent to prison for seven years, but that does me very little good as far as ... [regaining] my autographs goes. I was very much vexed as you can easily imagine, but it does no good I find.

Such beginnings seem inauspicious. Certainly for the next thirty years, Pierpont Morgan was chiefly concerned with matters other than collecting books and autographs. Fortunately for our knowledge of this period, the bookseller Joseph F. Sabin compiled in 1883 a **Catalogue of the Library of Mr. J. Pierpont Morgan.** Unquestionably the finest unit listed in this catalogue is the set of the Signers of the Declaration of Independence which is designated as number 14 in the Charles F. Jenkins census of 1925, and number 10 in the Joseph E. Fields census of 1948. The set was not listed in the Lyman C. Draper census of 1889.

Thomas Lynch Autographs

The star piece of this first Morgan set is the autograph note written in the third person and signed "Thomas Lynch, Captn in the 4th Company, 1st Regmt." It informs Lynch's commanding officer, Colonel Huger, that Mr. Baker, surgeon of the First South Carolina Regiment, had failed all the previous day to attend the sick at the hospital or in barracks, "tho his assistance must have been much wanted, the Room at each place being full of Patients." It carries on the verso an endorsement in the hand of Henry Laurens stating that Colonel Huger had presented this complaint to the Council of Safety.

This, and Dr. Emmet's famous letter from Lynch to Washington now in the New York Public Library, seem to be the only signed autograph letters of Lynch in existence. The scarcity of Lynch material is not due entirely to his early death, as is revealed in our library's extremely interesting letter from Rev. Dr. Samuel Gilman of Charleston, South Carolina, to Israel K. Tefft of Savannah, Georgia, one of the earliest collectors of autographs of the Signers. The letter is dated April 5, 1845, and reads in part as follows:

My dear Friend,

I took the first opportunity after your letter to call upon my friends the Misses Bowmans, and enclose you herewith the precious results of my visit. They tell me that a large trunk of their uncle's papers was burned at the time Gen. Hamilton's house was destroyed by fire a few years since. You may be aware that their mother was a sister of Lynch the signer . . . .

My precious enclosures are most undoubted reliques. Mr. Lynch was educated at Eton College, and when there he used a book of translations from the Latin, writing the Latin on one side, and his own version on the other. It appears to be an extract or condensation from one of the ancient classics. The book is now in the possession of the Miss Bowmans, and I cut these specimens from it. There are probably 40 pages in his own handwriting. The cover is of brown paper, on one leaf of which he had written the autograph I send you, and a little below, his name in a much larger character. On the other cover of the book, he printed his name in large handsome letters. The other autograph which I send was written alone on the first page of the book; all the rest of that page is blank. But I cut it out so as to give you a further specimen of the young student's handwriting on the opposite side . . . . The ladies intimated to me that repeated applications had been made, which they had refused . . . . So that though proud of my success, I did not dare to ask for too much, nor to mutilate the book further than I possibly could help. They seemed to be more anxious to keep the interior manuscript whole, than to save the signatures which I abstracted. They tell me that a good many of his books were given to our Apprentices' Library, and have no doubt his autograph is there. I will take the first opportunity to examine for you . . . .

A month later, on May 2, Gilman reported to his friend the results of his visit to the Apprentices' Library:

My Dear friend,

Visiting the Apprentices' Library last evening, I asked the Librarian if he had any books with the inscription of T. Lynch Jr.'s name. He immediately brought me four volumes, from which I cut the enclosed. Two are veritable signatures of the Signer of the Declaration, which I cut out from books that he no doubt brought with him from Eton or England. The other two signatures must be his father's as the date is 1743 . . . . I have requested the Librarian to keep his eye on other books for the same signature, as he thinks there may be several in the Library. He will also try to look for a Middleton.

These letters show that within one month Gilman had tapped the two principal sources of Lynch signatures; they also reveal a prime example of the **bibliothecarius libris inimicus,** or librarian as enemy of books.

One autograph page of Latin from Lynch's Eton exercise book is now in the Morgan Library, having come to it with the set of Signers formed by Col. C. C. Jones, Jr., of Augusta, Georgia. Emmet, writing in 1890, considered this the best Lynch known, next to his own letter, but he was probably unaware of the existence of our autograph memorandum to Colonel Huger. What, one wonders, has happened to the remainder of that forty-page exercise book so carefully treasured by the Bowman sisters? With its identifying Lynch signatures cut away by Gilman, may it still be gathering dust somewhere, a small fortune in unrecognized Lynch handwriting?

Sets of Signers

The Jones set of Signers was acquired by J. Pierpont Morgan in 1893 or 1894. It is number VIII in the Draper census, number 7 in the Jenkins list, and number 9 in the Fields list. Its great treasure is the Button Gwinnett will, entirely in his hand and signed by him. Morgan once owned a third set of the Signers, which had been formed by David McN. Stauffer. Morgan's generosity in disposing of this last set caused considerable chagrin to his librarian, Belle da Costa Greene.

Herbert Putnam, librarian of Congress, visited Morgan at his library one morning in November 1912. While being shown the manuscript treasures in the vault, Putnam remarked that the Congressional Library had no set of Signers of the Declaration of Independence. With "inspiring simplicity and directness" (to quote Putnam) Morgan immediately offered one of his three sets to the nation, and two days later President Taft wrote from the White House acknowledging the generous and patriotic gift on behalf of the people of the United States.

Privately, Greene wrote to Putnam, with the forthrightness and pungency of expression that throughout her life have compelled both admiration and fear:

> I am very glad that Mr. Morgan has seen fit to make this addition to the Library of Congress and can only hope in return that your next visit to this Library may be one of pure joy to us all and unalloyed by any wants in the Library of Congress.

Three days later, Putnam, in announcing the proposed visit of a colleague to 36th Street, took pains to placate the redoubtable custodian of Morgan's treasures:

> Be assured that Mr. Hunt comes with no predatory design whatever! (As little indeed did I the other day; and the thing that happened was as much of a surprise to me as it was a cause of gratification. Not to take prompt advantage of it would, however, have been more--or less-- than human.)

> With keen appreciation of **your** promptness and goodwill, and the best of wishes, believe me

> Very sincerely yours,
> Herbert Putnam

Need it be said that these two great librarians became firm friends, and cooperated on many worthy projects?

The "Set" Virus

Collecting autographs by sets is a time-honored custom. For all I know, the Romans may have done it. Certainly people in the United States have been forming sets of the Signers of the Declaration for 125 years, and we are still hard at it. Morgan was not immune to the "set" virus. In addition to his bishops and his Signers, he had sets of the members of the First Continental Congress (formed for him by Emmet), the signers of the Articles of Confederation, the generals of the American Revolution, the signers of the Constitution, the presidents of the United States, and the rulers of England. He had the autographs of many of the popes, one of which he solicited personally. In April 1908, he had a brief audience at the Vatican with Pope Pius X. Morgan prevailed upon His Holiness to write out his autograph on a sheet of his personal stationery, which is beautiful all-rag Fabriano handmade paper, watermarked with the papal seal **and** the papal portrait. We have it today in the library, and the message above the signature has a sly humor:

> We give heartfelt greetings to Mr. Pierpont Morgan, and every good wish for his prosperity.

I hope those who like to collect sets will dream of new sets to conquer. Too many buyers seeking the same commodity are likely to push the price up too far beyond its value as an historical document. For instance, it strikes me that it would be interesting, entertaining, and inexpensive to collect the autographs of **un**successful candidates for the presidency of the United States. The collection would include some of our greatest leaders and some of our greatest crackpots, but all of them vital people likely to have written good letters.

Another collection that would much intrigue me would be a set of famous illegitimates. It might be a little expensive to start with the signed manual of William the Conqueror, whose mother was the daughter of a tanner at Falaise, or the signature of the Conte de Dunois, commonly called the Bastard of Orleans, who was Joan of Arc's brave companion-in-arms. And it is hard now to get autograph material of Leonardo da Vinci, the illegitimate son of a notary employed by the Medici family. But no difficulties would be presented by Alexander Hamilton, or Audubon, or the Alexander Dumas who wrote **La Dame aux Camelias.** And some of the preparatory research would be fascinating.

Literary Autographs

At this point I must confess that my own preference in the autograph field is for the original manuscripts of works of the imagination, and for the intimate letters of literary figures. Fortunately for me, both Pierpont Morgan and his son liked these eighteenth and nineteenth centuries. Colonel Isham's Boswell Papers were acquired by Yale last summer, so perhaps it is timely to mention that we have some Boswell papers of our own. They are one hundred of Boswell's letters to his great friend, the Reverend William Temple, and if ever one man told **everything** to another, Boswell did so in this correspondence, which extended over a period of thirty-six years, from youth to death. George Birkbeck Hill, Thomas F. Madigan, and Mary A. Benjamin, in their books about autographs, all mention the miraculous rescue of these letters from wanton destruction, but the story has never, to my knowledge, been fully told.

When William Temple died in 1796 (a year after Boswell), the only one of his sons who was of age at that time was absent in America. One of the executors, Mr. Powlett, took possession of all Temple's books and papers. By the will they were to be divided among the children. But because most of the children were minors and one was absent, Powlett simply kept the papers and when he went to reside in France soon afterwards he took them along with him. There he died, and the papers disappeared until about 1850, when a certain Madame Noel, who kept a small shop in Boulogne, was found to be using Boswell letters to wrap up her merchandise (described as fish by Madigan and butter by Benjamin). It was learned that the paper was part of a large parcel that had recently been purchased from a hawker, and the whole parcel was immediately secured. But meanwhile some of the letters had been lost forever. I might add that, but for Powlett's careless performance of his duties as executor, all the letters might have been destroyed, considering their frankness and the fact that Temple's descendants included two archbishops of Canterbury.

There is a good deal to be said for giving institutional security to important letters and manuscripts. Scholars have so far paid little attention to Gilbert and Sullivan, but I venture the prediction that the remarkable collection of the partners' work that is being given to the Morgan Library by Reginald Allen will see much service in the decades to come.

Our three holograph manuscripts of novels by George Meredith, **The Amazing Marriage, Lord Ormont,** and **Diana of the Crossways,** were purchased by Morgan from Meredith's gardener-valet for 800 pounds some forty years ago. Meredith has been quite out of fashion for many years, and these manuscripts are now of little concern, but an institution can wait generations for scholarly interest to arrive. Since the last war we have witnessed an increasing interest in the Rossettis, Ruskin, and Swinburne, and highly important manuscripts and letters of these writers that have been lying virtually unheeded in our vaults for years are now in demand by scholars both here and abroad.

When, in 1907, Pierpont Morgan was offered for $150,000 Stephen H. Wakeman's remarkable collection of American literary manuscripts--the best in the world for Hawthorne, Thoreau, Poe, and Whittier--he found it difficult to convince himself that American literature could be worth spending that much money on. George S. Hellman says that the presence among the manuscripts of Longfellow's **The Children's Hour** provided enough sentimental appeal finally to persuade him. With the great surge of interest in American literature after World War I, the Wakeman material came into prominence, and it has been in constant use by scholars ever since.

And that brings me to one last comment about the Morgans as autograph collectors. They were always happy to make their material available to competent scholars for publication in a form compatible with its importance. The fetish of the unpublished has never been held in excessive regard at the Morgan Library. We are mature enough to know that the scholars of thirty or forty years hence will want to do over the work that their predecessors are doing today. As long as the original material is preserved, scholars will continue to make productive use of it. In the long run, the value of autograph collectors to society is to make available today and to preserve for the future these invaluable original records of our past.

Teaching with Autographic Material*

Virgil Y. Russell

Through the use of autograph documents, photos, and letters, I have stirred my students' interest in the study of what is often called the dullest subject in school. I hope that by briefly outlining my uses of this firsthand historical material, I may inspire others to use these and similar methods to enliven history classroom discussions.

A framed document signed by President Abraham Lincoln that hung in the front room of my family's little Kansas homestead accounts for my being a school instructor in history. It was the appointment of my father's uncle, David Floringer, as assistant surgeon of volunteers and was dated February 27, 1863. The parchment document was also signed by Secretary of War Stanton. I was taught to revere the document, signed by a president of the United States, second only to the old family Bible.

Soon after I started teaching I learned what I had often feared: that my students did not take the interest in history that I had at their age. When I asked them why they were in the class, they sheepishly replied, "Because it is required." When asked what they wanted from the course, they invariably replied, "a credit."

These answers worried me and I started to inquire why they did not like American history. I received the following reasons: "It's too dry," "These things happened so long ago," "I do not like to memorize dates."

Lincoln Started It

I recalled the framed Lincoln document. I asked for it and, after much persuasion, my father took it from the wall and sent it to me. I have often thought of the void it must have left in the room and in the hearts of my parents.

The document was transferred to a conspicuous place in my domain-- usually called a schoolroom. It created a great stir of interest when the students realized that Lincoln had actually signed that piece of parchment

---

*Originally published in 1951.

with his own hand. I placed a large picture of Lincoln over the document. It seemed to me that my history students soon began to look down upon the history students in the other classes. I began to feel like Archimedes, who shouted "Eureka!" when he noticed that his body displaced its own bulk in water and thus discovered the law of specific gravity. Like Archimedes, I felt I had the answer to my problem.

If that autograph document had such an effect on my life, and it was already having a noticeable effect upon my students, why not try to collect a number of autograph documents, photographs, and letters of prominent people?

My first step was to ask my students, "Do you or any members of your family know any prominent men? If so, it is just possible that they would sign and give me their photographs for our room."

I was surprised one evening after school when a little girl came in and said that her uncle was Edward White of the Supreme Court. "I am his favorite niece and I am sure I can get you many signed pictures from Washington, D.C." I could hardly believe my good luck!

My first request was for President Wilson! Yes, I got it. So, with her help, the autograph photographs started pouring in: General Pershing, Henry Cabot Lodge, William Jennings Bryan, Alexander Graham Bell, Arthur Brisbane, President Taft, Charles Curtis, Herbert Hoover, Adm. William S. Sims, and many others.

By now, I had some material, but how was I to use it? I finally worked out the following plans, not in a day, a month, or a year, but over a long period of time. Some plans I tried and discarded, but I found the following the most productive.

How to Use Material

First, I placed a letter, document, or autograph photograph on the board each week. Whenever possible, I used a picture of a man prominent in the news of the week. I gave the students a few interesting facts concerning the man and encouraged them to find more and report to the class.

Second, I had a glass frame made and placed a letter or document in it and passed it around the class. "Does this man's writing look like anyone's you know?" "What does a man's handwriting show?" "What was he doing at the time he wrote this?" "Where did he live?" "Why was he great?" "For what is this man noted?" I asked these and other provocative questions. With an opaque projector I can throw these pictures on a screen and reveal intimate details of the signatures.

I have encouraged my students to draw pictures of prominent people and send them in for signatures, if they are good works of art. I have often thought how well this method would work in art departments. The teacher would assist the student in securing the signature on the picture as a reward for an outstanding drawing. Most great men seem to be willing to encourage youth.

I once received a letter from Newton D. Baker that I prize. He wrote:

I take pleasure in sending you, under separate cover, a photograph which I shall feel honored to have added to your collection. If these pictures serve to arouse an interest in the study of history among your students they will serve a valuable national purpose. As the interests of men and nations become more intimately associated, the background of a knowledge of history is essential to safe and sound action by citizens who in a democracy constitute the government.

My room is always open after school. I encourage the students to come in and see other material, talk things over with me, and make suggestions and criticisms.

When the Freedom Train carrying historic documents was scheduled, our superintendent and principal were very enthusiastic about it. They asked me to prepare a "Course of Study" for all of the schools of Casper. We studied copies of the documents on the Freedom Train long before it arrived. We knew what we were going to see when we entered that patriotic shrine. It was with much pleasure that I noted a decided increase in the students' interest in history following the visit of the Freedom Train.

I believe I now have one of the best collections for teaching history. I have about six hundred autographed photographs, documents, and letters from famous people. I find most useful my presidential collection, consisting of some item from every president from Washington to Truman. It helps to give the students a continuing thread through the maze of United States history, dividing periods by men and their administrations. Each man is more real to the students because in the autograph they see something the president actually wrote or signed.

Some Prize Acquisitions

The students seem to enjoy the story I tell them about my Benito Mussolini autographed photograph.

On a cold, dark, and stormy night, I was alone. There was a knock at the door. I opened it. Standing there was a mysterious-looking fellow, with piercing dark eyes.

"Professor Russell?" he asked. I replied in the affirmative. "Well, may I come in?" he asked. I hesitated, but he stepped forward and I let him in. The mysterious atmosphere was heightened by his first question.

"Why did you write to Benito Mussolini for his autograph photograph?"

How could this stranger know that about two months before I had dared to write to Mussolini? I finally replied, "All right, I'll tell you why if you will tell me how you know. Is that a bargain?"

"It is," he answered. "Go ahead."

I asked him to excuse me a moment. I went into my den and returned with a number of photographs and documents and started showing them to him. Here was an eager and interested "student." We spent an hour going over the numerous items. "And, now, my friend, you see why I want Benito Mussolini's picture to go into a great collection like this."

He smiled slowly. "Yes, I see. I'll explain why you wish the photograph and I am sure you will receive it. The purpose is good! Oh, yes, I was to tell you how I knew. Well, when you wrote to Mussolini, he had his agents in Rome contact New York City. They notified Denver, who notified some of the Italians here. I was appointed to call on you and see why you wanted his picture. We thought you might be writing a book about Mussolini. If it were favorable we would help you and if it were unfavorable--" he hesitated a moment--"we would try to stop you!"

"How?" I asked.

"Who knows, my friend! Who knows! There are many ways to accomplish various things."

I received and still have the autographed photograph of Mussolini.

An item that always amuses the students is the following verse written in English by the German kaiser in 1921: "If you know the truth, speak out and tell! Would you refuse, then go to hell!"

A statement of General Allenby's seems to inspire them: "Remember that anything worthwhile is difficult, but nothing worthwhile is impossible."

To indicate to my students that they must never give up, I relate the following incident. I wrote to Marshal Foch of France six times over a period of two years. I first praised France and her great efforts in World War I and asked him to sign a photograph which I enclosed. No reply. Time passed; I sent another photograph and letter in which I paid great tribute to Marshal Foch himself. No reply. I then tried paying great tribute to Lafayette. Still no reply. And so it went, with no results. I then wrote a brief letter, enclosing another photograph, and told him of my history collection and how I used it, and asked for his signature. He signed and returned all six photographs with the brief comment in French, "Why don't you say what you want!"

This also is a good lesson to youth; be brief, and come to the point. Do not beat about the bush.

My Interview with the FBI

My students always enjoy hearing about the time I was investigated by the FBI for requesting the autographed photograph of Attorney General Homer S. Cummings. I was called into the office of Superintendent Hicks and was introduced to a member of the FBI. He asked me, "Do you have this collection of autograph documents and photographs of famous personages which you claim to have?"

"Why, yes," I said, "let's go over and see them. It will be a pleasure to show them to you. May I be excused to show my collection, Mr. Hicks?"

"Certainly, Mr. Russell," he replied, and I am sure he looked relieved.

"No," replied the FBI man, "you are too eager. I am sure you have the collection." I could not talk him into coming to see it; he said he had too much to do. "Investigating you is relatively unimportant anyway. We only wondered if you had the collection. If not, it would come under the heading of securing material through the mail under false pretenses."

Much to my disappointment, I had to return to class without showing my collection. That was my interview with the FBI.

How to Obtain Material

How did I obtain my collection? I owe a great deal to my thousands of students, who have always been on the lookout for me, to get an item or make a contact. I also owe much to my wife, who has always encouraged me and never hesitated to have me spend money on stamps and documents instead of clothing for herself.

I certainly will not deny that I have purchased material from reliable autograph dealers to fill in my collection. These dealers, by tireless effort and years of research, unearth material we would never find--material that otherwise might be lost or destroyed. By paying fair prices they can get people to dig historical items out of attics and trunks. They classify, arrange, and prepare these items so that we may have them for our use. A penny saved here and a nickel there, and even a schoolteacher will soon have enough saved to buy an historical item!

I also owe more than I can ever pay to the hundreds of great men and women who have listened to my appeal for help and have signed a photograph or written a letter to me. It has been wonderful to live in a world where a humble history teacher may dare to write to any of the really great, without fear, and even with hope that the request may be granted!

I have tried to repay these obligations to society by inculcating in my students a desire to observe historical events, a respect for law and order, an appreciation for greatness--wherever it may be found--and a gratitude toward American citizenship. If I have encouraged my students to pursue worthwhile activities in the years to come, then I feel my mission as a teacher has been fulfilled.

My one wish for today's youth is that they should live in, and understand the historical background of, a period of history as wonderful as the first half of the twentieth century.

Confused Identities*

Joseph E. Fields

Identical names have been a minor curse upon the autograph world since collecting began. General collectors, collectors of sets, dealers, exhibitors, historians--all need to be aware that there may be several people bearing the name of their subject specialty. Collectors are far more likely to acquire a mistaken identity than a forgery (which are actually quite rare). Old and experienced collectors such as L. J. Cist, Edward H. Liffingwell, and the Reverend William Sprague made a number of errors of confused identity. I daresay there is no dealer in autographs, in fact, who has not been victimized by confused identities--not once but numerous times.

It is not my purpose to provide a list of names of all the mistaken identities that one is likely to encounter. Instead, I shall reaffirm a few well-known principles. There is nothing new or startling in what I have to say. By repetition of what the reader already knows, I hope I may instill not a fear of confused identities, but a healthy respect for them and a curiosity about them. My aim is to help readers avoid costly mistakes as well as to add to their enjoyment of collecting.

The inclusion of a confused identity in a collection is usually an innocent error on the part of both seller and purchaser. I can recall no instance, in all the anecdotes in the history of autograph collecting, in which a dishonest person has intentionally pawned off a "wrong person" upon an unsuspecting collector. Perhaps there have been some instances, but the dealer is generally as unsuspecting as the buyer. He sincerely believes that he is selling an autograph of the right person of the given name. But, because of lack of knowledge, he unwittingly sells an autograph of the right name but the wrong person.

There is still another way in which a mistaken identity may intrude into a collection. A dealer may offer for sale a document that he has described, identified, and catalogued quite correctly. But, a prospective buyer, through lack of knowledge or carelessness, may make the purchase, blissfully ignorant of the fact that the autograph is of the name desired, but not of the person desired. For instance, the buyer may want a letter of Benjamin West, the artist, and may be purchasing a letter of Benjamin West, the mathematician, astronomer, and almanac maker.

---

*Originally published in 1950.

To most collectors the inclusion of a mistaken identity is a serious matter, for it detracts from the collection. Also, there may be a monetary loss attending confused identities, for usually one of a group of identical names is in greater demand, is more collectible, and brings a higher price.

The Thomas Lynches illustrate my point. We know of five men of this name. The most collectible of them is the Signer of the Declaration of Independence, whose autograph is very rare and costly. Of much greater importance to his country was the Signer's father, of the same name. His autographs are not common and, because he was not physically able to go to Independence Hall and put his name to the Declaration, his autograph brings a mere pittance compared with that of his son. Of much less value and importance, autographically speaking, are the autographs of Thomas Lynch, grandfather of the Signer; Thomas Lynch, a New York merchant; and Thomas Lynch, royal governor of Jamaica.

Thus it can easily be seen that a collector who is under the impression he has purchased a signature of Thomas Lynch the Signer, and has paid accordingly, would be considerably out of pocket should he later discover that the autograph is of the Signer's father. His set might be rendered incomplete and less attractive. Undoubtedly the collector would be very annoyed with his dealer and this member of the trade might conceivably lose by the transaction, not only by having to refund the collector's money but by losing good will.

A somewhat less serious but nevertheless considerable loss would be incurred by inclusion of the wrong George Rogers Clark, the wrong John Penn, or the wrong Arthur Middleton. Of course, there are many similar examples. Fortunately, the financial losses in most instances are not so severe as in those mentioned.

Ways to Avoid Confusing Identities

Let us now consider how we may avoid such pitfalls and thus make collecting more enjoyable.

First, and axiomatic, is the rule of buying from dealers who have a reputation for honesty and fair dealing. They will not intentionally attempt to sell "the wrong person." Such a practice is no less serious to the collector than the dealer. The customer may condemn the dealer, justifiably or unjustifiably, for selling a piece of merchandise that is not what it was represented to be. This may reflect upon the integrity of the dealer, who, in most instances, is innocent of any wrongdoing. A buyer need not be perturbed by purchase of "the wrong person." Once an error has been discovered, a buyer need only call it to the attention of the dealer and return the merchandise. Most dealers will gladly rectify their errors--in fact, they guarantee to do so, and the postal regulations will back up a purchaser's claim, if the merchandise is not as described.

Second, know the biographical details of the person whose autograph you desire. Special stress should be placed upon dates of birth and death, nature and terms of public office, and, if possible, place of abode at various periods of life. For this information I recommend Appleton's **Cyclopedia of American Biography** and the **Dictionary of American Biography,** as well as the usual biographies. I have found the sketches in Appleton's readily available works to be concise and usually accurate.

Let me further illustrate this point by citing the case of the three John Penns. The autographs of all three are highly collectible. The eldest was John Penn, son of William Penn, founder of Pennsylvania. He was known as "The American." He was born in 1700 (the only son of the founder to be born in America) and died in 1746. From his mother he received half the proprietorship, but he spent little time in America. Most of his autographs bear an English dateline. John Penn, nephew of "The American," was born in 1729 and died in 1795. He was a member of the Provincial Congress, member of the Albany Congress, lieutenant governor, and afterwards governor. Following the enactment of the first constitution of Pennsylvania he retired to private life. Of no relation to the foregoing was John Penn, Signer of the Declaration of Independence. He lived from 1741 to 1788 and through most of that period was a resident of North Carolina. He served in the Continental Congress and then after the war served as receiver of taxes for a short time. Both before and after the Revolution he practiced law in North Carolina. It is easy to see that familiarity with these biographical data will materially aid in determining which John Penn wrote any particular autograph. Distinguishing among these men of the same name is quite important, for autographs of John Penn the Signer are rare in any form and bring good prices.

Third, become familiar with the autograph you are thinking of purchasing. I cannot stress sufficiently the need for meticulous attention to catalogue descriptions. As a rule they are accurate. Again, let me illustrate my point by using the Penns. In my early days of collecting, I was naive enough to begin collecting Signers of the Declaration of Independence. By the time I had the autographs of about twenty-five Signers, I had many of the common ones and the remainder were coming a bit too slowly. I discovered in the catalogue of a dealer the following autograph listed: "Penn, John, Governor of Pennsylvania. Last of the 'true and absolute proprietaries.' Fine vellum document signed in 1774. Deed of a tract called 'Hemphill', complete with unusually fine example of the pendant paper seal." In my enthusiasm I was sure this could be none other than **the** John Penn, Signer of the Declaration of Independence. I promptly bought the item, overjoyed that I had added one more Signer to my collection. It was some time before I realized that I had been guilty of purchasing the autograph of the wrong man. Worse than that, I had been guilty of not reading the catalogue description accurately and carefully. To my superficial glance, the name of John Penn meant just one thing--**Signer.**

If you are undecided or hesitant, inquire of the dealer or order the item on approval. If it is the autograph you desire, then all that is required is a check. If it is not, then send it back promptly. There is no obligation to buy.

A further word of advice. Do not belittle dealers' listing of items such as "Hancock, John, Signer of the Declaration of Independence." The listing is not done to sneer at the reader's lack of elementary knowledge of history and biography. Dealers are trying to tell readers not that Hancock signed the Declaration, but that this specimen is the Signer's, and not that of some other John Hancock (there were at least four in America before 1800). **Read dealers' lists carefully!**

Fourth, know the physical characteristics of the handwriting desired. This may be learned from photostats, facsimiles, reproductions from dealers and auction catalogues, and comparison with known specimens, as well as from the usual references of bibliographical nature.   Compare the known handwriting of the individual whose autograph you seek with the handwriting on the item you are considering. Of course, take into consideration the usual discrepancies in date.

Finally, if there is any doubt in your mind, question the dealer who has supplied you the document. He will gladly make a serious attempt to verify the document, one way or another, for it is to his advantage to have a satisfied customer with no shadow of doubt in his mind. Consult the various experts, collectors, or professionals who may be authorities in the field in which you are working. Your fellow collectors include experts in many fields of interest. Seek them out and they will help you to the best of their ability. Go to the people who know what you desire to know, for they are most generous with their knowledge. Again, let me make a plea for a compilation, a gallery of examples, a list of places where such facts may be learned and questioned examples submitted. One person cannot fill that bill.

What Every Autograph
Collector Should Know
About Prices*

Mary A. Benjamin

How reputable and experienced dealers set prices on autographs has always been and unquestionably still is a major conundrum to most collectors. Yet there is no mystery about their method. It is, or should be, like that of a modern IBM computer into which certain facts are fed and from which come answers based on those facts. Conscientious dealers do not pick prices at random and slap them on items. Quite the contrary. They reach a decision only after mature deliberation. The value they place on a manuscript is generally the ultimate result of a series of considerations based on their individual knowledge and experience.

Since every autograph letter or document is unique, there can obviously be no absolute standard, and even dealers will necessarily differ in their opinions about values, depending on their individual holdings and clientele. It is surprising, however, to learn how often dealers do agree on valuation. Gathered together after some auction sale, they will be overheard to refer to prices as "very low," "astronomical," "wild," "very fair," and so on. Such unanimity implies that there are recognized norms to prices of autographs, and that the adjectives used are based on such norms.

Basic to the merchandising of all goods is first the rule of supply and demand. Dealers in autographs are bound by this principle as are dealers in any other field. When evaluating their holdings in relation to supply, they naturally take into consideration only those items on the open market that may be bought and sold. A plentiful supply of a man's letters permanently housed in the vaults of an institution is of no concern to them and will have no bearing whatsoever on current prices. Such letters are not for sale, never will be, and cannot possibly affect market valuations. I mention this as it has been my experience to have a librarian protest an "exorbitant" price on the grounds that his or her institution has a large mass of a certain character's letters. Common sense should point out that the greater the collection of a given person held by an institution, the fewer are the items of that person remaining available on the open market. And the more famous the name and the greater the demand, the more likely it is that prices will increase progressively through the years.

---

*Originally published in 1959; price estimates updated by the author in 1982.

Considerations in Pricing Autographs

To understand how a dealer goes about setting a price on a specific item, consider a fictitious letter of Washington, say an ALS, one-page quarto size, Mount Vernon, March 7, 1786. How would I go about pricing this?

First I would check the supply. How many Washington items similar to mine have been offered of late in other dealers' catalogues, at auction, or on the European market, and at what prices? How many do I personally have in my own stock? If six or eight, the supply has apparently been plentiful, the demand slow, or my price conceivably too high. I am not anxious to hold material indefinitely, and a reasonably quick turnover at a fair profit is, under most circumstances, sound business. My holdings suggest the wisdom of shading prices downward in the hope of rendering the material more attractive to collectors.

If I lower prices, however, I may find myself running short. What then are the chances of securing more? Do I know of sources not known to others where I may replenish my stock? Is there any likelihood that some large collection, privately owned, will come on the market? Or has a known supply recently been acquired by an institution, reducing the total of items available in the future? All these points must be weighed before I make my decision.

In the case of the Washington letter, I may decide that current supply should not cause any undue variation in the prices that have been standard during the past few years.

This question settled, I must next consider the demand--a far more complex problem. As far as salability is concerned, I need not worry, for Washington letters are always wanted by collectors to fill their sets of either the presidents or the great leaders of the American Revolution. Who a man is, and how famous, is directly reflected in the demand for his letters and has a proportionate bearing on their valuation. This fact is so obvious that it seems hardly worth mentioning. Lincoln and Poe, for example, are understandably in greater demand than William Jennings Bryan or Lydia Sigourney, and their letters will accordingly sell for far higher prices. But there are other factors besides that of identity which may affect the degree of demand and hence the valuation of any one item. I refer to content, date, condition, and length.

Generally speaking the content and date of a letter--it is difficult in most cases to consider them separately--will affect its valuation more than any other factor. An LS with fine content may sell twice as quickly as an ALS that says nothing. And content that is intensely interesting to one collector may not appeal to another. Collectors occasionally overlook this fact and are prone at times to question the dealer's price, not realizing that in determining values the dealer is considering not just one person's tastes but all possible interests of **all** collectors, as a good salesman must. The greater the clientele of a dealer, the wider the variety of tastes he must be prepared to satisfy. A dealer who has no customer interested in letters referring to early Indian matters will price his letters on that subject very low. Another dealer who may have five hungry customers searching for just such material will, of course, ask higher prices because of the demand and competition. Doing so is ordinary good business practice. It is also an argument in favor of collectors' not limiting their purchases to any one dealer.

As good content may cause prices to double, so date added to content may push prices even higher. I have repeatedly found, when considering purchase of some letter, that I instinctively look first at the writer's name and then at the date. Take a letter of a Civil War general. If the man is well known and the date is of the war period, I know it is a good item. If, in addition, the contents are exceptional, I have struck the jackpot. A war-dated letter of a general is worth many times the price of the same letter written either before or after the war. The letter of a Signer of the Declaration of Independence dated in the magic year of 1776 will fetch at auction many times the price of the same letter dated in either 1775 or 1777. In the literary field, early letters of poets and authors, written during the period when they were doing their most creative work and struggling for recognition, will command far higher prices than later examples of these same writers long after they have become successful. In the field of music or science, letters by composers and scientists on their own subjects, and written at crucial periods in their careers, are in much greater demand than are letters written late in life and on inconsequential subjects.

What, then, about my Washington letter? What about its content and date? The content is mediocre, relating to crops at Mount Vernon. And the date is a poor one. By 1786 the Revolution was well over and yet Washington was not yet president. The letter comes between the two periods of Washington's career that are of greatest interest to collectors. These aspects of the letter are not too good, and it looks as though I would have to put the price low if I am going to find a market.

However there are still the other factors to consider. What is the letter's condition? Fortunately, it is excellent, and both writing and signature are bold and clear. This is definitely an asset, for the average collector, who limits himself to securing only one example of any famous character in history, usually makes this point a major requirement. Some collectors even go so far as to sacrifice content and date to condition. Not so the specialist and the librarian, who tend to consider content above condition and who will rarely object to such defects as blurring, waterstain, or cracked folds, or even to letters written in pencil or signed with initials or not at all, if what the writer has to say is significant. But a letter of no consequence and in poor condition finds almost no buyer, private or institutional. And since private collectors far outnumber institutional collectors, items in poor condition will as a general rule be priced considerably lower than those that are better preserved.

Finally, the length of a letter does not so much affect value as it does salability. Many collectors desire items for framing or for exhibition. Such items usually must not exceed one page in length so that the entire contents and the signature are visible. Letters that cover two or more sides of a letter sheet are a nuisance to frame, requiring double glass, and even then part of the letter is out of sight.

The fact that my Washington letter covers only one page is perhaps its greatest asset. Such letters are not common. The general was a prolific writer, had much to say at times, and often said it at considerable length. Had it not been for this one factor, which greatly increases the demand for my letter, I might have considered the letter a somewhat undesirable example because of its poor date and content.

Summing up all the pros and cons, I would feel justified in placing a valuation on this Washington item of $3,000. Had the letter been of either presidential or Revolutionary date **and** with very fine content, it might have been worth $7,500 to $15,000 and up.

It is obvious, then, that pricing autographs is not a simple matter. Only the dealer, who handles great quantities of material, has contacts all over the world, and is in constant touch with colleagues, is in a position to gauge the market accurately. Others can at best only hazard a rough guess--often misleading and incorrect.

In the foregoing analysis, I have deliberately omitted the most important matter of all. I refer to authenticity. There is no happy medium on this score. If a letter is not genuine it is worthless. Reputable dealers' knowledge of the field and ability to guarantee what they sell naturally come before all else. There must be complete trust between dealers and collectors. Dealers are not infallible, but at least if they make honest mistakes they will at once refund whatever money is involved. As collectors rely on the dealers' knowledge and honesty with regard to authenticity, to the same extent must the dealers have confidence in their estimated valuations of the material they offer for sale.

Buying by Mail: Pointers for Beginners*

Forest H. Sweet

The primary pointer for buying by mail is to buy what really interests **you** and is priced within your budget. Your collection is for **your** satisfaction-- it should consist of things **you** like and can afford.

I urge you to buy from dealers' lists. The lists come by mail. There is no enthusiasm other than that aroused by the description of the item itself. Unless it is something you really want, you are likely to go on reading.

I read dealers' lists the minute they arrive, pencil in hand. I mark all I think I want. Then I read them over a second time, more carefully, and note defects, check with what I already have and what others offer, perhaps check price records, and prune my list to fit my budget. Then I write an order and mail it. When the items arrive, I go through the whole process again, and write a check. People who buy by mail using this cool, calculating, leisurely method are subject to no sales pressure except quality and worth.

Some people seem to think nobody else buys from catalogues--that catalogues are made solely for them. They are disturbed if they do not get all they order. Do not let yourself be so disappointed. You would be foolish to buy from a dealer--if there were such a dealer--who set all prices so high that nobody but you bought anything. There is no such dealer.

Buy something occasionally from each of the dealers--do not stick solely to one. You need the dealers just as much as they need you. It is smart to be on the customer lists of all of them. It may be easier to put all your business in one dealer's hands, but if you do, you will not see so wide a range of material to select from. An order or two a year--and it is hard to find a dealer whose lists do not offer any collector an item a year--will keep you on the dealer's customer list.

Some collectors believe that dealers can find anything anytime. We cannot. I have looked for years in vain for chances to buy inexpensive items to fill special wants. Willingness to pay several times what an item is worth does not always bring it out. The patience of Job is often necessary. After a long wait one day you may find it listed. After you phone for it, you may hear "Sorry, it's sold," and begin over; or you may be lucky and get it.

---

*Originally published in 1959.

Buy your letters and documents; do not let anybody sell them to you. Buy them for their own merit in your estimation.

If there is a "story," get the story in writing lest you forget it and later find you have something that looks ordinary but cost a fancy price. This is particularly true if you are subjected to high-pressure sales talk. Generally it is better to hunt up the story for yourself and put it in the folder with the letter. If, for example, you buy a Lincoln pardon, find out at least who the man was, what he did, and, if possible, what he did after discharge from the army. The ordinary pardon document then becomes more interesting to you. Dealers cannot always provide the story.

If you buy what you are not sure of from your own knowledge (and a beginner as well as an old-timer is sometimes tempted), buy it on representations of the seller through the mail. Honest mistakes can easily occur and are easily corrected; people who engage in fraud usually avoid the mails because the old gentleman with the striped trousers, star-spangled vest, and whiskers likes to keep his mails free from frauds.

However, no dealer or anybody else can absolutely **know** that Washington signed this or Lincoln signed that. Both died before anybody now living was born. We never saw either of them write. So our knowledge is secondary. It is informed opinion--informed by seeing and handling many letters and documents, enough to acquire a "feeling" for what is right and what is wrong.

Dealers' prices are erratic enough to make shopping worthwhile. That is why I suggest that you be provided with other dealers' current listings, so you can examine them for price variance at leisure. I urge you to get them sent to you regularly and read them as soon as they arrive. The bargain-priced specimens go quickly--the early bird catches the worm.

Leaders or intentional bargains are put into a list purposely; another kind of bargain is a sleeper--an unintentional bargain resulting from ignorance of the cataloguer or typographical error. You cannot build a collection on such buys but you can have a great deal of fun and pleasant recollections with the few you do get. It is a mistake, though, to think that the market price for all dealers or even for any dealer permanently falls to the lowest-ever quotation.

One dealer, by error or intent, listed a Charles Dickens check at $2.50. For a long time after that, any dealer offering a specimen of Dickens's autograph ran an equal chance of having his customer mention that absurdly low price, wondering whether the bottom had really fallen out of the market for Dickens.

Look for your desired items under headings for other specialties; a collector may miss a good item if he reads only the listings in his own line. Really good items have appeared in the least expected places.

Once you acquire the knack, it is easy to glance quickly through a whole autograph catalogue. The key words of your own interests will seem to jump out of the text prominently. Only then will you stop and read carefully. You will read lists as you do your newspaper, hastily, but missing little that interests you.

Sometimes you can judge a letter by its catalogue description, but often you cannot. The catalogue maker may ignore the very point of most interest to one particular collector. Most dealers ship on approval, provided the unwanted material is returned promptly, well packed, and with remittance for items kept. If in doubt, order on approval. You will generally find the item at least as good as it was described in a catalogue.

You can find out which are the best dealers for you by keeping a record of what you buy, where and when you buy it, and what you pay for it. Contents and values of individual letters vary widely, but if you average your purchases from each dealer you can form a fair judgment of which dealers serve you best. Such an alphabetical list of your autographs, with price data, is frequently highly useful; if you also keep a record of offerings in your lines of collecting that you do not buy, so much the better. In a short time you will be able to judge prices and values for yourself.

Get to know other nearby collectors who collect along some of the same lines as you; keep in contact with distant collectors of similar interests by mail.

You cannot get all the finest items no matter what you pay; you cannot collect with money alone. Collecting must be mixed with brains and a wide acquaintance. You can collect without money, except for postage on letters asking living celebrities for autographs. It requires a considerable investment of time and brains to write a letter good enough to earn a good reply, and not just an autograph on a card or photo.

Beginning collectors often ask, "Should I collect one individual only, or a whole subject?" Most people are interested in more than one individual, more than one subject. If beginners collect generally, not trying to specialize in any individual or any one subject, and buy only what is of interest to them, they will acquire experience that will be highly useful when they are ready to specialize.

Perhaps you watched Babe Ruth hit a ball out of the park, many years ago. If possession of a Babe Ruth autograph brings back a pleasant memory, then include it in your collection. (I make no apology for keeping one in my "sundry letters" file along with autographs worth a hundred or a thousand times as much money.) Autographs do not quarrel, however mixed the company the collector makes them keep.

As for specialization, avoid it until you cannot help it. The best training at first is to buy letters and documents of general interest that attract you, and look up all the references you can find to them. When you are ready to specialize, you will have a fair basis of knowledge on which to build a specialty collection.

The exception is the specialist who turns to manuscripts to go on past the boundary of printed sources. It is surprising how soon the collector of a specialty passes the frontier of recorded knowledge and begins to enjoy the pleasures of discovery.

Look for content, not form. That is the best rule I can offer collectors. Autographs should be collected for pride of possession, for enjoyment, for the creation of a new world into which, in imagination, the collector can go at will. An interesting letter brings far more pride and enjoyment than a mere signature card.

As a general collector, you will soon find your own special line of interest, but, before embarking on it, seek many dealers' advice on what the market is likely to hold for you: what the price range is likely to be, the extent of your probable competition, and so on. There are many wide-open lines for specialization at all times. Generally the most satisfaction comes from picking an unfashionable line and building up a good collection quietly before your open purchases attract enough attention to make it popular. There are many neglected people and periods in history. Your general collecting and your own interests will lead you to them.

Keep ahead of your collection in knowledge; never let it become financially burdensome. Then collecting can be a joy, if not forever, at least for a long time, because most collectors live long lives. They have to live long in order to get all the autographs and manuscripts they want.

Leaves from a Dealer's Notebook*

Gordon T. Banks

I want to discuss here a number of matters related to autograph collecting and selling from my perspective as a dealer.

Authenticity

With respect to fakes and mistaken identities in autograph material, I have felt for some time that we might fall into the position of a Chamber of Commerce which, while stressing a safety campaign, so publicized the hazards of the town highways and so magnified the incidents and accidents that people began to move out to a safer place. Both as a dealer and collector, I feel very strongly that these troubles are of strictly minor importance and, if over-emphasized, may be of harm to all of us. I would even go so far as to suggest that an impressive majority of collectors could completely ignore these difficulties or could at least set them back so far in their minds that the pleasures of collecting are not dulled. This reasoning is based in part on the fact that few collectors have the facilities or experience or perhaps even the time to engage in the detection of fakes or the consideration of forgeries. The question might even be raised as to whether the dealers have technological facilities to engage in the long and trying examinations required to settle positively questions of authenticity.

This may sound as though I am suggesting a measure of avoidance and trying to laugh off the frequent and very real appearance of bad material. Although forgeries are widely publicized, their actual frequency is trifling as far as the collector is concerned. I am confident that the average experienced dealer finds less than one item in five thousand that taxes his normal ability and leads to complicated examination. Also, the great majority of questioned autographs can and should be avoided. The average collector should not concern himself with any piece about which there is considerable doubt. To my mind, a letter or document that requires a deposition of an expert or depends on the preponderance of evidence of four out of seven experts should be left alone. I rule out, of course, those institutions that have well-equipped laboratories to check books, prints, and documents and those collectors who wish to adopt such examination as a hobby or who find detective work

---

*Originally published in 1950.

engaging and wish either to do the work themselves or to have those who are technically proficient do it for them. But the average collector must rely first on a responsible dealer who will screen the facsimiles and the recognizable forgeries, and advise against the doubtful pieces. The average collector should always deal with people who will be responsible for their merchandise and will prefer to have a questioned item returned than to have it kept by their customer.   Any dealer of experience and integrity should bring to his customers a sense of confidence, assuring them that every care has been taken to provide only authentic merchandise and that if any reasonable doubt exists, a prompt and full adjustment will be made. This can promote a peace of mind that permits the collector to temper his worries from this source.   This obligation of the dealer is only one of many, but none is more important, for without mutual confidence the pleasures of this avocation are limited.

Confidence

My selection of the word **confidence** may be ill-advised, for there have been confidence men engaged in selling commodities from the Eiffel Tower to the Brooklyn Bridge. Sometimes the dealer is so unbeloved as to be placed in this class by some thoughtful customer.   However, confidence also means conviction, reliance, trust, or faith. Down through the ages has come to us that best of all definitions of faith, "The evidence of things not seen." Strangely enough, it is not only the customer who expects fair and responsible dealing. It is very evident that every dealer needs and expects an equivalent fairness in his transactions with collectors. I will describe some of my own experiences to illustrate the unnecessary misunderstandings that break down the mutual confidence between dealer and customer. Even as I pointed out the infrequency of the bad autograph, so may I emphasize that these random experiences are not at all typical of collectors as a whole, but serve merely as danger signals. In describing these incidents, I tamper with dates, amounts, and geography, but the essential details of each case are accurate.

My desk is scarcely ten feet off Beacon Street in the shadow of our statehouse. Even the architect, in restoring our interior, hung the door so that practically every visitor is directed to my outer desk. I enjoy these contacts and probably would not change my location from choice except when the press of cataloguing and similar work drives me to a less accessible cubicle. Our theory at Goodspeed's is that many collectors wish a courteous reception and recognition and then desire to be left alone to enjoy poking around among the books and autographs. However, quite to the contrary is the occasional visitor who prefers a person at his elbow constantly in attendance. This attention we always give to those who desire it, but in general it is more helpful to lay out the material and leave the customer to enjoy the contents without constant interruption.   Conversation distracts, and many an owner has suffered some financial loss by constantly interrupting me as I tried to read the long and important letter that he wished to sell. Such interruptions prevented my full appreciation of the letter until after the owner had left the shop (with a little less than we might have paid).

One rainy day in March I was busy with a customer. A woman entered, leaving her husband outside, parked in a place where parking is not permitted. Since she had only about three to five minutes before she expected interference from a police officer, she interrupted our conversation and asked for a framed autograph for not more than ten dollars. Considering framing costs today, you can imagine what we could put under glass for ten dollars. It would be either a common example of a good name or possibly an interesting letter of an extremely common name. A Longfellow letter marked down to $7.50 seemed to be the only appropriate specimen. Next, would we erase the price? Would we send it to Florida? I pointed out that if it were to be shipped to Florida, there would be a charge for building a box and shipping the autograph.

Then the fun began. The lady in question, with some spirit, demurred at this charge; she said she assumed that we would take care of such an expense. At that exact moment her eye lit on a quite attractive framed autograph at $17.50. She immediately forgot the Longfellow and fixed on the new piece. This did not have our frame, but she insisted that we send to the fifth floor for one of our framing labels to be pasted on the back of this framed autograph. I pointed out that it was not framed at Goodspeed's and should not be so described, but I promised to get a label and clip off the indication that it was framed at Goodspeed's. Down came a boy with the label, the offending words clipped away. The lady grabbed label and autograph and, running to her car where her husband was frantically signaling the approach of the officer, she called back over her shoulder, "I'll mail it myself."

With some relief I turned back to customer A, who had patiently waited to tell me of a group of very important letters he had picked up from a family upstate at an attractive price; he therefore was not interested in the solitary example of the same colonial figure that I had laid aside for him. Here were two customers. To one we made a sale of $17.50 after some amusing difficulties. The other customer, delightful to talk with and an old friend, spent an hour with me to no avail. In the fifteen years I have known him he has not purchased enough material to reimburse Goodspeed's for my time. Even so, as a dealer I think I am right in giving this time freely and avoiding any discourtesy that would indicate that my time may have been needed elsewhere. This is not simply a matter of common courtesy but a business practice that over a period of fifty years or more, I am told, has brought dividends of good will that we enjoy and continue to cultivate.

One-Way Mail

All dealers are troubled with one-way mail. Here is an example drawn from our February correspondence. "Have you any Hancock letters? Please send copies. Last fall you had a few Adams letters on your list. Have you one now?" This lead sounded good, so about an hour of secretarial time was spent in transcribing six long items and a reasonable amount of background was dug out for presentation in the accompanying letter. Seven weeks later another letter from the same person asked, "Have you any Lincoln letters? Will you please send copies of all you have." No mention was made of either Hancock or Adams, nor had there been during the seven weeks. Now, the first inquiry cost us approximately four dollars, according to our accountant. We provided this service willingly as a good venture in both merchandising and courtesy, but you can see why we were tempted to give only a sketchy response to the inquiry for Lincoln material, and in the future this individual will receive the briefest of replies. I feel that all dealers would give more complete service more frequently if at least they received a courteous "thank you" when material is offered and not purchased. On top of the thanks there should be some explanation as to why the merchandise was unsuitable or the price out of range.

The "Important" Customer

Last fall I had a telephone call from some distance asking for photostats of all examples of royalty that we had--before 1800. The collector is well known and was able to purchase anything that we could offer, and there again, the potential seemed high. Within twenty-four hours we sent a package of photostats costing us approximately fifteen dollars and covering a wide variety of examples in both interest and price. To this day we have never received any acknowledgment or a return of the photostats. Perhaps this person wonders why, although letters in the meantime have been answered, we never seem to have anything in his field. Now, this photostat episode was not the first with this particular customer. He had entailed labor without results several times before, but since last fall he has missed triple A material that has gone to those who compete in his field and have better habits. In one case he found this out and objected because we had passed him by. Collectors of any experience soon learn that there is always a dearth of really fine material and that if they are truly in love with their hobby, it is of great importance to them to have first preference in their field. A variation on the same theme is the unfair bargain hunter who always quibbles about price and in the long run will invariably miss the better material, which will go to the collector who recognizes a fair price and is willing to pay it.

The Customer You Cannot Refuse

Last August I received a wire from an internationally known collector requesting a list of items in his field and current price information on a standard, widely offered type of document. Normally it is our policy to refuse to value any material offered by a competing dealer to our customer or any other kind of material that we cannot see. But the answer was so simple in this case and the person so prominent that we could not tactfully refuse. We were not only able to supply the information by return mail, but we sent a descriptive list of autographs of major interest to him, including one item the like of which he will never again have the opportunity to purchase. Here again, there was no acknowledgment of our letter or of our follow-up, although we have had correspondence since that time. This lack of response does not promote good service.

Delayed Returns

Every dealer should give his mail customers opportunities similar to those enjoyed by "in-town" customers. A key aspect is a liberal return policy. This is an expensive privilege and should be used carefully. If a customer fails to report promptly, another customer may be annoyed because the dealer can give no definite report.

We have had items returned as late as nine weeks from day of shipment. This should never happen.

Careless Packing

In January we sent "on approval" a fine letter well protected by careful packing. It came back promptly, but enclosed simply in a manila envelope. Corners creased?--yes. A little crumpled?--yes. Will it be marked down?-- yes. Generally it is not the financial loss that hurts so much as the feeling that a fine autograph has been abused.

The Angry Customer

I have left for my last example the type of difficulty that it is almost impossible to adjust, for anger, even when it has cooled, leaves scars that cause embarrassment for an indefinite period. A few years ago a customer whom I had not seen for some time visited us. I was busy examining and studying a new collection we had purchased the day before. As a practice, we price all of our merchandise; at least, we intend that it shall be all marked, but none of this material had been priced. However, this series of letters was so interesting that I handed a few over for the customer's enjoyment, at the time having little or no expectation of making a sale. This collection was purchased as a unit, and I intended to sell it as a unit, all the material being closely knit together.

The customer matched my enthusiasm letter for letter and picked out the finest individual piece. Much against my will I was persuaded to consider selling this letter separately, and much against my better judgment I was urged to set an immediate price for this piece. Under the circumstances my enthusiasm may have affected the price, but bear in mind that this was a key piece. The customer purchased the letter and was apparently very happy about the purchase. Going to another city, he found other letters of the same individual at half the price that I had set for this unusual letter, and he gained the impression in conversation with others that our price was excessive. Shortly afterward, I received an abusive letter expressing his opinion about the price and making other statements that were completely unsupportable. The letter was followed by a telephone conversation of similar content.

To my knowledge, Goodspeed's has rarely refused to accept the return of any merchandise for any reason if the customer makes known his wishes within a reasonable time after the purchase. If it is a question of authenticity, a reasonable time is a **lifetime,** but the average circumstances of price, condition, or content may be adjusted within a proper time. This was equally true in this case. Had this customer written or phoned or talked about the problem in a temperate manner, we would have parted the best of friends. I would gladly have accepted his opinion that I might have set the price too high, although I still believe the letter to be worth the amount he first accepted. We took the letter back and gave him full credit, but after the serious and unwarranted charge detailed in the letter to me, I told the person that in the future we would prefer to make no sales to him except from our published catalogues, and at the published prices. We may suffer somewhat in the diversion of his business to someone else, but ultimately the highly selective, rather obvious sort of merchandise that he bought could easily be placed with a dozen other collectors. Customers often do not understand that what is important is not our loss of business with this particular customer but our loss of friendly contact and his loss of a preferred source of material that he wants.

Rewards of the Job

The real joy of this business is the generous spirit of customers who write expressing their satisfaction after a transaction or those who shake hands as they leave and can honestly say that they had a great time and found something choice to take away with them. One of my favorites is a retired lawyer who comes in weeks after a purchase to tell me of new insights he has gained through studying his last purchase, sometimes checking over details that I had missed. Year after year, his collection has filled in against the loneliness of his later life, and he says collecting has kept him young. The door also swings wide for a surgeon who collects strictly in his own chosen field but enjoys immensely each new and interesting letter and probes through the text, pointing out with his professional knowledge names and places unknown to me. My top drawer always has treasures laid away for his next visit. These people inspire dealers to set their standards high in order to deserve this high confidence, making a profession out of what can be merely merchandising. They promote the confidence and good will without which we operate at a loss, no matter how great the profit.

I will close with a decalogue for the cultivation of happy collecting.

Ten Suggestions

1. Do not buy autographs as a speculation. You can do better in the stock market.

2. Buy autographs as you "buy" opera or "two on the aisle" or possibly the newest iris or a hybrid rose for your garden or greenhouse. Pay what you can afford, know a good value, and then forget the price.

3. Buy the best in its field. If you cannot afford Poe, buy Holmes. Buy one significant letter rather than three ordinary letters. Cheap autographs are not necessarily good values.

4.   Keep within your means. Budget your hobby and maybe you will have the strength of mind to avoid money worries.

5.   Do not bargain unless you know your field and have something to offer. It takes two to bargain, and you will lose every time if the bargaining is one-sided.

6.   Pay cash or the near equivalent, and many sellers will share their savings with you with advance quotations, occasional savings, and other services.

7.   Avoid the habitual return. Approvals will generally be freely granted, but, as a courtesy, returns should be made promptly and the reason given.

8.   Write your dealer (or dealers) once a month; visit your dealer once a year. Provide specific want lists to get in ahead of the catalogue.

9.   Have a plan. Diversify if you wish and can afford it. Better still, specialize and become expert on "your" period, event, or person.

10.   Join the Manuscript Society, get together with other collectors, and profit by the experience of others.

Philately and Autographs*

Herman Herst, Jr.

Cigarette manufacturers, eager to increase their market, found that they could double their sales by offering their wares to a group of potential customers never before tapped: the female of the species. Through skillful propaganda, they succeeded in making smoking a feminine vice as well as a masculine one. The annual sales figures show the extent to which they have been successful.

Autograph collectors have a similar opportunity to bring about a tremendous increase in their numbers, and with that, an almost limitless increase in the demand for material. It does not require any pioneering, for the seeds were planted years ago. It merely requires careful nurturing. I refer to the philatelic demand for autographs, a demand that few autograph dealers have made any attempt to satisfy.

It is not often that two hobbies possess so many common roots. In former years, stamps and coins went hand in hand, and the collector or dealer in one field was often interested in the other. For a number of reasons, stamp collecting in the past two decades has become such a popular hobby that it has far outstripped the collecting of coins, and now, except for the juvenile collector, the average philatelist is not a numismatist.

Philatelists are, however, collectors of stamps and things relating to stamps, notably postal history. But they are more than collectors: they are seekers of knowledge, not only about the stamps that they are collecting, but about the stories behind the stamps. They know some important American composers, for five of them (Foster, Sousa, Herbert, MacDowell, and Nevin) were honored on our stamps in 1940. They know some of our greatest military heroes (Washington, Greene, Andrew Jackson, Scott, Sherman, Grant, Sheridan, Lee, and "Stonewall" Jackson) for they were honored philatelically in 1936. They are well versed in people and in events.

Time was when the average philatelist went down to the local bookstore and picked out an album. The album had a multitude of little squares in it, some with pictures, and the goal was to fill the squares up. It was a lot of fun, but it did not teach too much. When one set or page was completed, the philatelist moved on to the next.

---

*Originally published in 1950; updated by the author in 1982.

Collecting today is somewhat different. Although the printed album, as it is called, still outsells the blank album by far, advanced collectors now refuse to be dictated to in their collecting. They buy what interests them, and they are not bound to putting an item in a book because there is a space for it. In any major stamp exhibition today, better than 90 percent of the exhibits are on blank album pages, which the collectors arrange according to their own desires, and not those of a publisher. The reason is apparent: today serious stamp collectors collect more than stamps.

There is no question that a collection of stamps picturing Lincoln, a very popular philatelic subject, is enhanced by a portrait of the subject. Add to it a campaign ribbon, and perhaps a Civil War patriotic cover picturing the martyred president, and the collection takes on an added luster. But include with it an autograph, even a mere "cutout" from a document, and the collection has in it an actual living part of the subject that will instill not only life, but interest and value as well.

The philatelic possibilities are tremendous. Survey after survey has shown that no hobby outranks stamp collecting. The estimated number of devotees ranges from 1 million to 10 million, the latter figure being supplied by no less an authority than former Postmaster General James A. Farley--and that estimate was made in 1935, when it was not nearly so popular a hobby as it is today. What women did for the cigarette industry was no more promising than what a linking of the autograph hobby with the stamp hobby could accomplish.

Already there are signs that this marriage is taking place. A number of prominent stamp collectors have taken membership in the Manuscript Society, primarily with the aim of advancing their own stamp collections.

The parallels between the two hobbies are surprising. The average autograph collector regards a franked signature as of secondary interest and value compared with a signed letter; the philatelist holds the contrary view. Prior to the use of stamps for the franking of letters in the 1840s, the autograph of a person authorized to send a letter free was the equivalent of a stamp; even today, the signature of the president of the United States (though he seldom avails himself of the privilege) will take the place of the first-class postage that the average user of the mail must affix.

Since the early days of collecting, franked letters have been in philatelic demand. Some facsimile signatures, placed on tiny bits of gummed paper, were actually sold by postmasters in the early days of the issuance of stamps. Today they are as rare to stamp collectors, and as valuable, as the rarest autograph is to autograph collectors. Even the commonest of franks, such as those of Henry Clay, Daniel Webster, and Albert Gallatin, possess far greater value to the stamp collector than to the autograph collector.

Stamp collectors have the same temperament, patience, knowledge, and instinct for collecting that autograph collectors do. Their dealers for the most part have a zeal that is already making itself felt in the autograph field; almost any autograph dealer can tell of the increasing number of philatelic contacts that he is making. In the past two years alone we have even had the unusual spectacle of stamp auctioneers offering for sale entire groups of autographs, many of them not the least bit valued for their philatelic associations.

The ideal marriage is one in which bride and groom each bring something to the other. So it should be, and so it will be, in a liaison between these two hobbies. More and more autograph collectors are finding that an occasional postage stamp brightens their own pages. No longer is it necessary to mount the tremendous steel engraving of Thomas Jefferson with the holograph; now, for a few cents, one can visit the nearest post office and purchase a beautiful mint steel engraving of our third president. And for an expenditure of less than two hundred dollars, one can complete a set illustrating every deceased president, postal custom forbidding the picturing of a living person on a stamp issued in his honor. A stamp dealer can sell the same set in used stamps for little more than a dollar!

Illus. 1. A Jefferson frank.

How to Mix Collecting Hobbies

How best to accomplish this proposed marriage of the hobbies? Probably the best way is through publicity. Philately has a wonderful press: a half-dozen or more weekly magazines, all thirsting for news of anything pertaining to the hobby. Several of these have circulations of thirty thousand or more. There are two prominent stamp societies, one with about fifty thousand members, the other with fifteen thousand. Both publish monthly journals, and both seek outside contributions. Among these tens of thousands of stamp collectors are an unknown number of autograph collectors; most of them do not even know of the existence of the Manuscript Society. Many of them do not even know that there are dealers who make a living from the purchase and sale of autographs, just as stamp dealers of their acquaintance earn a similar living from the purchase and sale of stamps.

The field is largely untapped, and it awaits discovery by enterprising autograph collectors and dealers who want to do the pioneering.

I can only hazard a guess as to the probable results if the number of autograph collectors in this country were even doubled. Items now plentiful would become much scarcer; items already scarce would become rare. But the value of every autograph collection would be doubled, perhaps trebled; the value of every dealer's stock would increase proportionately. Collections offered for direct sale or at auction would find a tremendously increased audience awaiting them. With a far more active market, both dealers and collectors would benefit.

But the autograph field would also benefit in other ways. With more people interested, more material would be found. Stamps, the existence of which was never supposed, are being turned up daily; with more collectors and dealers on the search for autographs, it is certain that material now hiding in garrets and basements would come to light. It was a philatelist who turned up the tremendous number of letters written by Alexander Stephens, vice president of the Confederate States of America; it well might be a philatelist who similarly turns up a cache of Robert E. Lee letters, for example.

There is also the benefit of the thorough and painstaking research that philatelists have tended to give their hobbies. No students of the Confederacy were better informed on that Lost Cause than Van Dyk MacBridge and August Dietz. Edward Stern's work on presidential and cabinet franks was outstanding. Philately's greatest students such as Stanley Ashbrook, Dr. Carroll Chase, Elliott Perry, and John A. Luff have all left their lifetime studies in their books. Manuscript collectors who do not use these works as source material are missing a good deal.

What Should I Do with My Collection?*

Joseph E. Fields

With apologies to Miguel Cervantes and the late Randolph Adams, "Naked we come into this world, and naked we go out of it." Much as we would like to do so, we cannot take our collections with us. Practically speaking, it would serve no purpose. Regardless of where we may land in the hereafter, there will be many opportunities for autograph collecting; great names abound on the far side of the River Styx and inside the Pearly Gates.

Every collector, no matter how modest, should come face to face with the question, "What shall I do with my collection?" May I urge you to give some thought to this problem while you are still among the living? Do not leave your decision to the courts. If you do make your own disposition, your estate will owe less in taxes. You yourself should have the say as to what is done with the collection.

A collector of autographs is fundamentally a sentimentalist. Without sentimentality no collector can be either successful or serious. Autograph collecting is a highly personal hobby; every item collected is unique. Nothing can bring you closer to the great figures of the past. You gain a knowledge of them that no other living person may have.

Let me illustrate with an anecdote from the lives of two of our great collectors of the past--Dr. Thomas Addis Emmet and Augustin Daly. In April 1889 Emmet was persuaded by Walter R. Benjamin to part with the great Lynch ALS which Benjamin then sold to Daly. Emmet was devastated by the loss of his prize item and subsequently appealed to Daly, as a matter of sentiment, to allow him to purchase it back, directly. With great magnanimity Daly allowed Emmet to purchase the letter back for $3,250, plus a cut Lynch signature, a Thomas Heyward DS, and a Hancock ALS. Within eight days, seven letters passed between the two men. Their letters indicate that these men who lived in the same city never met personally.

One does not need to have a Lynch ALS in order to feel as the good doctor did. All collectors feel as he did about their collections. If you doubt it, try to pry even a trivial item away from a collector. Autograph collectors, being sentimentalists, are more than cognizant of the dilemma of disposing of their collections.

---

*Originally published in 1953.

You have four choices if you are trying to decide what to do with your collection. First, you may give it to an heir, or to any other individual, during your lifetime. Second, you may will it to an heir on your death. Third, you may present it to an institution. Fourth, you may sell it privately or at public auction.

Let us take up each of these choices in somewhat more detail.

A Gift during Your Lifetime

Since 1976, U.S. law has permitted you to give up to $10,000 in one year to an individual without having to fill out any gift tax forms. The gross amount not subject to gift tax in 1983 was $275,000, rising in annual increments to a total of $600,000 in 1986 and thereafter.

Will to an Heir

If a collector has a legal heir who appreciates his collection, who will add to it, and who will make use of it, then the collector has a moral duty to dispose of it in this fashion. Unfortunately, all too seldom do we find the offspring of collectors sufficiently interested to be entrusted with the care, nurture, use, or disposal of an autograph collection. Before you will your collection to an heir, ask yourself whether the recipient is worthy of it. Will he use it? Does he appreciate its intrinsic and monetary value? Will he care for it properly? Only after carefully weighing these factors can you possibly make this decision. I speak from experience when I say there is nothing that gladdens the heart of a collector more than to pass on his collection to a son or daughter who will continue to use it, enlarge it, and give it the loving care it deserves.

Present to an Institution

In the absence of an appropriate individual recipient, you may decide to present your collection to one of the many institutional depositories. This is more likely to be the preferred choice if your estate is so sizable that it would be advantageous to so dispose of it as a means of decreasing inheritance taxes. Giving a collection to an institution is not to be taken lightly. It requires more study and investigation than the two choices already discussed.

If you are thinking of presenting your collection to an institution you should consider these questions:

1. Is the institution capable of caring for your collection? Does it have the physical and custodial facilities to care for it or is it like the well-known New England historical society that has the papers of one of the prominent Revolutionary War generals stuffed into twelve large cardboard cartons in a completely helter-skelter fashion--all because there is no one available to arrange, catalogue, and index the material?

2. Will the institution make appropriate use of your collection? Will the material be made available for study by students? Will it be put on exhibit regularly and in an accessible place so that the public may view it conveniently? (May I draw this to the attention of the federal government, which has seen fit to deposit our three great state documents in the National Archives? A more difficult, inaccessible, and inconvenient place could not be found if they had tried.) Or will the institution do as 98 percent of the institutions have done--entomb the collection on its shelves and there let it remain unused, unpublished, unindexed, and unavailable?

3. Will your collection be appreciated? Will you and your gift soon be forgotten? The ivy climbs thick over the name of Wiebold at the University of Chicago, and the pigeons roost comfortably and serenely on the statue of James Buchanan Duke. Will you receive public recognition for your generosity or will you merely receive a short TLS from the librarian, accepting your gift? Recently one of the large New England universities received from an alumnus a handsome gift consisting of numerous fine examples of first editions by an American author.   All were desirable rarities.   To this day the donor has received no recognition in the annual report of the library, while lesser contributors with more famous Back Bay names have received mention. Needless to say, the university probably will not receive the remainder of the extensive collection.

4. Will your gift serve the best interests of collecting, from the standpoint of both the private as well as the institutional collector? Cooperation between collectors and institutions is not a one-way street. The cooperation should flow freely in both directions. There has been an uninterrupted flow of autographic material into the files and shelves of institutions. This should not and must not be. There is no more certain way of sounding the death knell of collecting than by forever incarcerating autograph items in an institution.   It was private enterprise, manifested by such early collectors as Sprague, Tefft, Emmet, Gilmore, Gratz, and Dreer, that focused the attention of others onto the delights and pleasures of collecting. The result of the precedent and the course they set has been that for the past century most of the historical societies and similar public institutions have been conceived and perpetuated at the hands of collectors.   Few of our great libraries and societies would exist today without the private interest manifested by collectors and their pursuits.   Without such men as Morgan, Brown, Huntington, Folger, Clements, and many others, of what would our institutions consist?   The custodians would have nothing to "custode." Probably there would not even be custodians. The private interest and rugged individualism of the collectors have served the institutions well.

The Consequences of Institutionalization

What will be the result if the steady procession of material into institutions continues and the source becomes dry? The desire to collect will be destroyed.   There are evidences of atrophy setting in today.   With the incentive to collect gone, values will decline rapidly.   The already groaning shelves of the institutions will be weighed down with paper in a mess so chaotic that it will defy all human efforts to untangle it. No institutional budget could withstand the strain of hiring the experienced help necessary to catalogue, transcribe, index, and file the material. I can name today a large number of institutions, including state and national archives, in that very predicament. If the trend continues, we may well be in the process of killing the goose that laid the golden egg.

Is planned destruction of material by institutions the answer to the problem? Who among us would be willing to decide whether a letter or document should be destroyed? If it is a matter of limited housing, restricted funds for hiring proper personnel, or shortage of time, then surely there are other more practical, economical, and moral solutions than destruction.

Some Solutions

I would like to suggest that institutions sell duplicate and unwanted items. This would serve the public as well as the private interest. Certainly these items will bring more revenue at public or private sales than as scrap paper. In addition, they would provide abundant material to promote the private interest and perpetuate the system. Serving the private interest will more than repay the institutions by a greater enthusiasm and better support for their program. Their membership will increase--not with dead freight but with good, lively, and working members who will be a credit to the organization and have a genuine interest above and beyond merely participating as a civic duty.

Many institutions are hamstrung by legal restrictions imposed upon them by donors who forbid them to dispose of the gifts through sale or to trade them for other more desirable items. Some are even forbidden by the terms of the gift to allow removal of items from the library for purposes of exhibition. Do not shackle an institution with such provisos. Fields of interest change with time. What may be desirable today may in the future be of secondary interest and better sold or traded so that another more desirable item may be acquired. Make your gift with but one restriction--that the institution forever have its red carpet out to all deserving collectors and students, to anyone who is interested enough to stop, look, and listen. Permit the sale of your gift if it best serves the interest of the institution. Let the ultimate decision rest with the director. This implies faith in the management that your best intentions are carried out. The following deed of gift ensures that the spirit of your gift will be honored:

I, _____, hereby give to the trustees of the University of _____, for the use and benefit of the library, (here follows a description of the property). The said gift is to be without any conditions whatsoever and the donee shall have absolute discretion to retain the property herewith conveyed or to sell or to exchange the same or to make such other disposition of said property that shall seem wise and prudent to the director of the said library.

I should like also to advocate the appointment of collectors to the governing boards of institutions and libraries. Not many have, at the present time, done this. Collectors will help ensure the continuance of the best interests of collecting, private as well as institutional. They would be invaluable assets to the libraries they serve, for they have valuable insights into the problems of purchase, acquisition, rarity, value, authentication, and desirability, and other problems common to private as well as institutional collectors. The institutions have long wooed collectors as benefactors. Very few have thought well enough of them to place them at or near the helm.

Sale or Auction

Assuming you have no suitable heir and there is no institution meeting the requirements you have established, then there is but one other course open to you--to sell your collection privately or at public sale. At least you may then be assured of several facts:

o The new owner will give the document loving care.

o The item will be appreciated.

o The item's sentimental value will be greater to the private collector than to the institutional collector.

o You will pass along to a fellow collector the pleasure you once enjoyed.

o You will have the personal satisfaction of placing your autographs on the public market where they may continue in the realm of public interest rather than being forever removed from a competitive market.

o By promoting a continuing interest in others you will bring about competition and thereby increase the value of autographs.

o You will have the personal satisfaction of dispersing material that will spread the word of our American heritage.

Perhaps all this has been best put by the familiar quotation from the will of the great French collector, Edmond de Goncourt:

My wish is that my drawings, my prints, my Curiosities, my Books--in a word, these things of art which have been the joy of my life--shall not be consigned to the cold tomb of a museum, and subjected to the stupid glance of the careless passer-by; but I require that they shall be dispersed under the hammer of the Auctioneer, so that the pleasure which the acquiring of each one of them has given me shall be given again, in each case, to some inheritor of my own tastes.

* * * * *

Robert F. Metzdorf

There are too many factors involved for anyone to give a categorical answer to an inquiry about what to do with an autograph collection. Some collections, by their nature, might well be destroyed when the collector is finished with them; others should be preserved at all costs. Some should be broken up and redistributed; still others should remain intact. The collector himself is faced with these and with many other problems, depending upon the nature of the collection under consideration, his own financial situation and the tax laws at the time of decision, his family obligations, his preferences, and even his prejudices. Collecting, to my way of thinking (and I became a collector before I became a curator), is one of the last strongholds of individual enterprise: you can collect whatever you choose, and nobody can tell you what you have to do with the things later on.

What are some of the considerations you should bear in mind when you are attempting to decide for yourself? Perhaps the only bit of advice that holds true for all cases is this: decide carefully, coolly, logically, and unemotionally after studying the collection, considering possible destinations for it, and securing the best advice available.

En Bloc or Piecemeal Disposition?

Let us assume that you are about to make your will, or that for some reason you wish to dispose of the collection during your lifetime. If the reasons for the latter course are financial, you will wish to realize all you can from the material by selling it. The question immediately arises whether to sell **en bloc,** or piece by piece. In selling a collection as a unit, you may sell it to a dealer, who will propose either to remarket it as a unit, thus preserving the identity of the collection (at least for a time), or to break it up and sell the contents individually. You may sell the material to an institution with the understanding that the autographs will be kept together as a unit (in which case you might have to shade the price a bit); or the institution may separate the items, intercollating some with its own holdings and selling other items.

Or you may sell the collection piecemeal. It may be put up at auction, with the more important items offered separately and the less important items grouped in lots. This has often been done, and I do not think the auction business is about to give up the ghost, so far as manuscripts are concerned, for want of suitable material to offer for sale.

Collectors feed principally on the products of attics and storage files. If the great and sometimes greedy institutions of our country seem to swallow up the entire available supply of one type of material, you may be sure that the collecting instinct is so strong, interest in the past so intense, and respect for the memory of the great so well founded that collectors will find new fields in which to satisfy the collecting urge, as well as the competitive instinct. The history of collecting proves it, as does the history of trade. I cannot tell you, of course, exactly what the new fields will be, but there are indications of some new directions that collecting will take. One such field is business and labor documents.

Another way of disposing of items one by one is to sell them to dealers or to other collectors. But bear in mind that, once the gems of a collection are gone, the remainder may be difficult to market.

The decision in selling a collection, no matter what method is used, should be based on the purpose the collector originally had in mind and on the financial situation of the vendor. Cost of acquisition as well as cost of dispersal should be considered, as should special tax situations that may exist at any given time and location. The advantages that can accrue through careful study of the tax laws and one's own financial position are many and varied, and no one should overlook them. If you are going to have an auction, get the soundest and coolest advice you can about the probable total of the sale; then figure the deductions of auction expense, and decide what to do.

You might go to a friendly librarian who is experienced in such matters, or you might very well go to a dealer. Happy are collectors who have dealer friends with whom they can talk over such problems! And happy are the dealers with collecting friends who bring such problems to them!

If the decision is favorable to continue with the plan, secure a favorable date for the sale, and do not accept a sale date without studying the other offerings of the season (in other auction rooms as well as the one you propose to use), competing public events, and any other factors that may apply. Instruct your executors to do all these things, if you do not plan to be around when the decisions are made. And be sure you have a clear title to all goods that you offer!

The Gift

If you are considering disposal by gift, there are other questions you should put to yourself. If you cannot come up with the answers, you should seek some trustworthy advice.

Where will the material be of most use to the public, and to that specialized branch of the public called scholars? Where will the manuscripts get the best care; that is, where will you find trained personnel, proper storage conditions, and good exhibition facilities? Will the new owner add material to the collection, and will the collection take on new life, instead of remaining static? Is there material already in the depository that will dovetail with your gift, making each of greater usefulness and interest? If the gift is made in your lifetime, will you be able to see it from time to time, work (or play) with it, add to it, and be sure it is getting proper care?

That is a fairly long series of questions. But the question method does underline one of my main points: nobody can tell you what to do with your collection, and no one should try to do so. My own opinion is that, if you have been smart enough to conjure up the idea of a significant collection of manuscript material, enterprising enough to secure the money to realize your ideal, diligent enough to learn the necessary background material, thoughtful enough to care for the collection properly, and clever enough to compete with others operating in the same field, then you are presumably perfectly capable of studying the situation and deciding what you want to do with your own collection.

Let us imagine that you have decided to give away your collection, either directly or by bequest, and that you have a preference about where it should go. You may favor a local historical society, a hometown library, your alma mater, a great library of national reputation, a particular institution that already possesses supplementary material (which means the things you wish you had in your own collection!), or a neighboring institution with which you have friendly relations. My advice would be that you talk over the matter with the librarian of whatever place you have in mind. Take along an inventory.

Then sit back and listen. You may be surprised. Not all librarians are insatiable octupuses, snaking in with greedy arms everything they can encompass. In fact, beware of such librarians, for their libraries may be storage places, historico-literary graveyards, not libraries for use. If you canvass your own experience, I think you will agree that most librarians are honest people, specialists who work for a living at their specialties, interested in historical and literary materials and concerned about the fate of them more than they are with their own prestige or any fleeting monetary rewards that acquisitiveness may bring them. Your particular librarian may be very frank and tell you that he appreciates your offer, but that he cannot accept it--and he will be very sure to tell you why. He may not be able to meet your conditions, for example. If you wanted a separate room for the collection, and he does not have the space or does not agree that your collection deserves such a monument, he will have to say no. If the acceptance of the collection means taking on financial burdens that the library cannot assume--such as additional storage facilities, additional staff positions, or expensive reorganization--he will have to refuse. In such a situation, if your mind is made up, you will need to consider "buying your way in," literally, as others have occasionally done, figuring out a cash gift or an endowment fund to supplement the donation of material, or otherwise overcoming obstacles. It is not always so easy to give something away as many people assume! There are, of course, many collections that any administrator in the country would give his eyeteeth to secure. But we are for the most part considering the average collection--if such a thing exists.

On the other hand, your adviser may tell you that your collection obviously belongs somewhere else. It may supplement an existing concentration of papers elsewhere, and should join it to complete a group that should never have been separated. Let me make a plea for the collections that should never be broken up--either by sale, gift, or sheer inadvertence. The advantages of having a person's papers in one place, for example, are too many to list: those who have worked with Emerson material at Harvard, the Boswell papers at Yale, or the William Henry Seward collection at Rochester (to mention but three that I have myself used) can testify to the truth of this. One of the great tragedies in this field in recent times was the sale some years ago of Sir Isaac Newton's papers, which are now scattered over several continents and can never be studied in one place.

Putting my advice into a slogan, I would say, "Discuss before you disperse, study before you select, and think before you get thanked."

* * * * *

Thomas R. Adams

Joseph Fields and Robert Metzdorf have thoroughly covered the various problems of what to do with one's collection. I completely agree with most of what they have said. As a commentator, therefore, I am reduced to picking but a single point from Dr. Fields's remarks in which I find I disagree with him. He objects to the steady flow of materials into the shelves of institutions. He sees in this a drying up of the sources for autograph collectors, a destruction of the whole race of men like the Morgans, Browns, and Huntingtons, and, in general, a "sounding the death knell of collecting."

If I may say so, this sounds very much like the group of booksellers who, in this century, have bemoaned the drying up of Americana as a field of collecting, as the Columbus letters and Bay Psalm books have disappeared into institutions.   Yet right under the very noses of these men the Edward Eberstadts and John Kohns have, with their customers, discovered a whole new field of collecting in western Americana and American literature.

Autographs, like books, have the capacity to grow both in number and in collectibility as the years go by. Collectors have always been in the vanguard of scholarship by searching out new fields to collect and providing the raw materials for new and enlarged study and understanding of our history. Just as the work of Peter Force was invaluable in creating collections for research in early United States history, so we shall always be deeply indebted to William Robinson Coe for his great collection of contemporary journals describing the opening of the American West.

The areas of human activity are so wide that all the archives and libraries in the country could not begin to cover them all by their own collecting.   The recent growth of social, economic, and local history has opened vast new areas in which the historian badly needs the help of the collector. This, of course, is to say nothing of the whole field of literary scholarship.

The items one collector will cast aside in contempt another collector will eagerly seize upon. It is said that Wisdom, in assembling his collection on Thomas Wolfe, took every scrap of paper that might have some bearing on that author. And I am sure that he included things which many self-respecting autograph collectors would discard as unworthy. Yet the result is that today at Harvard there is the core from which most work on Wolfe must begin.

We all know that behind every great library from the Vatican to the Huntington lie many stories of the energy and devotion of collectors. The library is the product of the collector, and the institution serves him by providing a place in which his work will be preserved. Our institutions are not perfect, and they do not always carry out their functions properly. I hold no brief for the New England historical society that has allowed the papers of the Revolutionary War general to remain unsorted in cardboard boxes, but I would like to point out that at least they are **there**! There are many stories of important finds in overcrowded and understaffed libraries and archives. Had these same papers been in attics or barns, the chances are good that they would long since have been lost as wastepaper.

I recently found in the University of Pennsylvania Library a bound volume of manuscripts that contained President Monroe's veto of the Cumberland Road Bill. We know that it was given to us by Bloomfield H. Moore, a Philadelphia merchant of the 1870s, but we cannot discover how he got it. The federal government was notorious for the mishandling of its public papers during the nineteenth century. This major document of Monroe's presidency might well have been carted away by the trashman had it not been for a collector who saw its importance and the library that, despite its failure to recognize it for what it was, at least kept it from harm.

I fully agree with Dr. Fields that cooperation between institutions and collectors is not a one-way street. When the collector gives the results of his time, money, and knowledge to an institution, he should receive in return the assurance that his work will continue to live after him in the hands of scholars and to grow in the hands of the librarians. The institution should encourage and cooperate with the collector, not by providing him with things to collect, but by providing him with a background against which his collection will have some measure of security and stability in this troubled world.

* * * * *

Forest H. Sweet

"What shall I do with my collection?" This question is often asked of a dealer.

Dr. Fields is a collector. Mr. Metzdorf was a collector. Mr. Adams is the son of Randolph Adams, who, though he posed as a librarian, was the greatest collector I have known--and his son Tom was brought up on a collector's diet.

But there is another type of librarian, the so-called professional librarian, trained in a library science school and decorated with a bachelor's, master's, or doctor's degree in the mechanics of handling vast quantities of movable objects (books and manuscripts) and in the use of indexes, card catalogues, bibliographies, and other tools of the trade.

Librarians are schooled in making these tools and in administering their use by other employees. But a review of the curriculums of the various library schools shows no courses designed to give these students any knowledge of, or sympathy for, the collector's viewpoint. Graduates have proudly proclaimed to me, when I have asked whether they had any philosophical or sentimental or inspirational instruction, that theirs is a science, an exact body of knowledge.

Probably this kind of training is altogether fitting for work in a public library, a business or industrial library, the average state library, and some parts, at least, of university libraries, where the work is largely the mechanics of moving books from shelf to reader and back to shelf with a minimum of time and effort and expense, and where administration is devoted largely to keeping the employees reasonably happy on inadequate salaries, trying to have the books on the shelves ahead of the demand for them, and giving acceptable alibis when they are not. General Motors finds similarly "scientific" training advantageous to the nimble-footed young gentlemen who scurry about amongst the bins and shelves of the parts department to gather up the pieces necessary to put your car back into operating condition after you have wrapped it around a tree or worn it out by inadequate lubrication. They, too, have the indexes, the catalogues, the numbers, and other finding aids.

But while General Motors does not let these men design your car, similarly trained library technicians are sometimes put in control of fine collections. It happens easily. The president of the university is chosen because he is a good administrator and businessman. The library schools have to find jobs for their graduates, especially their Ph.D.'s. A Ph.D. is supposed to know everything, especially in university circles. The library job is open, a Ph.D. is out of work, the president is busy with ninety-seven other problems-- so the appointment is made and that is one problem off the president's mind. What happens when library science, or any other science, is applied to your collection?

You can restrict the gift of your collection so that it must be kept, but you cannot restrict the gift so that it will be appreciated, used, sympathetically cared for, and enlarged by additions.

I have two suggestions to collectors asking what to do with their collections.

1. If you insist on giving your collection to an institution, buy a set of false whiskers and a wig and investigate the library or libraries you have in mind. Find out how they operate, what they have done with other collections that have been given them. Inquire into all their gift collections, not just one or two. If you are too busy to do that, hire spies to investigate and report to you.

2. Sell your collection for the highest price obtainable. If it ought to be kept together, the highest price should come from the library best equipped to make proper use of it. Appreciation is best expressed in a treasurer's check. The library worthy of having the collection can raise the money for what it really wants. Human nature being what it is, we all appreciate anything in direct ratio to the amount of effort necessary to get it.

Then, later, if you want a tax deduction as a benefactor of a learned institution, give them back the purchase money, with additions if possible, to carry on the collection and to prolong and extend its usefulness.

Did you ever see a dearly bought collection in cold storage?

* * * * *

Cecil K. Byrd

Mr. Sweet employs in his remarks a cliche that has become synonymous with laughter in American folklore: the librarian as a well-meaning, slightly addle-brained do-gooder. But there is some progress; he gives the present-day librarian a new personality. Today the professional librarians are pictured as officious busybodies hurtling their way through libraries, filled with misinformation, destroying in their feverish activities the precious heritage of our past as represented in books and manuscripts. Were it not that I know Mr. Sweet to be something of a humorist and that there may be more than a grain of truth in his remarks, I would be more heated in my rebuttal of his accusations.

Mr. Sweet accuses library-science-school-trained librarians of not being prepared emotionally, philosophically, historically, or esthetically to care for and administer collections of books and manuscripts. Trained on a diet of managerial science, they are equipped only to page and shelve books. The library schools have nothing in their programs designed to give the students an appreciation for the collector's viewpoint.

I do not know what Mr. Sweet means by "the collector's viewpoint." To me, a person who has a knowledge and appreciation of the origins of writing, and the historical development of the book in manuscript and printed form, and who realizes that many of our great libraries of today started with the books of a great collector, must, in some degree, have the collector's viewpoint. Each year at Indiana University I have an eager group of graduate students working for library science degrees who meet with me in the library twice each week for a course labeled, for want of a better name, "History of Books and Libraries." In this course we study human records from the primitive to the refined form, the manuscript and printed book in their physical and spiritual aspects, and the great collectors and collections of the past and our own age. Surely this is proper background to make the professional librarian appreciate the private collector and his collection. Most other library schools offer similar courses.

There is a most important trend in professional library management that, if it continues, will lead to greater cooperation and mutual understanding between the librarian and collector. I refer to the growing practice in many libraries of employing staff with a minimum of professional library school training and a maximum of subject background in English and American literature, history, economics, and other related subjects. Perhaps these subject specialists who have fed but lightly on the library-school curriculum can properly administer and nurture this hypothetical collection under discussion, even to Mr. Sweet's satisfaction.

Mr. Sweet has suggested that some collections that have been given to libraries have been placed in cold storage, where they languish, unloved and neglected. We all know of collections so treated. In some instances a collection receives this treatment because the collector is grievously at fault in the selection of a final repository for his collection. If an institution is known to have any interest in the subject represented by your collection and has given evidence of that interest by employing a staff who teach and do research in the area, the chances are good that your collection will not be given the cold-storage treatment. You are inviting the neglect of your collection by giving it to an institution that has never shown any curricular interest in your subject.

Actually, the problem of what to do with your collection is not a difficult one. If you can afford to give it away, there are enough libraries in this country who have demonstrated their ability to house, administer, and use every conceivable kind of rare book and manuscript collection. If you cannot afford to give it away, there are numerous competent, informed dealers from coast to coast who can advise you on marketing your materials.

Part 2.
AREAS IN WHICH TO COLLECT

A. U.S. POLITICAL HISTORY
Colonial Rarities*

John F. Reed

The purpose of this article is to list the various degrees of rarity of autographs of the American colonial period. The lists do not deal with the various **forms** of autographs (e.g., ALS, LS), but with the rarity of the autographs in any form. For purposes of comparison, the autographs may be arranged in the following categories of rarity: the unfindables, the excessively rare, the extremely rare, the very rare, and the merely rare.

The colonial period, because of its increasing antiquity, undoubtedly contains more unfindables and near-unfindables than any other era of Americana. Time and accident (and sometimes incomprehensible intention) have an inexorable way of eliminating many of the precious relics of the past. Autographs, especially since they are fragile, are certainly no exception to this rule. Also, the number of unfindables and near-unfindables is doubled by the gradual (sometimes rapid) assimilation of autographs into public archives, where they are removed forever from the open market. The unfindables--the early navigators, explorers, and conquerors, as well as John Smith, John Carver, Myles Standish, Johan Printz, Peter Minuit, Roger Bacon, Peter Zenger, and perhaps a few others--need not be discussed. Only those autographs that are at all obtainable and of major importance, whatever their rarity, are of current interest. As Gordon Banks writes, "The list could be almost endless, but soon takes off into relatively unknown characters. I think it would be wise to submit the lists as outstanding examples, rather than even approaching the stand of a complete listing."

A simple listing of major autographs under their various categories of rarity should, therefore, suffice. No attempt at evaluation will be made. Even the best experts can sometimes fail considerably in their evaluations of autographs, especially rarities, in the present, especially auction, market--a market that is witnessing rapidly increasing values as a result of augmented interest and competition, plus the dwindling supply of autographs in certain fields of collecting.

The listing of important colonial autographs and their present autographic rarity (though in some instances the rarity may be at least

---

*Originally published in 1966.

temporarily dissolved by unexpected discoveries of "new" material) naturally commences with the category "excessively rare" and continues through the lesser degrees of rarity.   Only those historical persons whose names may have appeared on the market within the past decade or two are listed.   Those persons, particular colonial governors, who spent only a part of their lives in America are, for the most part, also included.   The listings in each category are alphabetical.   The indispensable assistance of Gordon Banks in compiling these lists is gratefully acknowledged.

Excessively Rare

William Bradford, second governor of Plymouth Bay Colony
Dutch governors (Wilhelm Kieft, Peter Stuyvesant)
John Eliot, the "Apostle of the Indians," translator of the first Indian Bible
French governors and explorers (Champlain, Du Luth, Frontenac, La Salle)
Roger Williams, founder of Rhode Island
Edward Winslow, governor of Plymouth Bay Colony
Very early (prior to circa 1630) Jamestown material

Extremely Rare

John Alden of Plymouth Bay Colony
Sir William Berkeley, early governor of Virginia
Charles Calvert, third Lord Baltimore, governor of Maryland
Leonard Calvert, governor of Maryland
Jacob Leisler, usurping governor of New York
Marquis de Montcalm, French commander in French and Indian War
James Oglethorpe, founder of Georgia

Very Rare

Sir Edmund Andros, governor of Massachusetts, New York, etc.
George Croghan, Indian agent under Sir William Johnson
Sir William Johnson, British Indian commissioner
Earl of Loudoun, British general in French and Indian War
Massachusetts witchcraft judges (Sewell et al.)
Cotton Mather, Massachusetts divine and author
Increase Mather, Massachusetts divine and author, father of Cotton Mather
Sir Henry Vane as governor of Massachusetts Bay Colony (fairly common
     of later date in England)
Conrad Weiser, Pennsylvania Indian agent
John Winthrop, governor of Massachusetts Bay Colony

Rare

John Endecott, governor of Massachusetts Bay Colony
Andrew Hamilton, Philadelphia lawyer, defender of Peter Zenger in famous
     freedom-of-the-press trial
Charles Mason and Jeremiah Dixon, surveyors of the Mason and Dixon Line
     (Note: Mason and Dixon usually signed together)
Maj. Gen. James Wolfe, captor of Quebec in French and Indian War
Numerous royal governors of various colonies

Revolutionary Rarities*

John F. Reed

This article deals with the rarity of the autographs of persons associated with the American Revolution. It deals only with individual autographs per se, not with contents, condition, or format.

Because of the great current interest in collecting American Revolutionary autographs--an interest that, unless quantity is lacking and prices are overdone, will undoubtedly ascend as the bicentennial of the Revolution approaches--it is becoming increasingly difficult to estimate the present rarity of many of these autographs. Only a few years ago many of those that are today becoming rare would not have been so classified. Indeed, almost all Revolutionary autographs except perhaps those of Washington are becoming scarce. Some Revolutionary autographs, of course, have always been and (barring the discovery of some long-hidden cache of material that might be turned loose on the market) will always be rare. Other Revolutionary autographs are rare only because some institution or private collector specializes in the autographs of certain persons, and dealers therefore naturally tend to funnel those autographs to known customers rather than presenting the autographs to the occasional uncertainties of the open market. This statement is also valid concerning certain periods of the Revolution; as a result, an autograph of one period may be much rarer than that of another. Also, many Revolutionary autographs that are common of postwar, and sometimes of prewar, date may be exceedingly rare of war date, since less time was allotted during the war for letter writing and document signing. In certain cases in the succeeding lists, note will be taken of this fact.

The following lists--and only the autographs of reasonably prominent persons that have appeared on the market within the past two decades or so are included--will be divided into the categories "excessively rare," "extremely rare," "very rare," and "rare." There will also be a further division (except in the case of foreigners serving in each particular service) into nationalities: American, French, and British. The last division may facilitate understanding by the neophyte collector. The lists also, in some cases, include the years directly preceding the Revolution, since those years were the formative period of the Revolutionary outbreak. Except for a brief acknowledgment of the assistance of Gordon Banks and the suggestions of Paul Lutz, all further explanations will be found in the lists themselves.

---

*Originally published in 1967.

AMERICAN

Excessively Rare

Philip Freneau, "The Poet of the Revolution"
Button Gwinnett and Thomas Lynch, Jr., two Signers of the Declaration of
    Independence (Gwinnett rarest in total forms, Lynch rarest in any form
    except cut signatures)
Nathan Hale, American spy hanged in 1776
Nicholas Herkimer, mortally wounded at Oriskany
Ebenezer Learned, general in the Continental Army
George Mason, author of the Virginia Bill of Rights
Haym Salomon, financial backer of the Revolution

Extremely Rare

Ethan Allen, captor of Fort Ticonderoga in 1775
John Barry, founder of the American Navy (of war date only; fairly common of
    later date)
George Rogers Clark, conqueror of much of what was later to be known as the
    Northwest Territory
Louis L. Duportail, French volunteer and military engineer (of war date only;
    merely scarce of later European date)
John Paul Jones, naval hero
John Laurens, aide to Washington, special envoy to France, killed in 1782
Hugh Mercer, general killed at Princeton
Richard Montgomery, general killed at Quebec
Francis Nash, general killed at Germantown
Casimir Pulaski, Polish volunteer killed at Savannah
Jethro Sumner, general in the Continental Army
Many of the foreign volunteers in the American service, several of whom have
    not even appeared on the market during the past two decades (Chevalier
    Armand, Prud Homme de Borre, Philip Du Coudray, Frederick de Woedtke,
    et al.; Matthias De Fermoy virtually impossible to obtain)

Very Rare

Caleb Gibbs, Major, commander of Commander-in-Chief's
    (i.e., Washington's) Guard
Esek Hopkins, naval hero
Tadeusz Kosciuszko, Polish volunteer (virtually impossible to collect of war
    date; very rare of postwar European date)
John Stark, hero of Bennington
Thomas Sumter, partisan leader in the South
John Trumbull, poet, author of "McFingal," famous Revolutionary satiric poem
Joseph Warren, general killed at Bunker Hill
William Woodford, general captured at Charleston, South Carolina, died in
    British prison

Rare

John Armstrong, Sr., general in the Continental Army and of the Pennsylvania
    Militia
Johan DeKalb, German volunteer general, killed at Camden, South Carolina
Mordecai Gist, general in the Continental Army
Francis Marion, partisan leader in the South
Thomas Paine, famous Revolutionary writer and philosopher (rare of late;
    formerly only scarce, but collector interest has virtually removed him from
    the market)
William Prescott, fought at Bunker Hill
Israel Putnam, general in the Continental Army
Alexander Scammell, adjutant-general of the Continental Army, killed at
    Yorktown
John Sullivan, general in the Continental Army
Also a number of only moderately known generals of varying rarity, such as
    Joseph Spencer, Thomas Conway, Adam Stephen, John Thomas, Rufus
    Putnam, David Wooster, William Smallwood, John Eager Howard, and
    William Maxwell; also certain members of the Old Congress

BRITISH

Excessively Rare

John Andre, co-conspirator with Benedict Arnold, hanged as a spy
Baron Wilhelm von Knyphausen, Hessian general
Most other German officers

Extremely Rare

Lord Cornwallis, British general (of war date only; rather common of postwar
    European and Indian dates)
Lord Germain, secretary of state for the colonies
Baron von Riedesel, Hessian general captured with Burgoyne
Banastre Tarleton, British cavalry officer

Very Rare

British Peace Commission of 1778: Lord Carlisle, William Eden,
    Gov. George Johnstone
Lord Dunmore, last royal governor of Virginia, raided coasts in Chesapeake
    Bay area
Thomas Gage, military governor of Massachusetts (of war date only; rather
    common of prewar date)
Samuel Hood, British admiral

Rare

John Burgoyne, British general captured at Saratoga (of war date only; somewhat less rare of postwar European date)
Sir Guy Carleton, governor of Canada (of war date only; less rare of later date, especially as Lord Dorchester)
Charles James Fox, member of Parliament, defender of American rights
Sir William Howe, British general (of war date only; merely scarce of later date)
Sir William Pitt, earl of Chatham, prewar prime minister, member of Parliament, defender of American rights
Sir Francis Rawdon, British general (of war date only; fairly common of later date, usually signed as earl of Moira)

FRENCH

(Note: None of the French autographs is really excessively rare, although most are extremely rare signed in America, 1778-83.   Many of the officers, both naval and military, were involved in the French Revolution and French Republican wars and are obtainable of these dates.)

Very Rare

Count de Barras, French admiral
Count D'Estaing, French general and admiral, executed in French Revolution
Count de Grasse, French admiral, blockaded Cornwallis at Yorktown
Count Jean Baptiste de Rochambeau, commanded French land forces in America (of war date only; rather common of later European date)
Chevalier des Touches, French admiral

Rare

Most of the French generals and other officers who served under Rochambeau, especially of war date (Count Deux Ponts, De Lauzun, St. Simon, Viomesnil, et al.; Counts Dumas and Custine occasionally obtainable of later European date); also the Chevalier de la Luzerne, second French ambassador to the United States

Signers of the Declaration of Independence: A Well-Defined Collecting Area*

Within the confines of one collecting category, there is certainly no finer cross section of early American history than that represented by the Signers of the Declaration of Independence. At least this is true if one's plan is to select a category that is well defined and not of such unlimited scope as "great Americans," "prominent statesmen," or "American military leaders." There were but fifty-six Signers, and they are all identified. Their signatures put them beyond quibbles of whether the individual was great, was ever actually commissioned, or was appointed and did not serve.

The spectacular prices often publicized and linked with the names of Gwinnett and Lynch have dampened or washed out the enthusiasm of many would-be collectors during the past several decades. In 1980, an indifferent example of a Lynch signature--his surname clipped from the flyleaf of a book--sold at auction for $3,600. One year earlier, a routine financial document signed by Gwinnett sold for the incredible price of $100,000, the highest price ever paid for an autograph as of that date.

It is always a temptation to arrange these fifty-six statesmen in the order of their rarity, but, unfortunately, innumerable qualifications may lead to a false position in the rating of the upper third, and most of the others are sufficiently easy to find to make their relative scarcity unimportant. The Signers are divided here into three groups. One could state almost without fear of contradiction that it would be wise to acquire almost any example that becomes available in the top group (group A). In any purchase, whether it is an oriental rug, a car, or a manuscript, a careful buyer always examines the asking price and then makes certain that it is within a fair range. If an owner points to the exorbitant record for a Button Gwinnett, this is no justification for a $30,000 price for a document that would be appraised on the current market for $10,000. On the other hand, somewhere between these two values the price may seem high but not excessive if the buyer prefers not to chance waiting or has any other reason for paying a "long price."

In the three groups of Signers below, it is sometimes necessary to overlook the relative scarcity of special forms of the particular Signer and simply to generalize on the possibilities of obtaining some example for a

---

*Originally published in 1960; updated in 1982 by the editors. For an article on Thomas Lynch, Jr., and his autograph, see part 4 of this volume.

complete collection. The individual eccentricities will be briefly catalogued in the checklist at the end of this article. The first group is small and expensive. Examples of these Signers may require five to ten years or more to locate.

Group A

1. Button Gwinnett
2. Thomas Lynch, Jr.
3. George Taylor
4. William Hooper
5. John Penn
6. Joseph Hewes

Most signatures in the second group should be available within a five-year span. Many are comparatively easy to find in the less satisfactory forms, but some would fall into the top group if a purchaser insisted on having an ALS with significant content.

Group B

7. Arthur Middleton	19. James Smith
8. George Wythe	20. William Floyd
9. Francis Lightfoot Lee	21. Abraham Clark
10. John Witherspoon	22. Francis Lewis
11. Lyman Hall	23. Samuel Chase
12. Richard Stockton	24. John Hart
13. Carter Braxton	25. Edward Rutledge
14. Matthew Thornton	26. John Morton
15. Thomas Nelson, Jr.	27. Lewis Morris
16. Thomas Stone	28. George Ross
17. William Whipple	29. Benjamin Harrison
18. William Paca	30. James Wilson

All signatures in the third group should be available with not more than a few months' delay. It would take more time, of course, if top content, top condition, or the magic 1776 date is required.

Group C

31. Richard Henry Lee	44. John Hancock
32. Philip Livingston	45. William Williams
33. Benjamin Franklin	46. Francis Hopkinson
34. Samuel Adams	47. Samuel Huntington
35. Robert Treat Paine	48. William Ellery
36. Stephen Hopkins	49. Thomas Heyward, Jr.
37. Benjamin Rush	50. Caesar Rodney
38. John Adams	51. Thomas Jefferson
39. Josiah Bartlett	52. Charles Carroll
40. Roger Sherman	53. George Clymer
41. Thomas McKean	54. George Read
42. Oliver Wolcott	55. George Walton
43. Elbridge Gerry	56. Robert Morris

No attempt has been made to pinpoint prices of the foregoing names, but price is one of the first things that a serious collector should study. At best any advance information is a rough approximation. Robert Morris, at the bottom of the list in a sense, could write a letter of such length and importance that it would become more valuable than a document of Joseph Hewes, who rests in the top half-dozen. Furthermore, the more easily an autograph can be obtained, the more important is its condition. Many in group C can be picked up in worn or tattered documents at almost nominal prices; they usually deserve to be acquired only in attractive condition. Prices throughout the three groups will be turned topsy-turvy if the content is truly "magnificent," or if the 1776 date appears either on an ordinary document or in combination with good condition or content.

The following alphabetical tabulation is somewhat more exact and would at least form a starting point subject to annotations or contradictions on the part of experienced collectors or dealers who may differ and are willing to express their differences.

1. John Adams (Massachusetts)--always available. More common in letters from $1,500 to $2,500. Moderately difficult to locate in low-priced examples.
2. Samuel Adams (Massachusetts)--usually available in document form, $250, plus or minus. Scarce in letters, $500 and up.
3. Josiah Bartlett (New Hampshire)--usually available at moderate prices, $200 and up for documents.
4. Carter Braxton (Virginia)--usually appears in letter form. Moderately scarce. Not usually found in low-priced examples.
5. Charles Carroll (Maryland)--quite plentiful in all forms.
6. Samuel Chase (Maryland)--hard to find in acceptable examples. Letters chiefly in the $750-and-up range; routine documents, $400 and up.
7. Abraham Clark (New Jersey)--available in DS, but letters are scarce.
8. George Clymer (Pennsylvania)--rather plentiful in low-priced documents. Letters available in the $150-to-$250 range. Scarce with good content.
9. William Ellery (Rhode Island)--easily available at modest prices.
10. William Floyd (New York)--scarce in all forms. Books from his library with his autograph occasionally available (frequently confused with books signed by his son, of the same name). Letters, $750 plus.
11. Benjamin Franklin (Pennsylvania)--frequently available but high priced. Almost anything is $1,500 and up.
12. Elbridge Gerry (Massachusetts)--easy to locate at modest prices.
13. Button Gwinnett (Georgia)--the most famous rarity; even a good forgery will bring $200 and up.
14. Lyman Hall (Georgia)--scarce in any form. Quite valuable in letters.
15. John Hancock (Massachusetts)--usually available with a very wide range in price; documents go for $400 and up. In popular demand. Was also president of the Continental Congress.
16. Benjamin Harrison (Virginia)--growing in scarcity, particularly in fine examples, but still available at a modest price.
17. John Hart (New Jersey)--frequently available in the New Jersey currency at $150, plus or minus. Very scarce in documents. Rare in letter form.
18. Joseph Hewes (North Carolina)--scarce in any form. Usually $1,000 and up for documents; beware of those liable to replevin by North Carolina.

19. Thomas Heyward, Jr. (South Carolina)--very common in document form at low prices. Extremely rare in letter form.
20. William Hooper (North Carolina)--much the same range as Hewes.
21. Stephen Hopkins (Rhode Island)--documents generally cost $200 and up, letters from $500.
22. Francis Hopkinson (Connecticut)--common in document form, not too scarce in unimportant letters. Prices usually moderate.
23. Samuel Huntington (Connecticut)--easily found in ordinary or the better examples.
24. Thomas Jefferson (Virginia)--almost always on the market. Most common in presidential documents, $500 and up. Prices of letters rising. Acceptable examples, $1,250 and up.
25. Francis Lightfoot Lee (Virginia)--scarce in any form; a clipped signature recently sold for $450.
26. Richard Henry Lee (Virginia)--usually available, considerable range in values, most often seen in letter form, $750 and up.
27. Francis Lewis (New York)--not easily found. Difficult to obtain in attractive, moderately priced examples.
28. Philip Livingston (New York)--usually available in the under-$300 price range.
29. Thomas Lynch, Jr. (South Carolina)--seldom on the market. Clipped signatures, $500 to $1,000. Autographed books occasionally available, $3,000 to $4,000. Only a handful of documents and one letter are known to exist.
30. Thomas McKean (Pennsylvania)--common in document form, chiefly as governor of Pennsylvania. Letters moderately scarce.
31. Arthur Middleton (South Carolina)--quite scarce in any form. Frequently found in unsigned or initialed letters. Scarcer in signed documents, and extremely rare in letters bearing his full signature.
32. Lewis Morris (New York)--not easily found in interesting, attractive examples. Routine ALSs, $400 and up.
33. Robert Morris (Pennsylvania)--easily obtainable in a number of forms. Plentiful in letters, with prices often under $200.
34. John Morton (Pennsylvania)--difficult to find in any form except legal endorsements and signed Pennsylvania currency, of which examples are moderately scarce.
35. Thomas Nelson, Jr. (Virginia)--difficult to find in any form. Attractive documents, $500, plus or minus. Letters, $1,000 plus.
36. William Paca (Maryland)--growing quite scarce. Difficult to find in any acceptable form under $400.
37. Robert Treat Paine (Massachusetts)--usually appears in legal writs for $150 and up.
38. John Penn (North Carolina)--very scarce in any form. Letters, $1,000 and up. As with the other North Carolina signers, beware of documents subject to replevin.
39. George Read (Delaware)--fairly common in ordinary material, particularly in unsigned or initialed legal manuscripts.
40. Caesar Rodney (Delaware)--fairly common in low-priced examples. Scarce in good letters.
41. George Ross (Pennsylvania)--fairly common in low-priced examples. Increasingly scarce in good letters.

42. Benjamin Rush (Pennsylvania)--usually on the market, but price is increasing. Attractive documents, $400, plus or minus. Letters, $750 and up. A popular name.

43. Edward Rutledge (South Carolina)--increasingly scarce, although occasionally obtainable at moderate cost. Good letters, $500 plus.

44. Roger Sherman (Connecticut)--usually available at moderate prices. Most common form is in legal documents.

45. James Smith (Pennsylvania)--becoming increasingly scarce. Most frequently available in so-so examples that rate under $250. Good letters are scarce.

46. Richard Stockton (New Jersey)--not always available but still not too difficult. Letters, $750, plus or minus.

47. Thomas Stone (Maryland)--becoming increasingly scarce in good examples.

48. George Taylor (Pennsylvania)--the third-rarest signer; very scarce in any form. Minimum, approximately $2,000.

49. Matthew Thornton (New Hampshire)--becoming more difficult to locate. Ordinary examples, $400 and up. Good letters, $1,000 and up (rare).

50. George Walton (Georgia)--common in document form. Prices low. Good letters not easily found.

51. William Whipple (New Hampshire)--rather scarce in any form. Good but ordinary examples, around $400. Letters, $750 and up.

52. William Williams (Connecticut)--almost always available at moderate prices. Fine letters rather scarce.

53. James Wilson (Pennsylvania)--not too hard to find in document form, $150 and up. Good letters rather scarce.

54. John Witherspoon (New Jersey)--scarce but not rare. Almost any acceptable example, $50 plus. Letters, $1,500 plus.

55. Oliver Wolcott (Connecticut)--plentiful in ordinary examples. Good letters can bring $500 to $750. Often confused with his son, the secretary of the treasury.

56. George Wythe (Virginia)--scarce in any form. Rare in fine examples of either condition or content, often $1,000 and up.

Note: Suggesting standard prices on any collectors' item is very precarious. The same document will vary widely in price depending on its condition (ranging from "shabby" or "separated at the folds" to "immaculate"), location and condition of the signature, whether the document is a single-page or a multiple-page item, and whether the document is too small to be impressive or too large and cumbersome to be readily displayed. These details assume even greater importance for letters, with the added factors of length and significance of content, or the occasional letter addressed to another Signer and, of course, the prized letter that has both content and the 1776 date. Bear in mind that auction records may not be and really cannot be consistent. Prices may approach high retail prices if purchases are commissioned by collectors. They may even be low wholesale prices when items are purchased at auction by a dealer for resale under limited competition.

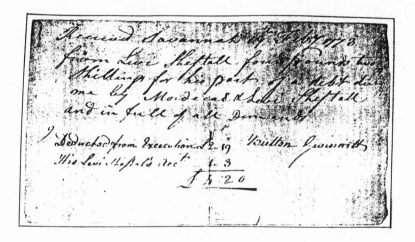

Illus. 1. A financial document signed by Button Gwinnett. It sold at auction for $100,000 in 1977, the highest price ever paid for a single autograph as of that date.

The Autographs of Arthur Middleton*

Joseph E. Fields

One of America's great statesmen during the Revolutionary period was Arthur Middleton of South Carolina. Middleton, a Signer of the Declaration of Independence, was a leader of the radical revolutionary party of South Carolina and served his state and nation faithfully, wisely, and unselfishly. His untimely death was a lamentable occasion, for the young nation was deprived of the outstanding capabilities of this relatively young man.

No full-length biography of Middleton has ever been written, although he warrants such treatment.[1] Few men in South Carolina went to such extremes in support of the radical revolutionary party and its aims. The character of the man and his unusual career make an intriguing story.

Had it not been for the great rarity and value of his autographs, which have served as an incentive to preserve them in sets of the Signers, we would today know little of Middleton and still less concerning the behind-the-scenes action of the Revolutionary cause in South Carolina. Middleton autographs are third rarest of those of the Signers, being exceeded in that respect only by Button Gwinnett of Georgia and Thomas Lynch, Jr., a fellow South Carolinian. When autographs of a person of prominence bring the substantial prices that Middleton's have brought, and when within the past year serious doubts have arisen concerning the authenticity of certain letters attributed to Middleton, it is time to examine the record. This is particularly true because one such letter has an auction record of $2,700. The writer believes the facts should be published for all to see, not only as a protection to collectors and dealers but as an aid to students of American history.

A Prominent Political Figure

Arthur Middleton was born at Middleton Place, St. Andrew's Parish, South Carolina, on June 26, 1742, the son of Henry Middleton and Mary

---

*Originally published in 1952; since that time, Middleton may have slipped somewhat in relative scarcity. See the article immediately preceding.

[1]Katherine Elizabeth Crane, in her biographical sketch of Middleton in the **Dictionary of American Biography,** states that Middleton left little impress upon the records of the Continental Congress, that he was absent frequently, and that he sat in the 1782 session of the Jacksonborough Assembly. The first two statements are open to serious question and the last is a misstatement of fact.

Williams Middleton, heiress of John Williams.   In 1754 young Arthur accompanied his uncle, Thomas Middleton, to England.   There he attended the well-known schools of Hackney and Westminster and afterwards enrolled at St. John's College, Cambridge.   He was admitted to the Inner Temple in London, on April 4, 1757.[2]   Middleton arrived back in South Carolina in December 1763 and the following August was married to Mary Izard, daughter of Walter Izard. The young Middletons settled at Middleton Place, the ancestral home on the Ashley River near Charles Town.[3]   Middleton became a justice of the peace and from 1765 until 1768 served in the Commons House of Assembly for St. Helena's Parish and St. James' Parish, Goose Creek.   In May 1768 the Middletons sailed for England and the south of Europe, where they studied art, music, and literature.   While they were residing in London their first child, Henry, was born, and there Benjamin West painted the family portrait.[4]   The family arrived back in South Carolina in September 1771.   Shortly thereafter Middleton was reelected to the Commons for Prince William Parish, where he soon became a leader of the American Party.

In January 1775 Middleton was elected to the first Provincial Congress from Charles Town and served in both the first and second sessions. After this he was elected a member of the Council of Safety and, with his neighbor William Henry Drayton, became a member of the group that urged violent measures in dealing with the governor's group and in enforcing the nonimportation agreements.   In August 1775 he was elected to the second Provincial Congress and again attended both sessions.   Middleton was one of the committee appointed to prepare a constitution for South Carolina.   On February 16, 1776, he was elected a delegate to the Continental Congress. The constitution he had helped formulate was adopted on March 26, 1776, and thereafter Middleton journeyed to Philadelphia to take his seat with the other delegates.

Middleton supported the Resolution on Independence and signed the Declaration on August 2. In January 1777 the General Assembly returned him as a delegate to the Congress. In February 1778 Middleton was not reelected as a delegate. But in March of the same year, when John Rutledge resigned the presidency of the state, Middleton was elected president by the General Assembly. He declined the office. In November 1778 he was elected to the House of Representatives and in January 1779 the General Assembly sent him as one of South Carolina's delegates to the Continental Congress. He was reelected the following year.

---

[2] A. S. Salley, **Delegates to the Continental Congress from South Carolina** (Columbia, 1927), pp. 10-16.

[3] The gardens at Middleton Place have been world famous for their beauty for almost two hundred years.

[4] The original portrait is now in the possession of Dr. Henry Drinker, Philadelphia, Pennsylvania.

In May 1780, while serving with the militia at the siege of Charles Town, Middleton was taken prisoner by the British when the city fell into their hands. He was paroled as a prisoner of war but this parole was soon revoked and he was sent to the dungeon at St. Augustine, along with many of the other civil and military officers. After his exchange in July 1781, he resumed his seat in the Continental Congress and was reelected the following year. Middleton was elected a senator from the parishes of St. Philip and St. Michael to the Jacksonborough Assembly, which was convened in January 1782.[5]

After Middleton's return from the Continental Congress late in 1782, he occupied himself with the rehabilitation of his property and the recovery of his fortune. During the war his home had been ransacked and burned by the British and his slaves carried away. He died suddenly while at his plantation at Goose Creek, South Carolina, on January 1, 1787, and was buried in the family vault in the gardens at Middleton Place.

A Rara Avis of the Autograph World

The papers of Arthur Middleton are in the possession of the South Carolina Historical Society. The small collection consists of letters written by Middleton, retained copies of letters, as well as notes and resolutions he made while a member of the Continental Congress. Some of this correspondence has been published by the South Carolina Historical Society.[6] Much of importance was omitted and no definitive study of his writings has ever been made. Aside from the manuscripts mentioned above, the remaining Middleton autographs are either in sets of the Signers or are in the hands of several members of the trade.

Middleton autographs have always been difficult to obtain in any form. This is particularly true in ALS form. Lyman C. Draper, in his essay on the sets of the Signers[7] published in 1889, describes the difficulties experienced by the collectors in obtaining Middleton signatures, and he lists but six known ALSs. They were located in the collections of Dr. Thomas Addis Emmet, Simon Gratz, Ferdinand J. Dreer, E. H. Leffingwell, Rev. T. Stamford Raffles, and Col. Frank Etting. Even today the majority of the Middleton autographs are in DS form. They are dated from Philadelphia during the years 1781 and 1782, when Middleton was serving a third term as a delegate to the Continental Congress. They are to John Ross, a prominent Philadelphia merchant who at that time was acting as financial agent for South Carolina. These documents are authorizations to Ross to pay to certain people money

---

[5]Middleton did not take part in the Jacksonborough Assembly, being in Philadelphia attending the sessions of the Continental Congress.

[6]"The Correspondence of Arthur Middleton," **South Carolina Historical Genealogical Magazine,** vol. XXVI, no. 4; vol. XXVII, nos. 1-3.

[7]"Essay on the Autographic Collections of the Signers of the Declaration of Independence and of the Constitution," New York, 1889.

due them by the state of South Carolina for services rendered. In addition to Middleton's signature, most of them also bear the signature of John Rutledge and Dr. David Ramsay. A few are also signed by the other South Carolina delegates, including Thomas Bee, Jacob Motte, Nicholas Eveleigh, and John Mathews.

Of the eighty-six Middleton autographs the locations of which are known, thirty-three are of the DS type. There are, in addition to these thirty-three, five clipped signatures and one address leaf in the handwriting of Middleton.

There have been thirty-four Middleton autographs sold at auction since 1895. Fifteen of these are in the nature of the signed documents just described. Two of the thirty-four auction items were clipped signatures.

A Census of Important Middleton Documents

Following is a list of the autographs of Arthur Middleton that are of considerable interest, importance, and value.

1. Library of Congress. The original Declaration of Independence, signed "Arthur Middleton."
2. Library of Congress. The Agreement of Secrecy, signed "Arthur Middleton."
3. New York Public Library (Emmet 1654). ALS, signed with initials "A.M." Charles Town, August 5, 1775. To William Henry Drayton, concerning events taking place in the Council of Safety.
4. New York Public Library (Emmet 1655). LS, 1 p., folio. Philadelphia, October 7, 1776. To the Convention of New York from a committee of the Continental Congress. Signed by Arthur Middleton, Robert Treat Paine, Josiah Bartlett, William Ellery, William Williams, George Wythe, William Floyd, Lyman Hall, and George Ross, all Signers of the Declaration of Independence (see illus. 1).
5. Historical Society of Pennsylvania (Gratz Collection). ALS, signed "A. Middleton." Charles Town, October 18, 1779. To Thomas Burke, concerning events taking place in Charles Town, with respect to the war and his impending trip to Philadelphia.
6. Historical Society of Pennsylvania (Dreer Collection). ALS, signed with initials "A.M." September 13, 1783.

Illus. 1. Full signature (courtesy of New York Public Library).

7. Historical Society of Pennsylvania (Dreer Collection). ALS, signed with initials "A.M." April 13, 1784.

8. Historical Society of Pennsylvania (Dreer Collection). AD, with a signature pasted thereon. Philadelphia, September 9, 1782. A resolve that General Greene stay in the Southern Department.

9. Historical Society of Pennsylvania (Dreer Collection). ALS, signed with initials "A.M." May 16, 1783.

10. Historical Society of Pennsylvania (Dreer Collection). AN on a document concerning slaves taken from the Savannah River region by Commodore Barkley in 1776.

11. Historical Society of Pennsylvania (Etting Collection). ALS, in the third person. March 23, 1786. To Mr. Simons concerning his flute and music.

12. Haverford College (Roberts Collection). AD. Philadelphia, October 26, 1774. A manuscript copy of the petition from the Continental Congress to King George III.

13. Huntington Library. ALS, 1 p., 8vo. Baltimore, January 28, 1777. To Samuel and Robert Purveyance. The document is a request for blankets and is written on the verso of an order by Richard Henry Lee, Francis Lewis, and William Whipple to furnish blankets to Middleton. The letter is written in the third person, the name "Mr. Middleton" appearing once in the text and the initials "A.M." appearing twice in the text.

14. Proctor Institute, Utica, N.Y. ALS, signed "A. Middleton," 3 pp., 4to. Cedar Grove,[8] March 1, 1783. To Lyman Hall, concerning the recovery of a slave carried off by the enemy.

15. John W. Garrett Library, Baltimore. LS, signed "A. Middleton." Philadelphia, October 13, 1776. A letter introducing Mathew Falconer to Gov. John Langdon of New Hampshire. The letter is also signed by John Hancock, Robert Morris, William Ellery, Josiah Bartlett, Thomas McKean, Richard Henry Lee, and William Hooper.

16. George A. Ball, Muncie, Indiana. ALS, signed "A. Middleton," 1 p., 4to. Charles Town, July 17, 1783. To John F. Grimke. A financial letter.

17. Robert C. Norton, Cleveland. ALS, signed with initials "A.M.," 4 pp., folio. Charles Town, August 22, 1775. To William Henry Drayton. A highly important letter concerning news of the Council of Safety.

18. Anonymous owner. ALS, signed with initials "A.M.," 1 p., folio. Philadelphia, September 18, 1776. To William Henry Drayton, concerning important military and political affairs.

19. St. John's Seminary, Camarillo, California (Estelle Doheny Collection). LS, 1 p., folio. Philadelphia, July 12, 1776. A letter signed by Arthur Middleton, Button Gwinnett, John Hancock, Robert Morris, Francis Lewis, and George Read. In 1927 this famous autograph sold at auction for $51,000.

20. William Emerson Fields, Joliet, Illinois. ALS, signed with initials "A.M.," 1 p., folio. Philadelphia, January 26, 1782. To Edward Rutledge, giving news of events in Congress.

----

[8]Cedar Grove, the ancestral home of Mrs. Middleton, was located near Dorchester in St. George's Parish.

21. Dr. Joseph E. Fields, Joliet, Illinois. AL, 2 pp., folio. Charles Town, September 15, 1775. To William Henry Drayton, concerning news of the Council of Safety. It is signed, "Veni, Vidi, Vici."
22. Dr. Joseph E. Fields. ALS, signed with initials "Ar.M," 7 pp., folio. Charles Town, August 4, 1775. To William Henry Drayton, concerning the affairs of the Council of Safety (see illus. 2).

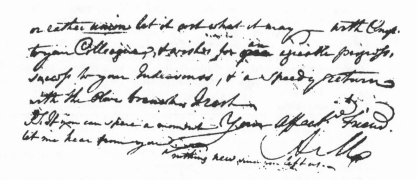

Illus. 2. Autograph letter signed with initials (author's collection).

23. Dr. Joseph E. Fields. ALS, signed "Andrew Marvell," 4 pp., folio. Charles Town, August 12, 1775. To William Henry Drayton, concerning the affairs of the Council of Safety. This is the only known manuscript bearing the signature "Andrew Marvell" (see illus. 3).
24. Dr. Joseph E. Fields. AL, 2 pp., 4to. Philadelphia, July 10, 1776. To William Henry Drayton, conveying to him the news of the passage of the Declaration of Independence.
25. Dr. Joseph E. Fields. Signature on the title page of Edmund Burke's **A Philosophical Enquiry Into the Origins of our Ideas of the Sublime and Beautiful** (London, 1761). The signature is written "Arthur Middleton 1761" (illus. 9).
26. Society of Colonial Dames in San Francisco. ALS, signed with initials "A.M.," 1 p., 4to. Ashley River, July 12, 1783. To Colonel Hammond, concerning the recovery of a slave. [9]
27. Anonymous owner. AL, 4 pp., 4to. Philadelphia, September 14, 1776. To William Henry Drayton, concerning news from the Continental Congress, the American retreat on Long Island, and the peace conference with Lord Howe.
28. Goodspeed's Book Shop. ALS, signed with initials "A.M.," 2 pp., 4to. Charles Town, August 5, 1775. To William Henry Drayton, conveying to him further news of the Council of Safety.

[9]"Ashley River" refers to Middleton Place, which was situated on the Ashley River.

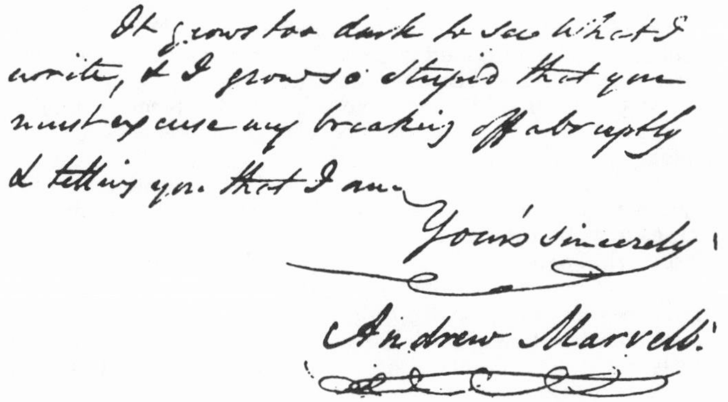

It grows too dark to see what I write, & I grow so stupid that you must excuse my breaking off abruptly & telling you that I am
Yours sincerely!
Andrew Marvell.

Illus. 3. Autograph letter signed with pseudonym "Andrew Marvell" (author's collection).

29. Goodspeed's Book Shop. ALS, signed with initials "A.M.," 3 pp., 4to. Baltimore, October 20, 1782. A report of his trip from Philadelphia to Baltimore on the journey back to South Carolina.
30. Goodspeed's Book Shop. ALS, signed with initials "A.M.," 2 pp., 4to. Ashley River, August 23, 1783. A letter upbraiding an overseer and threatening to discharge him.
31. Forest H. Sweet, Battle Creek, Mich. ALS, signed with initials "A.M.," 1 p., 8vo. Cedar Grove, June 29, 1783. A letter concerning the crops on his plantation.
32. Forest H. Sweet. ALS, signed "M," 1 p., 8vo. Cedar Grove, June 29, 1783. Acknowledgment of money due Colonel Eveleigh and his assurances that he will pay it as soon as possible.
33. Forest H. Sweet. AD. A copy of the articles of capitulation of Pensacola, entered into between the Spanish commander de Galvez and the British commander Gen. John Campbell, on May 9, 1781.
34. Forest H. Sweet. AD, 2 pp., folio. The original draft of an address to the king of France following Cornwallis's surrender.
35. Forest H. Sweet. AD, 1 p., 4to. A draft of a resolution to make immediate payment of deficiencies to General Greene's men and to put them on the same basis as those of Washington.
36. Forest H. Sweet. AD, 1 p., 4to. Draft of a resolution that Washington request the British commander in chief to liquidate the accounts due for keeping the British prisoners.
37. Forest H. Sweet. AD, 1 p., 8vo. Draft of a resolution threatening reprisals upon the British prisoners.

38.   Forest H. Sweet. AD, 1 p., 8vo. Draft of a resolution concerning the return home of the South Carolinians who had been sent away by the British in violation of the articles of capitulation of Charles Town.
39.   Forest H. Sweet. AD, 1 p., 4to. Draft of a resolution calling for the death penalty and forfeiture of property for illicit trading with the enemy.
40.   Forest H. Sweet. AD, 1 p., 4to. Draft of a resolution that the agents of Connecticut be informed that Congress does not have the power to determine the New York-Connecticut boundary.
41.   Forest H. Sweet. AD, 1 p., 8vo. Draft of a resolution calling for the revision of instructions to the American commissioners for the making of peace.
42.   Forest H. Sweet. AD, 2 pp., folio. Draft of a resolution concerning the importation of goods for British prisoners, calling attention to certain abuses of that system.
43.   Forest H. Sweet. AD, 2 pp., folio. Memorandum entitled "State of Finances." A report of the financial status of the United States and of the money owed France and Holland.
44.   South Carolina Historical Society. AL. September 17, 1782. To Edward Rutledge, concerning the prospects for the evacuation of Charles Town by the British and the prospect for peace.
45.   South Carolina Historical Society. AL. April 7, 1782. To A. Burke, concerning confiscation of Loyalist properties.
46.   Rosenbach Company. DS, 1 p., 4to. South Carolina, October 13, 1775. The appointment of Mathew Singleton to be a captain in the militia, signed by Middleton and the members of the Council of Safety.
47.   Justin G. Turner, Los Angeles. DS. March 1, 1776. Signed by Middleton, Thomas Heyward, Jr., Henry Laurens, John Rutledge, Charles Cotesworth Pinckney, Thomas Ferguson, and Rawlins Lowndes. It is a printed form of a military commission. It sold in 1932 for $825 and again in 1941 at the Gribbel sale for $200.
48.   Forest H. Sweet. AMs, dated 1781, concerning paper money of the Continental Congress and of the states of New Jersey, Maryland, Pennsylvania, New York, Virginia, Massachusetts, and New Hampshire.
49.   Forest H. Sweet. AD. September 10, 1782. Quotas of the respective states as assessed and fixed by the grand committee, and agreed to by Congress.
50.   Forest H. Sweet. ANS, signed with initials "A.M." The text is illegible because of fading.
51.   Forest H. Sweet. ALS, signed with initials "A.M." June 29, 1783. A business letter addressed to P. Smith.

The locations of three Middleton manuscripts sold at auction are unknown. They are of considerable interest and are listed below.

52.   Autographed letter unsigned. December 12, 1781. To John Rutledge, advising him to have a census taken. Sold in 1941 for $40.
53.   Autographed letter unsigned. March 4, 1782. To John Rutledge, concerning prizes taken by Commodore Gillon and the sailing of the British transports from New York. Sold in 1941 for $90.

54.   Autographed note of 110 words on a letter dated January 27, 1782, from the South Carolina members of the Continental Congress relating to the admission of Vermont as a state. In 1941 it sold for $22.

The remaining examples sold at auction either have already been mentioned or are documents signed by Middleton and addressed to John Ross. They are of interest only insofar as they are examples of Middleton's handwriting and will not be further considered. Four other letters, allegedly written by Middleton, have been sold at auction and these will be discussed shortly.

Autographic Anonymity

Probably Middleton's inclination not to sign his letters in any way, or to merely initial them, may be explained by the fact that to have signed them might have jeopardized his personal safety as well as that of the radical revolutionary cause in South Carolina. Middleton did sign his letters to his casual acquaintances. But to such close associates as his brother-in-law Edward Rutledge, his fellow radical, William Henry Drayton, and John Rutledge, no signature was necessary. At most, initials were sufficient. To these men the identity of the writer would be evident from both the handwriting and the content of the letters. The letters to Drayton seem to be of two periods: those written from Charles Town while Drayton was on a mission into the "back country," attempting to induce the citizens there to sign the association pledging them to the patriotic cause, and those written while Middleton was a member of the Continental Congress. The letters to John and Edward Rutledge were written while Middleton was serving in the Continental Congress (1781-82).

Most of the biographical sketches of Middleton tell of his exploits as a pamphleteer during the Revolution, writing under the pseudonym "Andrew Marvell."[10]   Despite a diligent search, no pamphlets, political tracts, newspaper articles, or essays bearing such a signature have been discovered. The writer possesses the only known letter signed in this way (illus. 3). The letter has been quoted in several histories of South Carolina and it is perhaps because of this that the belief has arisen that Middleton often wrote under this pseudonym. If he did so, no other examples are known to have survived.

Specters of Doubt

Within the past year doubts have arisen concerning a number of alleged Middleton letters that for many years have been regarded as authentic. Such

---

[10]A few of these sketches are as follows: **Delegates to the Continental Congress,** Salley, p. 14; **South Carolina Historical Genealogical Magazine,** vol. 1, p. 243, and vol. 27, p. 125; **Encyclopedia Americana; Appleton's Cyclopedia.**

grave doubts concerning their authenticity have arisen that a thorough investigation seems advisable. Since at least one of these questionable letters has an auction record that mounts into four figures, it becomes even more important that the question be resolved for the protection of collectors in the future.

Several members of the trade who had had an opportunity to examine the photostats of the set of Signers formerly owned by Colorado College had expressed their suspicions to one another of the Middleton letter in that set of Signers, notwithstanding the fact that accompanying it was a sworn statement of Thomas Madigan that the letter was a juvenile letter of Middleton. Then, in the April 1950 issue of **The Collector,** Mary A. Benjamin presented an expose of this letter together with an additional letter, showing they were both written by the same person and expressing the opinion that they were not written by the Signer, but by a woman.[11] The text of the letter from the Colorado College set of Signers (illus. 4), addressed to a Mr. Walsh, is as follows:

Yr. long absence from
this (place) has bin wonder'd
at since wee pretent to understand Mr. Walsh (at least) so
farr as to Judge our company
may be preferred to a mother's
& sisters but I wish wee had
bin in a mistake & that some
fresh dairy maid had kept you
from us rather than a pain in
yr stomack. how to remove
that disturber of yr ease I
know not but I hope tomorrows
post will bring me a cordiall
for yr distrest heart; but
well or ill I expect you shall
fetch it. Adieu.

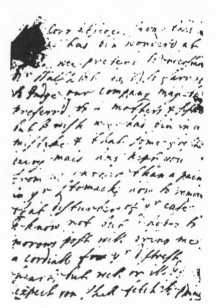

Illus. 4.   Letter from the Colorado College set of Signers (courtesy of Walter R. Benjamin Autographs).

---

[11] **The Collector,** vol. 63, no. 4, April 1950.

It should require no stretch of the reader's imagination to reach the conclusion that this is a bantering letter of affection written by a woman to a Mr. Walsh. The letter is unsigned and the identity of Mr. Walsh has not been ascertained. The letter has no previous auction or sale record.[12]

The second letter described by Mary Benjamin is an ALS dated December 27, (n.y.) (illus. 5). It is signed "A. Middleton." The text is as follows:

> Galantry is so naturall to Mrs. Walsh, that let her subject bee ever so plain, shee can give it a fair glosse; I will not then give way to vanity, (that constant attender on (your sex) but reasonably conclude yr letter spoake (not what I am but) what I shou'd bee, not that I wont grant myself infinitely oblig'd to you for the caracter you have given me; since I hope 't will make me strive to deserve it; now are you quite affraid of what you have done, least it shou'd prique me upon setting up for a witt; & upon tormentting you with the effects of it; oh! horid apprehension which I in good nature will remove, by asuring you; I never did, or shall pretend to more than common sence; & that as plainly express'd as is possible; for (affter all) **will in a woman is like Inglish grapes never in perfection; & I have the pride not to aime at a thing I cant compasse;** & to be sincere **you men so little expect (or desire) a good understanding in one of our sett** that when ever such a miracle is mett with, she is rather fear'd than valew'd; for a pretty naievety is the powerfullest charm & (gennerally speaking) prudence the choquings thing in a woman; now a meane is what I pretend to, for as too great a share of the first woud expose me to much to the **fluttring adresses of yr sex;** so a full share of the last wou'd draw on me the formidable name of xxx from wch good Ld deliver

> Yr very humble servant
> A Middleton

> I dont believe you can read this hideous scraule but my head akeing must excuse both hand & penn. [Emphasis mine.]

Mary Benjamin concluded, from a comparison of the handwriting of these two letters, that they were written by the same person and were part of the same general correspondence. A study of the paper placed them circa 1760. She rightly concluded the foregoing letter was written by a woman to a man. This decision was, of course, based on such phrases as "that constant attender on your sex," "will in a woman is like Inglish grapes never in perfection; & I have the pride not to aime at a thing I cant compasse," "you men so little

---

[12]The set of Signers that formerly belonged to Colorado College was sold to William Philips early in 1950. The alleged Middleton letter was withdrawn by Mary Benjamin. Upon Philips's death, the set of Signers was bequeathed to Haverford College.

expect (or desire) a good understanding in one of our sett," and "prudence the choquings thing in a woman; now a meane is what I pretend to, for as too great a share of the first woud expose me to much to the fluttring adresses of yr sex." Benjamin felt the most likely writer to be Anne Barnwell Middleton, wife of Col. Thomas Middleton, uncle of the Signer. Bear in mind, Benjamin did not know from where the letter was written or to what point it was sent. She acquired the letter as part of an incomplete set of Signers. It has no auction record.

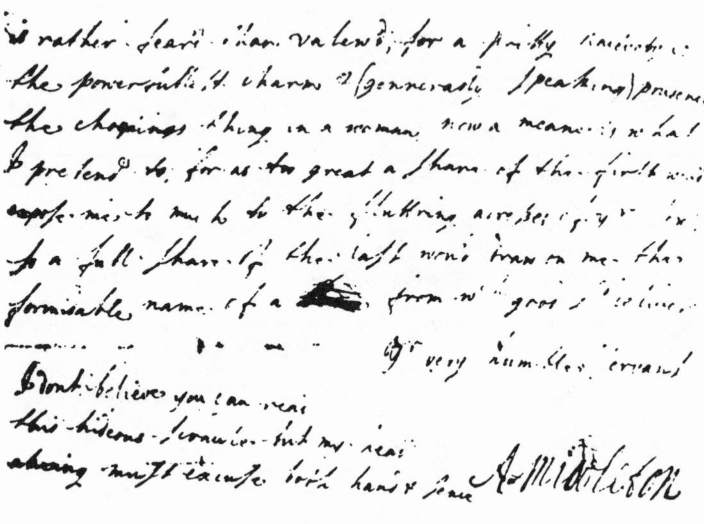

Illus. 5. ALS dated December 27 (courtesy of Walter R. Benjamin Autographs).

Further Suspicions

At the time of the publication of the foregoing letters in **The Collector,** I had also become suspicious of certain alleged Middleton letters that had appeared at auction and particularly one in my own collection. The letter in my possession had not been purchased as an authentic Middleton letter, but had been thought to be a letter of Arthur Middleton, grandfather of the Signer. It was sold at auction in the Dormitzer Collection in 1921 as an authentic ALS of the Signer and brought forty-five dollars. The letter is of two pages, quarto, and dated December 14, (n.y.). It is addressed to "Mr. Walsh lodging at Mr. Hyrons hous near the Kings head in King Street by St. James Square London." It is signed "Arthur Middleton" (illus. 6).

The text of the letter is as follows:

If you dont think I answer yr letter soon enough this time I know not when you will be pleas'd **espitialy when you consider how disgustfully it began by asuring a lady that you had seen another who you thought pritty.** O'horrid falce stepp in galantrey lease to be pardoned than that wch occasioned Mr. Poultneys dewell with you: & to say this in a time when yr eyes shou'd have bin blear'd with weeping for our late parting, **were this ill conduct publish'd I fear the world wou'd either think us not marred** or we shoud appear out of fashion in these days of conjugall fondnesse. Thro Sr John Dillon has comitted an Irishment for Cuckoldom is grown such a customery thing that a well bred discreet persen no more resents it as an affront than he wou'd do a mans not bowing twice when he drinks to him; but there will be quarellsome fools, as well as fantastic ladys; I supose thos you mention, will in some time revive the primitive dress of figg leaves, wch I shall as soon follow as that you describe. As for smiling Bentley or any other Philosophy has quite routed them, & if the Rev'rend Sparke dose but chuse a lady of his own sweet temper, he may save coler for I'le warrant the house will be hot enough, if not too hot to hold em (a very good Joake I'le vow) & now Sr be it known to you that I shall begin the New Year in London (a sure sign of my brothers being upon the mending hand) you are however desir'd to continue your correspondence to this family where you have as many friends as there are inhabitents & I desire you will place in the first rank of 'em

Yr Humble servant
Arthur Middleton

My brother desires you will remember ye books.   [Emphasis mine.]

A careful examination of this letter leads to several conclusions. First, the handwriting is identical with that of the letters described by Mary Benjamin. Second, the paper and ink of the three letters are identical. Third, the locale is England. Fourth, in spite of the fact that the letter is signed "Arthur Middleton," a close examination of the letter will reveal that it, too, was written by a woman. Such phrases as "espitialy when you consider how disgustfully it began by asuring a lady that you had seen another who you thought pritty" and "were this ill conduct publish'd I fear the world wou'd either think us not marred [married] or we should appear out of fashion in these days of conjugall fondnesse" make it evident the writer was female.

A Letter of Explanation

Accompanying this last letter is a letter by Dr. Charles E. Rice. Rice's letter is of considerable importance, since it serves to shed some light on the origin of the letters in question. It reads as follows:

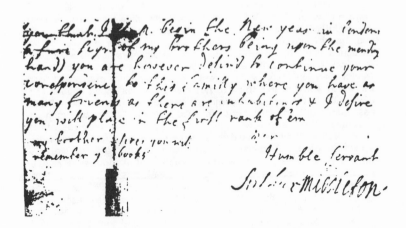

Illus. 6. ALS dated December 14 (courtesy of Goodspeed's Book Shop).

May 21, '15

I enclose the Art Middleton letter and am sorry it is so dilapidated. Why did you never say "Middleton" to me before? I had a number of Middleton relics--bought directly from the family. I knew old Eliza Middleton when she was considerably past 80 years of age (this was 20 years ago) & from her I obtained several things of value. Amongst them several very early letters of Arthur the Signer--3 or 4 of which are unsigned--but none the less genuine. The enclosed is a very boyish letter written when he was a school boy in England--as early probably as 1758. As you know he spent several years there and returned in 1753 [sic]. Mrs. Middleton also sold me a very fine tea pot . . . .

Sincerely
Chas E. Rice

Rice, a resident of Alliance, Ohio, was himself an autograph collector. When his collection was dispersed at auction by Stan V. Henckels in 1917, a Middleton letter was sold from it. According to the catalogue description, it was an ALS, three pages, octavo, April 10, 1762. It was described as being weak in the folds. It was sold to an unknown buyer for $320. The whereabouts of the letter remained a mystery until recently, when it was discovered in the Bamberger Collection of Signers at the New Jersey Historical Society. The Middleton letter in this collection exactly fits the description of the letter sold in the Rice Collection.

The Bamberger letter is an ALS, three pages, octavo, April 10, 1762 (illus. 7). It is very weak in the folds. The letter is addressed to "Mr. Walsh at Mrs. Noels house over against St. Jameses place in St. Jameses Street London." The text is as follows:

You have acquitted yr self in so deligent & prudent a manner of the commission I entrusted you with, that were speeches alowable among friends I shou'd make severall; but as it is, I shall only wish, our great Ministers of State were (but half) as faithfull & capable of discharging their dutys as you have been in this affair yr relation concerning Strephon made me laugh, to observe with how much caution you touch'd upon every part of his behaviour when in good truth the poor wretch was very sincere, & spoake exactly what he thought, without any of those nice turns which you put upon him; my fair friends wou'd modestly interpret things otherways, (espitialy Har:) but I am realy prouder of his short caracter than you can believe since my being sencible (I mean reasonable) must include my being indifferent to him, as upon my word I am, & therefore I freely release you from any farther trouble on his account. & now I desire to know (what is of much more consiquence) whither you have yet seen (or heard anything of) yr cruell Philis, I wish I cou'd return your curtesy by serving you there, as for news tis always wellcome, for it serves to intertain others tho not ones self; let us then know how Plays, Musick & parkes, goe forward; who ogles who; for such slight affairs may be heard by us Philosophers; a propos have you seen our Shick yet, whos even cariage deserves that name, as time will show.   Rose Har: is here, so what with chatter, work, & whisk; our hours passe on with much sattisfaction; my brother tis true is pretty weary of us; & we are so well bred as to desire to exchange him, tho a spark newly returned from Travail for a certain Deputy Lieutenant, Justice O th peace, & Capt of the Melitia of this County who is stray'd from us to London, where the poor Countrey soul will make a sad figure tho he is preferr'd here to because Bradford if you can persuade him to return, twill be an obligation to all, but chiefly to his very

Humble servant
Arthur Middleton
April ye 10th 1762

To the reader it will be evident that the writer of this letter is identical with the writer of the three previous letters, the signatures and handwriting being the same. The recipient is again Mr. Walsh, and the subject matter the same chitchat that characterized the previous letters. It is not the type of letter one man is likely to write to another.

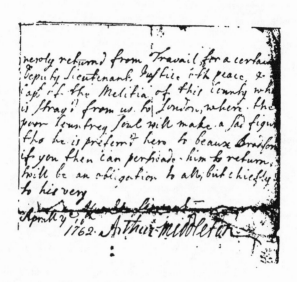

Illus. 7. ALS dated April 10, 1762.

The Mystery Deepens

On May 18, 1926, the fine set of Signers formed by the late Dr. George C. F. Williams was auctioned.   An ALS, supposedly written by Signer Middleton, was sold to the late Kenyon V. Painter of Cleveland for $2,700. Unfortunately, the complete text of the letter cannot be given since the present location of the letter is not known.   Nevertheless, the auction catalogue describing the item gives us some important information concerning the letter:

> 763 Middleton (Arthur, Signer from South Carolina). A.L.S., 2 pp.
>
> 12 mo. N.p., n.d. (Cambridge, ca 1761). To Mr. Walsh . . . A very rare example of an early holograph letter by Arthur Middleton. With the letter is a guarantee by Joseph Sabin with a sketch of its history: "It was obtained from Mrs. Eliza Middleton-- widow of Charles Middleton (descendant of the Rev. Middleton family, but cannot say if a descendant of the Signer). The item was obtained in 1880 when the old lady was in her 84th year. The collector obtained other Middleton relics from the same source . . . ."

Sabin's letter of authentication, of course, refers to Rice, who not only obtained the letters from Eliza Middleton, but also claimed to have received china from her that once belonged to the Middleton family.

The auction catalogue of the Williams sale, in addition to the foregoing, gave a short excerpt from the original letter as well as the closing lines and signature in facsimile. The excerpt is as follows:

> To answer y'r inquirey about betty she is now in princes Court
> ... with a Scotch Lady Naiper, but this is only while my Sister is retyred for a short time out of town to avoyd the Cerimone of Court which (?) upon an accasion gives her so dire a greefe as to Kingstons death. When she comes bake betty will resume to her new house in Southampton Square . . . .

The facsimile of the closing lines of the letter and the signature are reproduced in illustration 8. The text is as follows:

> ... thing halfe so entertaings; I have Just now had letters she
> is very well and Mrs hartop hopes well in her new sarrows.
>
>   Arthur Middleton

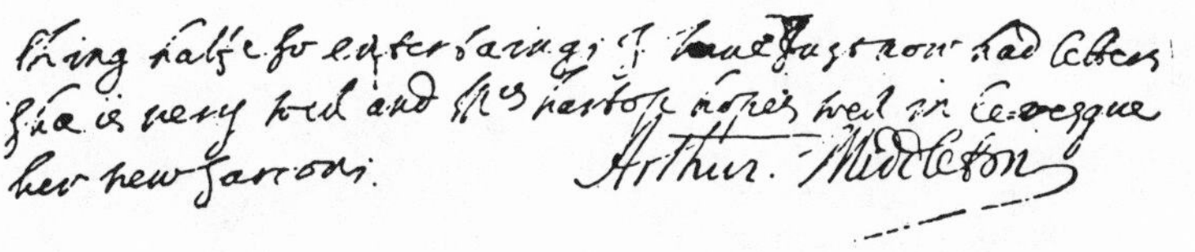

Illus. 8. Closing lines and signature of ALS in the Williams sale.

It will be noted that the handwriting and signature are identical with those of the other examples.

In retrospect, the five letters discussed above were written by the same person. From the text of two of them we may conclude all five were written by a woman, notwithstanding that three are signed "Arthur Middleton." Each of the letters is addressed to Mr. Walsh and the gossipy, bantering, half-scandalous tone is common to all.

Denouement

Let us consider why these letters could not have been written by the Signer. First, the errors in spelling, punctuation, sentence structure, and general use of English are far removed from Middleton's usage. The writer of these letters uses a liberal sprinkling of apostrophes and parentheses and seems to have a total disregard for the common and accepted usages of the times. We have established the time of composition as 1762. By this time Middleton, the Signer, was a young man of twenty years and not a juvenile. He had been a student in England since the age of twelve, having attended the schools of Hackney and Westminster. Later he entered St. John's College,

Cambridge. In 1757 he was admitted to the Inner Temple in London, the great seat of English legal learning. His known letters are masterpieces of the English language and are characterized by a profusion of Latin phrases and quotations, for he was an accomplished Latin and Greek scholar. He could not have become so with the meager knowledge of basic English demonstrated by the letters in question. Likewise, Middleton was a master in the art of allegorical writing and in the use of invective. Most of his letters contain such a style of composition. The Signer, after receiving the finest education and culture that England could provide, would never have written such a gossiping mumbo jumbo and literary hodgepodge as appear in these five letters. They are the writings of a person of little education and culture.

What of the handwriting characteristics? These letters are not in the handwriting of a recent graduate of the English public school system, one who had intelligence and ability enough to graduate from the greatest of the English law schools. The handwriting is hesitant, cramped, and jerky, while the Signer's handwriting is smooth flowing, mature, precise, and easily legible.

Further Evidence

Further evidence that these letters are not by the Signer can be found in a signature of the Signer written at the same period as the questionable letters. The signature, item 25 in the census, is reproduced in illustration 9. We may conclude that this is the Signer's signature on the title page of a book from his library, since there is an inscription on the title page, above the signature, to the effect that the book was presented to John Wilcocks, Jr., by Henry Middleton, eldest son of Arthur Middleton. We are quite justified in comparing this signature of the Signer with those in question, since they were written just one year apart. Comparison will show they are not the handwriting of the same person.

If these letters were not written by the Signer, then who was the writer? In her original article, Mary Benjamin said she believed that these letters were written by one Anne Middleton. Subsequent research into the Middleton family genealogy has convinced both Benjamin[13] and the writer of this article that such was not the case. First, three of the five letters were signed "Arthur Middleton." The accused Anne would hardly have signed her name in such a way. Second, there are three Anne Middletons and one Anna Louise Middleton in the South Carolina family. The first Anne, referred to in Benjamin's original article as being the most likely candidate for authorship, was the second wife of Col. Thomas Middleton, uncle of the Signer. She was the daughter of Nathaniel Barnwell and married Middleton in August of 1760. Colonel Middleton spent 1753 and 1754 traveling abroad and there is no record that he ever again visited England. Following his return to America he engaged in commerce, finance, and a military career. During 1760-61 he was totally occupied in the wars with the Cherokees. There is neither sailing notice nor record of travel abroad by Anne Barnwell Middleton or her husband

---

[13] The Collector, vol. 64, no. 2, February 1951, footnote 22.

after their marriage. It is extremely unlikely that she would have visited England alone while her husband was engaged in the Indian wars or tending to his business affairs in Charles Town.

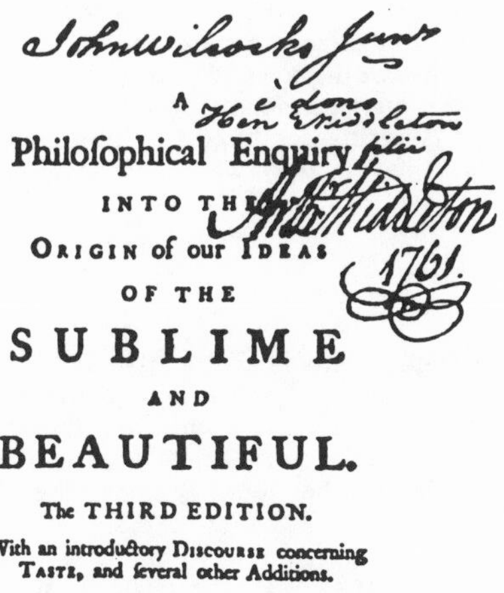
A
Philoſophical Enquiry
INTO THE
ORIGIN of our IDEAS
OF THE
SUBLIME
AND
BEAUTIFUL.
The THIRD EDITION.
With an introductory DISCOURSE concerning TASTE, and ſeveral other Additions.
1761.

Illus. 9. Middleton signature (author's collection).

A Second Anne

The second Anne, daughter of the above-mentioned Anne, was born in 1766, too late to have written the letters. The third Anne, wife of Thomas Middleton, brother of the Signer, was a daughter of Peter Manigault. She did not marry young Middleton until 1783 and hence also can be eliminated as a possible author. Anna Louise Middleton was the daughter of Arthur, the Signer. She was born in 1778, long after the letters were written.

It will be noted that in both Rice's and Sabin's letters considerable stress is laid on the fact that the source of these letters was Eliza Middleton, who was in her eighties toward the end of the nineteenth century. Examination of the Middleton genealogy does not reveal any such Eliza or Elizabeth Middleton at this date and age.[14] Sabin states Eliza was the widow of Charles Middleton,

---

[14]The nearest approach would be (1) Eliza Carolina Middleton (1774-1792), daughter of the Signer, who died unmarried, and (2) Elizabeth Izard Middleton (1815-1890), daughter of Henry Middleton and granddaughter of the Signer. She married Joshua Francis Fisher of Philadelphia in 1839 and lived in Philadelphia.

a descendant of the Reverend Middleton family. Search of the genealogy of the South Carolina family before 1900 reveals only two Charles Middletons. One, an unmarried lad of nineteen, was drowned in 1895. The other died in 1900 at the diminutive age of four months. In the entire genealogy of the illustrious Middleton family I find no reference to a Reverend Middleton, nor do I find any record of a member of the family, prior to 1900, who became a man of the cloth.

It is my opinion that the Eliza, Charles, and Reverend Middleton referred to are not members of the well-known South Carolina family, nor are they direct descendants of the Signer. In all probability they belong to another Middleton family, either American or English. Sabin hints at this in his letter when he states he cannot say if they were descendants of the Signer. This family has not been identified.

Caveat Emptor

The writer is thoroughly convinced the five letters were not written by the Signer, but were written by a woman who used the name Arthur Middleton as a pseudonym to cover her identity, should her letters fall into the wrong hands. The very nature of the letters would give a plausible excuse to any young female to wish to conceal her identity under the cloak of pseudonymity or anonymity.

Undoubtedly, Charles Rice was the source of distribution of these letters, since none of them has a sale record prior to the time Rice was active as a collector. By his own confession, he supplied Dormitzer with a specimen. Sabin's letter refers to Rice, by inference, as the source of the letter in the Williams sale. It is quite likely that Rice also supplied Madigan and Dr. Williams with examples. There must be other letters of this type in existence, for Rice stated in his letter to Dormitzer that he had three or four unsigned examples, and it is quite likely that he disposed of these to other collectors or dealers. And thus, dealers, collectors, librarians, and auction houses will do well to investigate thoroughly any Middleton letter, signed or unsigned, that is offered for sale. With true Arthur Middleton letters selling for from $250 to $1,000, it would be most unfortunate to sell or purchase a false example.

This writer recommends that collectors and dealers be content with DSs and unsigned letters and documents by Middleton. Middleton, always of prime rarity, is becoming more so, and it is doubtful if any full ALS will turn up. Some of the finest Middleton letters extant remain unsigned or are signed with initials. Even Dr. Thomas Addis Emmet, a collector of Signers for sixty years who had the choice of the best for as many years, was satisfied with a Middleton signed with initials. Emmet could not have the full signature and good content also. He chose content. For those who would insist on a full signature, let them then acquire one of the signed documents as a companion piece.

Hartford Convention, 1814-15*

Walter N. Eastburn

When a dealer friend in the spring of 1954 suggested that I buy from him an incomplete set of autographs of the twenty-six delegates to the Hartford Convention held in 1814-15, I naturally wondered, as you probably did on reading the title of this article, just what it was all about.

To answer that question, let us go back to 1784. The Revolutionary War had been won, a peace treaty had been signed, and the thirteen original states were free and independent, altogether too independent and jealous to help one another.

Congress, under the Confederation, could legislate, but could not enforce its acts. It had no power of taxation and could only beg the states for money. At times, the states grudgingly responded; at other times they ignored the appeals.

The patriots in each state and the younger members, many of whom like Madison and Hamilton were in college when the war began, busied themselves in such endeavors as forming state governments and adopting constitutions for their states. They soon realized that the Confederation was not a nation and that the states must be more closely knit together or they would soon be at one another's throats.

Largely by the efforts of Madison and Hamilton, a convention of five states met at Annapolis, Maryland, in 1786 and soon decided to call a general convention of all the states to meet in Philadelphia, in May 1787.

The avowed purpose was to--

devise such provisions as shall appear necessary to render the constitution of the Federal Government adequate to the exigencies of the Union, and to report to Congress such an act as, when agreed to by them and confirmed by the legislatures of every state, would effectually provide for the same.

The convention met and deliberated for four months, and on September 17, 1787, the Constitution was adopted and signed. Even its best friends

---

*Originally published in 1960.

realized it was not perfect, for many compromises were necessary to effect results.   But it was a good beginning and the First Congress, by proposing twelve amendments, ten of which were adopted and became the Bill of Rights, perfected the Constitution.

One staunch patriot, Thomas Jefferson, author of the Declaration of Independence, was out of the country while this was going on, Congress having sent him to Paris to strengthen American representation there.   He was in France from 1784 to 1789.   The horrors of the French Revolution turned Jefferson from an aristocratic leader here into a sympathetic believer in the rights of the common people against any form of tyranny in government. Despite his acceptance of the office of secretary of state under President Washington, he did not hesitate to voice his discontent over the new Constitution, feeling that it gave the central government too much power.

Two parties emerged after adoption of the Constitution: the Federalists, supporters of and largely the authors of the document, and the Anti-Federalists, or Republicans (in other words, the "ins" and the "outs"). Jefferson soon became the acknowledged leader of the Republicans.   He and Hamilton were constantly at loggerheads while they were in the cabinet. When John Adams was elected to succeed Washington, and his vice presidential candidate was defeated, largely through Hamilton's efforts, a violent feud developed between Adams and Hamilton, which ended in the breakup of the Federalist Party.   This led to the defeat of Adams for reelection and put Jefferson in office for two terms.

The governing principle through Jefferson's terms and those of his successor, Madison, who had been Jefferson's secretary of state, was friendship for France and enmity for Great Britain.   When Napoleon became the power in France he pressed hostilities against England so vigorously that both nations laid blockades against each other.   The United States, trying to be neutral, was in the middle of the controversy; its trade with Europe was stifled while the war was on.   To bolster its navy and maintain its supremacy of the sea, England had for some time been stopping American vessels on the excuse of looking for British sailors, and impressing American seamen into the British navy.   Both Jefferson and Madison unsuccessfully tried to stop this practice. When the blockade shut down American commerce, Madison took the side of France and asked Congress to declare war upon England.   This was done on June 18, 1812, though America was wholly unprepared to fight a war.

President Madison issued a call on the states for 100,000 militia troops to be mustered into federal service outside their own states and manned by federal officers.   Connecticut and Massachusetts refused compliance, on grounds that the Constitution plainly called for such troops to be headed by their own officers.   The government then withdrew the federal troops which had been guarding the seacoast in those states and refused to pay the expense of the militia who took over the job.

In 1814 the situation became alarming, with invasion threatened from the sea and also from Canada.   British depredations in the southern states were evidence of their intention to ravage the whole Atlantic Coast.   The Massachusetts legislature received pleas for relief from many towns.   On

October 16 and 18 the two houses of the legislature voted to appoint twelve citizens as delegates to meet and confer with delegates from other New England states.

Connecticut appointed seven delegates to meet with others at Hartford on December 15, 1814.   Rhode Island appointed four delegates, two county conventions in New Hampshire sent two delegates, and one county in Vermont sent one delegate.

The convention met on the date agreed upon. It was decided that the sessions would be held behind closed doors.   President Madison became so alarmed at this news that he sent a Federal Army officer and a company of troops to Hartford to see that things did not get out of hand.

The convention adjourned on January 5, 1815, and its report, including seven specific suggestions and recommendations for amending the Constitution, designed to strengthen states' rights, was immediately published. Its temper was mild, its tone moderate, and its sentiments liberal and patriotic.

Shortly thereafter the country was surprised to learn that a peace treaty had been signed with Great Britain, even before the battle of New Orleans was fought.

The convention's report and copy of the secret journal of its activities were published in the "History of the Hartford Convention" by Theodore Dwight, the convention secretary. The convention's original report, signed by all of its delegates and the secretary, is on file in the Archives of the Commonwealth of Massachusetts, in Boston.

My dealer friend, knowing that I had retired from business, urged me to purchase his incomplete set of delegate autographs. He felt certain that, "with my spare time and energy," I would soon be able to acquire the two missing items that he had been seeking for ten or more years! They were Edward Manton of Rhode Island and William Hall, Jr., of Vermont. They were both businessmen, as were three other delegates, while the other twenty-one delegates were lawyers. A further argument used was that, on completing the set, I could then write this article telling what the Hartford Convention was and how I went about acquiring the two missing items.   So I bought the incomplete set. That was in June 1954, five and one-half years ago. The quest was a time-consuming one. Whenever a new idea occurred to me, or a new lead developed, I followed it through.   I contacted dealers, many of our members, family descendants, the New England historical societies (state, county, and local), college libraries, and the state and local governments. I also engaged the services of genealogical researchers in both Rhode Island and Vermont. My efforts resulted in—

o   Preparing fourteen research memorandums,

o   Sending out 135 letters of inquiry, and

o   Receiving 121 replies, all negative except two.

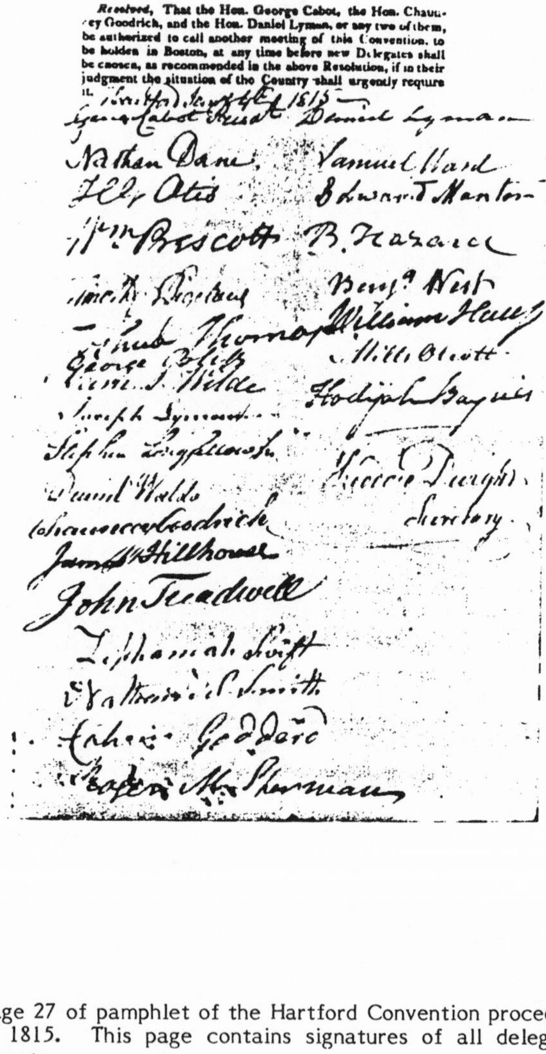

Resolved, That the Hon. George Cabot, the Hon. Chauncey Goodrich, and the Hon. Daniel Lyman, or any two of them, be authorized to call another meeting of this Convention, to be holden in Boston, at any time before new Delegates shall be chosen, as recommended in the above Resolution, if in their judgment the situation of the Country shall urgently require it.

Illus. 1. Page 27 of pamphlet of the Hartford Convention proceedings printed in 1815. This page contains signatures of all delegates and the secretary.

Early in 1959 my researcher in Rhode Island acquired for me a DS of Edward Manton.

In Vermont, my researcher had sent me a photostat of a document signed by William Hall, Jr., and others, on file in the secretary of state's office, petitioning for the opening of a highway. Finally, after exhausting all possible leads, I wrote to the editor of state papers, Allen Soule, rehearsing my efforts to obtain an original autograph of William Hall, Jr., and asking if he could help me obtain one. He evidently took pity on me and sent me a list of some early Vermont officials whose letters would be welcomed and several pamphlets of early legislative acts that were missing from the state library. He informed me that if I would supply one or more of these I could have a Hall!

I contacted dealers and old bookshops in New York but could find nothing mentioned on the list. In one shop I did find a two-volume set of **History of East Vermont,** by Benjamin H. Hall (New York, 1865), in mint state, of which only fifty copies have been printed. I asked the editor of state papers if the library had it. He replied they had an old set almost worn out by too much handling and that if I would send him the set I had seen, the secretary of state was willing to give me the original of the document of which I had the photostat. A photostat would serve their purpose, though not mine.

So I closed the deal and my set is complete. With two duplicates, it consists of twenty-two ALSs, one LS, one ADS, and five DSs.

I took a census of the number of complete sets, in addition to mine, among our members. My inquiries of all probable sources have thus far disclosed the existence of only two other complete sets. One is in the Gratz collection in the Historical Society of Pennsylvania, and the other is an 1815 pamphlet of the convention proceedings, on page 27 of which all the delegates and the secretary signed their names (see illus. 1). The pamphlet is in the Connecticut Historical Society at Hartford.

John Brown's Letters and Documents*

Boyd B. Stutler

Through the first fifty years of his troubled and turbulent life, there seems to have been little reason why anyone, other than members of his family, should have preserved or treasured letters written by John Brown of Hudson, Ohio, later of Osawatomie, Kansas, and Harpers Ferry, West Virginia. He had been a farmer, tanner, shepherd, wool merchant, real estate promoter, and whatnot, with most of his ventures ending in financial failure. Of course there were some creditors who carefully filed away evidences of debt in the hope that his fortunes would take a turn for the better at some distant day and that something could be realized from unpaid debts and accounts.

Brown was an antislavery exponent throughout his life, a loner who had little confidence in the organized antislavery societies. It was not until the Kansas troubles broke out in 1855, when he had reached his fifty-fifth year, that he attained any national prominence. He won the sobriquet "Osawatomie Brown" in the summer of 1856, when he made a losing defense of that town against the attack of Missouri Border Ruffians. In that same year Brown became known as a daring and ruthless Free State guerrilla leader. He then had but three years to live, climaxing his career and winning his measure of fame (or infamy, depending altogether upon the point of view) by his abortive raid on Harpers Ferry, then in Virginia but now in West Virginia, on October 16, 1859.

It was not until after Brown had been heralded in the newspapers as an uncompromising Free State leader in Kansas--and as a guerrilla captain with a somewhat blood-stained record--that he made his most important contacts with a group of radical abolitionists in the East, notably at Boston, and with the Concord group headed by Emerson, Thoreau, Alcott, and other leaders in cultural and reform movements. It was with this latter group that Brown carried on an extensive correspondence during a period of conspiratorial activities from 1857 down to the eve of the Harpers Ferry raid, with letters dated from places in Kansas, the northern states, and Canada. Only a fragment of this correspondence remains. Most of the letters were destroyed immediately after the raid as a measure of self-protection by his correspondents, thus leaving great gaps in the series that has been preserved. But there are other reasons why John Brown's letters have disappeared, and the principal one was of his own making. But more of that later.

---

*Originally published in 1954.

Few Letters Remain

Brown was a voluminous letter writer.   During his lifetime he sent thousands of letters to hundreds of people--just how many is anyone's guess. He filled a number of notebooks with memorandums, business notes, names of his prize buck sheep, quotations from books and letters that struck his fancy, and a plethora of pithy observations of his own. He also signed his name to hundreds of documents, from deeds for property to commissions to his captains in the Army of Liberation at Harpers Ferry. But of all this great volume that came from his busy pen, probably fewer than five hundred pieces survive. This is a rather liberal estimate based on a quick survey of the holdings of private collectors and of public and institutional libraries. It is conceivable, of course, that caches of letters may be found in the future--letters that are now hidden away in attics or in "grandpa's old trunk," that proverbial repository of unknown and undreamed-of treasures. But the chances are slim that any great number will come to light. It is more likely that known letters, now lost to view, will turn up.

Compared with the signatures or holograph letters of Signers Button Gwinnett and Thomas Lynch, Jr., John Brown's autographs are relatively common. Yet to today's collectors they are scarce enough to make the quest interesting and exciting. The person who in 1954 sets out to build up a series of original papers from the hand and pen of John Brown will need a great deal of time, the patience of Job, and more than a modicum of credit at the First National. A few years ago, John Brown material stayed in the files of dealers for a long time; there were few buyers and the prices were low enough that the low-income collectors could obtain fine letters at a cost within their autograph expenditure budget. But times have changed, and so have tastes and demands in the autograph-collecting field.

The new collector in 1954 will face some stiff competition, not only from fellow collectors who are intent upon building up their antislavery and Civil War collections, but from institutional and public libraries that have awakened to the historical importance of the old antislavery crusaders and to the practical value of collections of their papers to present and future students of history. The competition of institutional and public libraries does not usually come in the marketplace where items are bought and sold, but the pieces libraries receive by gift or trade become captive, reducing the number of free pieces available to the private collector.

As early as 1891 Frank D. Andrews, a noted collector in his day, suggested in **The Collector** (New York) the desirability of rounding up letters and documents of the sixty-two signers of the "Declaration of Sentiments" adopted at the organization of the American Anti-Slavery Society at Philadelphia in 1833. He named Whittier and Garrison as leaders, then for good measure threw in the name of John Brown, who was not a signer of the document and who never belonged to the society. "Letters of John Brown are scarce; they command the highest price of the anti-slavery agitators," he said.

Deeds Not Words

When Andrews wrote he was probably thinking of the bales upon bales of letters and papers of the abolitionists through which autograph dealers and librarians were patiently searching for a few prime nuggets. He knew, too, what a gabby, windy bunch these early reformers were, and how they poured out their troubled souls in a constant stream of pleas, prayers, protests, and petitions. All things concerned them, from the eradication of human slavery from the American scene, to temperance, tobacco, bloomers, and women's rights, up through a series of crackpot theories and pet ideas, to the upper realms of ethereal frets and fancies.

Brown had little use for the talking campaigns of the reformers. His personal plans after he popped into some national prominence called for action--direct, militant action that in recent years has made him a darling of Communist propagandists. But however rash he was in his forays to free the slaves, he was cautious with his pen. In his "war" letters to his fellow conspirators and to members of his family, he frequently indulged in double-talk, but there is no known instance when he resorted to the device of a cipher or code. "John Brown's cipher," nonetheless, has been up for sale in various forms for several years. One of the ciphers offered by a dealer turned out to be the Viginere Napoleonic code, which later was used not only by the U.S. Army and War Department, but also by the Confederate State and War Departments.

Brown's script was distinctive and legible, with letters small and clearly formed, though a bit pinched and pointed. There was little change in the general characteristics of his handwriting from early manhood to the time of his death. As with everything else he touched, he impressed his dominating personality into his script, and he had his own peculiar notions about spelling and punctuation, sometimes adding an extra letter or giving phonetic rendering to the most common words. He invariably used the ampersand; it would take a long search through his writings to find a single instance of use of the word "and." Throughout his letters he liberally sprinkled colons, semicolons, and dashes without reference to any need for a punctuation mark of any kind.

Brown's Early Writings

Brown's letter writing probably began in the fall and winter of 1816-17, when he spent a few months in study at Plainfield, Massachusetts, and at Morris Academy, in his native Litchfield County, Connecticut. But none of this correspondence has been found. The earliest known signature is affixed to a deed dated in 1825, now owned by Dr. Charles W. Olsen of Chicago. A series of fifty-five letters to Seth Thompson, a business associate--including his earliest letters, starting in 1826---are in the files of Atlanta University, Atlanta, Georgia. It was during the correspondence with Thompson, from 1828 to 1835, that Brown served as postmaster at Randolph (now New Richmond), Pennsylvania--his only public office---and not only signed and franked his own letters, but placed his signature as postmaster on all the letters written by his neighbors. These franks are excessively scarce. Atlanta University has eighteen in the Thompson series, but they are captive and presumably are forever removed from the channels of barter and sale. Only two are known to be owned privately: one by Olsen (coming from the Oliver Barrett collection) and the other by Dr. Clarence S. Gee of Lockport, New York. Long and patient search has failed to turn up other letters or franks of the Pennsylvania interlude. Most of the letters known were written after 1840, though there are several pieces in private collections dated in the 1830s.

Long absences from home after 1838, ever-widening business interests, bankruptcy, the Kansas wars, and later conspiratorial activities accelerated the flow of letters and kept Brown pretty well occupied at his traveling writing desk (which had a habit of getting lost). Even after the Harpers Ferry debacle and during the thirty days in Charles Town jail between sentence and execution on December 2, 1859, Brown turned out more than one hundred letters. Naturally, these letters are the prime desiderata of collectors, but comparatively few are found on the free market or in the hands of private collectors. Libraries and institutions have gobbled up the lion's share of the survivors. Six of these prison letters are included in my own file of ninety-eight John Brown letters and documents. The prison letters run from the first letter written to his family after the failure of the Harpers Ferry raid, telling of the raid, the death of his two sons, and his trial and sentence to be hanged, to one written about his temporal affairs to his half-brother Jeremiah late at night before his execution. Curiously enough, this last letter to Jeremiah was held in Tokyo by a Japanese autograph collector for many years before and during World War II.

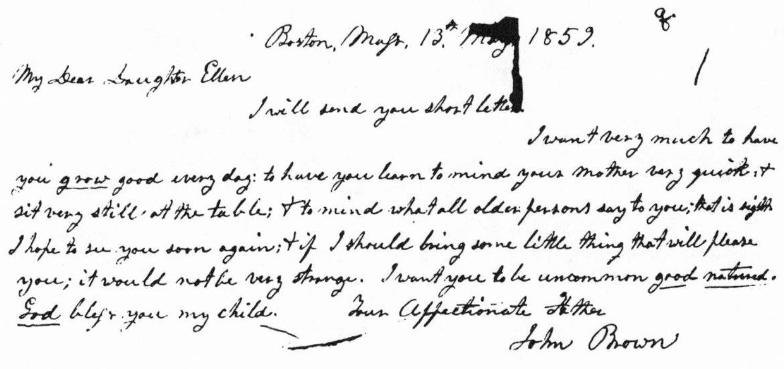

Illus. 1. John Brown's letter to his daughter Ellen, then five years old. It was written six weeks before he went to Harpers Ferry to plan his raid. Ellen, later Mrs. James Fablinger, lived in California until her death in 1916. From the author's collection.

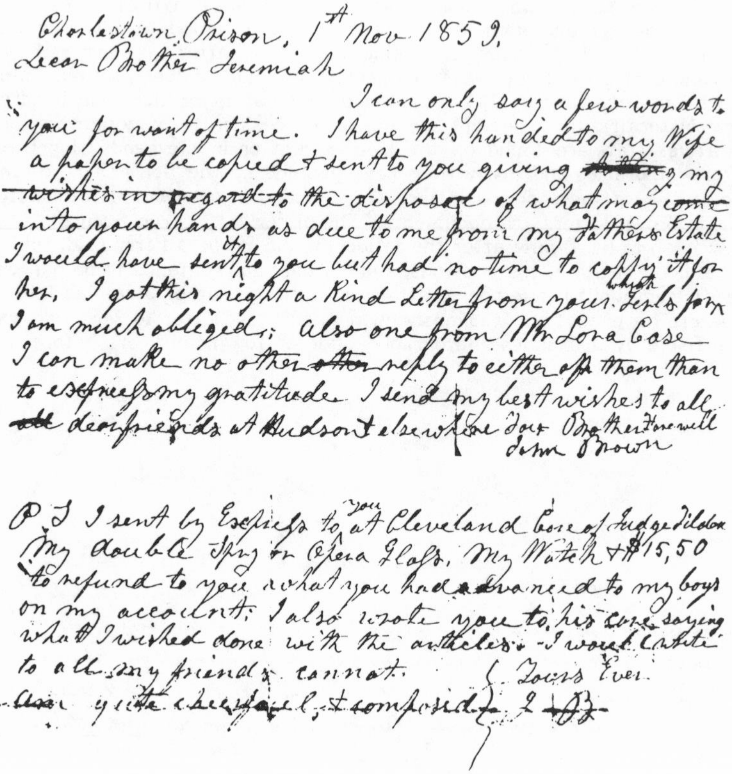

Charlestown, Prison, 1st Nov 1859.

Dear Brother Jeremiah

I can only say a few words to you for want of time. I have this handed to my Wife a paper to be copied & sent to you giving ~~a copy~~ my ~~wishes in regard~~ to the disposal of what may come into your hands as due to me from my Fathers Estate I would have sent to you but had no time to copy it for her. I got this night a Kind Letter from your Girls for which I am much obliged; also one from Mr Lora Case I can make no other ~~other~~ reply to either of them than to express my gratitude I send my best wishes to all ~~old~~ dear friends at Hudson & elsewhere Your Brother Farewell

John Brown

P S I sent by Express to you at Cleveland Care of Judge Tilden My double Spy or Opera Glass, My Watch &$15,50 to refund to you what you had advanced to my boys on my account; I also wrote you to his care saying what I wished done with the articles - I would write to all my friends cannot.   (Yours Ever.

Am quite cheerful, & composed) J B

Illus. 2.   This letter was owned by a Japanese collector and passed through World War II in Tokyo. It was bought by the author in 1951.

Destruction of Letters

The natural hazards of all written papers--fires, floods, war, and carelessness of individual owners--have taken a heavy toll through the years. From the burning of the homes of Jason and John Brown, Jr., by Border Ruffians in Kansas in 1856 down to the blitz over London in the early days of World War II, violence of man and nature has slowly reduced the number of Brown's writings. But most destructive of his letters was the great purge of 1859, when many of Brown's closest associates, and certainly those with whom he had had the greatest volume of correspondence, ran to cover after the Harpers Ferry rebellion. Gerrit Smith, Frank Sanborn, Dr. Samuel G. Howe, and others scoured their files and destroyed every scrap of writing that would identify them with the man or his raid. Fortunately a great number of letters were out of the hands of these men at the time of the raid and thus escaped the furnace. The existing pieces--a considerable number from the family archives--have had a hard time to survive.

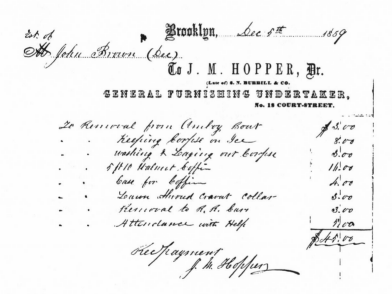

Illus. 3. Undertaker's bill for caring for the body of John Brown in New York, including a new coffin, amounting to $45 in all. Burials were cheaper in 1859.

Noms de Guerre

The diminishing number of pieces in the market is generally attributed to the hazard of years and to this great purge, but John Brown himself set up a hazard that has caused the unwitting destruction of an unknown number of pieces. He had the habit of signing with a nom de guerre or an initial that might not be his own, or of not signing his letters at all, leaving his correspondents to identify the writer by content or by his distinctive script. Dozens of letters were signed "James M. Bell," "Nelson Hawkins," "James Smith," "Shubel Morgan," "Isaac Smith" (for the Harpers Ferry plotting), or with initials such as "N.," "H.," or "J." Princeton University has a letter written from Chicago signed "Old Hundred," and a series (none now known to exist) went out from Chatham, Canada, signed with the firm name "Calm & Still." "I. Smith & Sons," a firm organized for a peculiar business, received mail and freight at Chambersburg, Pennsylvania, after the Army of Liberation rendezvous had been established at the Kennedy farm, near Harpers Ferry. Brown's practice of using a name not his own worked in later years to cause the destruction of many pieces for which collectors today would be glad to pay hard cash. Dealers and owners who were not entirely familiar with the pinched, old man's hand could not associate the signature, if any, with the firebrand of Kansas and Harpers Ferry.

Also, Brown's name was a common one that was legitimately borne by someone in nearly every community in the country. For a quarter of a century he moved restlessly over the country, buying wool, driving sheep and cattle from New England to as far west as Illinois, surveying in West Virginia, making overland wagon trips to Kansas and back to the East, conspiring in Canada, and later ranging over a number of the antislave states in the interest of his "greatest or principal object"--the abolition of slavery.

Thus, Brown's letters are dated from various places in many states, even from England and the European continent in 1849. That, too, has caused loss because many dealers and others who would prize a letter written by the old raider did not identify John Brown of Rockford, Illinois, who has cattle to sell, or a man bearing the same name at Chatham, Canada West, who writes about cutting cedars on a farm at North Elba, New York, as the same man who "led a little company of his own" in a midnight raid on a proslavery settlement in Kansas, in which five men were called from their homes and cut down with broadswords.

"Bobtailed" Letters

Members of Brown's family did not burn his letters, but some of them fell into the habit of chopping the signature from the sheet for the gratification of pestilent "autograph collectors," most of whom wanted only a signature to paste in an album. As a consequence of yielding to these pleas, even after the number of such requests became burdensome, dozens of good family letters were mutilated and their sale value immeasurably impaired. Brown was a thrifty soul who used both sides of his writing paper; thus, when the signature was clipped a good part of the letter on the opposite side was destroyed. As an example of how far this vandalism went, the papers of John Brown, Jr., in the library of the Ohio Historical Society at Columbus may be cited. Of sixty-seven original letters written by the crusading antislaver now held in these files, the signatures of twenty-five have been clipped or hacked out. In my own holdings only three of the ninety-eight letters and documents are bobtailed, but many are unsigned, or signed with a nom de guerre. There are a good "Shubel Morgan," written during the last stay in Kansas in 1858, and several "Isaac Smiths," dated from Chambersburg, Pennsylvania, but probably written at the Kennedy farm near Harpers Ferry.

The great number of bobtailed letters held in collections and in the hands of dealers at one time seemed to indicate that there had been a systematic campaign to destroy all the writings of John Brown. Years ago there was a story, which could not be traced to its source, that some southern partisan was responsible for the mutilations. But that theory seemed hardly logical for the simple reason that if anyone had been so interested in cleaning house he would not have contented himself with chopping off the signature, but would most certainly have destroyed the whole letter. The answer was found some time later, when a letter written by Brown's daughter Ruth Thompson turned up in the catalogue of a New York dealer. "How thoughtless all our family were to cut out of father's precious letters his autograph, without in many instances even a postage stamp to pay for sending it," Ruth wrote in 1893 to Frank C. Logan of Chicago, by way of apology for sending him a clipped letter. Logan's fine collection of John Brown autographic material, including this bobtail cripple, was presented to the Chicago Historical Society some thirty years later.

Other letters from family members confirm Ruth's statement, so the family was, in fact, responsible for the mutilations. Southern partisans were thus fully absolved.

Signature fiends were not the only people importuning the Brown family for letters. Several serious collectors wrote the sons and daughters, the great majority offering blandishment and soft soap but rarely cash, and a great number of them were obliged. It may be said that members of the family did not sell letters until many years after the Harpers Ferry incident, when old age and economic necessity forced them to dispose of remaining letters at prices that now seem pitifully small.

Location of Existing Letters

A survey of holdings upon which the estimate of five hundred surviving pieces is based discloses that my own collection heads the list with ninety-eight letters and documents and three letter books used by the firm of Perkins & Brown at Springfield, Massachusetts, for the first half of 1849. One book contains 216 letters in Brown's own handwriting, nearly all pertaining to the wool business. The Ohio Historical Society, the repository of the extensive John Brown, Jr., papers, is second with sixty-seven items and one Perkins & Brown letter book containing some 1,300 letters in various hands, many of which are John Brown originals. Atlanta University is third on the list with its long run of fifty-five early personal and business letters to Seth Thompson and one or two family letters.

The Kansas Historical Society, which became the repository of the family's Kansas papers in 1881, holds thirty-five original letters and documents, most of which relate to Brown's Kansas interlude.   The Dreer Collection in the Pennsylvania Historical Society, Philadelphia, has twenty-five items, including the codicil to Brown's will and memorandum for inscription on the family gravestone, both written on the morning of execution. The Dreer Collection is also rich in material relating to the trial of Brown and his associates and in letters from both northern and southern people to Gov. Henry A. Wise reflecting public reaction to the raid, trial, and sentence.   Most of this lot consists of "archival estrays" removed from the Virginia state files during the Civil War.

Other important collections that the student and researcher should not overlook are the following: Henry E. Huntington Library, San Marino, California, twenty items, including two memorandum books; Chicago Historical Society, nineteen items, including the little strip of paper Brown handed Hiram O'Bannon while on his way to execution, which is usually called "John Brown's Prophecy"; Boston Public Library, thirteen letters and two memorandum books; Massachusetts Historical Society, Boston, five letters; Villard Collection in Columbia University Library, six items; Yale University Library, five letters and a book of letters received by Perkins & Brown in the fall of 1849.

Other important holdings of from one to five letters are those of the Library of Congress; New York Public Library; Reis Library at Allegheny College, Meadville, Pennsylvania; and some two dozen other libraries. Private collectors scattered over the country hold some of the most important items.

All these collections afford fertile fields for the student and researcher, for in each library the few original John Brown letters and documents are only supplemental to a mass of related materials. This is particularly true of the Library of Congress, the Villard Collection in Columbia University Library, Huntington Library, and the two Massachusetts libraries mentioned.

The Prices of Brown's Letters

It seems that the crassly commercial angle should be discussed if for nothing more than to satisfy the academic interest of readers who have no thought of cornering the market. John Brown's auction-room performance has not been very impressive. Many of the very best and most important items, however, have never found their way into the auction room; the old covenanter has fared much better in person-to-person and dealer-to-collector negotiations, with some prices ranging into the four-figure mark--such as Brown's letter to Lora Case, which was written about an hour before he left the prison for the execution grounds (now in the Berg Collection, New York Public Library), and the codicil to his will and final note to his wife (now in the Dreer Collection, Pennsylvania Historical Society).

An analysis of the record as set down in **American Book Prices Current** (ABPC), covering sales from 1894 to 1953, reveals that 126 John Brown autograph items have been put on the block. Of this number, however, twenty-five were repeaters (two items appearing three times each), which reduces the total to 101 separate items. An average of slightly more than two sales were made per year for the sixty volumes examined. This should prove something as to general scarcity. These figures, it might be added, are not guaranteed to be entirely accurate as to the number of sales, for in the early years ABPC paid little attention to autograph sales; in many instances the sales were not listed, and even when they were listed the notation was often inadequate and unsatisfactory. Fortunately for the craft, that situation has been corrected.

The prices realized were not startling enough to command headlines in the newspapers. The 126 sales reported fetched a total of $5,860.75, an average of $46.52 per item. The pieces ranged in importance from a detached cover of a pocket memorandum book, signed ($10.50), and a two-line, undated order for a package (later found to be spurious), to John Brown's will drawn on the morning of the execution and the original draft of the Provisional Constitution (location now unknown) adopted at the convention at Chatham, Canada, in 1858. The Provisional Constitution was filched from the files at Richmond after the fall of the Confederate government. It brought only $52.50 at the Col. John Trumbull sale in 1897. If it were offered again in these days of the fifty-cent dollar, the price would probably soar into the four-figure bracket.

The lowest price recorded is that for a letter to Mrs. Brown, undated and with signature clipped, which brought $4.25 at Bangs's in 1897. Two years later, when Stan Henkels put the same letter on the block, some economic royalist was willing to bid 25 cents over the previous price record. The highest auction price recorded is that for the will drawn by attorney Andrew Hunter and signed by John Brown on the morning of the execution, which Ralph Newman bought for the late Foreman M. Lebold of Chicago at the Oliver Barrett sale in 1950 at his bid of $625. Second highest was a prison letter written to Marie Sterns, Springfield, Massachusetts, which brought $352 at Anderson's in 1916, but the sale price dropped to $135 when the item again appeared in the William Harris Arnold sale in 1924. The same letter was catalogued at $660 by a dealer some two or three years ago.

Definitely John Brown is not in the auction-room class with Abraham Lincoln, George Washington, and other worthies who are much more frequently represented in the auction and dealer catalogues.

There is still hope that other important documents may come to light some fair day. Maybe it is too much to hope that among these documents will be Brown's long-sought instructions to his lawyers, written while he was on trial for his life. These were disregarded and cast on the floor of the Charles Town courthouse. Hobnailed heel marks will plainly show that the paper was trampled upon, and it will be smudged with dark brown spots. No, those brown spots were not made by the sprinkled blood of the martyr. The spots will be all that remain of some ninety-year-old tobacco juice.

Presidents and Books*

Alfred J. Liebmann

The history of our country may well be traced by following the lives of the presidents who have guided its destiny. It is, therefore, readily understandable that among autograph collectors the signatures of the presidents are very highly prized; and the gem of many collections is a complete set. Interesting and revealing as the individual signature can be, especially if it is affixed to a letter related to some important event or person or if it discloses some intimate traits of the writer, I have always shared the feeling expressed by Dr. A. S. W. Rosenbach, the great bibliophile from Philadelphia, that the book habits of the presidents--as of all people--will give a fascinating insight into their personalities, characters, and habits. In an article for the **New York Times Magazine** of April 16, 1935, Rosenbach wrote,

> People have always been interested in books from the libraries of Queen Elizabeth of England, Louis XIV of France, Ferdinand and Isabella of Spain, Queen Anne, Marie Antoinette and other notable persons in European history. I have often wondered why the same interest is not expressed in volumes from the libraries of the presidents of the United States. Some of our presidents formed great collections and were interested in the books they owned. No one should look upon a book from the library of George Washington, Thomas Jefferson, or Abraham Lincoln without a thrill, and I am sure no true book collector could resist adding a specimen from one of them to his own collection--that is, if he could find one.

All these reflections led me to look around for books which our presidents considered good enough to place in their own libraries and in which they inscribed their name, and for books they considered worth giving to their friends with a dedication or some other inscription.

Peculiarly enough, I soon found that books bearing presidential signatures are by no means common. I have been seeking and tracing them for more than fifteen years and I am still missing books for seven presidents. Collectors and other students of history may be interested in hearing about the group I have assembled and about a few of the sometimes amusing incidents connected with their acquisition.

---

*Originally published in 1955.

The Origins of My Collection

I have been collecting books for more than forty years, although some authors and subjects have received more affection and concentration than others. I found myself switching from general literature or history and science to finely illustrated or otherwise distinguished issues. I have always tried to obtain limited or autographed editions or to obtain the signatures of the authors or persons identified with the contents of the books.

Whatever the book or subject, having the book autographed somehow established a personal link between me and the author or other person who wrote his name in the book. Knowing that he must have touched it in order to inscribe his name, I felt I was almost shaking hands with the writer; and so, in getting together a set of books, all inscribed by the presidents, I have not only relived the history of our country but I have somehow entered into a personal relationship with all the men who have helped to shape it.

My collection of "presidential" books now comprises thirty-seven volumes, with the autographs of twenty-six presidents. I shall briefly describe the collection, leaving out some of the less important duplicates.

As I write these lines, there have been thirty-three presidents, two of whom are living ex-presidents and one of whom is the incumbent. I have tried to find out what they think of books and what influence books have exercised on their lives, opinions, and decisions. The result of my attempt will be described later.

It is reasonable to assume, however, that all the presidents, as educated and public-minded men, liked to live with books and used them with benefit. Therefore, there would apply to most of them-- at least to some degree--the characterization of book lovers that recently appeared in the "Topics of The Times":

A good book owned becomes his [the book-lover's] raison d'etre, for it connects him with the past, underscores his present and causes him to look with faith and reason to the future.

It is, of course, natural that works on history appear most frequently in my collection and that the books presidents gave to their friends had to do with their own personal lives or their literary and oratorical expressions.

Washington—The Collector

Washington was a great book collector.   Since he was a man of considerable means, he was able to indulge freely in this hobby, which his wife also shared. At the time of his death, an inventory showed 884 volumes. This library went under his will to his favorite nephew, Supreme Court Justice Bushrod Washington. The judge added many volumes and left them upon his death in 1826 to his two nephews, John A. Washington and George C. Washington. The latter, who received almost two-thirds of the collection, sold the books in 1847 to Henry Stevens of London. The following year a majority of them were purchased by public subscription of about $4,000 for the Boston Athenaeum, where they still are.

The part of the library Judge Bushrod left to his nephew John was finally passed on by him to his grandson, Lawrence Washington of Alexandria, who gradually disposed of the books between the years of 1876 and 1892. The majority, comprising a lot of 138 volumes, was sold by M. Thomas and Sons at Philadelphia in 1876 for the ridiculously low price of $2,000 for the entire collection.

My Washington book is the first president's own copy of a contemporary English account of the war with the American colonists and of all the events that led to it. Rosenbach considered it one of the most interesting association copies in the whole range of American history. I am deeply indebted for it to John Fleming, present director of the Rosenbach Foundation, who has, at all times, taken a kind interest in my collection. He must have felt a sincere pang of regret in parting with this item, which was one of his treasured ones.

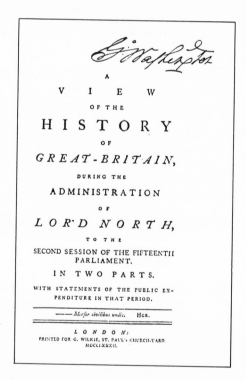

Illus. 1. George Washington's book of history.

The signature is written in Washington's usual bold style on the title page of the book. The bookplate inside the front cover is the armorial plate with the name George Washington and the motto "Exitus Acta Probat." Laid in the book is a one-page letter in the handwriting of Lawrence Washington:

Philadelphia. March 6, 1891

Lot No. 19 of the "Baker" Sale of books &c., in February 1891, made by Thomas Birch's Sons, Philadelphia: entitled "Views of the History of Great Britain during the Administration of Lord North to the Second Session of the Fifteenth Parliament, Etc. "London, 1782, bearing the autograph of Geo. Washington on title and his bookplate, I recognise as one of the books sold for my account in Philadelphia 1876 by M. Thomas & Sons.

This volume was inherited by me, and is from the Library of General George Washington at Mount Vernon.

(Signed) Lawrence Washington

In the course of a recent visit I paid to the Parke-Bernet Galleries, John Gaffney was kind enough to show me a very old catalogue of the Thomas sale that he has had in his possession for many years. The catalogue, which bears the title "Washingtoniana," is fully priced, and the North book is item no. 76. It sold for $13, but a marginal notation states that it was knocked down for $190 nineteen years later at the Baker sale and resold in Philadelphia, December 1892, to Luther Kountze for $290.

John Adams

John Adams was a graduate of Harvard College and was interested in books throughout his entire life, which exceeded ninety years. Despite the fact that he had one of the largest libraries in the colonies and was a constant collector, comparatively few of his books are now in circulation, because in his eighty-seventh year--in 1822--he gave practically his entire collection of 2,756 volumes to the town of Quincy, Massachusetts. In accordance with a stipulation to this gift, a printed catalogue was issued in the same year. Only the few books retained for his own reading and those he had given to his family and friends appear in circulation from time to time, but very infrequently. The one that I found, **History of Gil Blas** (London, 1744), was inscribed in 1767, indicating that Adams had started his accumulation of books in his early thirties.

Other Early Presidents

I have not yet been fortunate enough to acquire a Jefferson, but I feel that I should at least mention our great third president, who was an avid book collector. Always having an inquisitive mind and an irresistible thirst for knowledge, he accumulated books on art, literature, religion, architecture, philosophy, chemistry, and almost any other subject one could mention.

Jefferson's interest in his library was so intense that he personally compiled a catalogue that is now in the Massachusetts Historical Society. It bears the notation "1783, March 6, 2540 volumes." On the third page of the manuscript, Jefferson wrote, "This mark denotes the books I have. Those unmarked, I mean to procure." Here we have the true collector, fixing the past with the books he has accumulated and looking toward the future by setting down the objectives he intends to attain.

Jefferson had started to accumulate books at the very young age of seventeen years while studying in Williamsburg. Ten years later, in 1770, most of his library was destroyed by fire. Not discouraged, he started again almost from scratch. After moving to Monticello, he accumulated a library of over seven thousand volumes, which he offered to the national government at a price much below its real value. Despite some irrational opposition founded chiefly on partisanship and jealousy, the government bought the Jefferson library for $23,950, a fraction of its value even at that time. The library was moved to Washington in May 1815, and a printed catalogue of 170 pages was issued.

After this sale, Jefferson collected a second library, which he brought up to about one thousand volumes and donated to the University of Virginia. However, it had to be sold to pay accumulated debts. From this second accumulation come the few Jefferson books that appear for sale from time to time.

Jefferson never used a bookplate, and he rarely wrote his full name into his books. Occasionally he marked them with his initials, or with just one of them. More often, he wrote these initials in all parts of the books, sometimes in connection with the page numerals, sometimes hidden in footnotes or other obscure places.

Madison was an able politician who worked closely with Jefferson on some of his most important projects, such as the Louisiana Purchase. He was a great reader and earnest collector, especially of historical material. My Madison item, **A History of the Dutch Republic**, belongs in this category. I own a second book from Madison's library bearing a dedication to him, but not his own autograph.

James Monroe is not as yet actually on my list. He appears, however, in a eulogy on his life written by John Quincy Adams and delivered at the request of the Corporation of the City of Boston on August 25, 1831, at his funeral. It is inscribed by Adams to his nephew Isaac H. Adams.

Van Buren is represented by "A Message from the President of the United States to the Two Houses of Congress at the Second Session of the Twenty-Fifth Congress, 12mo, Washington, 1837." The pamphlet is bound into a small volume that bears on the first page the inscription "With Mr. Van Burens Kind regards."

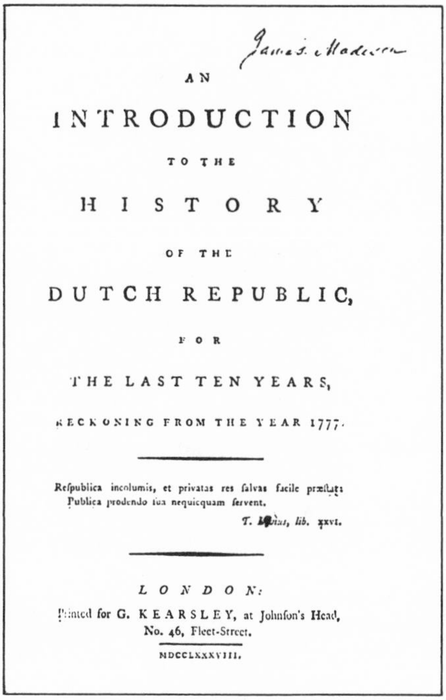

AN

INTRODUCTION

TO THE

H I S T O R Y

OF THE

D U T C H   R E P U B L I C,

F O R

THE LAST TEN YEARS,

RECKONING FROM THE YEAR 1777.

Refpublica incolumis, et privatas res falvas facile prællati
Publica prodendo tua nequicquam fervent.

T. Livius, lib. xxvi.

L O N D O N:

Printed for G. K E A R S L E Y, at Johnfon's Head,
No. 46, Fleet-Street.

NDCCLXXXVIII.

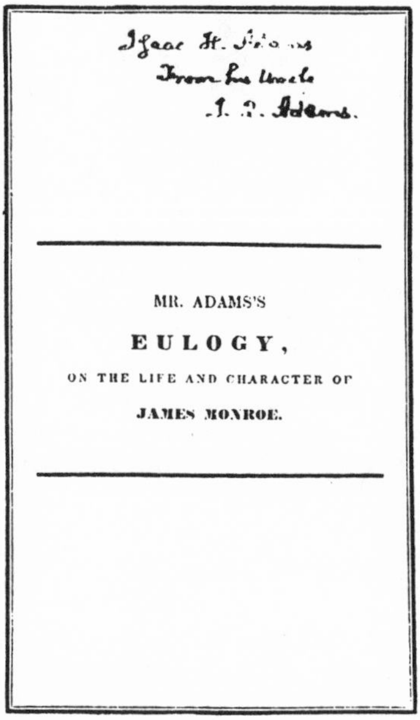

MR. ADAMS'S

EULOGY,

ON THE LIFE AND CHARACTER OF

JAMES MONROE.

Illus. 2. James Madison signed
a history book.

Illus. 3. John Adams signed
a book on Monroe.

The Rare Harrison

With William H. Harrison, I arrive at the most exciting and unusual chapter in my search for books of "missing presidents." It involves a lengthy correspondence with the diligent autograph hunter Forest H. Sweet of Battle Creek, Michigan. Considering the fact that Sweet writes all his letters in longhand with either a Chinese paintbrush or some similar instrument, thereby producing a most unusual manuscript, I have the feeling that he must have almost as much time invested in my collection as my devoted helpmeet, who conscientiously keeps it free of even the least speck of dust.

This is perhaps all the more remarkable since Sweet states that generally he concerns himself very little with books. However, his experience with historic American autograph material is probably second to none. I, therefore, appraise very highly and as most significant his comment "I have had few books of presidents, and only one collector." He informed me some time ago that he had acquired a few years earlier a book inscribed by William H. Harrison that he believed to be the only one of record with his genuine autograph. It was **A Historical Narrative of the Civil and Military Services of Major General William H. Harrison,** published in Cincinnati, 1824, by Moses Dawson, editor of the **Cincinnati Advertiser.** He told me that not only he but also Arthur Mitten, whose comprehensive Harrison collection forms the mainstay of the Indiana Historical Society, and the two librarians of the society had not seen a second book with a genuine signature by Harrison in the course of a search now carried on for nearly thirty years.

While my hunt has not lasted nearly so long and has not been anywhere near so extensive as that of the Indiana Historical Society, I can testify that no other such book has ever appeared. From time to time, some of my friends in the book world have told me of this or that collector who had a Harrison book. I wrote these collectors letters asking whether they might be willing to part with their proud possession. In every instance, the answer has been that they had no such book but most certainly would like to find one. Last year, Dave Kirschenbaum told me, with some satisfaction, that he had finally located a Harrison signature and that it was on the way to him. Conscientious connoisseur that he is, he advised me a few days later that he had received the book, but that he would not show it to me, being satisfied that it was not even a good imitation.

It is therefore understandable that Forest Sweet placed a quite high price on Harrison's rarity, so high, in fact, that even the Indiana Historical Society was not tempted. Needless to say, I was, and I tried to persuade Sweet to moderate his demand. One argument I used was that a New York dealer told me that he had actually seen a volume signed by Harrison in the possession of a Philadelphia collector, but had not been able to acquire the volume from him. This prompted an apparently somewhat irritated Sweet to make to me, just before Christmas of 1953, what is probably one of the most unusual propositions in the staid and stolid domain of autographs. He said that he would send his genuine volume to the treasurer of our society, Richard Maass, to be held in custody until I could show Maass either the alleged Philadelphia Harrison copy or any other book with a genuine Harrison signature, whereupon he would accept in payment one-third of the originally quoted price. My failure to produce such a duplicate would bind me to take over his volume at the original quotation. Since I am by profession a chemist and physicist, and therefore inclined to rely as much as possible on established facts and to bow in all things to the laws of nature, I found Sweet's proposition unrealistic; moreover, I felt that it might be unfair to expose innocent Rich Maass to a hot crossfire.

This ended the correspondence until I met Sweet's father last summer at the convention of our society in New Haven. I told him of my exchange of letters with Forest. The father stated that he quite recalled the book in question, and that if his son pronounced it genuine I should accept his judgment, since he was a most conscientious and, of course, qualified judge.

On my return from New Haven, I again wrote to Forest, telling him of my conversation with his father, asking him if he still had the book and if so, whether his terms had been in any way moderated. He responded with a repetition of last year's conditional offer good for the next two weeks, at the end of which he intended to go on vacation with the entire family for as long as the available bankroll would last. Seizing the opportunity (or perhaps I swallowed a carefully disguised bait), I offered to meet Forest halfway, adding that by accepting my offer he would certainly be in a position to extend his vacation. To finish this long story quickly, I now own the book. It is inscribed by Harrison to William L. Stone.

William Leete Stone, born in New Paltz, New York, was a soldier in the Revolution who later became a printer and editor of a number of newspapers in New York and Connecticut. He was delegated to accompany Lafayette on his tour of America in 1825. Harrison appointed him minister to The Hague, from which post he was recalled by Harrison's successor, John Tyler.

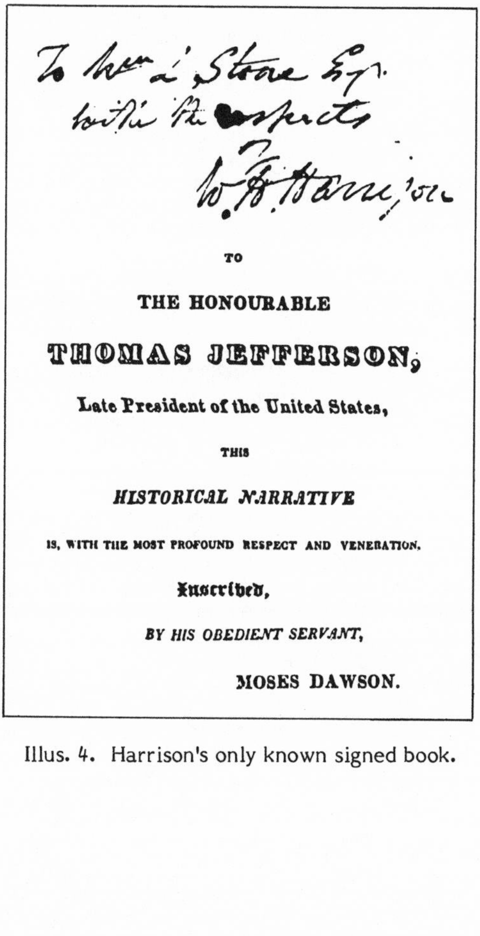
TO

THE HONOURABLE

THOMAS JEFFERSON,

Late President of the United States,

THIS

HISTORICAL NARRATIVE

IS, WITH THE MOST PROFOUND RESPECT AND VENERATION,

Inscribed,

BY HIS OBEDIENT SERVANT,

MOSES DAWSON.

Illus. 4. Harrison's only known signed book.

Tyler Through Buchanan

Tyler owned a rather extensive library, consisting chiefly of the classics. Most of these books were destroyed during the Civil War, causing his son, Lyon G. Tyler, to write in one of the remaining volumes, "This was one of the few books of his library preserved from the ravages of the Northern troops at his residence, Sherwood Forest, Charles City, Virginia."

Comparatively little is known of the literary tastes of Polk and Taylor, whose main interest was politics.

In contrast, Millard Fillmore accumulated a quite extensive library, consisting of more than five thousand volumes. Apparently he went to the trouble of inscribing his name in practically every one of the books he owned, so that volumes with his inscription are comparatively easy to find. I was able to obtain a five-volume set of biographies of the Signers of the Declaration of Independence, printed in 1828. Fillmore inscribed his name in each. I also have another fine little volume, **Tales from Shakespeare**, which bears a double inscription by Fillmore, on the front cover and the title page.

Pierce and Buchanan apparently were not greatly interested in books, although the former left about two hundred volumes, most of which are now owned by his descendants living in New Hampshire. From his library I have a copy of **The London University Magazine**, printed in England, May 1833, and inscribed on the flyleaf, "F. Pierce."

Buchanan was the only bachelor ever to occupy the White House as president. His niece, Harriet Lane Johnston, whose parents had died before she was nine, made her home with her uncle throughout most of her life and acted as mistress of the household. In my volume her signature appears below that of her uncle.

Lincoln

Abraham Lincoln was devoted to books throughout his life. His extensive library included books on subjects ranging from dictionaries and lexicons to the classics. The extent of his reading is reflected in his great command of the English language and in the unequaled way in which he could convey in words his thoughts, sentiments, and intentions.

In my hunt for a Lincoln inscription, I found one in 1946 in the catalogue of the then Anderson Galleries, and I immediately decided to attend the sale and acquire the book. It was no less than an account of the Lincoln-Douglas debates. I regret to this day that I was prevented at the last minute from attending the sale and I lost the book, which went for a very reasonable amount. This regret was all the greater because I succeeded later in obtaining another copy with an inscription by Stephen Douglas. The pair would have made a very interesting combination.

It was not until many years later that I found a good Lincoln sample in the incomparable Barrett Collection. It is a book of twenty lectures by W. B.

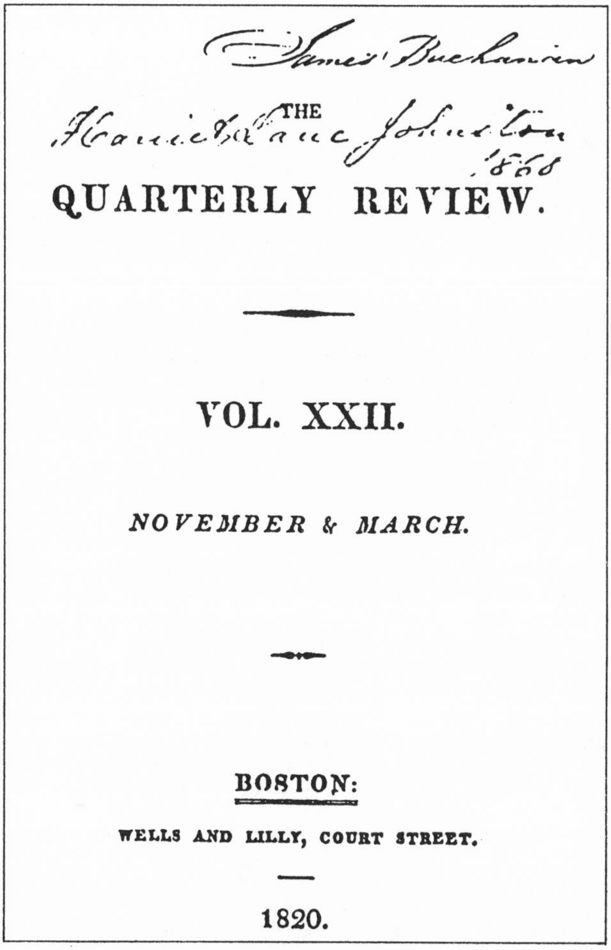

James Buchanan

THE

Harriet Lane Johnston

QUARTERLY REVIEW.

VOL. XXII.

NOVEMBER & MARCH.

BOSTON:

WELLS AND LILLY, COURT STREET.

1820.

Illus. 5. Buchanan and his niece signed this volume.

Thompson with two inscriptions inside the front cover. The first reads, "To Abraham Lincoln with my compliments from Wm. Springer, 1860." The second was written by Lincoln himself: "A. Lincoln, Springfield, Illinois November 30, 1860."

Johnson, Grant, and Hayes

Andrew Johnson had little interest in books. Ulysses Grant appears to have started, in a small way, on his library while a student at West Point. He invested two dollars in an illustrated book that he ordered shipped to the Academy at West Point. Grant is represented in my collection by the **Personal Memoirs of Ulysses S. Grant,** inscribed on the flyleaf: "These volumes are dedicated to the American Soldiers and Sailors--U. S. Grant, New York City, May 23, 1885."

Hayes had a library of more than eight thousand volumes, mostly Americana and western subjects. Practically the entire collection went to the Hayes Memorial Library at Fremont, Ohio. My book bears the title **Life, Public Services and Select Speeches of Rutherford B. Hayes.** It was printed in Cincinnati in 1876, and is inscribed on the flyleaf: "For Mr. H. C. Morton with the best wishes of Rutherford B. Hayes." Above the signature appears a stamp: Executive Mansion, March 4, 1881, which was Hayes's last day in office.

Garfield Through "T.R."

Garfield, who was a college president at the very young age of twenty-six, owned a quite impressive library covering a broad field. This collection also is practically intact at his former home in Mentor, Ohio. My copy of one of his speeches is inscribed with his initials, J. A. G.

Chester A. Arthur had an outstanding academic record at college. He was highly cultured and had a fine literary taste, which was reflected in his rather large library. I have two books inscribed by him. One is on a literary subject: **Library Notes,** signed on the flyleaf, "Chester A. Arthur, March 5, 1883." The other, which deals with the subject of war, is by Jonathan Dymond: **An Inquiry into the Accordancy of War** (New York, 1880). It bears on the flyleaf the following unusual and interesting inscription: "To Chester A. Arthur, Vice-President of the U.S.--with the best wishes, and kindly regards of the Central Tract Committee of New York Yearly Meeting of Friends. On behalf of the community--Robt. J. Murray, Sec'y." Inside the front cover there is the signature "Chester A. Arthur, July 11, 1882."

Cleveland apparently did not take a great interest in books, but nevertheless accumulated a quite respectable library that is still intact in his house at Princeton. Volumes with his signature do not appear frequently, but I was able to obtain collections of his public papers of both administrations with dedications and autographs.

Benjamin Harrison was a lawyer, and his library--still almost intact at Indianapolis--reflects his leaning toward the law and related subjects. My book is **Kate Sanborn, a Truthful Woman in South California** (New York, 1893). It is inscribed on the flyleaf: "Miss Jessie Mellis from her friend, Benjamin Harrison, December 25, 1893."

Relatively little is known of the literary pursuits and inclinations of McKinley. He left only a small library in his residence at Canton, Ohio, which was divided by his widow at random among heirs and relatives. My volume contains **The Speeches and Addresses of William McKinley** (New York, 1893) and is inscribed: "From William McKinley, Dec. 12, 1894."

Theodore Roosevelt was, throughout his life, a great scholar, an avid reader, and a collector of almost everything that came his way. His famous trophy room at Sagamore Hill had books stacked from the floor to the ceiling.

His special pride was in his books on big game, and he was convinced that this collection was second to none either in this country or in England. He expressed the opinion that book collecting did not measure up to game hunting or other manly sports. In this, he suddenly is at variance with Rosenbach, who wrote in the aforementioned essay, "Hunting after rare books has more thrills to the minute, in my estimation, than trapping wild animals in the jungle. The latter is child's play compared with it." I have done a bit of hunting myself, although never for lion, tigers, or elephants, but I certainly must side with Rosenbach.

My Teddy Roosevelt book, **Addresses and Presidential Messages,** is inscribed "with best wishes from Theodore Roosevelt," and pasted underneath is a visiting card of "Mrs. Theodore Roosevelt." Another book, **American Ideals,** was given to his "mother's friend," Charles Eliot Norton II, with his autograph.

Taft Through Coolidge

President Taft considered books chiefly as a source of information and reference in the exercise of his profession as lawyer and later as chief justice. Aside from his law library, which is still located in his former residence in Washington, he apparently owned comparatively few books. I have two volumes inscribed on June 30, 1924, by Taft for J. B. McGhee: **Presidential Addresses and State Papers** and **United States and Peace.**

Woodrow Wilson, in his capacity as a university professor, appreciated, and of course frequently used, libraries. He accumulated a modest collection that is still preserved in Washington. His book **Mere Literature** is in my collection. It is signed "Woodrow Wilson 1923." It very likely is one of the last such signatures before Wilson's progressing illness rendered him physically incapable of writing.

Warren Harding was interested in things other than books. Whatever small library he owned went with his other possessions to the Harding Memorial at Marion, Ohio. Books with his signature seem to be extremely rare. I was able to obtain only very recently a finely bound volume: **Life and Recent Speeches by Warren G. Harding,** by Frederick E. Shortemeier (Indianapolis, 1920). It contains an eleven-line inscription by Harding as president-elect:

> To Edward K. Uhler, Not in appraisal of utterances herein, but as an appropriate reminder of the campaign in "Our Town" when neighbors and friends worth while played the game and helped to win it. Gratefully Yours, Warren G. Harding, December 25, 1920.

Calvin Coolidge, with his almost proverbial punctiliousness, resorted to books on all occasions and liked them. Rosenbach relates that when he made his famous purchase of the original manuscript of **Alice in Wonderland** in 1928, the president invited him to lunch at the White House. Coolidge took with him to his home in Northampton well over four thousand volumes packed in forty large cases. He was a familiar figure sitting on the front porch of his modest house in a comfortable chair with a book in his hand. After he had completed his autobiography, I induced a young niece who was a student at Smith College to approach him there with the request for his autograph, which he graciously granted.

Hoover as a Collector

Herbert Hoover must be ranked as a book collector either close to or possibly ahead of Jefferson. Wherever he was on his world travels, he acquired books on many subjects and kept them. Stanford University became the recipient of one of the most comprehensive collections of books on China and the Chinese people.

Originally a metallurgist, Hoover became fascinated with the first book printed on metallurgy, the wonderfully written, printed, and illustrated **De Re Metallica,** by Agricola, published in Basel, 1556. The book was originally written in Latin, and Hoover and his wife, Lou Henry, undertook the laborious task of translating the work into English, which took them a number of years to accomplish. After returning from the Orient, where as a mining engineer in Burma and other places Hoover had been able to accumulate a comfortable fortune, he settled for a time in London. There he published his translated edition of Agricola with magnificent and true reproductions of the original woodcuts bound in white parchment. In my opinion, it is one of the most beautiful books ever published. I am proud to have a splendidly preserved copy that Hoover was kind enough to inscribe for me when he was president.

I have several other volumes with his signature, but none do I prize so highly as his **Memoirs,** which came to me under circumstances directly related to the writing of this article. As I stated earlier, I thought it would be of interest to know how our two surviving ex-presidents view books. So I wrote identical letters to Hoover in New York and Harry Truman in Independence, Missouri. I did not have much hope of hearing from Hoover, who had just a few days previously been appointed by President Eisenhower to head a committee for reorganization of certain government functions. Yet within forty-eight hours, I received from the Waldorf Towers a reply in which Hoover most graciously informed me that limitations to his time would not permit him to answer my request as fully as he would have liked. He pointed out, however, that his recently published memoirs contained a number of passages that described his attitude toward books. He stated that he had marked such passages in a copy of the book that he was sending me separately. The volume contained a most cordial presentation and his signature. Not only were all the passages referring to books marked on the margin with pencil, but Hoover had inserted a blue slip wherever these passages occurred.

With respect to my response from Truman, I heard first from his secretary, Miss Conway, to the effect that, "owing to a number of commitments and the time Mr. Truman must devote to his book," it would not be possible for him to comply with my request. Nevertheless, I undertook to write to Truman again about two months later and received a brief note to the same effect, but this time signed in his own hand. Of course I appreciated his preoccupation with more important matters, but I cannot help expressing the hope that when Truman has finished his memoirs, he will be kind enough to sign a copy for me.

FDR to Eisenhower

In this brief digression, the chronological order of the presidents has been slightly upset. Herbert Hoover was, of course, followed by Franklin D. Roosevelt, who was, like Teddy, a collector of almost everything that came his way. Mementos of every description cluttered his desk. He was particularly interested in maritime history, and he enthusiastically studied the early history of the American Navy. Documents, pictures, and models of ships--in fact, everything connected with ships--not only covered the walls of his study but every other available space as well.

Franklin Roosevelt began collecting manuscripts and books as a student at Harvard College and, in the course of his full and active life, he accumulated a respectable library. It is now installed as the Franklin D. Roosevelt Library at Hyde Park, New York, and has become a national shrine.

Roosevelt often employed some idle moments--of which there were not too many--by inscribing his name in some of his favorite books, but these were never dispersed. Although the number of letters and documents bearing Franklin Roosevelt's signature is at least as great as, if not considerably greater than, those of other presidents, books with his autograph are comparatively rare. He discouraged his secretaries and assistants from bringing to him books to be inscribed, except for a few very close friends and for specific reasons.

In direct contrast with Roosevelt, Harry S. Truman was not interested in collecting books or any other memorabilia. Whether because of his preoccupation with music and politics or some other reason, Truman's only real literary interest was in history.

With this, my pilgrimage beginning in the eighteenth century brings me to the current occupant of the White House, Dwight D. Eisenhower. His career has been so full that he could not have been expected to devote much time to books. First as a student at West Point, and later during his many shifts from place to place, he could hardly have accumulated a large library, especially not in Europe during the war.

Upon his return to this country, he was able to settle down for a relatively short time on Morningside Heights in surroundings more suitable for reflection, study, and the pursuit of a literary career. To this we owe his **Crusade in Europe.** After it appeared and even before his candidacy for the presidency had been seriously mentioned, I tried to get his autograph for my copy. I thought this would be easy since the bursar of Columbia University was a fellow trustee of Knickerbocker Hospital and a friend of mine. He gladly undertook the task of submitting the book to the president of the university with my request for his autograph. It came back to me in due time with a note from Kevin McCann, assistant to the president, explaining that "the physical difficulties involved in handling the books" had made it impossible for the "General" to sign the book itself. He enclosed, however, a notehead with the autograph for insertion in the book.

For the time being I had to be satisfied with this, but after the general and college head had become president of the United States, I renewed my efforts to obtain an actual inscription from him. A close personal colleague happens to be a classmate and intimate friend of one of the president's military aides and attending physicians, Col. Robert L. Schulz. His kind intervention secured for me a gracious presentation signature from the president.

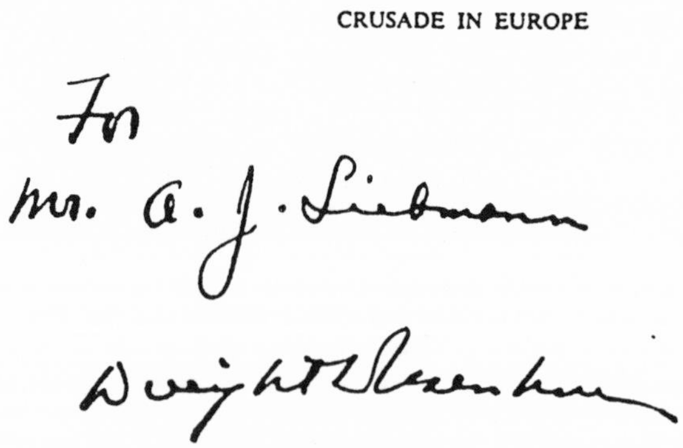

CRUSADE IN EUROPE

Illus. 6. President Eisenhower signed his own book for the author.

A U.S. Cabinet Collection*

Thomas J. Acheson

> He who is upright, kind and free from error
> Needs not the aid of arms or men to guide him
> Safely he moves, a child to guilty terror
> Strong in his virtue.

So wrote Robert John Wynne (1851-1922), U.S. cabinet member and presidential adviser, as he gave this statement of his guiding principle to an admirer. Reading the letter, one can only wonder which American president might be free from error and need not "men to guide him," including his postmaster general, Robert John Wynne.

At the time the Wynne autograph came to my collection, I was deeply involved in completing a set of presidential autographs, and anything unusual to add to the dossiers was, to put it briefly, as attractive as liver to a cat! So the Wynne letter was appropriately added to the file of President Theodore Roosevelt, with the thought that cabinet members have doubtless contributed more to presidential accomplishment than is generally acknowledged.

Right then was born a plan to see if it would be possible to complete a full set of cabinet members to add to the corresponding set of presidents. The thought that I had never heard of anyone accomplishing this, and that there were but thirty-two of the one and four hundred of the other did not, at the time, either occur or deter. But during the twenty years between 1934 and 1954, which I may call "the cabinet years," there were many occasions when the mere mathematical magnitude of the project became painfully apparent. More than once there was reason to think this particular group was more exclusive than Ward McAllister's famous social register, and I came to think some of these people must have "communicated only with God"! But in retrospect, compensations are seen; in such a quest one makes new friends, and many of the autographs come tagged with adventures of one sort or another, some humorous and some sad. I learned much about the way in which the American cabinet has functioned and about the many truly great personalities that from time to time have appeared in it.

---

*Originally published in 1954.

Growth of the Cabinet

One must remember that the cabinet, as a collective body, has no legal existence or power whatever. The Constitution itself does not contain a provision for a cabinet, and in 1789 when Congress, in its primary session, created the first three departments immediately necessary (i.e., State, War, and Treasury), it apparently did not recognize the possibility of a cabinet council composed of the heads of these departments. But George Washington began to require opinions from his several chief executive officials, and before long a cabinet, based on usage alone, became a part of the executive branch. By 1793 the term **cabinet** began to be generally accepted for this group of departmental presidential advisers. But then, as now, nothing was ever done with the cabinet's consent that could not be done without its consent, if the president should so decide.

Later in that first year of 1789 the offices of attorney general and postmaster general were added to the first three cabinet posts, but these last were not to be the heads of official departments for almost a century--in 1870 and 1874, respectively. The attorney general was considered a member of the cabinet from the beginning, however, and the postmaster general was invited into the "membership" by President Jackson in 1829. Other departments were added from time to time: in 1798, the Navy; in 1849, Interior; in 1889, Agriculture; in 1903, Commerce and Labor (divided in 1913 to the two separate departments); in 1947, Defense; and Health, Education, and Welfare in 1953.

The present practice is for the cabinet to meet at stated times, usually weekly, according to arrangements made by the president. These meetings are not public, and no record of transactions is kept; the discussions are confined to whatever the president sees fit to submit. The cabinet members usually are the president's personal selection, but each must be confirmed by the Senate. The president may dismiss any member at his pleasure, but in practice dismissals are rare and resignations frequent. The members are responsible to the president alone; they cannot be a member of either House of Congress, and they may not be heard from the floor.

Some Collecting Anecdotes

When I seriously turned to the collection of a cabinet set, one of my first experiences was a case of mistaken identity, with the autograph of Benjamin Franklin Butler, attorney general under Jackson and Van Buren. Having obtained a fine ALS of this name, I considered the matter closed. But through accident I obtained another Benjamin Franklin Butler, this one an LS, but with a signature entirely different from the first. There was no internal evidence in either letter to indicate identity, other than that both were evidently written by lawyers. Before long I bought a third specimen, on military affairs, and this signature matched the first of the three. Still in doubt, I bought a fourth specimen warranted "by the U.S. Attorney-General," and this matched the second specimen.

By the time I neared the end of my quest for cabinet autographs, I had discovered a fact that must be apparent to every experienced collector. It is often more difficult to obtain an autograph of good content from some contemporary than of his distinguished great-grandfather of a century back. And so, I hit upon the idea of writing directly to the official whose autograph I needed, choosing some subject that might be of interest to him. I kept my fingers crossed with the hope that some reply might be forthcoming that would express something of the signer himself, and thus please posterity as well as you and me. Writing thus to Secretary of Agriculture Benson, I politely enclosed a handsome, oblong California postage stamp of the color of ripening grain. Secretary Benson, peering through the tall grasses of my innocent obfuscation, evidently sensed my wishes for a plain garden autograph, but evidently misunderstanding the purpose for which I enclosed the postage, carefully and painstakingly inscribed his full signature in miniature on that tiny golden stamp itself, and mailed it back to a delighted recipient!

And then there was the case of Secretary Oveta Hobby, of Health, Education, and Welfare. Here I had the temerity to relate a dream--a dream that had actually occurred. The beautiful cabinet member (a fact that was purely coincidental to appointment) in the dream delivered a speech to the combined houses of Congress, in which she averred (this word is important here) that she considered Texas "a better state than California." When I related this matter by letter to the distinguished cabinet member, I myself averred, "Imagine such a thing occurring--even in a dream!" This letter brought a most valued, and nonsynthetic, autograph. (The term "synthetic autograph" was, I think, coined by the late Gen. H. H. Arnold, to indicate an autograph signed with permission by clerk or secretary.)

I vividly recall an embarrassing experience with then Secretary of the Treasury Fred M. Vinson. Obtaining from a New York dealer an inexpensive Vinson LS, I decided the very immature-looking signature was the product of either some schoolchild or some youthful secretary in the Treasury Department. So, sending the letter to Secretary Vinson personally, I bitterly complained of the decadent practice of having secretaries sign such purported signatures in the first place. I added, "I might mention that the signatures of American officials have been showing a steady deterioration for the past fifty years, and some effort might well be made to correct this at the same time." Vinson replied that I was quite mistaken in assuming the signature was not his standard effort, just as he always inscribed it, even if it was not satisfactory to me. But in any event he was carefully executing a current specimen, which I could accept or reject at my pleasure. The new one was almost an exact duplicate of the disputed item.

The Rarities

In seeking autographs of such a group of people prominent in public life, most of them with many friends and all with numerous official contacts, it would seem at first glance that all should be readily obtainable in autograph. Yet a surprising number turn out to be rarities. Surely any valued dealer could deliver the autograph of any president more easily than that of certain cabinet members. James Wilson Marshall, Grant's postmaster general for a short time in 1874, might be mentioned. This Marshall is not to be confused with the James Wilson Marshall who discovered gold in California, who was a contemporary.

Another difficult name is Albert B. Fall, the ill-starred secretary of the interior. For some reason Fall's autographs are almost as scarce as feathers on frogs; I do not recall a single Fall example appearing in dealers' published lists these past ten years. If experience may be one's guide, the best way to obtain a specimen of either Marshall or Fall is to pray to Santa Claus, for each of these items mysteriously appeared out of thin air during 1954 to complete entirely separate collections on opposite sides of the continent.

A third rarity, and quite possibly the most elusive of all, is that of Hugh S. Legare, attorney general between 1841 and 1843, and secretary of state, ad interim, in the latter year. Here the reason is more apparent. At age five, Legare was poisoned by an impure vaccination, which left his limbs permanently impaired.

Cabinet members of great prominence and interest include, among many others, Daniel Webster, W. H. Seward, W. J. Bryan, Alexander Hamilton, Henry Clay, and Charles J. Bonaparte, who was the grandson of a European king! Hardly to be overlooked are U. S. Grant, W. H. Taft, Herbert C. Hoover, Thomas Jefferson, James Madison, James Monroe, J. Q. Adams, Martin Van Buren, and James Buchanan--all once cabinet members who became presidents. Yes, a cabinet collection is very much worthwhile; it has color, interest, and history.

Mist'uh Speak'uh!*

Victor Jacobs

Who was John W. Taylor, or John W. Jones, or James L. Orr?

You would expect this question to be addressed to a perspiring contestant in an isolation booth on one of the late, unlamented quiz shows. But it seems hardly amiss to ask the question of the readers of **Manuscripts,** who, **ex hypothesi,** are familiar with history. So you do not know? They were all Speakers of the United States House of Representatives.

Why should anyone collect all the Speakers? The answers could be numerous: This is an unplowed field. It gives the collector an intimate sense of participation in practical American politics. It adds considerably to one's sense of humility to realize that these men--so sought after in their day--have slipped into oblivion. Besides, a collection of the Speakers is so inexpensive that it will drain only the slimmest purse.

But my reason for collecting the Speakers was none of the above. It was conceived in iniquity and later legitimized. My friend, Colonel X, has an item for which I would almost give my eyeteeth--an item twice signed by George Rogers Clark and once by Jefferson. I am interested in Clark, and all his autograph material is exceedingly scarce.

My friend, who was once a representative in Congress, had collected all the Speakers but one, John W. Davis. This Davis is from Indiana and is not to be confused with either the statesman of similar name from Massachusetts or with the Democratic nominee for president in 1924. He is hard to find.

Going over one of the New York auction house catalogues in November 1958, I saw the elusive Davis buried in a group of Speakers. My first thought was to authorize an agent to make the purchase for me and trade with the colonel, but wisdom told me that if the item could not be purchased cheaply it would be better not to buy at all. The item, consisting of approximately eighteen Speakers, might be a sleeper that I could bid for in pennies; otherwise, I did not want it. Fate smiled, and I picked up the lot at an average cost (including packing and postage) of $1.94 each.

---

*Originally published in 1960.

My sole purpose was to use Davis as a lever to pry loose the George Rogers Clark. But somehow I never drummed up my courage to make a pass in that direction. Admittedly, I boasted of my purchase and it was plainly obvious what I wanted, but the disparity of value was so great that I did not know how to proceed, and still do not.

I checked the handiest encyclopedia and found that there were only forty-three Speakers [as of 1960]. Remember this figure, because it is incorrect. Writing several of my dealer friends, I was amazed how quickly most of my wants were filled. I live in Dayton, Ohio, and I always wanted a Jonathan Dayton. I stretched a point and picked up a fine ALS for twenty-five dollars, which was perhaps higher than I had to go, in that I purchased other Jonathan Dayton items later for less.

In general, I was startled at the alacrity with which the dealers sprang to help. Even one dealer, who shall be nameless, who holds the record for the swiftness and completeness with which he loses one's list of wants, answered promptly. And the quoted prices were so reasonable that I had a sneaking suspicion that the dealers were delighted to unload on this lunatic items they had acquired with a bundle some years before. For example, an ALS of Theodore Sedgwick cost $3.00; a franked signature of Nathaniel Macon, $1.50; an autographed document signed by Langdon Cheves, $3.50; a clipped signature of John Bell, 75 cents; and an autographed document signed by William Pennington, $2.50. The two Speakers during Lincoln's administration, Galusha A. Grow and Schuyler Colfax, the former in an ALS and the latter on a large card signed as Speaker, cost $1.75 and $1.00, respectively. David B. Henderson, for a three-line signature, signed as Speaker, cost 75 cents. Robert C. Winthrop, Speaker of the House during Lincoln's term in Congress and for whom Lincoln voted, cost $1.75. And so the story goes. I purchased a rather poor signature of Linn Boyd (along with others even more unnoteworthy) for $1.00 and traded it, together with $2.50, to another dealer, making a total cost for Boyd of $3.50.

One of the relatively few persons who went forth from the Speakership to greater honors was James K. Polk. Unfortunately, I was unable to buy Polk at Speakers' prices because he later became president. But after fumbling around trying to buy an inexpensive Polk, I saw in an auction catalogue two documents signed by Polk as president, commending some forgotten soldier for his bravery in the Mexican War. So I bid $17.50 for either and fetched one for $15.00. Then I removed the clipped signature of Polk that I had in my collection of presidents, substituted the document signed as president, and inserted the clipped signature in my collection of Speakers.

Duplicates tend to be a problem in collecting Speakers. What do you do with the duplicates you acquire, particularly when, in buying a small group, you pick up an additional autograph of someone you already have? This problem I have solved by making "generous" gifts to my friends. These are always appreciated, and I know of no other way in which you can win so much gratitude, spending less than you would in buying a friend a lunch.

The obverse of the coin is whether one should duplicate autographs one has in another capacity. For example, Henry Clay was secretary of state, a presidential candidate, and a Speaker. Should one duplicate? If you want complete sets, the sets should be complete in themselves. For example, I bought a clipped signature of Henry Clay for $1.50 and then replaced it with a $15.00 ALS from another dealer and put the cheaper item with my collection of secretaries of state.

One stumbles on interesting facts along the way. A standard reference work spelled Milton Sayler's last name "Saylor." When I bought a Sayler autograph for $2.50 I was just about to return it on the fundamental principle that a man should certainly be able to spell his own name correctly. Then I checked the **Dictionary of American Biography** and found that the other reference work had goofed and that the dealer was correct. In place of a protest I mailed a check.

The list of Speakers, as already indicated, is open to question. Each of the Speakers who served nonconsecutive terms, such as F. A. Muhlenburg, Henry Clay, John W. Taylor, Thomas B. Reed, Joseph W. Martin, and Sam Rayburn, has always been counted only once. But the question of how many Speakers there have been depends on an interesting circumstance in American politics. The Speaker of the outgoing House of Representatives presides over the ceremonies for the swearing in of the incoming vice president of the United States.   Schuyler Colfax, the Speaker of the outgoing House of Representatives, was the incoming vice president under Grant as president. He resigned as Speaker on March 3, 1869, and Theodore M. Pomeroy was elected Speaker of the House of Representatives for one day. Some reference works include Pomeroy and some do not.

But the problem of who the Speakers officially are still exists. The **Congressional Directory** lists three Speakers pro-tem: George Dent in 1798, Samuel S. Cox ("Sunset" Cox) in 1876, and our friend, Milton Sayler, in 1876. Why these three Speakers pro-tem should be listed as Speakers is a mystery, but to conform with the list in the **Congressional Directory** it is necessary to collect three additional autographs.

After I had worked on my collection of Speakers since November 1958, I still lacked five autographs. I came to the conclusion that these autographs were hard to get, not because they were rare or costly, but because the individuals in question were so recondite and unknown that no one had bothered to save their autographs. I still needed Joseph B. Varnum, John W. Taylor, John White, John W. Jones, and the elected Speaker who served the shortest term in history, Theodore M. Pomeroy. Very recently, through the happenstance about which we collectors dream but which so rarely happens, I received a letter from a dealer friend who told me that he had come across an incomplete set of Speakers and that he had all five of my needs. Bingo! His price was ten dollars apiece for the five and I quickly snapped up the opportunity of completing my set.

A complete list of Speakers of the House of Representatives and their terms of office is appended:

1789-91	F. A. Muhlenburg	Pennsylvania
1791-93	Jonathan Trumbull	Connecticut
1793-95	F. A. Muhlenburg	Pennsylvania
1795-99	Jonathan Dayton	New Jersey
1798	George Dent	Maryland (pro-tem)
1799-1801	Theodore Sedgwick	Massachusetts
1801-07	Nathaniel Macon	North Carolina
1807-11	Joseph B. Varnum	Massachusetts
1811-14	Henry Clay	Kentucky
1814-15	Langdon Cheves	South Carolina
1815-20	Henry Clay	Kentucky
1820-21	John W. Taylor	New York
1821-23	Philip P. Barbour	Virginia
1823-25	Henry Clay	Kentucky
1825-27	John W. Taylor	New York
1827-34	Andrew Stevenson	Virginia
1834-35	John Bell	Tennessee
1835-39	James K. Polk	Tennessee
1839-41	R. M. T. Hunter	Virginia
1841-43	John White	Kentucky
1843-45	John W. Jones	Virginia
1845-47	John W. Davis	Indiana
1847-49	Robert C. Winthrop	Massachusetts
1849-51	Howell Cobb	Georgia
1851-55	Linn Boyd	Kentucky
1855-57	Nathaniel P. Banks	Massachusetts
1857-59	James L. Orr	South Carolina
1859-61	William Pennington	New Jersey
1861-63	Galusha A. Grow	Pennsylvania
1863-69	Schuyler Colfax	Indiana
1869	Theodore M. Pomeroy	New York
1869-75	James G. Blaine	Maine
1875-76	Michael C. Kerr	Indiana
1876	Samuel S. Cox	New York (pro-tem)
1876	Milton Sayler	Ohio (pro-tem)
1876-81	Samuel J. Randall	Pennsylvania
1881-83	John W. Keifer	Ohio
1883-89	John G. Carlisle	Kentucky
1889-91	Thomas B. Reed	Maine
1891-95	Charles F. Crisp	Georgia
1895-99	Thomas B. Reed	Maine
1899-1903	David B. Henderson	Iowa
1903-11	Joseph G. Cannon	Illinois
1911-19	Champ Clark	Missouri
1919-25	Frederick H. Gillett	Massachusetts
1925-31	Nicholas Longworth	Ohio
1931-33	John Nance Garner	Texas
1933-34	Henry T. Rainey	Illinois
1935-36	James W. Byrnes	Tennessee
1936-40	William B. Bankhead	Alabama
1940-46	Sam Rayburn	Texas
1947-48	Joseph W. Martin	Massachusetts

1949-52	Sam Rayburn	Texas
1953-54	Joseph W. Martin	Massachusetts
1955-61	Sam Rayburn	Texas
1962-71	John W. McCormack	Massachusetts
1971-77	Carl Albert	Oklahoma
1977-	Thomas P. O'Neill, Jr.	Massachusetts

B. EUROPEAN POLITICAL HISTORY
A Survey of Medieval
Royal Autographs*

Herbert E. Klingelhofer

If we were to draw a graph of the actual autographic writing done by eminent people throughout the years, decade by decade, we would obtain an ascending line reaching its peak during the early years of the present century. Its decline from this point is due to the increased use of typewriter, dictaphone, and telephone. The ALS has been vastly outdistanced by the LS-- and often we cannot be sure that the "S" is genuine.

If we were to plot a second graph, of that part of the writing that has been preserved to this day in desks, files, attics, and archives, the ascending as well as the descending curves would be somewhat steeper. Writing material is perishable--some more than others. Frequent handling, but also the sheer weight of age, is sure to take its toll. Few autographs are graven in brass or gold. The stationery of recent vintage is generally more acidic than that of an earlier era and hence more vulnerable to the ravages of time, but even the pure rag paper of yesteryear shows sign of age. Only small amounts of papyrus have survived, and even the tough and sturdy parchment can wear out.

It is no wonder, therefore, that most of the words that have been written have crumbled to dust and vanished. Human carelessness and disinterest account for more destruction. Luckily for autograph collectors, a considerable amount of material written by famous people in the past two centuries is available. How do we stand, though, when we go back through successive ages? We find that few sixteenth-century autographs are available, and that each preceding century offers less material. Giordano Bruno, Paracelsus, Palestrina, and da Vinci, for example, are extremely difficult to procure. In addition, there are people whose autographs do not come up for sale but specimens of whose handwriting can be viewed in museums and archives--for instance, William Shakespeare.

Let us give Father Time a rapid twirl and see how far back we can go and still come up with a genuine autograph of a known personality. What about Homer, Alexander the Great, Dido, Plato, St.Luke, Caesar? Nothing remains. Well, then, what about Pliny, Ovid, Horace, Tacitus, Marcus Aurelius? Nothing. It was assumed at one time that certain early manuscripts on papyrus were genuine, but it has been proven that they are copies made centuries later.

---

*Originally published in 1967.

What is the oldest genuine writing of a person of note? It now appears likely that a specimen of writing by Bishop Victor of Capua (541-554) is the most ancient. He corrected and amended a dictated version of his **Codex Bonifatianus.** It has been claimed that one copy of the Venerable Bede's **History of the English Church** could be in his own hand (673-735). It is at least very probable that some pages said to be written by St. Boniface actually were penned by him. There is supposed to be a Bible in Paris written by Hrabanus Maurus (died in 856). There exist some writings in the hand of Notker Balbulus (died in 912) and a French history written by Richer, a monk of St. Remi (died in 992).

In the second millennium there are specimens of writing by Ademar de Chabannes, Petrus Damianus, Eckehard of St. Gall, Guillaume de Jamieges, William of Malmesbury, and, later, Albertus Magnus, Thomas Aquinas, Bonaventura, Petrarch, Boccaccio, and Thomas a Kempis. Leaving the realm of writers and scholars, one of the great treasures of Spain is a specimen of the handwriting of the Spanish national hero, El Cid, written in 1096.

If only an infinitesimal portion of medieval scholars' original manuscripts or even of their signatures survives, the number of early royal autographs is somewhat larger. The main reason for this discrepancy is that, while to men of the past a clean and accurate copy of a manuscript was just as valuable as the original--or more so, if it was more easily legible--an original legal document or royal decree or letter was decidedly more important to possess and preserve than a copy. This is also the reason why the original poems and aphorisms of certain royal personages--such as Charles of Orleans, the Navarrase and Aragonese troubadours, and some of the philosophers on the throne--were lost, while some of their legal documents are still extant.

How is it that some kings signed their documents and others did not? This is mainly a matter of what was considered proper validation or authorization at the time. In antiquity a letter or document assumed full validity if it was signed and sealed. This habit of signing and sealing continued up to the eighth century A.D. In the ninth century signing lost its significance, but an increasing number of documents and letters were signed again from the year 900 up to the twelfth century, when once again signatures were not considered necessary.

The seal attained more and more significance, however. If during the twelfth of thirteenth centuries a prince or a bishop actually signed a letter or added an autograph subscription, the reason appears to be not so much the necessity of proving the letter's authenticity as the desire to show an unusual affection or attachment to the recipient. At other times the writer added in his own hand a few sentences that were too important to be dictated to a clerk--no third person was supposed to hear of the secret. If a seal was used to close the letter, the contents were to be kept from others' knowledge. If the seal was attached to the inside of the letter, it served merely as a token of authenticity. It was not until the end of the fifteenth century that actual signatures resumed their significance.

There were, of course, numerous ways of signing, but they can be grouped into four classes: signature, signum, sign manual, and monogram.

1. A **signature** is any combination of one's names, from a single initial to full first, middle, and last names, with or without rank and titles.   This includes self-chosen names, such as papal names.

Illus. 1. Example of a signature.

2. A **signum** is a simple design, having no connection with name or initials, most frequently in the shape of a simple or ornamental cross, drawn wholly or partly by the signer.

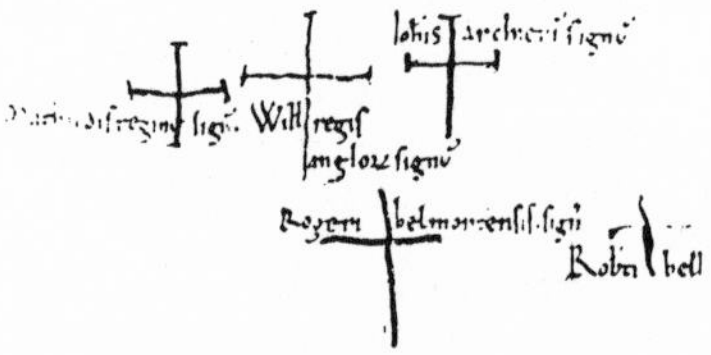

Illus. 2. Example of a signum.

3. A **sign manual** is an autograph design, usually consisting of initials of the signer's name and often of his title, combined by a number of loops and curved lines.

Illus. 3. Example of a sign manual.

4. A **monogram** is a fanciful design (often geometrical) drawn partly or wholly by the signer, which usually contains various letters of the signer's name--at times with the initial of his title.

Illus. 4. Example of a monogram.

Royal Literacy

Most of the Frankish kings of the Merovingian dynasty could read and write, and they signed their documents; but this practice was the exception rather than the rule during the early Middle Ages. In general, the practice of writing was thought to be ignoble. The king did not have to read for his entertainment; he had his harper and his poet to sing and play and recite. And he had his priest and his learned clerk to read to him and to write for him.

In England, the king who could read and write at all was an exception between 600 and 1100. The early kings were far from uncivilized, but the very idea of book learning was foreign to them. King Alfred began to study English and Latin at age thirty-eight, and it is likely that he was able to write as well. William I and William Rufus, in contrast, were completely illiterate. As rulers became familiar with reflecting on abstract thought, they also became aware of the importance of books in the communication of ideas. Between 1100 and 1300 the English kings learned to read Latin but they usually did not actually write it, even if they were able. During the next few generations they were taught early to read and write Latin, and they spoke French and English, of course.

In some instances, royal literacy on the Continent was more advanced. Emperor Frederick II, for instance, spoke nine languages and corresponded or wrote in seven. Autographic participation of monarchs in their own documents varied from country to country and from period to period. The popes' methods of giving validity to their bulls, charts, privileges, treaties, and letters also changed through the centuries.

The Popes

In Roman times, the popes had little occasion to compose documents. Their letters gradually became more formal in their construction, consisting of intitulation, inscription, and message. They bore the papal signature at the bottom of the page in the form of a greeting and wish and the date. The chancellor did not sign. Under Gregory I the letters named the writer and announced the papal signature; this, however, is exceptional.

At the end of the eighth century a change occurred: beginning with Hadrian I the officials were named and dates were given. The **Bene Valete** continued. Pope Leo IX, around 1050, changed the **Bene Valete** into a monogram, which, however, he did not write himself. He "signed" personally in shape of a rota. The rota consisted of two concentric circles surrounding the cross with letters in the four quadrants and within the ring formed by the two circles. The rota, incidentally, may be conceived as Christ's monogram. It is assumed that Charlemagne's creation of the cross monogram served as a model for the rota as well as for the monogram of the seal of the princes of Beneventum, a variety of other seals, and, most important, coins.

Illus. 5. Rota of Pope Leo IX.

After Leo IX, a few smaller changes occurred in papal letters and documents. The name of Alexander II was written in by an official. Pascal II started signing properly. His documents also bear the signatures of cardinals, as well as the rota, a monogram, and the large date. Beginning with Innocent II this custom became fixed. Under Innocent IV a new form was created. We see the papal bulls for the first time, in their inception only as decretalia and general decrees and excommunications. The first line of these documents ended with **ad perpetuam rei memoriam** or a similar formula. Martin V started to seal his secret letters, called brevia, with the fisherman's seal on wax.

During the later Middle Ages, the popes did not sign any documents except some less important **privilegia communia.** Innocent VIII introduced the custom of personally signing the **motus proprii,** unsealed documents, and from then on papal signatures became more common.   Strangely enough, they consisted of the Latin initial of the pope's original (not papal) first name.

$$fiat \cdot A \cdot$$

Illus. 6. Fiat A, signed by Paul III (the **A** standing for Alessandro Farnese).

The Holy Roman Emperors

The step from the Holy Roman Church to the Holy Roman Empire does not seem very wide, and there are quite a few similarities between them, at least theoretically, as seems natural between the temporal and spiritual aspects of the same organism.   There are also similarities between the two courts, the systems of the chancelleries, the scribes and notaries, and the documents.   Because both derived their traditions at least partly from the institutions of the Roman Empire, and because the empire of the early Middle Ages, as indeed all kingdoms, was dependent on ecclesiastics to staff the chancelleries and to serve as officials of all kinds, there is little wonder that there are also many formal similarities between the documents produced by both courts.

Since the kingdom of the Franks forms a link between ancient and medieval times, and a relatively large number of papers have survived in original form or as copies, let us see what we can learn about these first documents of the direct ancestor of modern European states.   These documents usually follow the same arrangement: the name is given, followed by the title **rex,** the **sub** (for **subscripsi,** or **subscripsit),** and one or two paraphs.   In the oldest documents, there is also a monogram between name and title.   It was the custom for the king to sign the orders and warrants personally, but not the decrees, and whenever the signature exists, it is authentic.   The chancellor or a similar official also signed.   Next to the incision made into the document for the seal, we find after the reign of Clovis II the **Bene Val,** which may have meant **Bene Valete** or **Bene Valiat,** "that [the document] may acquire validity."

The Carolingians did not sign their documents but used a signum, which their ancestors had used as mayors of the palace.   Pippin and Carlman used a simple cross, the unconnected four bars of which the king connected with two penstrokes.   Charlemagne introduced the monogram, a custom followed by his descendants.   The form varied between a diamond and shape of the letter **H** or **Y.** It consisted mainly of capital letters and was drawn at least partly by the monarch.   Charlemagne drew a diamond with the **A** at the top.   Louis the Pious and Louis the Stammerer used the letter **H** (for Hludovicus), drawing the bar of the **H** themselves.   Lothair also used a diamond, often shaped like a **Y,** the tail of which was drawn by the king.

The word **signum** came first, followed by the monogram, the king's name, and the **Rex Gloriosus.** Later this order was not necessarily followed. After 938, particularly important documents were supplied with a lead seal and also bore the word **Legimus** at the bottom of the page. This habit was copied from Byzantine documents. The chancellor usually also subscribed.

As the ninth century advanced, autographic participation of monarch as well as chancellor became less and less frequent. In France during the tenth century the principle of authenticating a document by the hand of king and chancellor was abandoned, the scribe also writing the subscription, but in Germany the opposite was true. Here also during the ninth century the number of unsigned documents about equals that of the signed ones, but after 900 the monarch resumed drawing or completing the monogram. It was not until the twelfth century that autographic participation by the emperor stopped altogether. At this time the seal rather than the signature had become the sign of authenticity.

Illus. 7.   Signum of Pippin.   Illus. 8.   Signum of Charlemagne.

Otto the Great and Otto II usually completed the monogram; Otto III wrote it in its entirety; Henry II at least in one instance wrote **"Ego Einricus imperator";** Conrad II signed no documents; Henry III and Henry IV occasionally wrote their complete signatures; Henry V returned to the form of the large signum. Between 1130 and 1250 the solemn privileges were personally signed by the emperor and often by the chancellor as well, but after 1250 most documents were not signed for the next two or three centuries. Charles IV and Rupert personally signed their letters to the popes, and Charles IV often wrote the word **aprobamus** on his documents. Wenceslas used the formula **"Rex per se"** several times. Sigismund and Albert II rarely signed. Frederick III personally sealed his letters and signed not infrequently either **"Praescripta recognoscimus"** or **"Nos Fridericus."** Maximilian I made personal signature the rule **(Per regem per se," "Maximillianus Rex,"** etc.), and all his successors signed their documents with their names.

During the thirteenth, fourteenth, and fifteenth centuries the monogram reigned supreme, although the autographic participation in it varies and is doubtful in most instances. The construction of the monogram changed at about 1272, when Rudolph I of Habsburg began to use a thin net "skeleton," and this practice persisted until the time of Frederick III, who returned to the original shaft style with the framework consisting of one or more strongly drawn capital letters. The monogram might appear anywhere on the document, but the tendency prevailed to place it near the center of the page. The use of the monogram ended at the moment when all documents began to be personally signed, in about 1500.

Illus. 9. An unusual type of signature used by Maximilian I.

Illus. 10. An example of the "skeleton" monogram like that used by Rudolph I.

Illus. 11. An example of the heavy capital letter monogram like that used by Frederick III.

The Kings of France

The earliest French kings used diamonds or **H** or **Y** signums like their German cousins. Here, too, the principle of autographic participation was not upheld. The Capetians continued to use the Y-shaped monogram for a while. Henry I and Philip I used a cross as signum; Robert, Louis VI, and several successors employed the monogram. The position of the monogram was variable here also, but under Louis VII it was placed in the last line of the document behind its announcement and in front of the subscription of the chancellery and the date. Louis VII serves as an example of the truth that during the Middle Ages a man might be able to read though not necessarily to write. The later Capetians did not autograph their documents but simply had them sealed by the chancellor. The color of the seal, incidentally, indicated the character of the document, green wax being used for more important documents of permanent validity, yellow wax on one string for short-lived measures, and yellow wax on two strings for documents of an intermediate status.

It is doubtful whether any French kings signed their names before Philip V, who wrote to Pope John XXII in his own hand. The letters or documents of Philip VI were not signed, even by the secretary. Most of the letters of John II were signed by a secretary, but three that he signed himself are in existence. Charles V occasionally signed himself, and this fact usually is especially announced, but dating is rare. A few of his **lettres missives** are partly or totally in his hand. His successors signed more and more frequently and even added postscripts. Charles VI signed quite a few of his letters, using successively two types of signatures, and all others were signed by a secretary. From the reign of Charles VII on, letters on paper were always written in French, signed by the king, and countersigned by a secretary, giving a date but no year and no place; from 1524 on, the year is given.

Illus. 12. Signature of Charles V
of France.

Illus. 13. Signature of Charles VI
of France.

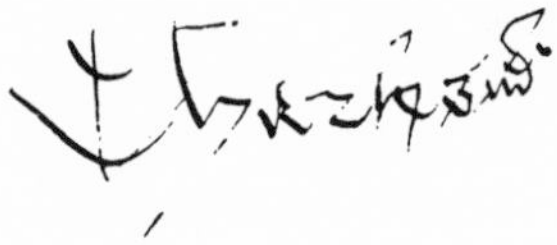

Illus. 14. Signature of Charles VII of France.

Louis XI employed two different signatures. Francis I wrote in French to the pope, the king of Scotland, and the duke of Bavaria, but in Latin to the emperor. The procedure of signing the letters went as follows: The king gave the command that a certain letter be written, or he dictated it. It was then copied, or engrossed, and submitted to the king for signing; the secretary often countersigned it and dated it. The signature of the king was the equivalent of a royal command.

From Louis XI on, secretaries often signed for the king, imitating his hand. In the seventeenth and eighteenth centuries they were known as **secretaires de la main** and were said to "have the pen." The genuine royal signature became very infrequent, though the letters sent by the king's cabinet were always signed by the king himself and not countersigned. Oddly enough, when the expression "I am writing to you with my own hand" occurs, this almost certainly showed that it was **not** the king's hand. When Louis XVI gave an order to pay, the secretary's signature **Louis** had to be vouched for by the king's writing below **Bon Louis.** Louis XVIII was the last king to have the secretary sign for him.

The Kings of England

As already stated, William the Conqueror used the cross signum on a few documents, and his sons followed his example. Henry II could read, but it is unlikely that he could or did write. Richard I spoke French and some "French English," and knew Latin. King John personally wrote an acknowledgment of the receipt of a book to the abbot of Reading, but this was an exceptional case. Almost invariably the kings dictated their letters to their scribes in French.

From Edward III on, there are samples of every king's handwriting, though the early ones are very rare. Edward's first autograph is dated 1330, when he was still a boy. He wrote to the pope that he had been forced to write letters and to seal them, but the pope would know that a letter was from him by the words **Pater Sancte.** The sign manual of Edward III first appeared in 1389 in a letter where the king also added in his own hand **Le Roy R.S. Saunz departyr.** Other documents of the time bear the royal initials or the full name. The sign manual was used on all documents from this point on and did not go out of fashion until the time of Queen Mary I. One of Richard II's sign manuals is still in existence. Henry IV was the first to use the initials **H R (Henricus Rex)**, and Henry V followed the custom with his **R.h.** While there seem to be only one or two of these specimens in existence, there are several of Henry VI, who was the first to spell out his name (Henry). The autographs of Edward IV are occasionally available commercially, either as signatures or as sign manuals. One DS of Edward V is known, signed **R. Edwardus quintus.** Richard III exists in the form of signatures, sign manuals, and monograms, and these are now and then offered in the trade. From Henry VII on, most royal autographs except for Edward VI are easy to find.

Illus. 15. Signature of Henry VI.

Other European Monarchs

The story of the Scottish royal autographs is similar to that of the English kings. Autographs of the last five sovereigns, James III, IV, V, VI, and Mary Stuart, while somewhat scarce, are obtainable, but any king before James III (1451-88) is a decided rarity in autograph form.

In most of the other realms of Europe the rulers started signing letters and documents in the sixteenth, and more rarely in the fifteenth, century. There are exceptions to this. The early Byzantine emperors wrote the word **"Legimus"** ("we read") at the foot of the documents using red ink. On rare occasions, when writing to especially high ranking monarchs, they used gold ink and various types of signatures. Several autograph signatures of Byzantine emperors of the end of the twelfth century and later are in existence.

In Italy, as might be expected, some rulers, such as those of Naples and Amalfi, signed their documents during the tenth, eleventh, and twelfth centuries. The Norman kings of Sicily also participated in the writing of documents. Roger I made the figure of a cross; William of Apulia and Roger II of Sicily signed personally. The margraves of Tuscany in the twelfth century drew at least part of their monograms. In northern Italy the first signature of a duke of Savoy was affixed in 1451 (Duke Louis).

In Denmark, royal participation in documents up to the end of the fifteenth century consisted of applying the various royal seals. In various periods, the chancelleries added a notice at the bottom of the page, such as **"dominus rex per se"** or **"ad mandatum domini regis."** Christian I is the first Danish king known to have signed a letter in his own hand. There are two documents in existence, one of March 16, 1479, to two Saxon princes and the other of December 1, 1480, to Queen Dorothy, both in the German language. From the reign of King John there are very few signed letters, the first one of the year 1503. After King John, examples of royal handwriting are more common.

The oldest royal charter in existence sealed by a Swedish king is one granted by King Karl Sverkersson between 1164 and 1167. In Sweden likewise the sealing of documents and letters with the royal seal constituted authentication until the end of the sixteenth century. During the reigns of Gustav Vasa (1521-60), Erik XIV (1650-68), and John III (1568-92) only the most important documents and letters to foreign kings were personally subscribed by the king. The Swedish National Archives has some royal letters that are believed to have been written, partly or entirely, by the Vasa kings themselves.

Perhaps on another occasion a study of the autographs of the Iberian kings will be undertaken. Of the latter, this much can be said now: There is a rather bewildering profusion of innovations and changes in the chancelleries of the several peninsular kingdoms, though autographic participation began quite early. The unusual habit of the kings of Spain to sign **"Yo el rey"** ("I, the king") is a Castilian invention and dates back at least to the fourteenth century. In Aragon, all kings since James II (1291-1327) signed personally, but before his time very infrequently.

Tables

The following lists attempt to tabulate the royal autographic participation in documents and letters. I believe that these are the first tables of their kind. I am quite aware of the pitfalls of such an endeavor. There are bound to

Illus. 16. Typical signature of a Castilian or Spanish king, **"Yo el rey."**

be mistakes, although considerable effort was made to avoid these and a good number of authorities were consulted. Trying to establish accuracy in the remarks made about rarity or nonrarity is problematic, as rarity is a relative term, hard to define at best; yet I feel justified in making the attempt and hope that the tables will be useful.

Coming to the tables themselves, if under "form of autograph" mention is made of an autographic occurrence, this, of course, indicates that the autograph can be found in a public or private collection. The numbers 0 to 3 show the occurrence in auction catalogues or dealers' stock:

0 = probably impossible to procure; not likely ever to occur
1 = almost impossible to procure; very rarely occurs
2 = hard to procure; occurs infrequently
3 = not very difficult to procure; occurs relatively frequently.

Obviously, in considering the possibilities of procuring autographs, we must make allowances for constantly changing circumstances that will affect the rarity of a given piece. Readers who are interested in prices should study dealers' catalogues and the price lists of auctions.

Reign	Form of Autograph	Occurrence
Merovingians		
Clovis I (481-511)	signum	0
Clotaire I (588-561)	signature, most documents signed	0
Clotaire II (613-629)	signature, most documents signed	0
Dagobert I (623-639)	signature, most documents signed	0
Clovis II (657-657)	signature, most documents signed	0
Childeric II (673-675)	signature, most documents signed	0

Reign	Form of Autograph	Occurrence
Merovingians (continued)		
Theoderic III (675-691)	signature, most documents signed	0
Childebert III (698-711)	signature, most documents signed	0
Dagobert III (711-715)	signature, most documents signed	0
Theoderic IV (720-737)	signature, most documents signed	0
Childeric III (734-752)	only two documents known, unsigned	0
Carolingians		
Pippin (751-768)	completion of signum, most documents signed	0
Carloman (768-771)	completion of signum, most documents signed	0
Charlemagne (768-814)	portion of monogram, most documents signed	0
Louis I the Pious (814-840)	portion of monogram, many documents unsigned	0
Lothaire I (840-855)	portion of monogram, many documents unsigned	0
Louis II (844-875)	portion of monogram, most documents signed	0
Berengar I (888-924)		0
Berengar II (950-961)		0
Charles II the Bald (843-877)	portion of monogram, many documents unsigned	0
Louis II (877-879)	portion of monogram, many documents unsigned	0
Louis III (879-882)		0
Carloman (879-884)	portion of monogram (3 types), most documents signed	0
Charles II the Simple (898-923)	portion of monogram, most documents signed	0
Louis IV d'Outremer (936-954)	portion of monogram, most documents signed	0
Lothaire (956-986)	portion of monogram, most documents signed	0
Louis V (986-987)		0
Louis II the German (840-876)	portion of monogram, most documents signed	0
Charles II the Fat (876-887)	portion of monogram, most documents signed	0

Reign	Form of Autograph	Occurrence
Carolingians (continued)		
Arnulf (887-899)	portion of monogram, most documents signed	0
Louis IV the Child (900-911)	portion of monogram, most documents signed	0
French Kings		
Hugh Capet (987-996)	portion of monogram	0
Robert (996-1031)	portion of monogram	0
Henry I (1031-1060)	portion of monogram	0
Philip I (1060-1108)	signum, sometimes portion of monogram	0
Louis VI (1108-1137)	portion of monogram, rarely signum	0
Louis VII (1137-1180)	portion of monogram	1
Philip II Augustus (1180-1223)	portion of signum	0
Louis VIII (1123-1226)		0
Louis IX (1226-1270)		0
Philip III (1270-1285)		0
Philip IV (1285-1314)		0
Louis X (1314-1316)		0
Philip V (1316-1322)	signature, body of letter	0
Charles IV (1322-1328)		0
Philip VI (1328-1350)		0
John II (1350-1364)	signature	0
Charles V (1364-1380)	signature	1
Charles VI (1380-1422)	two successive types of signature	2
Charles VII (1422-1461)	signature, somestimes postscriptum	3 (2)
Louis XI (1461-1483)	signature	3
Charles VIII (1483-1498)	signature*	3
Louis XII (1498-1515)	some letters in his own hand, signature*	3
Francis I (1515-1547)	some letters in his own hand, signature*	3
Henry II (1547-1559)	some letters in his own hand, signature*	3
Francis II (1559-1560)	some letters in his own hand, signature*	2 (3)

*Usually signed by secretary, imitating the king's signature.

Reign	Form of Autograph	Occurrence
French Kings (continued)		
Charles IX (1560-1574)	some letters in his own hand, signature*	3
Henry III (1574-1589)	some letters in his own hand, signature*	3
Henry IV (1589-1610)	signature,* some letters in his own hand	3
Louis XIII (1610-1643)	signature,* some letters in his own hand	3
Louis XIV (1643-1715)	signature,* some letters in his own hand	3
Louis XV (1715-1774)	signature,* some letters in his own hand	3
Louis XVI (1774-1792)	signature,* some letters in his own hand	3
Louis XVII (1792)	few samples of his writing, also signature	1
Napoleon I (1804-1814/15)	signature, letters in his hand	3
Napoleon II	letters, signatures	3
Louis XVIII (1814-1824)	letters in his hand, signature*	3
Charles X (1824-1830)	letters in his hand, signature	3
Louis Philip (1830-1848)	letters in his hand, signature	3
Napoleon II (1852-1870)	letters in his hand, signature	3
English Kings and Queens		
William I (1066-1087)	portion of signum	0
William II (1087-1100)	portion of signum	0
Henry I (1100-1135)	portion of signum	0
Stephen (1135-1154)		0
Henry II (1154-1189)	portion of signum	0
Richard I (1189-1199)		0
John (1199-1216)	several words in his hand	0
Henry III (1212-1272)		0
Edward I (1272-1307)		0
Edward II (1307-1327)		0
Edward III (1327-1377)	sign manual, several words	0
Richard II (1377-1399)	signature, sign manual	0

---

*Usually signed by secretary, imitating the king's signature.

Reign	Form of Autograph	Occurrence

English Kings and Queens (continued)

Reign	Form of Autograph	Occurrence
Henry IV (1399-1413)	signature (initial), portion of letter	0
Henry V (1413-1422)	signature (initial), portion of letter	0
Henry VI (1422-1461; 1470-1471)	signature, sign manual	0
Edward IV (1461-1483)	signature, sign manual, portion of letter	1
Edward V (1483)	signature	0
Richard III (1483-1485)	signature, sign manual	2
Henry VII (1485-1509)	signature, sign manual, ALS	3
Henry VIII (1509-1547)	signature, very rare letters	3
Edward VI (1547-1553)	signature, letters	3 (2)
Mary I (1553-1558)	signature, letters	3
Elizabeth I (1558-1603)	signature, letters	3
James I (1603-1625)	signature, letters	3

German Kings and Holy Roman Emperors

Reign	Form of Autograph	Occurrence
Conrad I (911-918)	portion of signum	0
Henry I (918-936)	portion of signum	0
Otto I (936-973)	portion of signum	0
Otto II (973-983)	portion of signum	0
Otto III (983-1002)	signum, monogram, signature, additional words	1
Henry II (1002-1024)	portion of monogram, signature	1
Conrad II (1024-1039)	none	0
Henry III (1039-1056)	portion of monogram, signature	0
Henry IV (1056-1106)	portion of monogram, signature	0
Henry V (1106-1125)	signum	0
Lothair (1125-1137)	portion of signum	0
Conrad III (1137-1152)	portion of signum	0
Frederick I (1152-1190)	portion of signum	1
Henry VI (1190-1197)	portion of signum	0
Philip (1197-1208)	portion of monogram	0
Otto IV (1208-1214)	portion of monogram	0
Frederick II (1214-1250)	portion of monogram, letters	0
Conrad IV (1250-1254)		0
Richard of Cornwall (1257-)		
Alfons (1257-)		0
Rudolph I (1273-1291)	portion of monogram	0
Adolph (1292-1298)	portion of monogram	0

Reign	Form of Autograph	Occurrence

German Kings and Holy Roman Emperors (continued)

Albrecht I (1298-1308)	portion of monogram	0
Henry VII (1308-1313)	portion of monogram, signature	0
Frederick (1314-1330)	portion of monogram	0
Louis IV (1314-1346)	portion of monogram	0
Charles IV (1346-1378)	portion of monogram, signature, "aprobamus"	1
Wenceslas (1378-1400)	portion of monogram	0
Rupert (1400-1410)	portion of monogram, signature	0
Sigismund (1410-1437)	portion of monogram, signature	0
Albrecht II (1438-1439)	signature	1
Frederick III (1440-1493)	portion of monogram, signature, **"Praescripta recognoscimus"**	2
Maximilian I (1493-1519)	signature, **"Per regem per se"**	3
Charles V (1519-1556)	signature, ALS	3
Ferdinand I (1556-1564)	signature, ALS	3

Popes

Earlier popes	form of greeting and wish and date, usually **"Bene valete"**	0
Gregory I (590-604)	same, but also signature	0
Leo IX (1049-1055) *	signature inside of rota	0
Urban II (1088-1099)	signature inside of rota	0
Pascal II (1099-1118) *	signature	0
Celestine III (1191-1198)	signature	0
Innocent III (1198-1216) *	very rarely signed	0
Sixtus IV (1471-1484)	very rarely signed	0
Innocent VIII (1484-1492)	**manus proprii** always signed	1

Hereafter often an autograph word or two followed by the varying
Latin initial of the pope's original first name (not papal name)

---

*All intervening popes also signed in this fashion.

Reign	Form of Autograph	Occurrence
Danish Kings		
Christian I (1448-1481)	signature (only two DSs known)	0
John (1481-1513)	signature (few in existence, none before 1503)	0
Christian II (1513-1523)	signature, a few words	1
Frederick I (1523-1533)	signature, a few words	1
Christian III (1534-1559)	signature, a few words	1
Frederick II (1559-1588)	signature, occasionally ALS	2
Christian IV (1588-1648)	signature, occasionally ALS	2
Swedish Kings		
Gustav Vasa (1521-1560)	signature	0
Eric XIV (1560-1568)	signature	0
John III (1568-1592)	signature	0
Sigismund III (1592-1599)	signature, occasionally ALS	1
Karl IX (1604-1611)	signature, occasionally ALS	2
Gustav Adolf (1611-1632)	ALS, signature	2
Kings of Castile		
Juan I (1379-1390)		0
Enrique III (1390-1406)	signature **"Yo el rey"**	2
Juan II (1406-1454)	signature **"Yo el rey"**	2
Enrique IV (1454-1474)	signature **"Yo el rey"**	2
Kings (and Queen) of Castile and Spain		
Isabella (1474-1504)	signature **"Yo la reyna"**	3
Felipe I (1504-1506)	signature **"Yo el rey,"** letters	2
Carlos I (1516-1556)	signature **"Yo el rey,"** letters	3
Felipe II (1556-1598)	signature **"Yo el rey,"** letters	3
Felipe III (1598-1621)	signature **"Yo el rey,"** letters	3
Felipe IV (1621-1665)	signature **"Yo el rey,"** letters	3
Carlos II (1665-1700)	signature **"Yo el rey"**	3

Reign	Form of Autograph	Occurrence
Kings of Aragon		
Jaime II (1291-1327)	signum	1
Alphonso IV (1327-1336)	signum	1
Pedro IV (1336-1387)	signum	1
Juan I (1387-1395)	signum, occasionally signature	1
Martin (1395-1412)	signature	1
Fernando I (1412-1416)	signature	1
Alphonso V (1416-1458)	signature **"Rex Alphonsus"**	2
Juan II (1458-1479)	signum	2
Fernando II (1479-1516)	signature **"Yo el rey"**	3

The Napoleonic Era*

William Marvin Spencer

In the entire realm of autograph collecting, perhaps no field is more interesting than the Napoleonic era. It presents amazingly absorbing and intriguing opportunities and, of particular importance, there is a wealth of material with which to work. It was a period of feverish activity and almost continuous war, so the writing and dictating of letters, the issuing of military orders and edicts, and the widespread distribution of signed documents in one form or another reached enormous proportions. In those days, even more so than now, it was customary to carefully preserve such material. Hence a vast amount of it is available to modern collectors.

The field, quite obviously, is dominated by the writings and dictations of the Emperor Napoleon. He was a prodigious letter writer. It is estimated that over his lifetime he wrote or dictated between fifty and sixty thousand letters, notes, orders, and memorandums. Whenever the mood struck or the situation demanded it of him, he would summon one or more of his secretaries and dictate for hours on end. One of his favorite times for dictating was early in the morning; when ideas came to him, he would frequently rout out a secretary from his bed and pour forth what was on his mind until the poor fellow literally dropped from exhaustion. Napoleon was, perhaps, the world's most impatient letter writer. He dictated at great speed and, to keep up with him, his secretaries were forced to invent a shorthand system all their own. He took great care to ensure the accuracy of the facts in his letters. Customarily in the morning he read over the dictations of the previous day or night; his meticulousness is indicated by the fact that so many of his letters contain corrections and postscripts or other notations in his own handwriting.

Holograph letters of Napoleon are extremely rare. He was too busy or too rushed to spare the time to write longhand letters. In fact, his hand never could keep up with the lightning-like speed of his mind, and the net result was a scrawl that in many instances is extremely difficult to decipher. Indeed, a few of his writings have yet to be interpreted. His most sought-after ALSs are those written to Josephine and Marie Louise, most of which have been published. Such letters rarely appear on the market and very few are in private collections.

---

*Originally published in 1951.

Family Letters

The writings and dictations of the emperor are by far the most interesting to the collector, but because of their volume they are by no means the rarest of the Bonaparte family.   The letters of his father, Charles Buonaparte (or "de Buonaparte," as he usually signed himself), are the most difficult to find and, in fact, are exceedingly rare, no doubt because he died at the age of thirty-eight (in 1785), years before his distinguished son became famous.   Napoleon's mother, Maria Letizia, an extraordinarily capable person from whom he inherited his strength of character and brilliance of mind, dictated a great many letters, but because she was a careless writer as well as a poor speller, few of her letters in holograph form are known to exist.   Of Napoleon's brothers and sisters--Joseph, Lucien, Louis, Jerome, Caroline, Elisa, and Pauline--the letters of Joseph are the most common, most of them being in holograph form. (Quite recently at Sotheby's in London, a collection of 117 of his holograph letters was sold at auction.   They were written over a period of years to his ailing wife in Europe while he was in exile in the United States.)   All members of the family, with the exception of Lucien, who was in disfavor because of a marriage that Napoleon did not approve, were given important political positions by their all-powerful brother at one time or another; as a result, there was a veritable stream of letters, orders, and documents written or signed by them.

Letters of Napoleon's immediate family, in themselves, constitute an interesting collection. Josephine's handwriting was clear and legible, and she expressed her thoughts in beautiful language, signing herself before the empire "Lapagerie Bonaparte," and later simply "Josephine."   Marie Louise, whom Napoleon married in 1810 after divorcing Josephine, wrote clearly but in tiny handwriting, signing herself "Louise" in personal letters and "Marie Louise" officially.   Most of their letters that come into the market are in holograph form.

His Children

It is not known generally, but Napoleon actually was the father of three children.   The first, born in 1806 to an actress, Eleanor Denuelle, was physically remarkably like his father, but in mind and character markedly dissimilar.   Named "Comte Leon" by his father, he had a notorious reputation as a gambler and meddler in speculations and politics.   He married the daughter of one of his servants in 1865 and died in 1881, leaving several children, at least two of whom were alive twenty years ago--the actual grandchildren of the Emperor Napoleon.

The Polish Comtesse Walewska was the mother of Napoleon's second son, Comte Alexander Florian Joseph Colonna Walewska.   He developed into a rather brilliant man, who for a time devoted himself to writing.   Under the Second Empire, he became a senator and a minister of foreign affairs. He held other important political positions until his death in 1868.

Napoleon's only legitimate child was Napoleon Francis Joseph Charles, born in 1811 to Marie Louise and usually known as Napoleon II, although he was created king of Rome by his father at birth. He was a boy of fine character but his life was a tragic one, and after the fall of Napoleon he was brought up in Austria as the duke of Reichstadt. His health was never robust, and he died in 1832 at the age of twenty-one. Letters of the three children are exceedingly rare and a collector who has them all is fortunate indeed.

His Marshals

One of the most popular collections of Napoleonic material to assemble consists of letters and documents of his marshals, of whom there were twenty-six--Augereau, Bernadotte, Berthier, Bessieres, Brune, Davoust, Grouchy, Jourdan, Kellerman, Lannes, Lefebvre, Macdonald, Marmont, Massena, Moncey, Mortier, Murat, Ney, Oudinot, Perignan, Poniatowski, St. Cyr, Sault, Serurier, Suchet, and Victor. Letters of most of Napoleon's marshals are not hard to find. For some reason, however, letters of Marshal Lannes are among the rarest of all Napoleonic material, and very seldom is one found in a public sale or on a dealer's list. Marshal Poniatowski, the Polish marshal, is the next most difficult to find--an ALS is extremely rare. The letters, orders, and memorandums of Berthier, Napoleon's chief of staff, are quite common and, because of the importance of his position, they often contain historical information of great interest.

Other sources of Napoleonic material are the writings and dictations of Napoleon's ministers, his aides, his secretaries, distinguished personages of the period, and his admirals and generals. There were something like twenty-five hundred of the latter and a complete collection probably would be impossible to assemble. Some of the more important were Caulaincourt, Clauzel, Desaix (one of Napoleon's closest friends, killed at the Battle of Marengo), Exelmans, Foy, Kleber (who commanded the army of Egypt after Napoleon's return to France in 1799), Lecourbe, Marbot, Moreau, Petit, Pichegru, and Vandamme. Letters of women prominent in public life during the Napoleonic era in themselves present interesting opportunities--the duchesse d'Abrantes, Mme. de Genlis, Mlle. le Normand, la Marechale Ney, Mme. Recamier, Mme. de Stael, Marie Walewska, and many others.

Chain of Command

Most of Napoleon's letters were obviously military in character. While he dictated rapidly, he was exceptionally careful in what he said. Rarely, if ever, would he dictate an order without checking it before signing. In issuing such orders, he was particular in following the correct "chain of command." Orders to his marshals and his brothers were usually issued directly. Other orders were routed through his chief of staff (Berthier) or the minister of war (Clarke), who were required to develop the details. When the military situation demanded prompt action, he would sometimes issue orders directly to subordinate officers, but a report of the action he had taken would be sent to the minister of war or other proper authority. Incidentally, Napoleon's letters invariably closed with what was then standard form: **"Sur ce je prie Dieu qu'il vous ait en sa sainte garde"** ("May God preserve you in His holy keeping").

In the early days of his ascendency, Napoleon frequently used writing paper with striking vignettes and this custom was followed by most of his marshals and subordinate officers. When he became emperor, he rarely, if ever, used a vignette although one might expect a most lavish and colorful one. It so happened that his marshals and generals developed the habit of vying with each other in the vignettes they used--the higher the rank, the more elaborate--until Napoleon ended this rivalry by abolishing all but the most simple forms. In fact, official letterheads of any kind during the period of the empire are a rarity. Napoleon, himself, used nothing but plain white paper.

Forms of Signature

The signatures of Napoleon are a story all their own. In his youth, he signed his letters "Buonaparte," the original Italian spelling of the family name. During this period his handwriting is reasonably legible. This form of spelling was supplanted in 1796 by the omission of the u and the adoption of the signature "Bonaparte." Occasionally he signed with his initials, "N B," as evidenced by an ALS that he wrote to Barras on September 19, 1797. When he became emperor, he used several forms of signature.   The complete "Napoleon" is a rarity; he usually reduced it to "Napole," "Napol," "Nap," or, most frequently of all, the simple "N." Some of his signatures are merely unrecognizable scrawls, typical of anyone signing his name under pressure or in a hurry.

The writing and dictations of Napoleon are widely diversified in form and substance. His letters to Josephine, so saturated with love and passion, are tender in the extreme. In the early years, his letters to his family were filled with concern for their welfare, but in time family members became mere pawns in his scheme of things and his letters became just as imperious as those to his ministers or marshals. Perhaps the exception were his letters to his elder brother, Joseph, for whom he had a deep affection.   To the man or woman who incurred his displeasure, it was quite a different story--then he became vitriolic and merciless in the extreme.

The great bulk of Napoleonic material is to be found in national archives, or in the libraries of colleges and public institutions. There is still, however, a large amount in the hands of private collectors. Rarely is there an important sale that fails to include several Napoleonic items. It is a field that is becoming increasingly popular with collectors. The man and the period are unique in the annals of history, and one can derive the greatest satisfaction and pleasure in assembling a collection of autograph material of the times and particularly of the one man who created and dominated them.

Illus. 1. Signatures of Napoleon. Left, top to bottom: postscript, 1811; First Consul, 1801; Captain, age twenty-four, 1793; Vienna, 1809. Center: Cairo, 1798. Right, top to bottom: Dresden, 1813; unusually bold signature, 1812; Paris, 1808; rare full signature, Munich, 1806.

More Signers—Of Israel's Declaration of Independence*

Walter N. Eastburn

On May 19, 1951, the **New York Times** published a dispatch from Tel Aviv, Israel, the first ten lines of which read as follows:

> David Remez, Minister of Education, died of a cerebral hemorrhage today in Hadassah Hospital in Jerusalem. He was 64 years old.

> Mr. Remez was the first of the thirty-seven signers of Israel's declaration of independence to pass away.

At that time I had just retired following an active business career of fifty-one years. For several years, my hobby of autographs had been sadly neglected, particularly the filing, indexing, and record-keeping part of it. Furthermore, I was still about a dozen items short of my objective of a complete set of our own Signers. But I put the clipping from the **Times** away for future consideration. I decided then and there that the next addition to my collecting objectives was to be a set of signatures of the thirty-seven signers of the Declaration of Independence of the Republic of Israel.

Drafting a Campaign Strategy

It was late November the following year before I had time to begin to plan the details of my campaign. Considering possible difficulties of language and a distance of five thousand miles between me and the source of my material, I felt it necessary to plan the various steps of my undertaking with much care. Then, to add to my difficulties, I learned that two other signers had passed away. It was May 1953, just after my set of U.S. Signers was complete, that I really got started on the Israel job.

The Declaration of Independence

The Israeli declaration was signed on May 14, 1948, the date of termination of the British mandate. In arrangement, particularly of the signing, the Israel declaration and that of the United States are alike. David

---

*Originally published in 1955.

Ben-Gurion, head of the People's Council and first premier, evidently signed first, just as John Hancock, president of the Continental Congress, did in our declaration.

Many members of the Jewish Council had been citizens of England or the United States and were familiar with our own Declaration of Independence, as a study of the two documents will show. Of course, the invention of the typewriter and advances in printing gave Israel advantages in bringing out its document.

Comparing the Two Declarations

The Jewish declaration, just as ours did, affirms the birthright freedom of nationality to which all people since the dawn of history have aspired. Both documents recite the hopes, the advances, and the setbacks in the long journey toward final realization of their aspirations.

Just as the original thirteen colonies that became the United States had to resist the efforts of Spain, France, Holland, and England to rule this continent in their own interests, so did the Jews, over a much longer period, have to resist neighboring tribes and suffer conquests by the Assyrians, the Philistines, and the Egyptians. After fleeing from captivity in Egypt, under the leadership of Moses, the Israelites became the dominant power in Palestine. For a while the tribes were consolidated, but after a century, unity gave way to the two kingdoms of Israel and Judah.   Later Assyria overran Israel, carrying the ten northern tribes captive to the Far East, never to return. Babylon captured Judah and took the larger part of the two tribes to Babylon, where they languished for about seventy years, when Cyrus, the Persian, allowed them to return to their homeland.

But freedom for the Jews was still far off, as first the Romans and then the Turks conquered and ruled the country for nearly a thousand years each. It was not until World War I, when the British drove out the Turks, and the Balfour Declaration of November 2, 1917 (reaffirmed in the subsequent mandate of the League of Nations to the British), that the great nations of the world gave international sanction to the right of the Jewish people to national rebirth in Palestine. This right had been proclaimed by the First Zionist Congress in 1897.

Conditions in Europe and the Near East remained unsettled. Then came World War II and, with its end, the founding of the United Nations.   On November 29, 1947, the U.N. passed a resolution calling for the establishment of a Jewish state in Israel. The declaration adopted and proclaimed on May 14, 1948, by the Jewish Council asserts this recognition by the United Nations to be irrevocable.

My Set of Signers Complete

On December 18, 1954, I received the last of the signatures of the thirty-seven signers, including the signatures of the three who had died, which were furnished by their families. I had prepared slips of paper for the signatures of the living signers. Two are reproduced here; illustration 1 shows the signature of David Ben-Gurion, premier for five years; illustration 2 shows that of Moshe Sharett, the current premier.

The Autograph Collection Of

Walter N. Eastburn

SIGNER of the Declaration of Independence of the Republic of Israel, adopted May 14, 1948.

Dated 1953 ______________________
David Ben-Gurion

D. Ben-Gurion
Sde Boker
13.1.54

Illus. 1. Example of form used, showing David Ben-Gurion's signature.

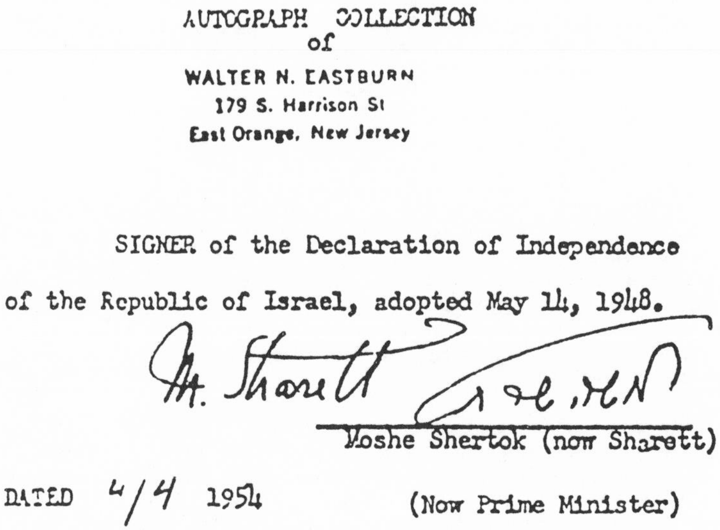

AUTOGRAPH COLLECTION
of
WALTER N. EASTBURN
179 S. Harrison St
East Orange, New Jersey

SIGNER of the Declaration of Independence

of the Republic of Israel, adopted May 14, 1948.

Moshe Shertok (now Sharett)

DATED 4/4 1954   (Now Prime Minister)

Illus. 2. Moshe Sharett's signature.

The signers, beside the two premiers, included many officials of the new government:

The president of Israel
Minister of trade and industry
Minister of labor
Minister of justice
Minister of finance
Minister of police
Minister for religious affairs and social welfare
Deputy minister of religious affairs
Minister for foreign affairs
A former mayor of Jerusalem
Three officials of the Jewish Agency
Minister to Sweden
Officials of Hebrew colleges and various societies, and many
  members of the Knesset, or Parliament.

Incidentally, of course, I sent an addressed envelope with return postage coupon with each of my letters of solicitation. I have saved the envelope that brought each response, so I have acquired a collection of Israeli postage stamps, many very attractive and colorful.

C. MUSIC AND LITERATURE
The Lure of Music Autographs*

Ray Rawlins

At the outset of this article I must make it clear that I write as an autograph collector and not as a musician or expert on music in any form. Nor, since I am a general collector, can I even claim to be a specialist in the autographs of the music world. My seven hundred or so music autographs represent only one-twentieth of my collection. Nonetheless, I often wish that when I started collecting autograph material thirty-eight years ago, I had gone in for specialization. At that time it would probably not have been music, but today it might well be.

Why the change of heart? There are two reasons, one good and the other, I suppose, not so good. First, the great men of music (especially the classical composers) have become more and more fascinating to me as I have read their letters and handled their original autograph music. I think it is the extremely colorful personalities of many of the more celebrated composers that I find so intriguing. There is so much variety in their lives. One moment they are poor and unknown, the next they are famous and acclaimed; and then some may fall again or, like Mascagni and Leoncavallo, never again come up to the standard of the work that made them famous.

The second reason, that of which I am not proud, is purely mercenary. There is no doubt whatsoever that collecting autograph material of famous composers and musicians is a wise investment. At present there is more demand in the autograph market for music material than for any other professional fields except literature and certain of the sciences. True, many great artists are sought after, but many (like the majority of Victorian Royal Academicians) are more dead economically than the proverbial dodo. Even the great historical names--and certainly most of the political ones among these-- are trailing well behind in commercial value. But more of this anon. So, it is a wise step to start collecting music autographs because they are exciting and a good investment. Who can ask for more?

What are the categories of classical music autographs? Briefly, I would say they fall into the following groups: composers, instrumentalists (e.g., pianists, violinists, cellists, organists), conductors, and singers. In addition,

---

*Originally published in 1969.

there are the fringe groups of ballet dancers, choreographers, and music impresarios.

When starting music autograph collecting (or any form of specialized collecting), you must decide whether you are going to collect musical material in general--in other words, material of all the groups mentioned above--or to go in for some form of specialization. Below are some examples of specialized categories. I give only a few. They can be combined and permutated ad infinitum:

Composers only
Instrumentalists only (or only pianists or violinists, etc.)
Conductors only
All autograph material connected with opera
All autograph material connected with ballet
Autograph music only (a suggestion for millionaires!)
Gilbert and Sullivan material
All music material of a certain period or century
All music material of a certain country (or countries)
Only signed portraits or photographs of musical people
Musical families or sagas (such as the Liszt-Wagner-Bulow-
    Countess D'Agoult set-up)
Recognized music composer groups (like "Les Six"--Poulenc,
    Milhaud, etc.)
The collection of material relating to one great musician only.

The last category is, of course, the ultimate in specialization and can be developed beyond the autographic stage. You can collect material relating to the man himself, his family, and his circle; the letters of other people to him and about him; printed original editions of his works; articles and books about him; portraits of him whether signed or not; and concert programs, posters, and tickets in connection with performances of his work. In the end I suppose it could be taken to the point of buying his favorite piano or hoarding a snip of his hair!

After you decide what to collect, the next step is to get the objects of your desire. This is not going to be easy with the demand as strong as it now is. As with all other autograph material, the cost depends on supply and demand. It also depends on condition, contents, length (of the letter or score), date written, and whether the score is published or unpublished.

If your means were limitless, what would you collect in music auto-graphs? The best is obviously holograph music (signed, if possible, though this is not strictly necessary). Certainly the full autograph score of some great opera would cost a fortune today, but even a few music bars (especially from a particularly well-known work) in the holograph of a great composer are most desirable and often most ornamental. Though musicians may not agree with me (remember I write as an autograph collector not a music expert), it is obviously more intriguing to have some autograph music from Johann Strauss's "Blue Danube" than from some virtually unknown work of his. Similarly, if Ravel quotes from his "Bolero" (which I understand many music critics scoff at), this would be a great acquisition.

Illus. 1. A medley of signatures: John Philip Sousa, Bela Bartok, Maurice
Ravel, Serge Prokofieff, Giuseppe Verdi, Sir Arthur Sullivan, Edvard
Grieg, Jan Paderewski, and Jean Sibelius surround an autographed
musical quotation of Franz Lehar from his operetta **Giuditta.** (This
and all other illustrations are from the author's collection.)

Illus. 2. Signature of Igor Stravinsky with opening bars from his **Rite of Spring**.

In my own collection, I have a card of Humperdinck with a picture of himself and of his villa at Boppard on which he has written a holograph greeting and a little piece of the music of his most famous work, **Hansel and Gretel**--signed and dated 1906.   This is a small item indeed, but it is very decorative, and this kind of thing can look particularly pleasing when framed and hung on a wall. So I would say that any form of holograph music from a complete score to a **feuille d'album** is a very satisfactory music autograph.

Illus. 3. Engelbert Humperdinck's autograph on a card with autograph music from his **Hansel and Gretel** score.

Next in interest come other signed documents, such as letters and portraits. If a portrait contains a little holograph music as well, this greatly enhances its interest and monetary value. As to letters, obviously, although length is important, content is much more so. A letter about his own work or indeed any musical subject from a great composer is of the greatest overall value.

Another desirable form of music autograph, if you cannot afford (or get hold of) an autograph score, is printed music signed by the composer. This can be a good deal more exciting than it sounds. I would like to give two examples from my own collection. They concern the scarce autographs of Chopin and Haydn, neither of which I could afford in the form of holograph music (even if I could find it!). The Chopin item is the original print of four mazurkas by him, and on the top of the page of the first mazurka (Opus 30) the celebrated composer has signed his name. Chopin's signature is both rare and very much sought after, but this item is made far more interesting by the fact that his friend Hector Berlioz has confirmed that this is Chopin's own signature by writing on the same sheet, "De la main de Chopin--Hector Berlioz."

Illus. 4. Chopin's signature.    Illus. 5. Haydn's signature.

I have a bound copy of the first edition of the three sets of Haydn's canzonettas. I am informed that there is only one other recorded copy of the third set in the British Isles, so that even the printed music is rare. But for me the thrill of this item is that Haydn, whose autograph is decidedly uncommon, has signed the dedication page of the first set. I also have signed dedications on their printed music by more modern composers, including Poulenc and the much sought-after Ravel. Collecting this sort of music autograph can, I suggest, be compared with collecting "association copies" of literary works, an interest indulged in by many collectors and obviously a very satisfactory way of building up a good library with the added autographical interest of the writers' signatures and perhaps a holograph dedication in the books concerned.

The question that must be in the mind of anyone deciding to collect music autographs is "How available are they, and at what price?" As this is so vital, I propose to deal with it at some length, but I must say at once that I shall not give prices. The reason is that these change so rapidly and vary so tremendously on the standards of each item that it is virtually impossible to be accurate. To quote prices of a commodity (an odd word with which to describe autographs, perhaps) is always dangerous, and I do not intend to set myself up as a target for the slings and arrows of those whose knowledge on this subject may be deeper than mine! Most of my fellow members of the Manuscript Society know all too well that all forms of autograph material are increasingly expensive these days--as indeed are antiquarian books, paintings, and similar items. Suffice it to say, then, that music autographs are going up in market value rather more rapidly than most other categories and this--as with anything that is bought and sold--is because of the trends in supply and demand.

How available are the autographs of, for example, the great composers? I take this group because I know more about composers autographically than I do about the great singers or instrumentalists, and also because on the whole it is this group that is most in demand and, to my mind, most rewarding to collect. I should say also that as a general rule (there are many exceptions, such as the great violinist Paganini, who is rare and highly desirable) the autographs of composers are more costly than those of their fellow music makers. Most of the great singers, for instance, are still inexpensive. Jenny Lind is perhaps an exception, but at least she is very easy to get. I do apologize, Jenny, I speak entirely autographically!

Even if you are a millionaire you will have the greatest difficulty obtaining anything of Monteverdi, Purcell, and Handel. It so happens that I have a very small Handel item myself, but I acquired it a very long time ago, and I am not absolutely certain that it is genuine anyway! Purcell and Monteverdi I have never seen, although I assume they exist in some institutions. Close behind these are the almost unfindable autographs of Rameau, Scarlatti, and Smetana, followed by the considerable rarities of Johann Sebastian and Carl Philipp Emmanuel Bach, Gluck, Glinka, and Haydn. After these I would say that, if you have the money to pay for them, you can still find--though the search may take some time--the highly prized letters of Chopin, Schubert, Bellini, Mozart, and Rimsky-Korsakov.

Illus. 6. Rimsky-Korsakov (in Russian).

Perhaps the most resounding name of all is that of the great Beethoven. His letters can still be found, but though he might not be quite so rare as the composers just mentioned, he might well be the most costly of all to buy. This time the reason lies entirely in "demand." I have nothing of Beethoven in my own collection. I would dearly love a single word--or a single letter of the alphabet--in his holograph, but, quite frankly, I cannot afford it. I am not unique among collectors and I am sure that the autographic demand for this great man is more than that for any other musical name. Once again, let me remind readers that I claim expertise as an autograph collector and not as a musician. As such I am prepared to stick my neck out and stand by my statement about the autographic desirability of the deaf genius of Vienna.

Comparatively scarce, but certainly available if one has the money, are the letters of Berlioz, Bizet, Debussy, Dvorak, Gershwin, Wagner, and Weber. Mendelssohn and Verdi also can be found, but here again the demand is considerable and the price accordingly high. These remarks also apply, rather surprisingly, to the comparatively modern Ravel and Sibelius and to the contemporary Stravinsky. Russian composers are very much in demand and on the whole both expensive and hard to get. Rimsky-Korsakov has already been mentioned, and Tchaikowsky would be equally expensive. Moussorgsky and Prokofieff are not easy to get and even Rachmaninoff, although available, is going up in price. Shostakovich, still very much alive at sixty-six [in 1969], is virtually unfindable in the West. Other modern Russian composers such as Gretchaninoff and Tscherepnin may be less known to the public, but they, too, are desirable autographically and not easy to find.

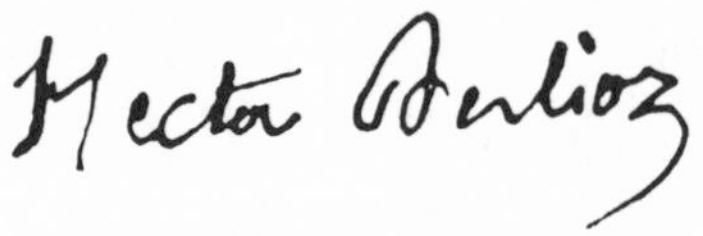

Illus. 7. Berlioz's signature. 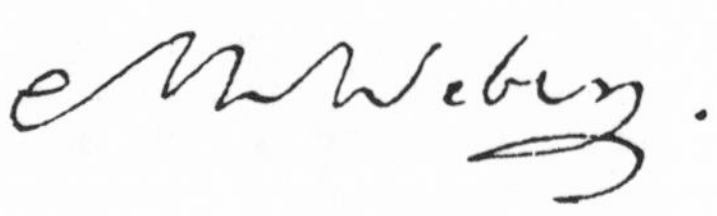   Illus. 8. Weber's signature.

I find the popular French and Italian composers--perhaps because of their Latin flamboyance--the most colorful group. Most of these are readily available, but many are in such great demand that they will not be bought "for a song"--to use an appropriately musical metaphor. Of the French, including those born elsewhere who lived and worked in France, Massenet, Gounod, Offenbach, Cherubini, Meyerbeer, Saint Saens, Faure, and D'Indy will be found with no difficulty, and the price that must be paid will depend entirely on the nature of the actual item itself. The members of Les Six may be a little more expensive, though Milhaud is still alive. The popular Italians may be a little more costly, but are not yet hard to come by. In this group one can list, inter alia, Leoncavallo, Mascagni, Puccini (higher priced), Rossini, and perhaps Donizetti, though the last is now getting more expensive.

Illus. 9. Puccini's signature.   Illus. 10. Donizetti's signature.

Of the great names in music from other nations, Liszt, Johann Strauss, Richard Strauss, and Lehar can be found without difficulty, but no longer so inexpensively. Bartok is much in demand and Grieg is not readily obtainable. British composers' autographs are not difficult to come by, and several would be well worth inclusion in a collection of most distinguished composers. The names of Delius, Elgar, Vaughan Williams, and Britten spring to mind, and there is now quite a run on Sullivan and his collaborator Gilbert. Among Americans I would say that the most autographically desirable include Aaron Copland, Gershwin, John Alder Carpenter, Victor Herbert, William Grant Still, and that very different but very popular march composer, John Philip Sousa.

I do not propose to offer advice on how to get these things, because most readers of this article are themselves constantly seeking for autographic material, and you must search for music autographs just as you do for any other kind. Apart from the usual dealers and auction rooms, there are a number of dealers who specialize in music material and are therefore more likely to be of assistance to the collector. But even a very rich collector will not be able to buy all he or she wants through these obvious sources, simply because many fine items never come onto the "public market" at all. Being lazy, I myself retired early in life and am more mobile than many of my fellow enthusiasts. I travel fairly extensively on the continent of Europe and even farther afield, always on the lookout for the letters and holographs of the great--very much including those of music. I buy for my own collection all I can afford to, but, alas, I cannot take all I find! Then again, like all autograph material, the supply of music autographs is diminishing, especially as the interest has risen so much; hence I view this type of material as a particularly good investment quite apart from the excitement of the chase after these spectacular personalities.

As for my own collection, I have a preference, already expressed, for the distinguished composers. Around a hundred of my music items come within this classification, but I have many items of the great singers, conductors, and instrumentalists. It is interesting to note that many instrumentalists were themselves composers. Statistically, I would say this applied in particular to pianists. Liszt, Thalberg, Paderewski, Rachmaninoff, Moscheles, Hummel, Anton Rubinstein, and D'Albert are examples taken at random from my own collection list. Successful composers also include the violinists Paganini, Lvoff, Sarasate, and Kreisler; the cellists Piatti and Casals; and the conductors Hamilton Harty, Toscanini, Weingartner, Messager, and Randegger. Organists such as Perosi and the British organists Elvey, Bridge, and Stainer tend to compose church music.

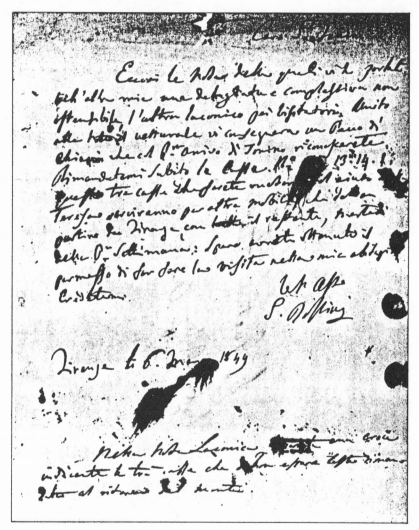

Illus. 11.   ALS of Gioacchino Rossini, 1849.   The wild flourishes and ink blots are typical of this brilliant and flamboyant Latin composer.

| Illus. 12.   Johann Strauss's signature. | Illus. 13.   Richard Strauss's signature. |

It is difficult to choose my favorite items among my collection, but I would say that two of my more prized letters are by Mendelssohn and Debussy. Debussy, a sick man, wrote a sad letter to his editor thus:

Sunday, 15 Jan 1899

Dear Mr Hartmann,

Here is a Nocturne! The others will be following rapidly.

Please excuse me but I have been in such misery recently and I must have been momentarily mad when I orchestrated the Nocturnes! I had to start them all again from the beginning. I know well that I should have invited you to come and see me but Destiny took charge so cruelly and intervened so much in my life that it would be very kind of you not to join forces with it against me!

That our friendship should not be abandoned is all that I dare to hope for, at present.

Most affectionately,
Claude Debussy.

Illus. 14. Debussy's signature.

Weakened by cancer and worn out by war, Debussy died in Paris during a German bombardment of that city in March 1918.

Felix Mendelssohn-Bartholdy, to give his full name, had a very good knowledge of English but because he wrote mostly in his native German, his letters in English are uncommon. Here is part of one in my collection:

My dear sir,

You will receive with these lines the copy of my Festgesang in which I have made a few remarks in those passages in which Mr. Bartholomew has two different versions, and also the arrangement of the whole for a Chorus with female voices. I think it will do well in this shape and have no objection to your publishing it; as I am to fix a price I would say four guineas. The orchestral parts are not published, but if you want to have them I shall send you a copy of them immediately. They are, as you presumed, for brass instruments only, 6 trumpets, 6 horns, 6 trombones and ophicleide (being two orchestras, the smaller of which consists of 2 tr, 2 horns and 3 trombones, and has to play the Echo in the passages marked thus *) I should not like the accompaniment to be called Pianoforte or Organ, as if it had been originally intended for those instruments, but if you should like to say adapted for Piano or Organ by the composer, you are very welcome to do so, as it is the truth . . . .

* * *

I think there ought to be other words to no. 2 the "Leid". If the right ones are hit at, I am sure that piece will be liked very well by the signers and the hearers--but it will <u>never</u> do to sacred words. There must be a national and merry subject found out, something to which the soldierlike and buxom motion of the piece has some relation, and the words must express something gay and popular, as the music tries to do it . . . .

* * *

The translation of all the rest, I like very much and it sings as well or better than the German. . . . Believe me always your very truly,

Felix Mendelssohn Bartholdy.

Leipzig 30 April 1843.

I take the liberty of enclosing a line to Mr Moscheles which I beg you will kindly forward to him.

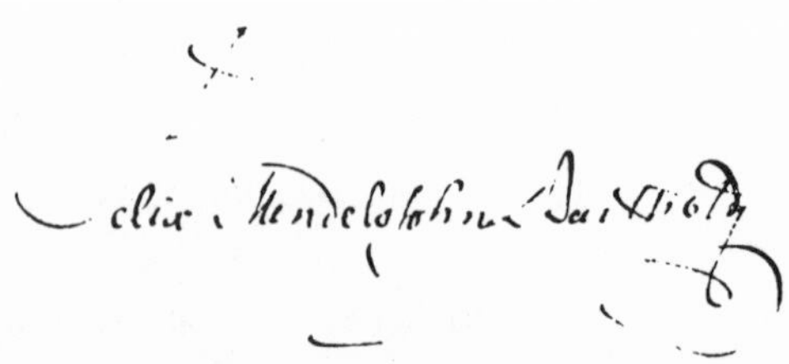

Illus. 15. Mendelssohn's signature.

Despite the composer's wish, some of this music did eventually become associated with religious words; for example, the inspiring Christmas carol, "Hark the Herald Angels Sing."

I also am fond of my letter of Carl Maria von Weber, whose autograph is comparatively scarce. Already a very sick man, he had come to England to write an opera for Covent Garden. At the age of thirty-seven he learned English specifically to do this. When he had adapted for the piano the first act of **Oberon**, he sent it to Sir George Smart with this little note now in my collection:

My dear sir!

According to your request, I have the honour to send you hereby the first act of Oberon adapted for the piano-forte. The second act is also ready and you can have it at any moment.

I am my dear sir,
Most sincerely yours,
C. M. Weber.

26 Marcn 1826.

The note, unimportant in itself, is more poignant than it appears. He finished the next act, but less than two months later he was dead from consumption. The fact that the letter is written in English (in which he cannot have written many letters) and the mention of his final work, **Oberon**, add considerably to this note's already increased value as one of his last letters.

Johannes Brahms is a highly desirable autograph and no longer common. He wrote to his publisher Simrock a four-page letter concerning a quatuor that had been printed without his consent. In this letter, he discussed his fellow composer Max Bruch and described himself as phlegmatic and lazy. (You can see from a remark I made earlier why I feel Brahms is a kindred spirit!) Leoncavallo, who never wrote another real success after **I Pagliacci,** wrote delightedly about its reception in Paris, while Delibes, composer of the famous **Coppelia** ballet, wrote in great detail regarding the staging of his opera **Le Roi l'a Dit.**

Robert Schumann's holograph is scarce. I have his autograph receipt for fifty pounds for twelve piano compositions (Opus 85). He appears to have sold these in London, as the receipt is dated there in 1850. At approximately four guineas for each piece, it is not surprising that this renowned composer was not a rich man! He, too, ended his life sadly, in a private mental institution.

Among music part scores or bars, I value the holograph extracts by Boito from **Mephistopheles,** by Massenet from **Herodiade,** and by Delibes from **Le Roi l'a Dit;** the score of a Paternoster by Gounod; and autograph music excerpts of the lesser work of Stravinsky and Offenbach. In addition, I find great charm in autograph music quotations from the well-known works of composers themselves not so well known, for example, Haydn Wood quoting from his "Roses of Picardy" and Ketelby from "In a Monastery Garden."

Illus. 16. Schumann's signature.

I also collect signed portraits. The finest is a very large one of Wagner with an autograph dedication to the famous piano maker Bechstein. I have a considerable number of signed photographs of composers, some with dedications and others with holograph music bars. These include Lehar, Rossini, Liszt, Rachmaninoff, Faure, Anton Rubinstein, and D'Indy. The one I find most amusing, however, is that of Norwegian composer Edvard Grieg. He wrote right across an excellent picture of himself, "This is not Edvard Grieg"!

Illus. 17. Musical excerpt in the hand of Jules Massenet, Prelude to the Fourth Act of his opera **Herodiade.**

Illus. 18. Excerpt from "In a Monastery Garden," signed by its composer, Albert Ketelby.

Also adding a touch of humor are the self-caricaturists. Caruso was famous for this, and his self-caricatures are a most desirable form of his autograph, for he always added his signature to them. I have such a portrait and also a signed self-caricature of the great Russian bass Chaliapin and one of Francis Poulenc. There are many other signed photographs in my music collection: the instrumentalists Cortot, Casals, Sarasate, and Paderewski; the singers Melba, Tetrazzina, and Patti; the conductors Toscanini, Koussevitsky, and Monteux; and a particularly fine example of Pavlova in her most famous role of the Dying Swan.

And, finally, to end on a human note, I must mention that most human and fallible of composers, the too good-looking, too brilliant Giacomo Puccini. A lady-killer par excellence, he was in fact indirectly responsible for one lady's drowning herself in Lake Como. I have a sad letter card with a cryptic holograph message written by a remorseful Puccini, who left his beloved Como for a sojourn in Rome because of this affair. I also have two of his autograph checks. Both were written in the same year, 1921. One is to his wife, Elvira, made out for 1,000 lire, the other to his lady friend, Laura di Ciolo, for 5,000 lire! Too human, too fallible? But Puccini, who took so much, also gave so much to the whole world through **Madame Butterfly, La Tosca, La Boheme,** and **The Girl of the Golden West.** If he brought sadness to a few, he gave joy to millions.

Illus. 19.   Signed self-caricature of Enrico Caruso, London, 1906. This one is particularly unusual, because most of Caruso's self-portraits were merely profiles of his bust.

The Autograph—Adjunct to a Literary Career*

A. W. Yeats

Writers sign copies of their works for one reason--to personalize the impersonal printed page. Autographed issues as a selling device came into vogue around the turn of the present century, and the practice has subsequently become in a measure established. Although two modern authors, George Bernard Shaw and Rudyard Kipling, have made almost phenomenal use of this book-selling device, Kipling's practice is the more interesting of the two.

Kipling's first book offered to the public[1] was in many ways prophetic of the scores to follow. **Departmental Ditties and Other Verses** (1886) first appeared in narrow tan wrappers designed to resemble an official British departmental franking form, complete with imitation seal and red cloth tape around the center. These envelopes were addressed to "All Heads of Departments and Anglo-Indians" in facsimile script. It is interesting to observe that the youthful Kipling anticipated later publishing practice, for this volume of verse bore his facsimile signature as assistant in the "Department of Public Journalism, Lahore District." That he was pleased with both the idea and its success is indicated in his remark that, "among a pile of papers (it) would have deceived a clark [sic] of twenty year's service."[2] The book sold rapidly and was reissued many times in more conventional form, but its author said of it:

> I loved it best when it was a little brown baby with a pink string around its stomach; a child's child, ignorant that it was afflicted with all the most modern ailments; and before people learned beyond doubt how its author lay awake of night in India plotting and scheming to write something that would "take" with the English public.[3]

---

*Originally published in 1952.

[1] **Schoolboy Lyrics** (1881) was printed for private circulation; **Echoes** (1884) and **Quartette** (1885) were family projects.

[2] Rudyard Kipling, "My First Book," **The Idler,** Christmas Number (London, 1892), the author's signed typescript of which is in the Rare Books Collection of the University of Texas.

[3] Ibid.

Plain Tales From the Hills (1888) carried no autograph identification, but the Indian Railway Library Series (1888-90)[4] that followed began a literary tradition without parallel in the records of English literature. Each of the six Kipling volumes in this series carried on its cover the head of an elephant; the head varied slightly from volume to volume, but each resembled the other five. From that time on, nearly every important Kipling volume, including his posthumous autobiography (1937), carried an elephant's head (a ganesha) device on its cover or single or multiple swastikas, which are also elephant symbols,[5] on its title page.   These symbols were omitted on many of the earlier American editions, and, naturally enough, they did not appear where their use would have been inappropriate, as on war publications and on books devoted to stories about other animals.

Rudyard's father, John Lockwood Kipling, designed or supervised the designing of the covers of the six books in the Indian Railway Library Series. His own volume, **Beast and Man in India,** shows clearly the elder Kipling's sympathetic interest in animals and his particular fondness for the elephant, and an attractive sketch of one graced the cover of his own book. Taking the cue suggested by his artist father, Rudyard chose **both** elephant devices as his identifying printed signature.

A Registered Trademark

By 1930 the ganesha had become such an individualized symbol that Kipling sought to protect his financial and literary interest in it by applying to the United States and British governments to register three[6] forms of the device as a personal trademark. His applications were granted, and to him goes the distinction of possessing the only literary trademark device registered by an author in this country and in England. The nearest parallel is Samuel L. Clemens's protection of the name "Mark Twain" for much the same reason. To American readers the most familiar form of the ganesha is that used by Doubleday, Doran and Company, Charles Scribner's Sons, and the Macmillan Company, the publishers of most of Kipling's works. The earlier forms of the ganesha that appeared on the Indian Railway Series, while protected by governmental registry, seem to have been largely abandoned in favor of the standardized form of later years.

Consciously or unconsciously, Kipling stamped his personality on the bindings and title pages of his books, rendering them as individual as their contents. Even the style of his autograph signature was personalized. His usual custom was to draw a line through his name as printed on the various

---

[4]**Soldiers Three, The Story of the Gadsbys, In Black and White, Under the Deodars, The Phantom Rickshaw,** and **Wee Willie Winkie.**

[5]See John Lockwood Kipling, **Beast and Man in India** (London, 1891), p. 232, for a discussion of the symbolism of these two devices.

[6]**The Kipling Journal,** no. 17, April 1931, p. 23.

title pages of his works and to place his signature immediately above or below the deletion.   When an inscription accompanied the autograph, it usually appeared above the title. [7]

This signature, in great demand from 1890 onward, is rare, for Kipling was by nature somewhat retiring and gave few autographs, except to acquaintances or to readers who wrote requesting them. His first gesture to an autograph-hungry public was as generous as it was humorous. According to one writer,

> Autograph collectors applied so frequently to Kipling for his signature that in self-defence he caused to be printed a little broadside or card, which stated that when he saw the applicant's name in the **New York Tribune** in the list of contributors of $2.50 to the "Tribune Fresh Air Fund," he would send his autograph. During the winter of 1894 and 1895 he distributed over two hundred to applicants. [8]

Illus. 1. Kipling's signature.

Deluxe and Limited Editions

Kipling's phenomenal popularity as a young author fortunately did no damage to his creative ability. He did not lower his artistic standards or stoop to capitalize on the demands for his signature. He preferred to earn his income simply by writing, and it should be said to his credit that he had a quarter century of steady writing behind him and a bibliography of 310 separate publications before his first autographed limited issue appeared in 1909. He was not, however, unmindful of the value of special printings, and eventually he capitalized upon them for a substantial profit. From 1892 to 1910, ten of his many publications appeared in limited issues in special bindings or on special paper. Four more appeared before his death. These issues were printed from the types set for the regular trade editions, the

---

[7] His characteristic style is reproduced in Flora V. Livingston's **Bibliography of Rudyard Kipling** (New York, 1927), p. 208.

[8] Ibid., p. 142.

number of copies usually being small--generally one or two hundred, never more than five hundred. He believed that his books belonged to the masses, and it was to the common man that he initially addressed his art. The books in the Indian Railway Library Series were paperback volumes that sold for one rupee, and this preference for the inexpensive volume continued throughout his career. He knew, however, that the discriminating purchaser preferred books with superior bindings and quality paper. It was to this type of purchaser that he offered the many deluxe issues and autographed editions of his works.

From 1909 onward he used the device of the special printing or the autographed edition with more frequency. Fourteen autographed special issues and autographed editions of his works have appeared, and shrewd business acumen seemed to guide him both in his business methods and in his selection of these works. In general, his practice was to follow up with special collected editions those of his works already popular in trade, taking care that the special edition was not a mere reprint. When new plates were made for the special edition, invariably the volume contained some hitherto uncollected work or a limited number of poems or stories published for the first time. Hence, each autographed volume became in effect a first edition. Much the same practice was followed in printing the more important editions of his complete works. The "Outward Bound" edition, the Edition de Luxe, and the Sussex edition of his complete works all vary somewhat in content. For example, the Sussex edition appeared posthumously and was limited to five hundred signed sets of thirty-five volumes. Each volume was bound in fine leather, printed on handmade paper, boxed in an individual slip case, and sold at the handsome price of fifty shillings. Yet the unique value of this edition lies not so much in its format but in the fact that it contains two volumes of uncollected material found in no other of the so-called complete works. His important collected editions, like so many of his autographed editions, are also first editions.

Bitter personal grief fell upon Kipling in his later years and did much to rob him of his natural spontaneity. Two of his children died tragically. The world war that he had so long predicted not only cost him his son but placed on him the public duty of serving the nation as a member of the War Graves Commission. On the physical side, the appearance of a duodenal ulcer caused him almost daily pain for the last two decades of his life, rendering him tense in body and troubled in spirit. During occasional periods when he found himself below the level of creative work, he turned as a sort of mental discipline to the task of revising and collecting his earlier works, a labor that accounts for many of his autographed and collected editions. While no figures are available, his earning power may well have increased rather than declined as age came upon him. He left a sizable estate acquired solely by the process of converting ink into ideas, and his success as a man of letters is ample evidence of his literary industry, his fine business acumen, and, in a more limited way, his wise use of the autograph.

For the benefit of readers who may be interested in the special and autographed Kipling issues, the following limited bibliography is given:

1892   **Lyra Heroica, a Book of Verses for Boys,** ed. by W. E. Henley. London: (two poems by Rudyard Kipling); 100 copies on large paper; 20 on Japanese paper.

1892   **Barrack-Room Ballads and Other Verses.** London: 225 copies on large paper; 30 on Japanese paper.

1896   **The Seven Seas.** London: 150 copies on handmade paper; 30 on Japanese paper.

1898   **An Almanac of Twelve Sports.** London: a few copies on Japanese vellum.

1898   **The Vampire.** New York: 500 copies on Enfield deckle-edge paper; 125 on Japanese paper.

1898   **Collectanea.** New York: 500 copies on Enfield deckle-edge paper; 100 on Japanese vellum.

1898   **Departmental Ditties and Other Verses,** 9th edition. London: 150 copies on large paper; 12 on Japanese paper.

1898-99   **The Dipsy Chanty.** New York: suppressed; about 60 copies in circulation from 100 illuminated copies and 950 plain copies.

(1899)   **The Betrothed.** New York: 500 copies on Strathmore deckle-edge paper; 100 on Japanese paper.

1903   **The Five Nations.** London: 200 copies on large paper; 30 on Japanese paper.

(1908)   **The Flag, the Book of the Union Jack Club,** ed. by H. F. Trippel. Contains Kipling's "The Marred Drives of Windsor"; 150 copies of the Royal Edition on handmade paper, bound in morocco, and presented to members of the royal family and to the contributors.

(1919)   **The Years Between.** London: 200 copies on large paper; 30 on Japanese paper.

(1929)   **The English Way.** London: a large paper edition in addition to a trade edition.

1929   **Lamentable Comedy of Willow Wood.** San Francisco: 100 numbered copies.

1897-1923   **The Writings in Prose and Verse of Rudyard Kipling,** "Outward Bound" edition. 30 volumes; 204 copies on Japanese paper.

Autographed Issues and Editions

1894-95   "**Tribune** Fresh Air Fund," (Broadside), signed; more than 200 given away.

(1909)   **A Song of the English.** London: 500 copies on special paper signed by the artist; 50 copies on vellum signed by artist and by author.

1910   **Collected Verse.** New York: limited edition of 150 copies; 125 copies on handmade paper, signed.

1912   **Collected Verse.** London: 500 copies on handmade paper; 100 copies printed on vellum, signed.

1913-19   **The Bombay Edition of the Works of Rudyard Kipling,** 25 vols. London: 1,050 sets, first volume of each set signed.

1918   **The Irish Guards.** New York: autographed edition of 100 copies, signed.

1919   **Inclusive Verse 1885-1918,** 3 vols. London: 100 sets on handmade paper, first volume of each set signed. New York: 250 sets on large paper, first volume of each set signed.

1920   **The Feet of the Young Men.** New York: limited edition of 377 copies, signed.

(1920)   **The Man to Watch.** San Francisco: limited edition of 170 copies, signed.

1926   **Sea and Sussex.** London: special issue of 500 copies on large paper, signed.

1927   **Songs of the Sea.** London: special issue of 500 copies on large paper, signed.

1929   **Poems 1886-1929,** 3 vols. London: 525 sets printed, first volume of each set signed. New York: 537 sets printed, 12 sets for presentation; 525 sets with first volume signed.

1934   **Collected Dog Stories.** New York: limited American edition of 450 copies signed by the artist, M. Kirmse; small paper edition containing a facsimile signature of Rudyard Kipling.

1937-39   **The Sussex Edition of the Complete Works in Prose and Verse of Rudyard Kipling,** 35 vols. London: limited, autographed edition of 500 sets, first volume of each set signed.

A Gilbert and Sullivan Collection*

Reginald Allen

I have been collecting Gilbert and Sullivan material for more than twenty-five years and have put together what is in all respects a triple collection: a Gilbert collection, a Sullivan collection, and a Gilbert and Sullivan collection. It must cover the prose, verse, and dramatic works of Gilbert as an author on his own or in conjunction with some collaborator other than Sullivan. It must cover Sullivan as a composer of innumerable songs, ballads, church music, and instrumental works, as well as works for the stage in which his collaborator was someone other than Gilbert. And it must cover, obviously, those fourteen collaborations between the two men, Gilbert and Sullivan, for a period of over twenty years.

Each of these three fields might easily make a field of collecting concentration by itself. I have only to outline the character of the general material that I have assembled to make this all too apparent. There are first those works in the actual handwriting of Gilbert and Sullivan, whether they be manuscripts of their creative efforts, letters, or miscellaneous signed or inscribed objects such as presentation copies of their works.

Next there is certainly the huge bibliographic field that involves the first issues of librettos or published volumes in the case of Gilbert; and sheet music, vocal scores, or full orchestral scores in the case of Sullivan. And from the fact that the Gilbert titles total more than fifty works for the stage alone and the Sullivan individual titles, including songs, are in the hundreds, one can see that this phase is in itself almost a life's work of collecting. It is also made doubly complicated because librettos and sheet music in the latter half of the nineteenth century were seldom dated. In the case of Gilbert, this situation is further complicated by the fact that he reduced his creative efforts to set-type early in his writing schedule very much the way the modern writer would move from one typewritten draft to another. We therefore have to face the possibility of prepublication, printed librettos in advance of the so-called first issue.

Then there are programs of the dramatic works of these two men. Naturally, first-night programs or programs of special performances form a necessary and attractive complication to this field for the collector.

---

*Originally published in 1953.

An already involved subject is rendered indescribably more complicated when one adds to his collecting sphere the American aspect of Gilbert and Sullivan, because here, with no international copyright restraining the potential items to be collected, there is a welter of unpredictable and largely undated material that still has background interest for one who wishes to study it.

Finally, the catchall designation of miscellany or ephemera in the field of Gilbert and Sullivan--especially in America--is a large and fascinating field in itself.   It contains such varied possibilities as trade cards, ad nauseam, inspired by the Gilbert and Sullivan operettas, paste figurines, china mugs, pressed glass, buttons, games, fans, and advertising handouts of infinitely varied description.   And this field is made even more attractive, and more exasperating, because these items are intrinsically almost worthless and are excessively hard to locate; yet they may well be in the attic or cellar of any family with seventy-five years behind it and thus may turn up in any small bookstore or antique shop, or even at a junk dealer's.

The Autographic Material

But now let us focus on one aspect alone: the Gilbert and Sullivan autographic material.   A few months ago, when I dropped in on my old friends the Drake brothers overlooking the public library in New York, they introduced me to George Matthew Adams, a collector of George Gissing.   For a moment, unaccountably, I felt at home in contemplating this man's field, although I am almost completely unfamiliar with Gissing's works.   Then I realized why.   I said to him, "You know I have always felt much more familiar with George Gissing than I have any right to feel.   Year after year, through hundreds of book and autograph-letter catalogues, I have thumbed quickly through the pages, always hopefully, until I come to Gissing, and the moment I reach that fateful name I realize there is nothing in the catalogue for me."   This is the basis for my feeling of familiarity with the works of Gissing.

In the field of Gilbert and Sullivan autograph letters, I had a nest egg left me by my father, a Philadelphia neurologist, who was himself a practicing Savoyard. He founded the Philadelphia Savoy Opera Company in 1901, a club that was then and is now dedicated to producing a Gilbert and Sullivan opera each year.   My father was the founder, stage director, and conductor.   My aunt, his sister, was the business manager and worked in the chorus.   My uncle was one of the male principals, and in their second production, **The Sorcerer,** my mother-to-be was one of the ladies of the chorus.   I do not believe I have to explain my interest in Gilbert and Sullivan any further.

My father was not a collector, but he had a collector's instinct for value, and as he was exceptionally interested in this field, he picked up in England in either 1911 or 1913 a letter from Sullivan to John Hollingshead, the man who produced **Thespis,** the first collaboration of Gilbert and Sullivan.   The letter is undated, although from interior evidence it can be dated to the day, probably July 31, 1879.   It is of particular interest and even importance, as it is one of the only surviving records of the existence of the score of **Thespis,** which has since disappeared without a trace.   The evidence that dates this letter so precisely is the sentence "I am retaining the parts of 'Pinafore' so that the Directors shall not take them away from the Comique tomorrow . . . ." This refers to the brawl staged by the directors of the Opera Comique when they tried to seize the scenery and properties of **Pinafore** on August 1, 1879, when their contract with D'Oyly Carte expired.

I inherited this letter from my father in 1918, and several years later, when I was an undergraduate in Cambridge, I made my first Gilbert collecting purchase: a pair of first issues of **Bab Ballads** and **More Bab Ballads** from Maurice Firuski, of the Dunster House bookstore, where I spent many pleasant hours.   My bibliographic appetite was trained and whetted by George Parker Winship at the Widener Library.   In fact, I blush to say that as a sort of thesis for him I prepared what I rashly called in those days a Gilbert bibliography, a feat for which today, twenty-six years later, I would hesitate to assume the qualifications.

From these beginnings, largely with the twenty-four-hour-a-day, year-round help of Mable Zahn of Sessler's, as friend, banker, and alter ego, I have amassed more than five hundred letters of Gilbert and Sullivan, in addition to a considerable number of other autographic items.   These letters seem to adhere pretty steadily to the ratio of three Gilbert to two Sullivan.   Despite the apparent relative scarcity of Sullivan items, it has also been apparent that, except in cases of exceptional merit, Gilbert's letters bring a higher price than Sullivan's.

Letters Reveal True Character

It is no new idea that through the accumulation of incidental letters of a creative genius, one can gradually build up a rare and vivid appreciation of the man himself, sometimes in better, truer focus than that which is distilled for us by the frequent and understandably biased pens of biographers.   I feel that I know the flavor, if you like, of William S. Gilbert and of Arthur Sullivan better from what I have of their own correspondence than from reading the many biographical and appreciative works written about them over the past fifty years.

For example, I have always been certain, based on my own collection rather than biographies, that Sullivan in his own way was a man of an extremely keen sense of humor, which not only translated itself into magnificent musical parody, but which necessarily matched Gilbert when the two men were in personal creative contact.   For example, I have a letter Sullivan wrote to Alan Cole, his close friend, and son of Sir Henry Cole, in which Sullivan starts out in what is apparently the most serious vein as follows:

My dear Alan:

I am not a rich man, but out of my small income I always contrive to set aside something for the relief of those not so fortunately placed as myself.

Your sad story touched me very much this morning, and if I claim the privilege of a friend and request your acceptance of the enclosed (which if to make things comfortable for all, and relieve you from the sense of obligation, we will consider as a loan that you can repay when and how you like), you will not, I trust, be offended but will accept it in the same friendly spirit in which it is offered.

In the meantime--work, my dear boy, work. Do not waste the precious golden hours of youth in the false, hollow existence you are now leading. Night into day--night into day, as the great father of a dissolute son used to say to him. (You have, of course, read "Sullivan's Personal Recollections of the Last 250 years.")

Be wise. Be earnest, ever striving after the ideal when men shall say hereafter, "He was awfully good form"!

Yours affectionately

A.S.S.

At the bottom of this letter there is a penciled note in the hand of Alan Cole, as follows: "enclosing a farthing wrapped up in paper."

In Gilbert's correspondence one repeatedly finds manifestations of the kindly man that many who knew him well have said he was. His kindness has been largely disregarded by biographers who are more interested in sensation achieved by carving individual sentences and episodes from their context. I have a letter in which Gilbert deliberately avoids a position in which he would be forced to be highly critical of his friend, the well-known actor Beerbohm Tree. What lends additional significance to this letter is that it recalls the famous Gilbert jest made at the expense of Beerbohm Tree. When Gilbert was asked his opinion of Beerbohm Tree's acting of the role of Hamlet, Gilbert is alleged to have remarked that Tree's Hamlet was "funny without being vulgar." Yet the same man wrote in a letter on May 16, 1886,

... but in any case I would rather not do that particular play for this reason. Beerbohm Tree (who will play "Paris") is an intimate friend of mine--I like him very much, but I detest his art, and in such a part as "Paris"--a blank verse lover--I am sure he will be entirely out of his element. I know I should have to abuse him, and this is just what I particularly do not want to do.

This is only an isolated instance that could be reproduced many times. Gilbert's true character was rather different from what one conjures in reading some of the highly colored passages describing his quarrelsomeness.

In my experience so far, autographed photographs of either Gilbert or Sullivan are very scarce, or at least they are certainly seldom on the market. The only autographed photographs I have of these two men cover their life spans with equal appropriateness. The first two Gilbert photographs, though undated, are from the 1870s; the final one is certainly only a few years before he died, possibly around 1908 or 1910. In Sullivan's case, the photographs are actually dated 1879 and 1899, respectively. A Gilbert photograph inscribed to Mrs. Alec Tweedy takes on a particular interest among autograph collectors because Mrs. Tweedy was herself a banner autograph collector in a very real sense. Her book **My Tablecloths** is a collection of reminiscences based on her predilection for having her dinner guests autograph the damask tablecloth of banquet size at which they sat, and which she apparently preserved.

The Mystery of the Middle Name

There is an interesting parallel between Gilbert and Sullivan in the story told by their letter writing, like the whorls in a slice of a tree trunk. Each used his middle name in his early career but abandoned it shortly thereafter. In Gilbert's case, his father, William Gilbert, was a Victorian martinet who wrote an enormous number of works in the latter half of the century but whose first work, oddly enough, coincided with the first work of his son, young William Schwenck Gilbert, in 1858. It is easy to imagine the older man's insistence that his son avoid using the name William; and since we can also appreciate the young Gilbert as a strong-willed fellow, it is equally plausible that he was damned if he would use the old man's name anyway. We therefore see the odd signature "W. Schwenck Gilbert" on the holograph manuscript of "My Maiden Brief," which he wrote for the **Cornhill Magazine** in December 1863. William Schwenck Gilbert is the illustrator of a book of verse called **An Algerian Monkey versus British Apes** (before he coined the pen name "Bab"). This name also appears in several individually published songs of the 1867-69 period. It also appears in the only known presentation copy of the first edition of **Bab Ballads** from the library of the late Carroll Wilson: "Cousin Annie from Cousin Schwenck."

Gilbert's use of his middle name appears to have been short-lived and does not intrude itself beyond the scope I have just outlined. I have never seen a letter of Gilbert's signed with it.

In the case of Arthur Seymour Sullivan, the young man up through his thirty-first year always signed his name as Arthur S. Sullivan, or Arthur Seymour Sullivan. In my collection I can place the change of this signature to within two weeks. The last date of a letter signed "Arthur S. Sullivan," or indeed any letter containing the middle initial, is October 8, 1873. I have a letter written on October 21, 1873, in which he signs himself "Arthur Sullivan," and from that date on I have no example of Sullivan's signature in which his middle initial or name is used. The explanation of this odd fact seems obvious, although it is partially conjecture, and I believe it has been suggested by one of his biographers. Sullivan frequently signed with his initials, and I have many such letters. It is suggested that some close friend, more than likely a young lady to whom young Arthur wrote a personal note signed with his full initials, called his attention to precisely what his initials spelled at the bottom of her letter, and young Arthur promptly stopped using them.

One finds that during June and July 1876 Gilbert actually made use of a primitive typewriter, one that had no lower-case letters. I have several letters typed on it--and I have only one other of Gilbert's that is typewritten, and that is one twelve years later when an upper- and lower-case typewriter was used. Sullivan apparently did not believe in the contraption. Sullivan, however, did believe occasionally, though infrequently, in having a secretary write his letters for him, and he merely signed. I have a number of such letters, particularly in 1893-94. Gilbert, except in some of his early manuscripts when possibly he wanted multiple copies, never resorted to a secretary for letter writing even though he was so plagued by gout on and off during the last fifteen years of his life that his handwriting became almost illegible and its execution must have been excessively painful.

Their Earliest and Latest Letters

The earliest Gilbert letter I have been able to obtain is dated May 30, 1863, when he was twenty-seven years old. For Sullivan my earliest letter is dated July 26, 1858, when he was only sixteen years old. This Sullivan letter is particularly interesting because it is to Sir George Smart, the musician and conductor, and really one of the most important leaders in British musical affairs in the first half of the nineteenth century. Sir George was instrumental in discovering the young Arthur Sullivan as a "wunderkind" and sending him to Leipzig, where he had the training from which he became immediately famous. Sir George really covered the field in that half-century--he conducted at the funeral service of George IV, at the coronation of William IV, and at the coronation of Victoria; and in his house Weber died, just a year or two after the opera **Oberon** was first performed in London.

A succession of other letters illustrates the key home addresses from which these two men habitually wrote. For Gilbert, the addresses were Essex Villas, 24 The Boltons, Harrington Gardens, and Grim's Dyke, his final home; for Sullivan, Claverton Terrace, Albert Mansions, and Queen's Mansions, his final home. My latest dated letter of Gilbert is a letter of May 7, 1911, twenty-two days before he died. In the case of Sullivan, it is an introduction for his nephew on a visiting card dated November 1, 1900, exactly three weeks before his death. Since Gilbert outlived Sullivan by eleven years, there are a greater number of interesting Sullivan letters in my collection from the early period and a greater number of Gilbert letters from the later period. The arbitrary point I set more than sixteen years ago for dividing the Gilbert and Sullivan letters each into two groups has proved to be practical and correct insofar as even division is concerned. I divide my Gilbert letters into those before Grim's Dyke and those during the Grim's Dyke period (dividing at 1890). For Sullivan they fall into those before Queen's Mansions and those during the Queen's Mansions period (dividing at 1882).

Presentation Copies

Presentation copies of Gilbert and Sullivan works are on the whole rather scarce, and presentation copies of their joint works are excessively rare. I have seen only one presentation copy of a Gilbert and Sullivan libretto

Illus. 1. With pun and picture Gilbert closed a letter of apology explaining
that an attack of gout would keep him from a friend's wedding.
Gilbert wrote, "I shall be physically unable to be present at your
wedding tomorrow. I have got it in both feet at once, which is
cowardly on the part of the gout, and if I presented myself in church I
would have to be on my hands with my feet in the air, which would
attract attention . . . . They call it 'gout,' and I can't g'out."

inscribed by Gilbert, and that is a prepublication copy of **The Pirates,** which
belonged to the late Carroll Wilson. In the case of presentation copies by
Sullivan of Gilbert and Sullivan operetta scores, I have seen only those that I
have in my own collection. There are five of them, three inscribed to Mrs.
Ronalds and two to her daughter, Mrs. Hay-Ritchie. I am very fortunate to
have these and two others associated with Mrs. Ronalds, who was the Boston-
born wife of Pierre Lorillard Ronalds. Mrs. Ronalds exercised a profound
influence on Sullivan throughout his entire adult creative life. No scrap of
autograph that passed between them has survived, even though they are said to
have written to each other every day. I have learned from Mrs. Ronalds's
granddaughter that the family house in London suffered a direct hit during the
blitz and was wiped out with everything in it. She was amazed to learn that I
had these treasures from her grandmother, which she recalled having seen in
the house before the recent war. I have no idea who removed them, and I am
only very glad they were removed.

The earliest dramatic work of Gilbert was a burlesque of **L'Elisir
D'Amore** entitled **Dulcamara, or The Little Duck and the Great Quack,**
December 1866. I have a presentation copy of this libretto inscribed by the
author to his sister-in-law-to-be, Grace Turner. This copy was part of a bound

group of librettos and therefore lacked cover- and endpapers. It is one of the rarest of the Gilbert librettos for the collector.

The late A. Edward Newton, in **The Greatest Book in the World,** wrote that the three volumes of Gilbert's collected plays in his library, each one inscribed with a complete stanza from one of the Gilbert and Sullivan operettas therein contained, were the only Gilbert presentation copies he had ever seen. I was fortunate enough to acquire these when Newton's wonderful collection was sold. They are all dated May 31, 1906. Newton refers to these as presentation copies to Captain Shaw, the head of the London Fire Department in 1882, who was immortalized in Gilbert's **Iolanthe** by the lines "Oh, Captain Shaw, type of true love kept under." I have always thought that Newton was overly hopeful in describing them as he did, and I think I understand his reason. The top line in Gilbert's hand reads, "Oh, Captain Shaw," and there is a pencil notation by some dealer on the facing endpaper that reads, "3 presentation copies to Captain Shaw." I can see no reason why, twenty-five years after **Iolanthe,** the aged Gilbert should suddenly be presenting such copies to the then aged Sir Eyre Massey Shaw, who died only two years later, especially when there is no reference in any Gilbert biography or letter which indicates that he and Shaw were friends. I should like to have proof of Newton's suggested provenance, but I doubt it can be proved.

All in all, my collection of presentation copies is peculiarly balanced by sheer coincidence. There are sixteen Gilbert presentation copies and seventeen of Sullivan. This is not quite a fair comparison because my Sullivan copies represent fifteen different works, whereas my Gilbert copies contain some duplication. The main reason for duplication in the field of Gilbert presentation copies, which must have escaped the notice of Newton, was the housewarming party the Gilberts had on October 30, 1890, at their new home, Grim's Dyke, when they entertained the cast of **The Gondoliers,** then playing at the Savoy.

It would appear that every guest received a copy of the newly published **Songs of a Savoyard,** each with an identical inscription:

To _____ with the author's kind regards and sincere thanks. 30th of Oct. 1890. Graeme's Dyke, Harrow Weald

The spelling of "Graeme's" in this inscription conforms with the embossing on the letterhead Gilbert used for the first year of his residence, after which his stationery was changed to "Grim's Dyke." I have three of these **Songs of a Savoyard.** The inscribed copies bear the names of Esther Palliser (Gianetta), Rudolph Lewis (Go-To and Old Adam), and Miss Watts (as yet unidentified). I know of four other copies, and I suppose there are a score or more still treasured privately in England.

Autograph Manuscripts

The field of holograph manuscripts, most important of all phases of autograph collecting, must necessarily be rather circumscribed in any Gilbert and Sullivan collection. Gilbert's virtually adopted daughter, Nancy McIntosh, has told me that it was his practice as soon as a new production was on the stage to sweep into the wastebasket next to his desk all the papers and notes concerning its creation. For this reason there have been preserved only such manuscripts as exist in the form of copybooks. McIntosh gave me one such copybook in which Gilbert set forth the story outline for his **Utopia Ltd.,** in which McIntosh sang the leading role. She also gave to the Pierpont Morgan Library a magnificent Gilbert copybook in which he developed **Iolanthe.** This book is probably the greatest surviving example of his painstaking method of creation, writing, and rewriting. I myself have his manuscript of the play **Great Expectations,** which he wrote from the Dickens novel, and another short comedy, **Highly Improbable.** Neither of these was ever published in his time, although both were produced in London. I have given these two to the Morgan Library, along with the original manuscript of one of his five grand opera burlesques, **The Pretty Druidess,** or **The Mother, the Maid and the Mistletoe Bough,** a parody of Bellini's opera **Norma.** For the most part, however, one must look to the D'Oyly Carte files in London for what remains of the original manuscript works of Gilbert and Sullivan operettas.

Sullivan's manuscript scores of Gilbert and Sullivan operettas are wholly unpublished. They were left in his will to his family and specific individuals or institutions, and of course complete working copies in manuscript are in the files of the D'Oyly Carte Opera Company. So far as I know, there is no such material in the hands of private collectors. For Sullivan's music manuscripts, the private collector must content himself with songs and church music and an occasional instrumental composition. Among other manuscripts, I have the manuscript of a song I have not yet identified that Sullivan apparently wrote and inscribed to Miss Mary Anne Harrold on September 13, 1864, at the time he was in Birmingham for the performance of his masque **Kenilworth.**

In addition, Sullivan was wont to embellish the memory books and guest books of his friends with bars of music, sometimes virtually complete songs, which occasionally come on the market for collectors.

I have two menus of particular Sullivan interest. One, dated July 21, 1893, is autographed by a distinguished company of musical personages including, in addition to Sullivan, Pietro Mascagni, Christine Nilsson, and Nellie Melba. The other, bearing the noteworthy date of May 13, 1900, is from Sullivan's last birthday party. It is an elaborate Savoy Hotel menu with the signatures of fifteen people close to Sullivan and the operettas, including Richard and Helen D'Oyly Carte, Mrs. Ronalds, Herbert Sullivan, Wilfred Bendall, Sullivan's secretary, and George Grossmith, who signed himself with the musical "G" repeated.

I have not mentioned the work of Gilbert the illustrator as a potential collecting field, and this should certainly not be overlooked. Unfortunately, there is little such material available. I believe most of Gilbert's originals for the **Bab Ballads** went straight from Grim's Dyke to the British Museum when he died. In some unaccountable manner the group of drawings he made for the **Ruddigore** lyrics, which appear in **Songs of a Savoyard,** became detached from the bulk of his illustrative material and fortunately arrived in my collection. I also have Gilbert's deft line-drawing of three costume sketches, presumably

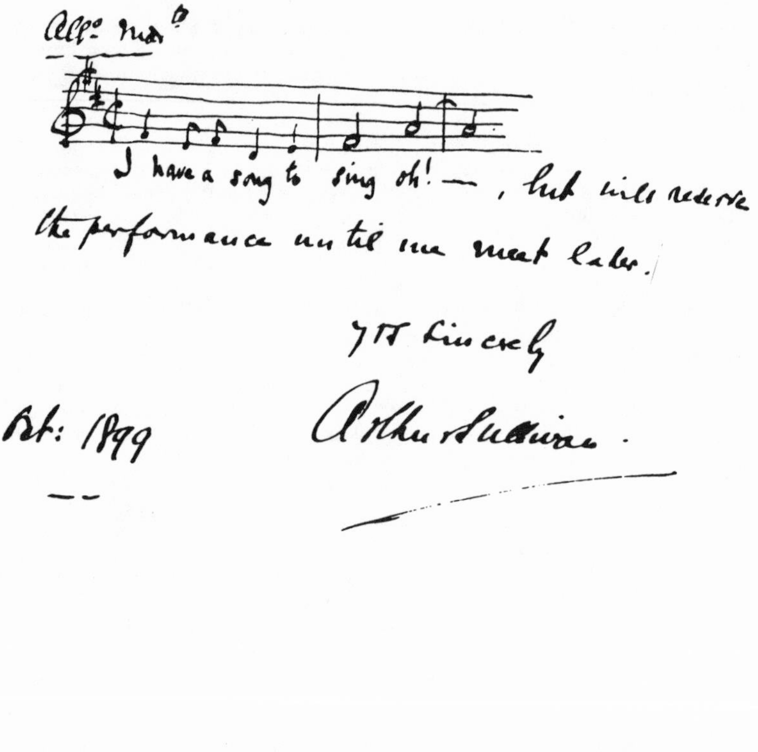

Illus. 2. A memory book page on which Sullivan obliged his friend Lady
Campbell Clarke with some notes from his popular duet from
Yeoman, "I have a song to sing oh!"

for the **Palace of Truth,** one of his early, blank verse plays that he wrote for John Buckstone in 1870.

My own favorite item, which occupies a position on my desk, is the original manuscript of "Is Life a Boon?", the lovely tenor aria from **Yeoman of the Guard.** This manuscript appears to have been sent by Gilbert to Sullivan signed only with his initials and bearing the day of the week, "Monday," without date. Sullivan wrote in his diary that he scored this song on Saturday, September 29, 1888. It is likely that my manuscript was sent to him on the Monday preceding, or September 24. Gilbert selected this quotation from their joint works as the inscription on the Sullivan monument that was erected on the Thames Embankment close by the Savoy Hotel.

At the request of Frederick Adams, director of the Pierpont Morgan Library, my collection is on permanent deposit there, and it is my aim to give the entire collection to that library in the course of the next few years. I hope this example may attract others who have material in this field so that there may be one great and permanent monument in the form of a comprehensive collection of the works of these two men available for study in this country as long as there are Savoyards to answer the call.

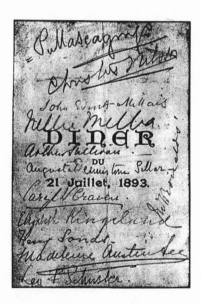

Illus. 3. Mascagni, Nellie Melba, Christine Nilsson, Millais (who painted Sullivan's portrait), and the ever-present Mrs. Ronalds were among the notables who were with Sir Arthur on this occasion and autographed this menu.

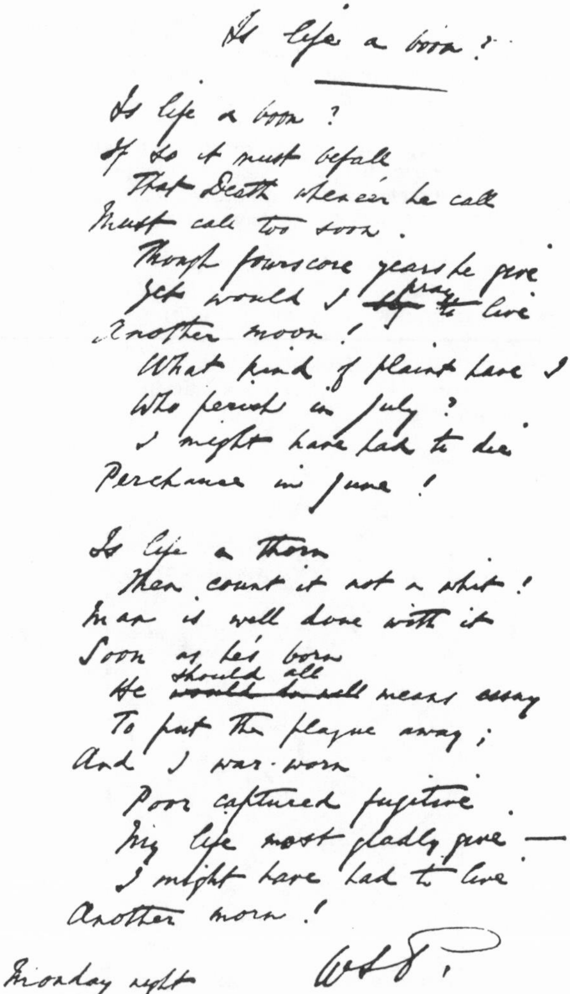

Illus. 4.   Original manuscript of "Is Life a Boon?" -- a beautiful tenor aria from **Yeoman of the Guard,** initialed by Gilbert and presumably sent to Sullivan in mid-September 1888 for him to set to music.

Illus. 5.   Gilbert embellished a friendly letter to his fellow dramatist Pinero with a deft cartoon of himself.

D. UNUSUAL COLLECTIONS
Franks, Frankers, and Franking*

Thomas J. Acheson

From the Old French word **franc** (free) comes the term applied to mail sent free of charge. Originally the privilege of "franking" was restricted to royalty, but by the late 1500s it was extended to various persons in the service of the king. In England, before the end of the reign of James I in 1625, franked mail was generally known as "King's Post." In 1660 there was introduced into the British House of Commons "A Bill for Erecting and Establishing a Post Office," and in the first year of the reign of Charles II we find the London General Post Office stamping the covers of franks with the month and day, enclosed in an outline. Forty-two years later (1702) post offices in the larger towns began to add the name of the town to the date.

The bill for establishing the first post office carried a clause providing that all letters to or by members of Parliament during that first session after the accession of Charles II were to be carried free. This clause was promptly stricken out by the House of Lords, but in its place was inserted a provision for free letters of the king and his great officers of state, and including single inland letters of the current Parliament. But the idea had taken hold that persons connected with the government, including members of Parliament, should be exempted from paying ordinary postal charges, all of which, incidentally, at this time were paid by the recipients of mail, not by the senders. Thus it came to pass that, more or less covertly, perhaps, many members of Parliament continued to use the privilege until 1764, when the practice was finally recognized by law.

Under the new statute, each member of the House of Commons or Lords was allowed to send ten or to receive fifteen free letters a day, each letter being restricted to one ounce and required to be mailed within the United Kingdom. However, the wording of the act failed to limit the free mailing privilege to letters actually **written by or to** the members; all that was required was the placing of the authorized signature on the cover by the ostensible sender. Flagrant abuses soon began to appear. Franking was on its way to becoming a wholesale business, as members supplied their families, friends, and constituents with stacks of presigned covers, to be used whenever they desired. It was not long before the practice reached the proportions of a

*Originally published in 1956.

major scandal. Huge packages, even men, women, cattle, and dogs were sent about the country post-free, with the result that the matter came up for heated debate in Parliament.

New and strict regulations were put into effect. All authorized frankers were required to write on their letters their signature, the full address of the recipient, the post town, and the day of the month. Letters were to be posted the same day or the day following within twenty miles of the address of the sender. The wholesale business suffered a sharp decline, but before long a new menace arose, even more sinister than the first. The wide distribution of signatures of important persons on open frank covers stimulated the interest of skillful forgers. Franking signatures were copied or even removed bodily from covers and at times were placed on such documents as promissory notes. These notes were then brokered or used as collateral by the forgers.

In consternation the members of Parliament hastily resorted to protective expedients. Some signed their franks in the most illegible script possible. From the very beginning to about 1720 it had been customary for a franker to write the word "Frank" over his signature; from 1720 the word "Free" was substituted. Now the word "Free" was combined with the signature, such as "Free-Grafton" or "Free-Orford"; or a line was drawn through the signature, as if to cancel it; or the "Free" was placed between Christian name and surname, as "Harold Free Tudor"; others wrote the word "Free" followed by Christian name and surname one above the other, or Christian name over "Free" over surname. Needless to say, specimens illustrating these devices are among the chief treasures of the collectors of franks. With the use of these unusual forms of signature, the menace of forgery began to lessen, and when a new law setting the penalty for frank forgery at death was followed by the execution of several persons convicted of the crime, offenses of frank forgery vanished almost completely.

Franks in America

Meanwhile, in America on November 8, 1775, franking had been introduced by act of Congress. At first the privilege was limited to the members of Congress themselves and to military leaders in the field. It was later extended to include the president, cabinet officers, senators, and some other government officials. Most American frankers added the familiar "Free" or their official title to their cover signatures, but it is noteworthy that George Washington sometimes wrote "President U.S." or "Pres.U.S." and omitted his signature. I have learned of no subsequent president who used this form. Of course, the American franking privilege was intended for official use only but, as in England, abuse soon became rampant. Economically minded first ladies were allowed to use this privilege of their illustrious husbands. Washington himself was not above "providing a cover" for a Mrs. Stuart on June 27, 1788, and Mrs. Lincoln used a frank to order a bonnet.

An act dated March 3, 1845, restricted franking to presidents, vice presidents, members or delegates in Congress, and postmasters. On March 3, 1863, the privilege was extended to the chiefs of executive departments, heads of bureaus, and chief clerks as designated by the postmaster general for their

Illus. 1. Lord Hotham (1799-1856), an Irish peer, franked a cover with a signature calculated to confound prospective forgers.

official business only; to senators and representatives for all correspondence; to senders of petitions to either branch of the legislature; and to publishers of newspapers for their exchanges. Since that time it has variously been allowed to new members of Congress before they take office, former members of Congress for the first nine months after their term expired, and to some other government officials. Also, by special acts, the privilege has been extended to the widows of Presidents Garfield, Grant, McKinley, Cleveland, Theodore Roosevelt, Harding, and Wilson.

In February 1873 an interesting innovation was introduced when attractive, adhesive departmental stamps were supplied. All franking was abolished as of July 1, 1873, but four years later the stamps seem to have been found to be a greater nuisance than the practice for which they had been thought a cure, and at this point the so-called penalty envelopes began to be used.

The Origin of Adhesive Postage Stamps in England

Returning to the late 1830s in England, we find a British schoolmaster named Rowland Hill, who noted the abuses of franking and the general confusion caused by collecting postal charges from the recipient. He conceived the idea of an adhesive postage stamp. Hill suggested, "Perhaps the difficulties might be obviated by using a bit of paper just large enough to bear the stamp, and covered on the back with a glutinous wash, which by applying a little moisture might be attached to the back of the letter." On January 10, 1840, Hill's stamps began to be used and parliamentary franking was abolished.

Two years later the postage stamp was adopted by a private postal service in New York City. The United States government issued its first stamps on July 1, 1847.

For the Love of Money*

Joseph E. Fields and Harley L. Freeman

Autograph collectors have long been familiar with those seemingly nondescript scraps of paper that once passed as the folding stuff of colonial and Revolutionary days. These notes are tolerated because many were signed by one or more of the prominent figures of the period, but autograph collectors usually do not rhapsodize over them for they bear only a signature of the famous person. The notes are taken somewhat grudgingly into the fold, either because of lack of a better example or because of a limitation on the funds to purchase better. Few of the signatures are rare. Thomas Lynch, Jr., Button Gwinnett, George Washington, and Benjamin Franklin never signed notes.

Most owners do not seem particularly concerned with the typography of their colonial notes, but there are those who treasure such currency, who collect it assiduously, and who are willing to pay prices that are continually mounting. The enthusiasm of the numismatist stems not from the signatures alone but from the significance the notes bear in our monetary, economic, and political history. The typophile is interested in them as examples of early typography and printing craftmanship. Ben Franklin is known to have printed many of the early Pennsylvania, Delaware, and New Jersey notes, and Paul Revere engraved the plates for the Massachusetts notes and bills of credit from 1775 until 1779.

Colonial and state notes were printed from economic, political, and military necessity. During Britain's struggle for world power in the seventeenth and eighteenth centuries, a high degree of self-sufficiency was believed essential for ultimate victory. We have come to call this "British mercantilism." It had as its goal the creation of an empire from which foreign trade and commerce were excluded as much as possible. The British colonies served a twofold purpose in this economic theory and their participation was essential for its success. Their first function was to supply the raw materials for goods to be manufactured in England. Second, the colonies were expected to consume a fair share of those finished products. The British merchant-manufacturers were thus in the unusual position of determining the prices they would pay for raw materials as well as the prices to be paid for the finished articles. Needless to say, they paid as little as possible for the raw materials and charged all the traffic would bear for the finished products. They leveled

---

*Originally published in 1959.

loaded muskets at the colonials while picking their pockets, and the various navigation and trade acts made it all quite legal and potentially enforceable.

The frequent colonial wars, in part financed by the colonies, made some type of financing necessary. With a shortage of hard money, created in large part by the mercantile practices, only one solution was possible--create more money via the printing press.

Colonial Currency Appears, and So Do Abuses

Colonial currency first made its appearance in Massachusetts. In 1690 the Massachusetts governor, Sir William Phips, planned an attack against Quebec. Insufficient money in the treasury made it necessary to borrow money in the colony to pay for the expedition. It was to be entirely a New England enterprise, for the mother country contributed no men, money, or material. It was hoped the booty captured would go far toward paying the costs of the enterprise. The expedition failed and the returning Massachusetts militia demanded their pay. There being insufficient money for the purpose, it was decided to create paper bills of credit to the amount of 7,000 pounds. Thus was created the first paper money put in circulation in British America. The bills were at first received skeptically but within a year were accepted as legal tender. The original issue was soon found to be inadequate, and in the following year, 1691, the limit of issue was set at 40,000 pounds. It was not long before all of British America got around to issuing paper currency.

Many abuses soon developed. Exports from England were largely financed by credit. By 1760 these exports were valued at about 2 million pounds annually. However, the debit side of the ledger showed 4 million pounds. Each year the debt mounted. The planters were at last obliged to pledge future crops of tobacco, rice, or indigo for additional credit. To make matters worse, the English merchants, in order to protect themselves, charged higher prices for their goods and higher carrying charges, and paid less for raw materials.

There were two ways out of the dilemma. The colonists could decrease their purchases or pay off their creditors in colonial paper currency. They either could not or would not do the former and thus chose the latter course. Inevitably, with no regulations in force, this course led to a deflation in the value of the currency and an inflation of prices, particularly in New England. For example, in 1702 it required 133 pounds of New England currency to purchase 100 pounds sterling, and by 1748, 1,100 pounds were required. The English creditors at last were sufficiently burned that Parliament in 1751 passed an act regulating and curtailing the use of paper notes in New England. Use of the notes as legal tender was forbidden. The notes could be used, however, for the payment of government expenses or in case of invasion.

By 1764 the notes had been declared illegal in the colonies, and they took on a diminishing role until 1775. All thirteen colonies made issues. Vermont, not one of the original thirteen, also produced an issue in 1781. There were eight Vermont denominations in all and these are among the rarest of all. With the outbreak of hostilities and the formation of the Continental Congress, the Congress also made a number of issues. They were known as Continental notes or currency and were to be acceptable in all of the colonies. After 1789 the states, under the new Constitution, were forbidden to coin money or issue currency. However, as late as 1835 some of the old notes were still being used as legal tender.

Illus. 1. Massachusetts forty-shilling note of 1708. On the original the monogram is overprinted in red. Only four examples are known, each of which is marked "counterfeit." The notes are genuine and it is entirely possible that this was an easy way for the colony to abrogate its obligation to redeem payment.

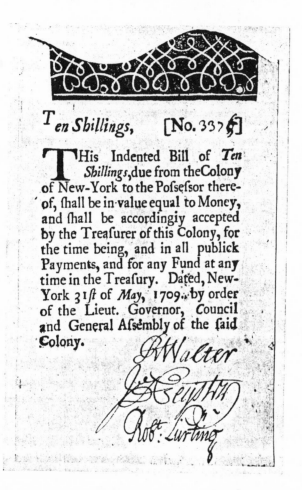

Illus. 2.   New York ten-shilling note of 1709, the first issue of that colony. It
was printed by William Bradford and is exceedingly rare.

Illus. 3.   Rhode Island half-crown (two shillings, six pence) note of 1743. Exceedingly rare.

Typography and Paper

Three types of typography were used on "the little brown notes," as they are affectionately called by the collecting brotherhood: engraved on metal and printed in intaglio, set in type and bearing type ornaments, and set in type with ornamentation engraved on wood. It is quite evident that these notes are far superior in design and letter styling to the currency issued by our present federal government, but that is a story in itself. Almost certainly the early issues of Maryland, South Carolina, and Georgia were made from plates engraved in England. Later, however, the plates were produced in the colonies.

The paper was of the best quality obtainable, but of course it was not reinforced by animal or vegetable fiber. Most of the paper was of rag content and was imported from the Wookey Hole Mill in England, although one Pennsylvania mill is known to have furnished paper. Some of the Virginia issues of a later date were printed on rice paper. Even Franklin had his thumb in the pie; he furnished the paper for the twenty-dollar Continental issue of May 10, 1775, the only note different in size and design of that entire series. The currency soon became dilapidated, and then began the practice of reinforcement by pasting paper on the back of the bill. Change was often made by halving and quartering the notes despite the efforts of the government to halt the procedure.

Illus. 4. Twenty-dollar note of the 1775 issue of the Continental Congress.
The paper was furnished by Benjamin Franklin.

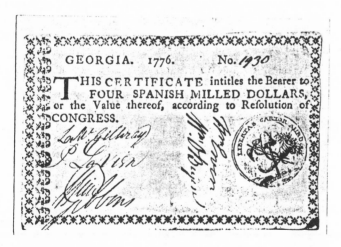

Illus. 5. Georgia note of 1776, printed in red and black with a vignette in blue.
Relatively common.

Illus. 6. Three-pound note of the 1776 issue of New Jersey. This is probably
the most beautiful note struck by any of the colonies. It is printed in
red, blue, and black.

Counterfeiting

Counterfeiting was first discovered as early as 1704. It continued to be
a problem regardless of all efforts to render the practice more difficult and
the punishments more unusual or severe. One of the early methods used to
prove genuineness was an "indentured" border. But because of wear and
mutilation this method proved of little value and the practice was finally
discontinued.   The numbering of the notes and the placing of qualified
signatures by hand before issue did serve to make the act of counterfeiting
more difficult and easier to recognize, but it did not wipe out the crime
completely.

Currency Collecting

To the best of our knowledge, between four and five thousand varieties
of currency (issues, denominations, plate letters, and minor variations) were
produced in the century from 1690 to 1789. The notes from New Hampshire
are the rarest. No collector has been able to build a complete collection and
there is little probability that at this late date the feat will ever be
accomplished. With the present scarcity of items and the substantial increase
in prices, a good collection consisting of 750 different items would be feasible.
Beyond that point the going is very rough, and depends on luck or wealth. It
should be noted that most collectors are willing to overlook indifferent
physical condition since most of the notes are badly worn and discolored and
the material is becoming scarcer.

It was probably the pioneer autograph collectors in America who first
became sufficiently interested in the notes to preserve them and build them
into collections. It is likely they were as much interested in the signatures as

they were in the typography and the interesting facet in American history they served to illustrate. And then there are those curious folks who will collect just about anything.

Two pioneer autograph collectors formed excellent collections: Dr. Joshua I. Cohen of Baltimore and Dr. Thomas Addis Emmet. Cohen's group was purchased a number of years ago by Henry Ford and is now at Greenfield Village. Emmet's collection, bound into several volumes, now forms part of the currency collection at the New York Public Library. Col. Theodorus Bailey Myers, an autograph collector of considerable repute, laid away a number of notes and these also are at the New York Public Library. Two other members of the autograph fraternity, Simon Gratz and Frank Etting, also gathered a respectable group, and these are now located at the Pennsylvania Historical Society.

One of the most extensive collections ever formed was that of Henry Chapman, a Philadelphia numismatic dealer. Chapman's collection was divided into two excellent groups. Following his death the best group was purchased by Frederick C. C. Boyd of Ringoes, New Jersey, the other by J. S. Spiro of Maplewood, New York. Shortly before Spiro died several years ago, he sold his collection to the American Antiquarian Society, sans the New Jersey notes.

The largest and finest collection ever formed was probably that of Frederick C. C. Boyd. The nucleus of his collection was the best of the Chapman collection supplemented by his purchase of the fine collection of T. James Clark of Jamestown, New York. Over the years Boyd added a large number of items. Our most recent list (1956), supplied by Boyd, revealed 2,029 different notes. By that we mean different issues, denominations, plate letters, or border varieties, but signature variations are not counted. If we were to count complete sheets and signature combinations, the total would exceed 4,200 items. This collection is especially strong in the very early issues of Massachusetts, New Hampshire, Rhode Island, and Maryland. What the disposal of this collection will be, following the very recent death of Boyd, is not known.

The second-largest collection, owned by Harley L. Freeman, includes about 1,720 different items. Counting the signature variants would bring the total to about 2,600 items. The collection is stronger than the Boyd collection in the southern colonies and states. It was formed by the purchase of several small collections and the addition of individual items over a long period.

Several other large collections have been formed. Otto C. Budde of Cleveland Heights, Ohio, has about 1,300 different issues. Wayte Raymond, a New York numismatic dealer, formed a fine collection, especially noted for the fine physical condition of the notes. Richard S. Rodney of New Castle, Delaware, has a fine collection of Delaware notes, consisting of about eighty pieces. George Wait of Glen Ridge, New Jersey, has about 450 varieties and a total of 1,100 specimens. A number of newer collections are being formed but it is doubtful if they contain more than five hundred different items. We are equally certain that collections exist of which we have no knowledge.

A number of institutions have good collections but in no way do they compare with the private collections. The American Antiquarian Society has probably the largest institutional collection, having acquired the Spiro collection to add to the society's existing group. The Ford collection, mentioned earlier, contains approximately 1,000 to 1,200 items. Of similar size is the New York Public Library collection, the nucleus of which consists of the Howes, Emmet, and Myers collections. Western Reserve Historical Society, Cleveland, has an impressive group of about 775 pieces. The American Numismatic Society, Massachusetts Historical Society, and New York Historical Society all have collections that contain approximately five hundred to eight hundred specimens. Only slightly less extensive is the Buffalo Historical Society collection. One of the better institutional collections is owned by the Chase Manhattan Bank, Museum of Moneys of the World, Rockefeller Center, New York. The collection consists of almost six hundred items, including a small number of duplicates.

The Connecticut Historical Society has a sizable collection consisting of about 950 different issues, collected by a former president of the society, Charles J. Hoadley. A list of the items was published in 1939. The Connecticut State Library also has a moderately large collection of about two hundred items, none of which have been surveyed. The New Hampshire Historical Society has a small group, the details of which are not available. The Essex Institute, Salem, Massachusetts, also is believed to have a moderately extensive collection but again an accurate appraisal is not procurable. The Massachusetts Archives Division has no currency in its files. The Rhode Island Historical Society has a fine collection, formed by the late Elisha Potter. It is particularly strong in the Rhode Island issues, and Potter published a monograph on the subject in 1880. The Rhode Island Archives Department has only a few unissued sheets of late date.

The New York State Library has only a few issues in its collection. The New Jersey Historical Society has a small collection of issues from that state consisting of thirty-six varieties. The New Jersey State Library has ninety-six pieces from several of the colonies.

The collection at the Pennsylvania Historical Society has already been mentioned. The Pennsylvania State Museum has a collection of about two hundred pieces, representing about fifty varieties. Both the Delaware Archives Commission and the Delaware Historical Society have small groups of notes from their colony and state. The Hall of Records at Annapolis has purchased a small group of Maryland currency. More extensive is the collection at the Maryland Historical Society which consists of about three hundred Maryland notes and about two hundred from other colonies and states. The Virginia State Library has a small collection of forty-two items, representing thirty-three separate varieties.

One of the best collections of Virginia notes is owned by the Virginia Historical Society. It consists of approximately 150 unduplicated issues with an additional 100 duplicates, the greater part of which was the gift of Dr. B. Randolph Wellford. A checklist has been published by the society. The North Carolina Department of Archives and History, which has about seventy-five pieces issued by that state, has published an interesting monograph on the subject.   The South Carolina Archives Department has an insignificant collection but in the near future may come upon additional issues among a quantity of as yet uncatalogued material that has recently come into its possession. The Georgia Department of Archives and History has no collection of currency issued by that state.   The Georgia Historical Society has only a small collection of Georgia and South Carolina issues, consisting of twenty-three varieties.

Few of the collections housed in institutions have been adequately appraised, catalogued, or integrated.   In several instances not even the exact number of items is known. Several well-known institutions seemed oblivious to their fine collections to the point of practically denying their existence.

The increasing interest and value of these colonial issues should serve as a challenge to the institutional owners to adequately survey and catalogue their collections.   Present microfilming and photostating techniques make it economically practical and physically possible for the task to be accomplished by any one of a number of experts.   A golden opportunity exists by which the desiderata of one institution might be satisfied by the sale or barter of duplicates from other institutions and private collectors.

Unfortunately there is no accurate list of all denominations, their dates of issue, and people authorized to sign them. A number of volumes have been written on the subject but not all the colonies have been covered and the information for some of those that have been is incorrect or incomplete. North Carolina, Georgia, and Maryland have never been accurately covered in any publication.   Rhode Island, New Hampshire, Massachusetts, and Connecticut issues warrant further study, especially as to the various overprinting of dates as additional issues were made.

Lottery Tickets—Where are They?*

Philip G. Nordell

I suffer from a rare disease--lottery ticket fever. It is not fatal, but it is incurable. The common symptoms are periods of chronic depression and insomnia mixed with fits of letter writing and research. Sometimes new medicine in the form of hitherto unseen and important tickets reduces the temperature and for a spell the worst of the symptoms may yield to seizures of hysteric enthusiasm. But these are not to be counted on. Depression and insomnia return. Brooding over those items that have eluded him, the distraught victim remains pervaded by a sense of futility.

The disease is hardly communicable. I have been instrumental in infecting only one other person--a prime authority in many fields, whose interests in Americana stretch from the little circular labels in old watches down to, or rather up to, letters of the Signers. He has now become so rabid on the subject of tickets as to be obsessed by various plate letters on some of them, a complication of the disease to which so far I am immune.

Another complication to be avoided is to work up more than an academic interest in the printers' ornaments that often distinguish tickets printed on the same sheet. Occasionally I have tried to assemble a set of such ornaments, when whole strips are not to be had, but the collector's health will be much improved by leaving them, as well as plate letters, alone; finding single tickets is enough of a job.

Rarity Plus Lack of Knowledge

Lottery ticket collectors are rarer than whooping cranes. I had an enlightening experience a year ago. Two dozen duplicate tickets of mine were returned by a good auctioneer for lack of bidders. And yet some of them were so rare that if they had been postage stamps they would have sold for hundreds of dollars each. You know the answer. If you own a brick from the front walk of the dwelling at Appomattox where two famous Americans faced each other, and if no one wants it, its market value--not its value to you--is nil.

In some cases, however, the prices of lottery tickets rise above the $2.98 level, and all autograph collectors are interested. At least, prices would rise

---

*Originally published in 1952.

and autograph collectors would be interested if only the tickets were to be had. All of you know of the Virginia ticket signed by G. Washington for the "Mountain Road Lottery" and the one signed by John Hancock for rebuilding Faneuil Hall. And there are those signed by William Byrd and by Lord Stirling. As lottery tickets go, they are common. There must be a dozen or two or three of each of these around. They must, it is true, form some of the foundation stones in any lottery collection, and yet they do not put a glint in my eye. They are old stuff.

But what of the other tickets signed by persons not forgotten by all of us? I know of three tickets signed by William Henry Stiegel. There is one extant signed by Stephen Hopkins. If I were living back in pre-Revolutionary days and took the notion to collect lottery tickets hot off the press, I would try to pick up some signed by George Ross, Caesar Rodney, Robert Morris, James Wilson, Benjamin Rush, George Mason, John Blair, Carter Braxton, Richard Henry Lee, Benjamin Harrison, Philip Livingston, and Benjamin Franklin.

Few Are Left

Where are they now? George Ross, for example, in his capacity as a lottery manager signed at least 340 tickets. None of the persons who should know has ever heard of one still in existence. Benjamin Franklin was a manager of several lotteries. To my knowledge, of the 44,000 tickets printed in these lotteries only four are now extant, and, unfortunately, none of these bears his signature.

At another time it is my hope to discuss such tickets with important signatures whether they are known to exist or not, but this article is on the rarity of tickets in general. The examples are presented with the warning that the figures used are "subject to change without notice." From 1770 to 1775, a rash of lotteries took place in New York, New Jersey, Pennsylvania, and Delaware. I have records of ninety-five of them. Of these I know of extant tickets in only twenty-four. Of the thousands of lotteries in all the colonies, provinces, and states, my guess is that there are known tickets in about the same proportion--one quarter.

For certain periods both before and after the Revolution, some very good runs of tickets could be assembled if all those known to exist were brought together. Perhaps tickets of Massachusetts could make the most impressive showing, but even here there are wide gaps. One may correctly infer from these statements that except for isolated strong spots, no collection of tickets is more than a scattering.

Up to about 1825, tickets of the southern states are far rarer than those of the northern. I know of only a few tickets of Louisiana, Georgia, South Carolina, and North Carolina before 1825, and yet those four governments authorized a total of about 200 lotteries before this date. Alabama, Mississippi, and Tennessee authorized a combined total of nearly two hundred lotteries, both before and after 1825, and yet I do not recall ever having seen one of their tickets.

Some Are Common

Most readers probably are familiar with the common lithographed and colored type of ticket in vogue after 1830 up to Civil War days. There are three different numbers on each, from one to seventy-eight, and combinations or permutations of these were used in determining the lucky winners in a matter of minutes. Like horse races in our enlightened age, lotteries were big business in those years, with a variety of drawings available to the plunger every day. Most of these "ternary" tickets are close to the dime-a-dozen class. But there are rarities even here. A blissful dream for any collector would be to find an album filled with Vermont and Maine tickets. And the Missouri State Lottery, with drawings based on either the ternary or single number plan, ran for years with drawings every day except Sundays. Millions of these tickets must have been printed, and yet I know of only one survivor. Somehow, I feel hundreds still exist in such repositories as old cigar boxes.

At this moment I believe all the tickets shown in the illustrations are unique. The Connecticut ticket (illus. 1) was issued at a time when New Haven still had dreams of being an important seaport. It was signed by Jared Ingersoll, the father of the signer of the Constitution of the same name. The New Jersey ticket (illus. 1) was for the benefit of St. Michael's Church of Trenton. Of the more than a dozen lotteries of this province prior to this one, not a single ticket has survived so far as I know. The Boston ticket (illus. 1) was to repair the very narrow neck of land connecting the Boston peninsula to the Roxbury mainland before the Back Bay was filled.

From the title one would never guess the "Biles-Island" ticket (illus. 2), undated but of 1771 vintage, was of a New York City lottery. The purpose of this lottery in part was to dispose of real estate in the present downtown section of the city. As a means of circumventing the lottery laws of the period it was drawn on Biles Island, in the Delaware River a little below Trenton, over which neither New Jersey nor Pennsylvania exercised any jurisdiction.

During the second half of the eighteenth century, Philadelphia was not only the largest and most important city in the American colonies but the second-largest city in the British empire. Illustration 3 shows two Philadelphia lottery tickets. The one signed by Philip Syng the silversmith is from a lottery to raise money to purchase a public landing at a point along the Delaware River and to pave some of the city streets. The lottery was run in four classes with a total of 20,000 tickets, but this is the only ticket I know to have survived.

Christ Church in Philadelphia has an honored history besides the fact Washington and Franklin were pewholders. The building itself is one of the priceless jewels of the city, completed except for the steeple more than two centuries ago. The church raised money for construction by means of two successful lotteries advertised in 1752 and 1753. There are various "Christ Church Lottery" tickets in existence and off and on during the last half-century it was supposed one or the other of these was for the benefit of this church, but they were connected with others of the same name. It can be definitely stated that the "Philadelphia Steeple Lottery" ticket shown in

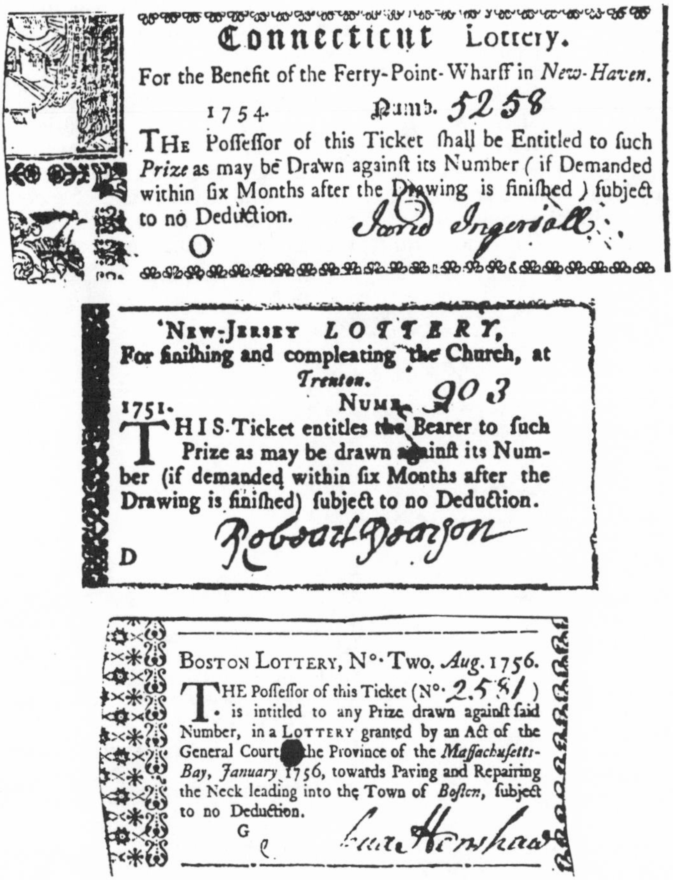

Connecticut Lottery.

For the Benefit of the Ferry-Point-Wharff in *New-Haven*.

1754.   Numb. *52 58*

THE Poffeffor of this Ticket fhall be Entitled to such *Prize* as may be Drawn against its Number (if Demanded within fix Months after the Drawing is finifhed) fubject to no Deduction.

O   *David Ingerioll*

'NEW-JERSEY **LOTTERY**, For finifhing and compleating the Church, at *Trenton.*

1751.   NUMB. *903*

THIS Ticket entitles the Bearer to fuch Prize as may be drawn againft its Number (if demanded within fix Months after the Drawing is finifhed) fubject to no Deduction.

D   *Robert Pearson*

BOSTON LOTTERY, N°. Two. *Aug.* 1756.

THE Poffeffor of this Ticket (N°. *2.5 81*) is intitled to any Prize drawn againft said Number, in a LOTTERY granted by an Act of the General Court of the Province of the *Maffachufetts-Bay, January* 1756, towards Paving and Repairing the Neck leading into the Town of *Bofton*, fubject to no Deduction.

G   e   *Henshaw*

Illus. 1.   Some rare lottery tickets.   The Connecticut and New Jersey tickets are from the Historical Society of Pennsylvania; the Boston ticket is owned by the author.

BILES-ISLAND LOTTERY.

N° *5202*]   O

THE Poffeffor of this TICKET, is intitled to fuch PRIZE as fhall be drawn against its Number.

Illus. 2.   Biles-Island lottery ticket.

illustration 3 is the only one that has come to light for either of the lotteries run by Christ Church on North Second Street, Philadelphia. It is purely coincidental that the number coincides with its date.

As already indicated, there are many hundreds of lotteries of which no tickets are known today. Where are they? The managers called in the prize tickets and usually, when the lottery accounts had been settled, these would be destroyed. But in the average lottery, less than half the tickets bring prizes. What happened to the blanks not turned in? Who saves raffle chances today? Once the turn of the wheel exploded the dreams of fortune, the piece of paper had less reason to exist than Continental money or old canceled checks.

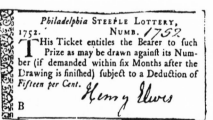

Illus. 3. Philadelphia lottery tickets.

Sometimes the managers preserved the prize tickets. And a few books remain of sheets of tickets unsold and undetached. But I imagine most of those that have come down to us were saved by the type of person who simply cannot throw things away, and as the heirs in each generation burned the family papers a few of these tickets escaped.

Collectors began attaching value to postage stamps by Civil War days, and thus great numbers of them were saved from the kitchen stove. And of course when letters were saved, the envelopes would often be kept with them. Uncanceled stamps retained their value. Stamps being everywhere, it was easy to start a collection. The more collectors, the greater the demand and the more diligent the search. In contrast, old lottery tickets could scarcely be regarded as other than utterly worthless. There were not enough to go around and to form competitive collections. Much more than stamps or letters or documents, they have gone with the wind.

Part 3.
HISTORICAL
DOCUMENTS

The Bogus Washington Commission*

Victor Hugo Paltsits

About a dozen years ago, in my official capacity as chief of the American History Division and keeper of manuscripts in the New York Public Library, I was consulted about some Washington manuscripts in the possession of the Washington Headquarters at Morristown, New Jersey. I identified one of the letters as a Robert Spring forgery; the others were genuine, but needed attention for preservation. I so advised Elbert Cox, then superintendent of Morristown National Historical Park. I understood that most of the Washington items, if not all, had been given to the headquarters by the well-known collector of autographs, Ferdinand J. Dreer of Philadelphia, who was known for his liberality.

On January 12, 1937, Clyde Potts, mayor of Morristown, wrote to me as follows:

> I am sending you herewith the following photostat samples of the handwriting of Timoth[y] Matlack. One dated June 12th 1775 was written within a week of the writing of the Washington Commission and the similarity is so striking that it would seem anybody could believe that it was his handwriting. The request of Matlack for a substitute to serve in his stead, I think, was written a year or so later--I am not sure of that. The other is dated, Philadelphia, July 2nd 1776 which was a little over a year later.

> I am enclosing a copy of the original printed Minutes of the Continental Congress which gives the wording of the Washington Commission as it was published. You will notice from this that the published Commission differs in a number of particulars from both the Morristown Commission and the Library of Congress Commission.

On January 25 Mayor Potts wrote again, in his own hand, as follows:

> Enclosed herewith is a first drau?ht of Mr. Albert S. Osborne's [sic for Osborn] Report on the Washington Commission. After you have finished with it I would be pleased to have you return it with your comments. We want to get it in final form at some early date.

---

*Originally published in 1948.

With the items sent to me by Mayor Potts, the alleged manuscript commission was placed in my custody. I had been told that the body of the alleged commission was written by Timothy Matlack, clerk in the Continental Congress, and that, since the document was folded to a square, it must have been folded so by Washington for convenience to carry it on his person, which could not be done with the large engrossed original commission he had received that is now in the Library of Congress. The signatures of John Hancock and Charles Thomson were considered to be genuine.

In my first studies of the alleged commission I soon rejected the idea that Matlack wrote the body. The signatures of Hancock and Thomson I compared with numerous undisputed originals. The Thomson raised a doubt in my mind, but the Hancock was a stumbling block because of the influence of the opinions that had been given me. I then set aside all opinions from other people. My independent conclusions, reported on March 13, 1937, are reprinted later in this article. But since that report was made, interesting evidence has come to my view, showing that just a century ago this alleged commission was the subject of an exchange of correspondence between David Ames Wells and Jared Sparks. Wells was born in Springfield, Massachusetts, on June 17, 1828, and graduated from Williams College in 1847. For a while in 1848 he was a member of the editorial staff of the **Springfield Republican,** and it was in that year that we connect him with the document in question. Wells, who became a distinguished economist and public man, died on November 5, 1898. Wells apparently wrote to Sparks about the document, for Sparks's reply, dated Cambridge, September 18, 1848, has survived. This original Sparks letter came from the Wells family and is now in the Manuscript Division of the New York Public Library. The full text is as follows:

> I have always supposed that when Washington resigned his commission at the close of the war, he actually gave back to Congress the identical commission he had received when he took command of the army. This commission I conceive to be the one, which is now in the Department of State.[1] I cannot say, however, that I have seen any positive proof that such are the facts, but, all the circumstances considered there is no doubt on my mind.

> How the commission you mention should be in existence I cannot explain. I think it certain there could not have been two commissions; but it is possible that a copy may have been sent to the Virginia delegates in Congress, especially as the commission was drafted by Richard Henry Lee, as chairman of the Committee of Congress appointed for that purpose.

---

[1] It was later transferred with other Washington manuscripts to the Library of Congress.

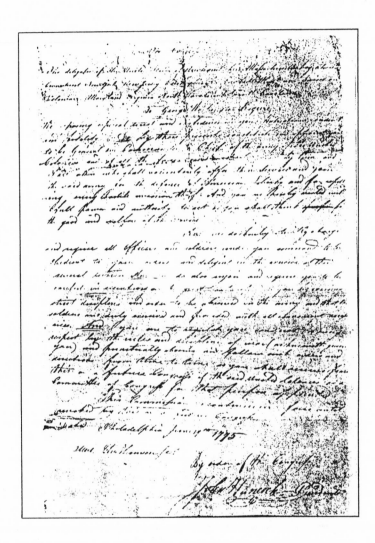

Illus. 1. The bogus Washington commission is in Morristown National Historical Park, New Jersey.

The Commission, as reported, is printed in the Journals of the Old Congress under the date of June 17th 1775. Why Hancock's signature should be affixed to such a copy, or why it should be written on parchment,[2] it is difficult to explain. The genuine commission was also attested by Charles Thomson as Secretary.

There would seem to have been no motive for forging such a document; and, without seeing it, I cannot form an opinion as to the genuineness of the signatures.

The commission as printed by Judge Marshall is an exact copy from the Journals of the Old Congress, except the omission of the word "do" in one instance.

The Report

I have been asked by Elbert Cox, superintendent of Morristown National Historical Park, and the Hon. Clyde Potts, mayor of the town of Morristown, New Jersey, to examine a certain folio sheet of paper, alleged to have written upon it a commission to George Washington as "General and Commander in Chief of the army of the United Colonies," and "Dated Philadelphia June 19th 1775," subscribed "By order of the Congress John Hancock President," and bearing "Attest Cha Thomson secy." In this report this folio sheet of paper will be referred to as "the Morristown manuscript." This paper has been mounted on a textile of linen or cotton, and the back has remnants of a paper edging, probably from a former framing of it. The face of the paper bearing the alleged commission has been heavily covered with a kind of varnish, greatly discoloring it. These mistreatments of the Morristown manuscript are disadvantageous to its fullest examination.

Potts submitted to me, for consideration in connection with the Morristown manuscript, four photostats, and thirteen typewritten pages of an unsigned "Report of Examination of Washington Commissions," stated by Potts to be "a first draught of Mr. Osborne's Report on the Washington Commission." In the Osborn report the Morristown manuscript is compared with the finely written, or engrossed, commission to Washington as commander in chief that is in the possession of the Library of Congress and is familiar from facsimile reproductions in books. This latter commission will be referred to as the Library of Congress commission.

The Library of Congress commission to Washington was engrossed by the same hand that engrossed in similar form and purport the commission to Horatio Gates as "Adjutant general," bearing the date of June 19, 1775, signed by Hancock and attested by Thomson. The original Gates commission is owned by the New York Historical Society.

---

[2]The document is covered with a varnish or other substance. As a result Wells mistakenly believed the document to be parchment.

The heading of the Library of Congress commission begins, "In Congress The delegates of the United Colonies," and, further on, the words used are, "constitute and appoint you to be General and Commander in chief of the army of the United Colonies." The same designation of "United Colonies" is given in the same related places in the Gates commission.

The Morristown manuscript begins, in the heading, "In Congress The delegates of the United States," and, further on, the words used are, "constitute and appoint you to be General and Commander in Chief of the army of the United Colonies." This discrepancy is a damaging fact.

My data relating to the journals of the Continental Congress refer to the printed volumes called **Journals of the Continental Congress . . . Edited from the original records in the Library of Congress by Worthington Chauncey Ford.** Dr. Ford says the journals of 1775, the year we are particularly considering, were "transcribed from the original record of the Secretary, Charles Thomson."

Washington was a delegate to the Congress and on June 14, 1775, was made one of the committee voted "to bring in a dra't (draught) of Rules and regulations for the government of the army." The next day (June 15) the Congress "Resolved, That a General be appointed to command all the continental forces, raised, or to be raised, for the defence of American liberty"; and then "The Congress proceeded to the choice of a general, by ballot, when George Washington, Esq. was unanimously elected." On June 16 President Hancock

> from the chair informed Geo: Washington Esqr. that he had the order of the Congress to acqu(ain)t him, that the Congress had by a unanimous vote made choice of him to be general and com(mander) in chief to take the supreme command of the forces raised and to be raised, in defence of American Liberty, and desired his acceptance of it.

The full report of Washington's response to the Congress is printed in volume II (1775), page 92.

When Washington had completed his address and acceptance, with qualifications, it was upon motion "Resolved, That a committee of three be appointed to draught a commission and instructions for the general" (ibid., p. 92). On Saturday, June 17, the Congress "met according to adjournment," and "The committee appointed to draught a commission to the general, reported the same, which, being read by paragraphs and debated, was agreed to and is as follows" (p. 96). Here follows the text of the commission "Dated, Phila. June 17, 1775." It was then also "Ordered, That the same be fairly transcribed, to be signed by the president, and attested by the secretary, and delivered to the General."

So far the printed journals carry the record. The Library of Congress commission is a "fairly transcribed" document. It was also dated by the engrosser "June 17" to conform with the date of the order. It was altered by Hancock when he signed the commission on the nineteenth by making a nine out of seven. The Gates commission was dated "19" by the same engrosser. Is it not reasonable to believe that both of these commissions came to Hancock for signature at the same time, and that he made them conform in date? It was on Monday, June 19, "Ordered, That the secretary get a number of commissions printed, with proper blanks, for the other officers" (p. 100). These were to be used for the rest of the military establishment that had been named on the seventeenth to expedite commissioning so many others.

At no time in the year 1775 or the first months of 1776 did the Continental Congress ever in its journals or other official records, whether written or printed, use the form "United States." They were always "colonies" or "United Colonies," or "the English colonies on this continent." It is so in the rules and regulations made in the Congress for the Continental Army, in the Declaration on Taking Arms, in the Militia Act, and in the Articles of Confederation. In fact, in the committee presentation on July 21, 1775, of the "Articles of Confederation and perpetual Union," article I reads, "The Name of this Confederacy shall henceforth be **The United Colonies of North America**" (p. 195).

The Declaration of the Congress to General Howe in January 1776 reads, "the Representatives of the United colonies." In the Address to the Colonies, in February 1776, the Congress answered the accusation of some that carrying on the war was "for the Purpose of establishing an independent Empire." The address stated, "We disavow the Intention. We declare, that what we aim at, and what we are entrusted by you to pursue, **is the Defence and Re-establishment of the constitutional Rights of the Colonies.**" In April, May, and June 1776, the designation "United Colonies" continued in use. At the end of June 1776, when separation was intended and drafts of the Declaration of Independence were being prepared, the delegates were called "Representatives of the United States of America." It was on July 2, 1776, that this separation was declared by resolution in the Congress, in these memorable words: "That these United Colonies are, and of right, ought to be Free and Independent States."

This was the first official order representing the colonies to be "States." It was later confirmed by the Articles of Confederation and perpetual Union, in the first article, reading, "Art. I. The Name of this Confederacy shall be THE UNITED STATES OF AMERICA" (**Journals,** vol. V, p. 546).

These records indicate that the words "United States" could not appear in an official manuscript issued in 1775 by the Continental Congress. Further, in his edition of the **Journals,** Ford (vol. II, 1905, pp. 96-97) writes in a footnote to the text of Washington's commission:

> The original is in the Library of Congress . . . . At the Washington Headquarters, Morristown, New Jersey is a paper which purports to be this commission, or its earliest form. It was found in a shoemaker's shop by David Ames Wells, and he gave it to George Washington Childs, from whom it passed to Ferdinand J. Dreer, who presented it to the Headquarters. It is of doubtful value.

This was a polite way of condemning the Morristown manuscript.

Examination of the paper on which the alleged commission is written is hampered by the mountings and varnish. But enough can be seen for the purpose of this inquiry. In one corner is visible, by holding up the paper before a strong light, early nineteenth-century writing, and these words can be made out:

to (   ) Keep ‡ quaere
Write to Balto immediately
pages 10 and 11 of (the) book of
                    Deeds

By holding the Morristown manuscript face forward with an electric light behind, avoiding certain daylight cross-lights, there is visible at the top the watermark of the paper manufacturer and the date, 1809. I have a hunch that the paper may have been made in Maryland or a nearby state, but an extended search would be necessary to confirm the true place of manufacture.

Oath of Allegiance, 1778

John F. Reed

In February 1778, Congress was enmeshed in seemingly insoluble debates at its place of exile in York, Pennsylvania, the British having ousted it from Philadelphia. In the course of these debates Congress passed a law that seemed to cast some doubt on its own faith in the result of the War of Independence. Although the law was aimed at civilian and soldier alike, the target in main was the military. Congress, being civilian itself, was obsessed with a need to control as it might the military situation. Civilians often misunderstand the actions of soldiers, and soldiers similarly misunderstand the actions of civilians. They rarely seem, as history shows, at one in the prosecution of war or in mutual trust when danger threatens. Each group unfortunately seeks the upper hand and tends to meddle in the affairs of the other. Chaos sometimes results, or nearly so. In this instance, however, such a result was happily averted since the weapon of law employed was not sharp-edged enough to slash the mutual bonds of liberty that bound civilian and soldier together.

Thus, on February 3, 1778, Congress, struck by the disease of mistrust, rose to meet the fear with a nostrum of law. Unjust, or seemingly unjust, law rightfully breeds another disease, discontent; and it was unjust law against which patriots were fighting. Fortunately the laws of Congress were held in less contempt, when contempt was present, than those of Parliament, or the Revolution might have ended by simple dissolution on many occasions. But Congress, fearing the insidious acts of traitors, whether real or fancied, bowed to the report of a special committee set up by Congress itself to devise effectual means to exclude the disaffected from the ranks of patriots, civilian and soldier alike. The committee and Congress believed that oaths of allegiance were the surest answer to the problem. A man's conscience, Congress naively argued, was perhaps a sufficient restraint from the breaking of such an oath. However, oaths, despite their value to Congress, **were** broken on occasion. Both Charles Lee and Benedict Arnold had taken them.

Although civilian oaths were often administered, we are here concerned with the military. Undoubtedly there was a good deal of grumbling about the statute in question. It specifically required that an oath of allegiance should be sworn or affirmed, as the declarer's conscience ruled, to the United States

---

*Originally published in 1961.

by every officer committed to the birth and defense of the infant nation. These oaths, a number of which survive, were generally printed, many by John Dunlap, the printer of the Declaration, on a scrap of paper measuring about 6-1/2 by 4-1/2 inches, but longhand oaths were employed whenever a shortage of printed forms occurred. The wording was duly prescribed by Congress as follows:

> I _____ do acknowledge the UNITED STATES of AMERICA to be Free, Independent and Sovreign States, and declare that the people thereof owe no allegiance or obedience to George the Third, King of Great-Britain; and I renounce, refuse and abjure any allegiance or obedience to him; and I do [swear or affirm] that I will, to the utmost of my power support, maintain and defend the said United States against the said King George the Third, his heirs and successors, and his or their abettors, assistants and adherents, and will serve the said United States in the office of _____ which I now hold, with fidelity, according to the best of my skill and understanding.

The oaths, as originally worded by Congress, closed with the prayerful phrase "so help me God," but this was soon deleted, for none of the forms surviving include it. The oaths were signed in duplicate. The swearer, or affirmer as the case might be, kept the original, which might be defined as a sort of passport to a patriotism already proved. The certified duplicates were returned to headquarters and entered the records to satisfy Congress. According to the records, no officer, from commander in chief to ensign, declined to sign, whatever his personal feelings regarding this palpable lack of trust by Congress may have been. Later such oaths became accepted as a matter of course, but not in 1778. A patriot's word and deeds, and the fact that he risked his life to keep the Congress alive, seemed oath enough. No printed or written oaths were needed; but oaths there were and oaths were signed.

Washington's orderly book states for May 11, 1778, that "The general officers are requested to meet at Head Quarters at 11 o'clock tomorrow, A.M., that they may take the oath appointed by Congress in a Resolution of the 3rd of February last, which was published in the order of the 7th instant." On May 12 the generals assembled at the gray stone house at Valley Forge where their leader held his headquarters. Since he was senior in rank, Washington himself was undoubtedly the first to sign. He set an example for the others, so that they could scarcely question the measure. One by one the ranking officers followed, probably in order of seniority, for a list exists reporting this manner of signing, though names of some who did not serve at Valley Forge are included. After each general signed, Washington witnessed the oath. Washington's own oath was witnessed by Stirling. All these oaths, fortunately, survived the fire in the War Department in 1800.

This was the official beginning of the taking of oaths, although some oaths apparently were taken earlier. According to the law, not only commanders themselves, but also major generals and brigadier generals could witness the oaths of the lesser in rank. On May 7 Washington had appointed the following officers to witness oaths:

Stirling, the late Conway's brigade (Conway had been relieved for
   involvement in the Conway Cabal)
Lafayette, Woodford's and Scott's brigades
De Kalb, Glover's and Learned's brigades
McIntosh, his own North Carolina brigade
Knox, the artillery and officers of military stores
Poor, his own brigade
Varnum, his own and Huntington's brigades
Paterson, his own brigade
Wayne, his own division (1st and 2nd Pennsylvania Brigades)
Muhlenberg, his own and Weedon's brigades
Greene, commissary departments (both purchasing and supply) and
   the medical department.

That oaths preceded the official commencement is proved by the surviving oath of Lt. Lewis Thomas of the 13th Virginia, witnessed by Muhlenberg, now in the author's possession. It is dated May 11, the day preceding the headquarters signings. The swearing and affirming went on through May into June. Many of the oaths signed in Wayne's division are datelined "Camp at Mount Joy" rather than "Camp at Valley Forge." Mount Joy is what proved to be a misnamed hill that juts from the western part of the encampment. Little did William Penn, who reserved this land for himself and named it thus, foresee the bitter humor in the name--a humor the troops themselves were wont to laugh at cynically.

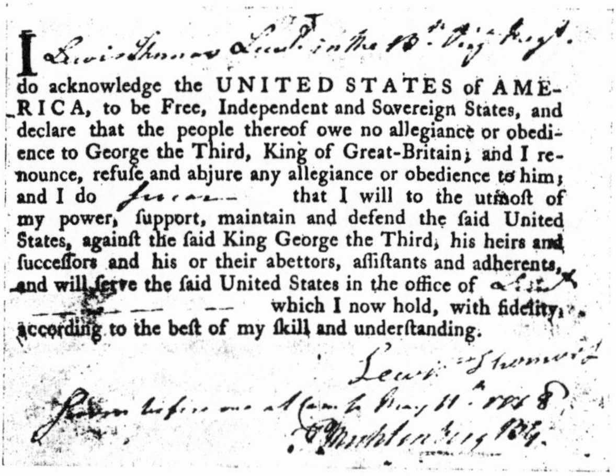

Illus. 1. The oath of Lewis Thomas, witnessed by Muhlenberg, is dated May
           11, the day preceding the signing of those very officers who were
           themselves authorized to witness oaths.

On many of the oaths the generals simply signed as witnesses, but on one of the author's examples Muhlenberg wrote out in his own hand, "Sworn before me at Camp May 11th 1778." On another de Kalb likewise wrote out the date and place, in a misspelled script: "Sworn befefore [sic] me June 9th 1778 Camp [the **m** with an extra loop] at Valley forge [again **sic**] The Baron de Kalb M.G." This he appended to the oath of Ens. Joseph Washburn of Col. Timothy Bigelow's 15th Massachusetts.

Illus. 2.   The Baron de Kalb witnessed the oath of allegiance taken by Joseph Washburn, in Colonel Bigelow's regiment. The curious spelling of "before" noted in the text of this article is found in this example.

Although the third of the author's examples was likewise signed at Valley Forge, Lafayette's attestation does not designate that unhappy ground. This oath, dated June 7, oddly enough predated the general's own oath by a couple of days. In fact, Lafayette's oath was taken a full four weeks after the generals' signings of May 12, but there was a reason. Lafayette, immediately after his return from New York, where Congress had sent him to lead an invasion of Canada that never got beyond the planning stage, was given a division of his own as he long had begged. On May 19 he and his division were pushed from the Valley Forge encampment to an advanced position at Barren Hill to watch for a British stir in Philadelphia. A stir soon came, and it was almost the Frenchman's undoing. On May 20 Clinton, who took command of the British since Howe was returning to England, launched a secret expedition that American scouts failed to note in time. Lafayette, finding a British column poking across his rear, drew out safely, then drifted back to his former position when the enemy column receded. Late in May he returned to Valley

Forge and began the taking of oaths among his officers. It was there that he signed for William White, lieutenant of the 7th Virginia, with the rare form of his signature, "The Marquis de," a title that he later discarded, simply signing "Lafayette." It was not until June 9, however, that the general got to headquarters to swear an oath for himself.

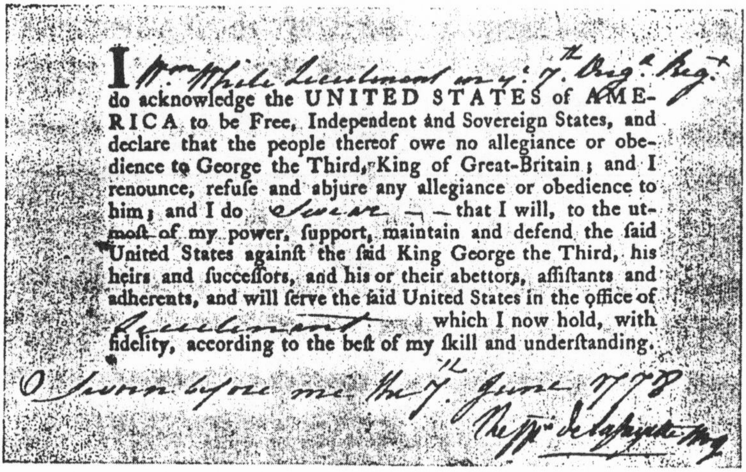

I Wm. White Lieutenant in ye 7. Virga. Regt. do acknowledge the UNITED STATES of AMERICA to be Free, Independent and Sovereign States, and declare that the people thereof owe no allegiance or obedience to George the Third, King of Great-Britain; and I renounce, refuſe and abjure any allegiance or obedience to him; and I do swear — that I will, to the utmoſt of my power, ſupport, maintain and defend the ſaid United States againſt the ſaid King George the Third, his heirs and ſucceſſors, and his or their abettors, aſſiſtants and adherents, and will ſerve the ſaid United States in the office of Lieutenant which I now hold, with fidelity, according to the beſt of my ſkill and underſtanding.

Sworn before me the 7th June 1778
The Mqs. de Lafayette M.G.

Illus. 3. The Marquis de Lafayette witnessed this oath of Lt. William White on June 7, a month after Lafayette's authorization to witness, yet two days before he was himself able to sign such a declaration.

The signings in Washington's army were not completed by the time the army abandoned the winter's encampment on June 19, for the business was still proceeding when the army, in August, squatted to the north and east of New York to watch Clinton commence his long hibernation on the tip of Manhattan. New and returning officers were constantly drawn to service, giving a reason for the extended task. As an officer had written from Valley Forge, the army was "daily increasing with Recruites from the Southward."

In all events, whatever the feeling at the time--oaths or no oaths--the results were the same. The officers, with the notorious exceptions of traitors Charles Lee and Benedict Arnold, were true to the cause, and Yorktown had a shining date with history.

The Discarded Inaugural
Address of George Washington*

Nathaniel E. Stein

Imagine an eminent educator, while in the process of compiling and editing the original Washington papers from Mount Vernon, giving away pages of the first president's unused first inaugural address to people whose fancy led them to ask for a page. It is hard to believe that such a wanton and senseless act really occurred, but it did.

In Cambridge, Massachusetts, during the third decade of the last century, Jared Sparks, editor and historian, was compiling his magnum opus, **The Complete Writings of George Washington.** This vast work was to be accomplished through the generosity of the first president's heirs, who made available to the author mounds of precious manuscript material and diaries from Mount Vernon. But Sparks's editorial methods were subject to grave criticism by modern standards. He blue-penciled freely, made omissions at random, standardized the spelling, and even attempted to improve Washington's English phraseology.

Working on the papers in his own home in Cambridge, the compiler loosely scattered the voluminous historical documentation all over his literary workshop for a number of years, and when his task was nearing completion, Sparks was made the willing prey of friends and prominent people who avidly sought some piece of Washington's handwriting. Thus he blithely disposed of the entire unused first draft of the first inaugural acting on the puzzling assumption that since the speech was not uttered, it had no official existence. Going one step further, when the requests became too numerous, Sparks calmly cut up whole pages to accommodate his persistent petitioners. In this scandalous manner, a manuscript of major historical significance was scattered to the four winds, with recovery in its original entirety an almost certain impossibility.

Many collectors in the past were inspired to bring together all these scattered pages, but such a goal was, and is now, unattainable because many pages are now the prized possessions of historical institutions and famous libraries. Despite this difficulty, the late Forest H. Sweet painfully and slowly gathered six sheets, or twelve pages, over a quarter of a century. I managed to purchase the collection from his estate. Those fragments, added to some I already owned, make up the largest individually owned portion of the original address.

---

*Originally published in 1958.

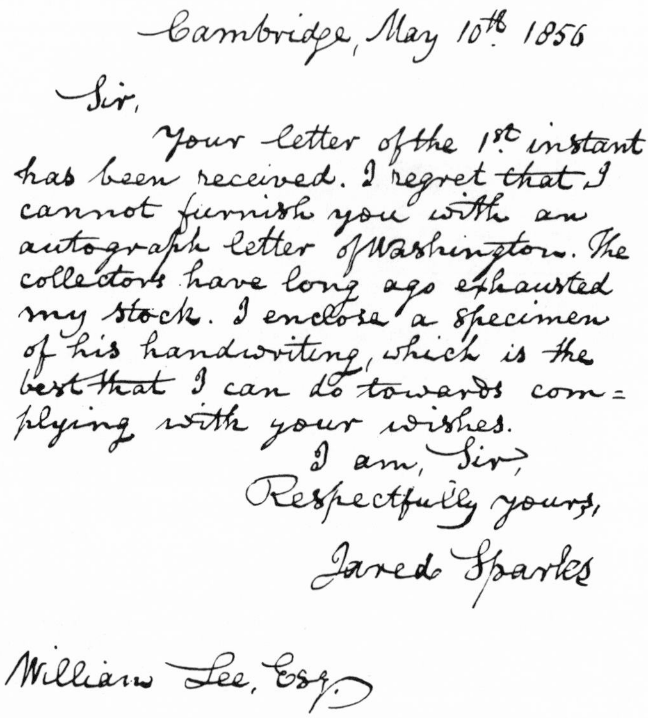

Cambridge, May 10th 1856

Sir,

> *Your letter of the 1st instant has been received. I regret that I cannot furnish you with an autograph letter of Washington. The collectors have long ago exhausted my stock. I enclose a specimen of his handwriting, which is the best that I can do towards complying with your wishes.*
>
> *I am, Sir,*
> *Respectfully yours,*
>
> *Jared Sparks*

William Lee, Esq.

Illus. 1.   One of Sparks's letters showing his continued compliance with the numerous requests for Washington's autographs even as late as 1856. He states baldly that "the collectors have long ago exhausted my stock." (Courtesy of Col. Ray Trautman.)

Fitzpatrick's major work of the writings of Washington lists some of these pages with the explanatory footnote that "they were part of the first inaugural or first message to Congress . . . but the scant few pages that survive make it virtually impossible to make sense and coherence." After the Sweet acquisition, I was convinced that the fragments were part of a proposed inaugural address, and I proceeded to gather photostats of the pages held by others in order to render a near-complete typescript of the speech. The resultant reading contained a fair degree of continuity, and its intent left no doubt in my mind.

Douglas Southall Freeman, in his **Life of Washington,** volume VI, has this to say on the moments before the first inaugural ceremony:

> The General and his assistants . . . were busy with last minute details that had to be set in order before the ceremonies began. Washington's inaugural address was not a concern. It was in final form, ready for delivery. **He had put aside completely the long statement of needed legislation he had written some weeks before at Mount Vernon, for presentation to Congress.** [Emphasis mine.] In its place, probably with some help from James Madison, he had prepared a paper that could be read at unhurried pace in less than twenty minutes. It was largely personal, with one recommendation only, and that one carefully phrased.

Other allusions to another prepared address are contained in letters to Madison and Hamilton during the early months of 1789. A careful comparison with the actual delivered address shows an underlying similarity of thoughts rather than words, although numerous recommendations to Congress appear in the unused draft. It is quite logical to assume, lacking evidence otherwise, that the replacement was used for two strong reasons: the original speech with its multiple recommendations to Congress was too radical and far too long.

For many months before the first group of electors assembled in 1789, Washington had been well aware that the public was single-minded in its determination to make him chief magistrate. His reluctance was set down in a letter to his friend General Knox, a man on whose sound judgment he had often relied:

> I have always felt a kind of gloom upon my mind as often as I have been taught to expect I might and perhaps erelong be called to make a decision. If I should receive the appointment, and I shall be prevailed upon to accept it, the acceptance would be tendered with more diffidence and reluctance than I have ever experienced before in my life.

Again, later, he wrote from seclusion in his beloved Mount Vernon:

> In confidence I assure you . . . that my movements to the chair, of the Government will be accompanied by feelings not unlike those of a culprit who is going to the place of execution; so unwilling am I, in the evening of a life nearly consumed in public cares, to quit a peaceful abode for an ocean of difficulties, without the competency of political skills, abilities, and inclinations, which is necessary to manage the helm.

This mood persisted even up to the very meeting of the electors, and when the first unanimous ballot was cast for president and vice president, it prompted his fellow statesman Richard Henry Lee to hurriedly pen a letter to him that described the balloting and continued with a fervent plea:

On Government of the People

"This Constitution is really in its formation, a government of the people; that is to say, a government in which all power is derived from, and at stated periods, reverts to them."

Before this period, I judged it might not be acceptable to speak my sentiments to you on this subject; but now I hope I may be permitted to express my ardent hope that your inclinations may correspond with the United wish of America, that you should preside over those councils which you have so greatly contributed to render independent. Indeed, I am sure that the public happiness, which I know you have so much at heart, will be very insecure without your acceptance.

The receipt of this letter must have dispelled all doubt from Washington's mind, and he forthwith made preparations to leave "a peaceful abode for an ocean of difficulties." It was during the interim of notification and the leavetaking from his abode on the banks of the Potomac that he must have completed the final draft of what he thought was to be his first official speech to the nation as president.

The delivery of the shorter inaugural took place on the portico of Federal Hall in New York City, and we are indebted to Fisher Ames, one of the great orators of Congress, for his vivid picture of the event:

I sat entranced. It was a very touching scene and quite of the solemn kind. Washington's aspect grave--almost to sadness; his modesty--actually shaking; his voice deep--a little tremulous, and so low as to call for closer attention; added to the series of objects presented to the mind, and overwhelming it, produced emotions of the most effecting kind upon the members (of Congress). I pilgarlic, sat entranced. It seemed to me an allegory in which Virtue was personified, and addressing those to whom she would make her votaries.

The reader would do well to ponder that most curious and intriguing word **pilgarlic**. Now almost obsolete, it was used then to describe an individual who was as bald as a peeled garlic, and thus by contemptuous application compared with the less formal phrase "poor creature."

Here are Washington's original thoughts that he so laboriously penned. This is the speech that was doomed by our overly conservative founding fathers, and later so recklessly given away as holographic souvenirs. Of the sixty-four pages, there exist today, as far as I know, twenty-two full pages, twelve half-pages, and two three-line fragments.

Fragments

(Three-line fragment owned by Col. Ray Trautman, probably from pages 1 and 2)

Upon the parent of all good. It becomes a pleasing commencement of my office to offer my heartfelt congratulations on the happy . . . .

(Three-line fragment on the reverse of the above)

Be [fore]we entered upon the performance of our several functions, it seemed to be our indispensable part, as national beings . . . .

Emergence from the Revolution

(Full sheet, two pages, owned by the Princeton University Library)

At the beginning of the late war with Great Britain when we thought ourselves justifiable in resisting to blood, it was known to those best acquainted with the different condition of the combatants and the probable cost of the prize in dispute, that the expense in comparison with our circumstances as colonists must be enormous, the struggle protracted, dubious, and severe. It was known that the resources of Britain, were, in a manner, inexhaustible, that her fleets covered the ocean, and that her troops had harvested laurels in every quarter of the globe. Not then organized as a nation, or known as a people upon the earth, we had no preparation. Money, and the nerve of war was wanting. The sword was to be forged upon the anvil of necessity: the treasury to be created from nothing. If we had a secret resource of a nature unknown to our enemy, it was in the unconquerable resolution of our Citizens, the conscious rectitude of our cause, and the confident trust that we should not be forsaken by Heaven. The people willingly offered themselves to the battle; but the means of arming, clothing, and subsisting them; as well as procuring the implements of hostility, were only to be found in anticipation of our future wealth. Paper bills of credit were emitted: monies were borrowed for the most pressing emergencies: and our brave troops in the field unpaid for their services. In this manner, peace, attended with every circumstance that could gratify our reasonable desires, or even inflate us with ideas of national importance, was at length obtained. But a load of debt was left upon us. The fluctuations of and speculations in our paper currency, had, but in too many instances, occasioned vague ideas of property, generated licentious appetites, and corrupted the morals of men. To these immediate consequences of a fluctuating medium of commerce, may be joined a tide of circumstances that flowed together from sources mostly opened during and after war. The ravage of farms, the conflagration of towns, and the diminuation (of industry) . . . .

On Appointments

"We should seek to find the men who are best qualified to fill offices: but never give our consent to the creation of offices to accommodate men."

Fragments

(Two-line fragment, whereabouts unknown, but collated by Fitzpatrick in **The Writings of George Washington**)

. . . reputation and a decent respect for the sentiments of others, require that something be said by way of an apology for my . . . .

(Nine-line fragment, ownership of which is attributed to John Ball, follows the above)

. . . myself with the idea it was all that would ever be expected at my hand. But in this I was disappointed. The legislature in Virginia in opposition to my express desire signified in the clearest terms to the Governor of that State, appointed me as a Delegate to the federal convention.   Never was my embarrassment or hesitation more extreme or dis . . . .

(Seven-line fragment owned by the Massachusetts Historical Society follows the "Ball" fragment)

. . . tressing. By letters from some of the wisest and best men in almost every quarter of the Continent, I was advised, that it was my indispensable duty to attend, and that, in the deplorable condition to which our affairs were reduced, my refusal would be considered a desertion of . . . .

(Seven-line fragment, the reverse of the above, owned by the Massachusetts Historical Society)

. . . rest, neither life or reputation had been accounted dear in my sight. And, from the bottom of my soul, I know, that my motives on no former occasion were more innocent than in the present instance. At my time of life, and in my situation, I will not suppose that many moments need . . . .

(Six-line fragment owned by Franklin H. Hooper, from page 15)

. . . situation could be so agreeable to me as the condition of a private citizen. I solemnly appeal and assert to the searcher of hearts to witness the truth of it, that my leaving home to take upon myself the execution of this office was the greatest personal sa [crifice] . . . .

(Six-line fragment, reverse of above, owned by Franklin H. Hooper, from page 16)

... to prove that I have prematurely grown old in the service of my country. For in truth, I have now arrived at the sober age, when, aside from any extraordinary circumstances to deter me from encountering new fatigues, and when, without having met with any par[ticular] ....

On the Presidency

(One sheet, two pages, owned by Nathaniel E. Stein, numbered 19 and 20)

[No words] need to be bestowed in exculpating myself from any suggestions, which might be made "that the incitement of pleasure or grandeur, or power have wrought a change in my resolution." Small indeed must be the resources for happiness in the mind of that man, who cannot find a refuge from the tediousness of solitude but in a round of dissipation, the pomp of state, or the homage of his fellow men. I am not conscious of being in that predicament. But if there should be a single citizen of the United States, to whom the tenour of my life is so little known, that he should imagine me capable of being so smitten with the allurements of sensual gratification, the frivolities of ceremony, or the baubles of ambition, as to be induced from such motives to accept a public appointment: I shall only lament his imperfect acquaintance with my heart, and leave him until another retirement (should Heaven spare my life for a little space) shall work a conviction of his error. In the meantime, it may not, perhaps, be important to mention one or two circumstances which will serve to obviate the jealousies that might be entertained of my having accepted this office, from a desire of enriching myself, or aggrandizing my posterity. In the first place, if I have formerly served the community without a wish for pecuniary compensation, it can hardly be suspected that I am at present influenced by avaricious schemes. In the next place, it will be recollected that the Divine Providence hath not seen fit that my blood should be transmitted, or my name perpetuated by the endearing, though sometimes seducing channel of immediate offspring. I have no child for whom I could wish to make a provision--no family to build in greatness upon my country's ruins.   Let then the adversaries of this constitution, let my personal enemies if I am so unfortunate as to have deserved such a return from ....

On the Nation's Future

(One sheet, two pages, owned by Princeton University Library, numbered 23 and 24)

... when they shall witness the return of more prosperous times. I feel the consolatory joys of futurity in contemplating the immense deserts, yet untrodden by the feet of man, soon to become fair as the garden of God, soon to be animated by the activity of multitudes, and soon to be made vocal with

---

On National Security

"As to any invasion that might be meditated by foreigners against us on the land, I will only say, that, if the mighty nation with which we lately contended, could not bring us under the yoke, no nation on the face of the earth can ever effect it; while we remain united and faithful to ourselves."

---

the praises of the Most High. Can it be imagined that so many peculiar advantages, of soil and of climate, for agriculture and for navigation were lavished in vain--Or that this continent was not created and reserved so long undiscovered as a theatre, for those glorious displays of divine munificence, the salutary consequences of which shall flow to another hemisphere and extend through the interminable series of ages! Should not our souls exult in this prospect! Though I shall not survive to perceive with these bodily senses, but a small portion of the blessed effects which our revolution will occasion in the rest of the world; yet I enjoy the progress of human society and human happiness in anticipation. I rejoice in a belief that intellectual light will spring up in the dark corners of the Earth, that freedom from enquiry will produce liberality of conduct; that mankind will reverse the absurd position that the many were made for the few; and that they will not continue slaves in one part of the globe, when they can become free in another.

Thus I have explained the general impressions under which I have acted: omitting to mention until the last, a principal reason which induced my acceptance. After a consciousness that all is right within and an humble hope of approbation in Heaven--Nothing can, assuredly, be so grateful to a virtuous man as the good opinion of his fellow citizens, tho the partiality of mind led them to consider my holding the Chief Magistracy as a matter of infinitely more consequence than it really is. Yet my acceptance must be ascribed rather to an honest willingness to satisfy the partiality, than to an overwhelming presumption upon my own capacity. Whenever a Government is to be instituted or changed by the consent of the people, confidence in the person placed at the head of it, is, perhaps more peculiarly necessary.

On the Constitution

(One sheet, two pages, owned by Nathaniel E. Stein, numbered 27 and 28)

[Shall I] set up my judgment as the standard of perfection? And shall I arrogantly presume that whoever differs from me, must discern the subject through a distorting medium, or be influenced by some nefarious design? The mind is so formed in different persons as to contemplate the same object in different points of view. Hence originates the difference of questions of the greatest import, both human and divine. In all institutions of the former kind, great allowances are doubtless to be made for the fallibility and imperfection of their authors. Although the agency I had in forming this system, and the high opinion I entertained of my colleagues for their ability and integrity may have tended to warp my judgment in its favor; yet I will not pretend to say that it appears absolutely perfect to me, or that there may not be many faults which have escaped my discernment. I will only say, that, during and since the session of the Convention, I have attentively heard and read every oral and printed information on both sides of the question that could be procured. This long and laborious investigation, in which I endeavored as far as the frailty of nature would permit to act with candour has resulted in a fixed belief that this Constitution is really in its formation, a government of the people; that is to say, a government in which all power is derived from, and at stated periods, reverts to them--and that, in its operation, it is purely, a government of laws made and executed by the fair substitutes of the people alone. The election of the differ't branches of Congress by the freemen, either directly or indirectly is the pivot on which turns the first wheel of the government. A wheel which communicates motion to all the rest. At the same time the exercise of this right of election seems to be so regulated, as to afford less opportunity for corruption and influence; and more for stability and system than has usually been incident to popular governments. Nor can the members of Congress exempt themselves from the consequences of . . . .

On the Function of Government

(One sheet, two pages, owned by Pierpont Morgan Library, numbered 29 and 30)

. . . any unjust and tyrannical acts which they impose on others. For in a short time they will mingle with the mass of the people. Their interests must therefore be the same, and their feelings in sympathy with those of their constituents. Besides, their reelection must always depend upon the good reputation which they shall have maintained in the judgment of their fellow citizens. Hence I have been induced to include that this government must be less obnoxious to well-founded objections than most which have existed in the world. And in that opinion, I am confirmed on three accounts; **first**--because every government ought to be possessed of powers adequate to the purposes for which it was instituted: secondly, because no other or greater powers appear to me to be delegated to this government than are essential to accomplish the objects for which it was instituted, to wit, the safety and happiness of the governed:--and thirdly, because it is clear to my conception that no government before introduced among mankind ever contained so many checks and such efficacious restraints to prevent it from degenerating into any species of oppression. It is unnecessary to be insisted upon, because it is well known, that the impotence of Congress under the former Confederation, and the inexpediency of trusting more ample prerogatives to a single body, gave birth to the different branches which constitute the present general government. Convinced as I am that the balances arising from the distribution of the legislative, executive, and judicial powers, are the best that have been instituted; I presume now to assert that better may not still be devised. On the article of proposed amendments I shall say a few words in another place. But if it was a point acknowledged on all parts that the late federal government could not have existed much longer; if without some speedy remedy a dissolution of the union must have ensued; if without adhering to the union we . . . .

On the Value of the Compact

"Should hereafter, those who are intrusted with the management of this government, incited by the lust of power and prompted by the supineness or venality of their constituents, overlap the known barriers of this constitution and violate the unalienable rights of humanity; it will only serve to show, that no compact among men (however provident in its construction and sacred in its ratification) can be pronounced everlasting and inviolable. And if I may so express myself, that no wall of words, that no mound of parchment, can be so formed as to stand against the sweeping torrent of boundless ambition on one side, aided by the sapping current of corrupted morals on the other."

On Constitutional Amendments

(One sheet, two pages, owned by the Massachusetts Historical Society, numbered 33 and 34)

. . . on the one hand, and an unalterable habit of error on the other, are points in policy equally desireable; though, I believe, a power to effect them never before existed.

Whether the constitutional door that is open for amendment in ours, be not the wisest and apparently the happiest expedient that has ever been suggested by human prudence, I leave to every unprejudiced mind to determine.

Under these circumstances I conclude that it has been the part of wisdom to admit it. I pretend to no unusual foresight into futurity, and therefore cannot undertake to decide, with certainty, what may be its ultimate fate. If a promised good should terminate in an unexpected evil, it would not be a solitary example of disappointment in this mutable state of existence. If the blessings of Heaven showered thick around us should be spilled on the ground, or converted to curses, through the fault of those for whom they are intended, it would not be the first instance of folly or perverseness in short-sighted mortals. The blessed religion revealed in the word of God will remain an eternal and awful monument to prove that the best institutions may be abused by human depravity; and that they may even, in some instances be made subservient to the vilest of purposes. Should, hereafter, those who are intrusted with the management of this government, incited by the lust of power and prompted by the supineness or venality of their constituents, overlap the known barriers of this constitution and violate the unalienable rights of humanity; it will only serve to show, that no compact among men (however provident in its construction and sacred in its ratification) can be pronounced everlasting and inviolable. And if I may so express myself, that no wall of words, that no mound of parchment, can be so formed as to stand against the sweeping torrent of boundless ambition on one side, aided by the sapping current of corrupted morals on the other. But . . . .

> **On Our Secret Resource**
>
> "If we had a secret resource of a nature unknown to our enemy, it was in the unconquerable resolution of our Citizens, the conscious rectitude of our cause, and the confident trust that we should not be forsaken by Heaven."

On Defense

(One sheet, two pages, owned by Nathaniel E. Stein, numbered 36 and 37)

It might naturally be supposed that I should not silently pass by the subject of our defense. After excepting the unprovoked hostility committed against us by one of the powers of the Barbary, we are now at peace with all the nations of the globe.   Separated as we are from them, by intervening oceans, an exemption from the burden of maintaining numerous fleets and armies, must ever be considered as a singular felicity in our national lot. It will be in our choice to train our youths to such industrious and hardy professions as that they may grow into an unconquerable force, without our being obliged to draw unprofitable drones from the hive of industry. As our people have a natural genius for naval affairs, and as our materials for navigation are ample, if we give due encouragement to the fisheries and the carrying trade; we shall possess such a nursery of seamen and such skill in maritime operations as to enable us to create a navy almost in a moment. But it will be wise to anticipate events and to lay a foundation in time. Whenever the circumstances will permit, a grand provision of war-like stores, arsenals, and dock-yards, ought to be made.

As to any invasion that might be meditated by foreigners against us on the land, I will only say, that, if the mighty nation with which we lately contended, could not bring us under the yoke, no nation on the face of the earth can ever effect it; while we remain united and faithful to ourselves. A well organized militia would constitute a strong defense; of course, your most serious attention will be turned to such an establishment. In your recess, it will give me pleasure, by making such reviews, as opportunities may allow, to attempt to revive the ancient military spirit. During the present impoverished state of our finances I would not wish to see any expense incurred by augmenting our regular . . . .

Fragments

(Eleven-line fragment, owned by Justin G. Turner, top half of page numbered 45)

. . . of this government, it may be proper to give assurances of our friendly dispositions to other powers. We may more at our leisure meditate on such treaties of amity and commerce, as shall be judged expedient to be propounded to, or received from any of them.

In all our appointments of persons to fill domestic and foreign offices, let us be careful to select only such as are distinguished for morals and abilities. Some attention should likewise be paid, when . . . .

(Thirteen-line fragment, owned by Walter P. Gardner, bottom half of page numbered 45)

. . . ever the circumstances will conveniently admit, to the distribution of offices among persons, belonging to the different parts of the union. But my knowledge of the characters of persons, through an extent of fifteen hundred miles, must be so imperfect, as to make me liable to fall into mistakes: which, in fact, can only be avoided by the disinterested aid of my coadjutors. I forbear to enlarge upon the delicacy there certainly will be, in discharging this part of our trust with fidelity, and without giving occasion for uneasiness.

(Nine-line fragment, owned by Justin G. Turner, top half of page numbered 46)

It appears to me, that it would be a favourable circumstance, if the characters of the candidates could be known, without their having a pretext for coming forward themselves with personal applications. We should seek to find the men who are best qualified to fill offices: but never give our consent to the creation of offices to accommodate men.

(Eleven-line fragment, owned by Walter P. Gardner, bottom half of page numbered 46)

Certain propositions for taking measures to obtain explanations and amendments on some articles of the constitution, with the obvious intention of quieting the minds of the good people of the United States, will come before you, and claim a dispassionate consideration. Whatever may not be deemed incompatable with the fundamental principles of a free and efficient government ought to be done for the accomplishment for so desireable an object. The reasonings which have been used to prove . . . .

On the Three-Fourths Rule (See illus. 2.)

(One sheet, two pages, owned by Nathaniel E. Stein, numbered 47 and 48)

. . . that amendments could never take place after this constitution should be adopted, I must avow, have not appeared conclusive to me. I could not understand, by any mathematical analogy, why the whole number of States in Union should be more likely to concur in any proposed amendment, than three fourths of that number: before the adoption, the concurrence of the former was necessary for effecting this measure. Since the adoption, only the latter. Here I will not presume to dictate as to the time, when it may be most expedient to attempt to remove all the redundances, or supply all the defects, which shall be discovered in this complicated machine. I will barely suggest, whether it would not be the part of prudent men to observe it fully in movement, before they undertook to make such alterations, as might prevent a fair experiment of its effects? And whether, in the meantime, it may not be practicable for this Congress (if their proceedings shall meet with the

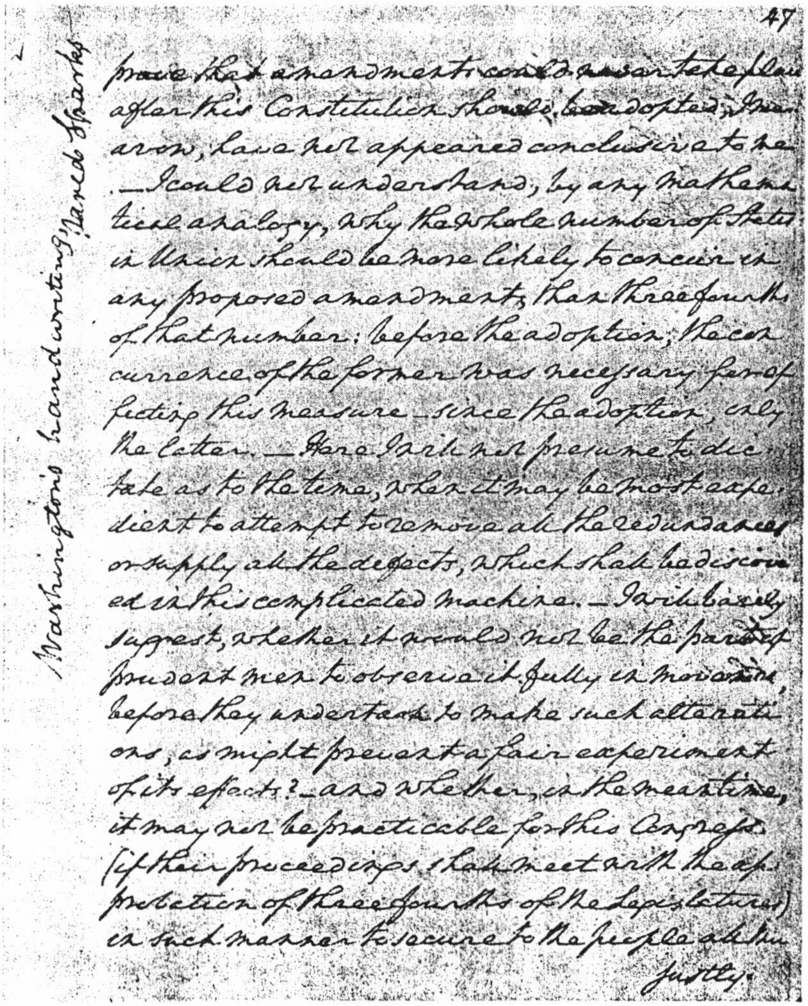

Illus. 2. A page of Washington's undelivered inaugural address in the author's collection.   The first president here discusses amending the Constitution. Sparks's authentication of Washington's handwriting is in the left margin.

> **On Separation of Powers**
>
> "Convinced as I am that the balances arising from the distribution of the legislative, executive, and judicial powers, are the best that have been instituted; I presume now to assert that better may not still be devised."

approbations of three fourths of the legislatures) in such manner to secure to the people all their justly esteemed privileges, as shall produce extensive satisfaction?

The complete organization of the Judicial Department was left by the constitution to the ulterior arrangement of Congress. You will be pleased, therefore, to let a supreme regard for equal justice and the inherent rights of the citizens be visible in all your proceedings on that important subject.

I have a confident reliance, that your wisdom and patriotism will be exerted to raise the supplies for discharging the interest on the national debt, and for supporting the government during the coming year, in a manner as little burdensome to the people as possible. The necessary estimates will be laid before you. A general, moderate impost upon imports; together with a higher tax upon certain enumerated articles, will undoubtedly, occur to you in the course [of your deliberation.]

On Commercial Intercourse

(Three sheets, six pages, owned by Nathaniel E. Stein, numbered 57, 58, 59, 60, 61, and 62)

. . . of the soil and the sea, for the wares and merchandize of other nations is open to all. Notwithstanding the embarrassments under which our trade has hitherto laboured, since the peace, the enterprising spirit of our citizens has steered our vessels to almost every region of the known world. In some distant and heretofore unfrequented countries, our new constellation has been received with tokens of uncommon regard. An energetic government will give to our flag still greater respect; while a sense of reciprocal benefits will serve to connect us with the rest of mankind in stricter ties of amity. But an internal commerce is more in our power; and may be of more importance. The surplus of produce in one part of the United States, will, in many instances, be wanted in another. An intercourse of this kind is well calculated to multiply sailors, exterminate prejudices, diffuse blessings, and encrease the friendship of the inhabitants of one state for those of another.

While the individual states shall be occupied in facilitating the means of transportation by opening canals and improving roads; you will not forget that the purposes of business and society may be vastly promoted by giving cheapness, dispatch, and security to communications through the regular posts. I need not say how satisfactory it would be, to gratify the useful curiosity of our citizens, by the conveyance of news papers and periodical publications in the public vehicles without expense.

Notwithstanding the rapid growth of our population, from the facility of obtaining subsistence, as well as from the accession of strangers, yet we shall not soon become a manufacturing people, because men are even better pleased with labouring on their farms, than in their workshops. Even the mechanics who come from Europe, as soon as they can produce a little land of their own, commonly turn cultivators. Hence it will be found more beneficial, I believe, to continue to exchange our staple commodities for the finer manufactures we may want, than to undertake to make them ourselves. Many articles, however, in wool, flax, cotton, and hemp; and all in leather, iron, fur and wood may be fabricated at home with great advantage. If the quantity of wool, flax, cotton and hemp should be encreased to tenfold its present amount (as it easily could be). I apprehend the whole might in a short time be manufactured, especially by the introduction of machines for multiplying the effects of labour in diminishing the number of hands employed upon it. But it will rest with you to investigate what proficiency we are capable of making in manufactures, and what encouragement should be given to particular branches of them. In almost every house, much spinning might be done by hands which otherwise would be in a manner idle.

It remains for you to make out of a country, poor in the precious metals, and comparatively thin of inhabitants, a flourishing State. But here it is particularly incumbent on me to express my idea of a flourishing state with precision; and to distinguish between happiness and splendour. The people of this country may doubtless enjoy all the blessings of the social state: and yet United America may not for a long time to come make a brilliant figure as a nation among the nations of the earth. Should this be the case, and should the people be actuated by principles of true magnanimity, they will not suffer their ambition to be awakened. They should guard against ambition as against their greatest enemy. We should not, in imitation of some nations which have been celebrated for a false kind of patriotism, wish to aggrandize our own republic at the expense of the freedom and happiness of the rest of mankind. The prospect that the Americans will not act upon so narrow a scale affords the most comfortable reflections to a benevolent mind. As their remoteness from other nations, in a manner, precludes them from foreign quarrels: so their extent of territory and gradual settlement, will enable them to maintain something like a war of posts against the invasion of luxury, dissipation, and corruption. For after the large cities and old establishments on the borders of the Atlantic, shall, in the progress of time, have fallen a prey to those invaders, the western states will probably long retain their primeval simplicity of manners, and incorruptible love of liberty. May we not reasonably expect, that, by those manners and this patriotism, uncommon prosperity will be entailed upon the civil institutions of the American world? And may you not console yourselves for any irksome circumstances which shall occur in the performance of your task, with the pleasing consideration, that you are now employed in laying the foundation of that durable prosperity?

It belongs to you especially to take measures for promoting the general welfare. It belongs to you to make men honest in their dealings with each other, by regulating the coinage and currency of money upon equitable

> ## On Foreign Policy
>
> "They (the people) should guard against ambition as against their greatest enemy. We should not, in imitation of some nations which have been celebrated for a false kind of patriotism, wish to aggrandize our own republic at the expense of the freedom and happiness of the rest of mankind."

principles; as well as by establishing just weights and measures upon an uniform plan. Whenever an opportunity shall be furnished to you as public or private men, I trust you will not fail to use your best endeavors to improve the education and manners of the people; to accelerate the progress of arts and sciences; to patronize works of genius; to confer rewards for inventions of utility; and to cherish institutions favourable to humanity. Such are among the best of all human employments. Such exertion of your talents will render your situations truly dignified, and cannot fail of being acceptable in the sight of the Divinity.

By a series of disinterested services it will be in our power to show, that we have nothing . . . .

Conclusion

(One page, two sheets, owned by Nathaniel E. Stein, two nine-line fragments unnumbered)

While others in their political conduct shall demean themselves as may seem dear to them, let us be honest. Let us be firm. Let us advance directly forward in the path of our duty. Should the path at first prove intricate and thorny, it will grow plain and smooth as we go. In public, as well as in private life, let the Eternal line that separates right and wrong, be the first to [guide us]. I have now again given way to my feelings, in speaking without reserve, according to my best judgment, the record of soberness and affection. If anything indiscreet or foreign to the occasion has been spoken, your candour, I am convinced will not inpute it to an unworthy motive. I draw now to a conclusion by addressing my humble petition to the [Lord].

The Five Manuscript Copies of the Gettysburg Address*

Justin G. Turner

Five copies of the Gettysburg Address, each in Lincoln's handwriting, are extant. Two are at the Library of Congress, and one each at the Illinois State Historical Library, Cornell University, and the Lincoln Room of the White House.

There has been considerable confusion on the part of researchers and historians not only as to the delivery, but also as to the writing and provenance, of the various versions of the address. Much has been written on the subject, a good deal of it erroneous and conjectural. An examination and comparison of the two versions at the Library of Congress is intriguing although not illuminating.

It is my considered judgment that what has hitherto been referred to by scholars and writers as the first version of the address is actually the second version. Upon rereading his second draft, Lincoln possibly thought that the latter part of the third paragraph and the first part of the sentence which followed it seemed repetitious, since each of these sentences contains the words **rather** and **dedicated:**

It is for us, the living, **rather** to be **dedicated** here to the unfinished work which they have thus far, so nobly carried on . . . .

It is **rather** for us to be here **dedicated** to the great task remaining before us . . . .

He therefore condensed the two sentences into one.

For purposes of clarification, I shall hereafter identify what is usually referred to as the second version as version A. What is referred to as the first version, I shall identify as B.

I would identify version A as the first known, or preliminary, draft. It is written in ink on two sheets of ruled bluish gray foolscap and contains three paragraphs of ten sentences. The first sheet consists of twenty-two lines and the second of eleven lines, the last eleven lines being blank. The phrase **That all men are created equal** is not enclosed in quotation marks.

---

*Originally published in 1964.

The following corrections, or changes, are found in the A copy. The penultimate sentence in the second paragraph originally read, "We are **met** to dedicate a portion of it as **the** final resting place **of** those who **have here given** their lives that that nation might live." It was changed to read, "We **have come** to dedicate a portion of it as **a** final resting place **for** those who **here gave** their lives that that nation might live." The substituted words have been inserted above the four words as first written.

The second sentence in the third paragraph was originally written, "The brave men, living and dead, who struggled here, have consecrated it far above our power to add or detract." Between the words **our power**, Lincoln inserted a caret, above which he placed the word **poor**, so that the phrase read, "far above our **poor** power to add or detract." In the penultimate line on the first page, Lincoln evidently neglected to include the word **work.** This he corrected by inserting it above a caret after the word **unfinished.** Similarly, in the lengthy last sentence, in the second line of the second page, he inserted the word **us** over a caret. The phrase **increased devotion to the cause** was changed in the fourth line to **that cause.** In the same line he wrote the word **gave** twice, and then lined out the superfluous **gave.** Thus, in this first version, there are nine alterations.

Certainly, this A version has all the appearances of a working copy. The interlineations, with the corrected words written immediately above those ruled out, clearly indicate that this draft was written prior to what is ordinarily referred to as the first version. The four other copies contain no such interlineations, nor the words originally used. Version A is the only one of the five that is mutilated by interpolations, with the exception of version B, which has pencil corrections on the first page.

The four subsequent versions read **in our poor power to detract** without any correction. Lincoln naturally reedited the preliminary draft, not only incorporating the corrections thereon, but making other changes and improvements as he continued to redraft the second version. It is certain that this first draft was written in Washington prior to his departure for Gettysburg.

The B version was written on two sheets of paper. The first page was written in ink on executive mansion stationery, consisting of nineteen ruled lines. The second page was written in pencil on foolscap similar to that of the A version. Ten of the twenty-two ruled lines are written on; the remaining lines are blank. Only the last three words in the last line of the first page were changed in pencil. They originally read, "it is rather for us, the living **to stand here.**" They were changed to read, "it is rather for us, the living **to here be dedicated.**" The last three letters **ted** in **dedicated** were inserted at the beginning of the second page. This is the only version in which, at the conclusion of the first paragraph, quotation marks are used for the phrase **all men are created equal.** In the second paragraph, in the phrase **but, in a larger sense,** commas are inserted that do not appear in the A draft. Lincoln also omitted the sentence, "It is for us, the living rather to be dedicated here to the unfinished work which they have thus far so nobly carried on." Notwithstanding the changes, the second version is little more than a copy of the first.

The first two versions, known as the Hay copies, were written prior to the delivery of the address and were in the possession of Lincoln's secretary, John Hay, whose children presented them to the Library of Congress in 1916.

The third copy, known as the Everett copy, was written at the request of Edward Everett. According to Thomas Madigan, Everett wrote to Lincoln, stating that he had promised to give the original manuscript of his own oration to Mrs. Hamilton Fish, head of the Committee of the Metropolitan Fair, which was to be held in New York in April 1864 for the benefit of wounded soldiers. Everett added, "It would add very greatly to its value if I could bind up with it, the manuscript of your dedicatory remarks if you have preserved it." On February 4 Lincoln wrote, "I send you herewith a manuscript of my remarks at Gettysburg, which with my note to you on November twentieth, you are at liberty to use for the benefit of our soldiers as you have requested."

This copy Everett had bound with his own, and in his own hand he carefully indexed it and wrote the title page. The volume was said to have been sold at the fair to an uncle of Sen. Henry W. Keyes of New Hampshire, for $1,000. It remained in the Keyes family for sixty-six years and then was acquired by Thomas Madigan in 1929 reportedly for $100,000. Madigan then sold it to James C. Ames, a Chicago banker, for $150,000. After the death of Mr. Ames, his widow had it appraised and agreed to sell it to the state of Illinois for the then appraised value of $60,000. In 1944, the schoolchildren of Illinois raised the money for its purchase, excepting the last $10,000, which was provided by Marshall Field of Chicago. The volume is now permanently housed in the collection of the Illinois State Historical Library at Springfield. The words **under God** appear for the first time in the Everett copy, and they also appear in the fourth and fifth copies.

The fourth copy was requested by George Bancroft for the benefit of the Baltimore Sanitary Commission Fair. Lincoln sent it to him on February 29, 1864, with an accompanying letter. Sanitary Fairs, the equivalent of our present-day Red Cross functions, were held during the Civil War in many cities. This copy, known as the Bancroft copy, was also acquired by Thomas Madigan in 1929 and was sold by him in 1930 for a reported price of $90,000 to Mrs. Nicholas H. Noyes. It was presented by her family to Cornell University in 1949. This copy, as well as the fifth, contains the word **on** instead of **upon** in the first sentence. Because this copy was written on both sides of a single sheet of paper and was not signed or dated, Bancroft, on March 6, 1864, wrote requesting another copy, which Lincoln sent him.

This latter copy, known as the Bliss copy and written by Lincoln on March 11, 1864, is the fifth known copy. It is written on one side of three sheets of blue ruled paper and consists of 272 words. F. Lauriston Bullard stated that Lincoln intended this copy to be the final one, as he had written on the top, "Address Delivered at the Dedication of the Cemetery at Gettysburg." Lincoln usually signed unofficial documents "A. Lincoln," but this version bears his name in full and is dated, November 19, 1863. Nicolay states that "this careful and deliberate revision" became the "standard and authentic text" and is the only version so headed and signed. It is now generally regarded as the official version of the Gettysburg Address.

This fifth copy was retained by George Bancroft and later by the family of Col. Alexander Bliss, a stepson of George Bancroft, from 1864 until it was sold at auction April 27, 1949, at the Parke-Bernet Galleries for the widow and daughter of General Bliss. It was acquired by Oscar B. Cintas, the former Cuban ambassador to the United States, for the bargain price of $54,000. Cintas died in 1957. His will provided that this copy of the address was to be deposited in the Lincoln Room at the White House "with his compliments." As a result of litigation by the Cintas heirs, the Court decided that the address should be surrendered to the White House, to which decision the heirs subsequently acceded.

This fifth copy was to have been reproduced and included in a specially bound quarto volume, "Autograph Leaves of our Country's Authors," issued by Col. Alexander Bliss and J. P. Kennedy. This book was also to have contained ninety-five holographic examples by American authors, including Edgar Allan Poe, Francis Scott Key, Washington Irving, Nathaniel Hawthorne, William Cullen Bryant, Oliver Wendell Holmes, Henry Thoreau, Herman Melville, and John Greenleaf Whittier. This edition of facsimiles was also to be sold for the benefit of the Sanitary Fair.

From one version of the address to another there are changes of wording. The only important difference in the last three versions is the insertion of the words **under God,** which are not found in the first two versions. The five copies of the address vary by a few words in length, the longest having 272 words.

The address was received with mixed emotions by the press. Some papers carried only a scant notice and others ridiculed the address. The **Copperhead Chicago Times,** for instance, stated, "The cheek of every American must tingle with shame as he reads the silly, flat dishwatery utterance of the man who has to be pointed out to intelligent foreigners as the President of the United States." **The** [London] **Times** remarked that "the ceremony was rendered ludicrous by some of the sallies of that poor President Lincoln." However, the **Springfield Republican** of Massachusetts reported,

> surprisingly fine as Mr. Everett's oration was, at the Gettysburg consecration, the rhetorical honors of the occasion were won by Lincoln. His little speech is a perfect Gem. Deep in feeling-- compact in thought and expression--and tasteful, elegant. **Turn back and read it over. It will repay study, as a model of speech.**

The only newspaper in the country to make Lincoln's address the feature of its Gettysburg report appears to have been the **Ohio State Journal.** In many papers, Lincoln's address was used as a shirttail to Everett's oration. Everett's speech took up so much print that there was hardly room for Lincoln's address.

Lincoln, at first, thought his address had been a failure. As time went on, however, he, too, must have sensed its durability and greatness. In the Robert Todd Lincoln Collection in the Library of Congress, there is a memorandum in Lincoln's handwriting to the effect that Senator Sumner showed him a letter from the duchess of Argyle, dated March 2, 1865, in which he stated, "She thinks the speech at the Gettysburg Cemetery must live."

"Long-Remembered," an excellent monograph prepared by David C. Mearns and Lloyd A. Dunlap, incorporates the gist of many of the theories and interpretations regarding the preparation, delivery, and writing of the Gettysburg Address. The authors state:

> The Gettysburg Address has long been the subject of research by Lincoln students. This investigation has established beyond doubt that the address was the outcome of Lincoln's careful thought and preparation. It was not, as was once popularly thought, an almost extemporaneous production. Beyond this incontrovertible fact, scholarly probing has produced little that can be said with finality. A notable failure has been the lack of an answer to the question of when and where Lincoln wrote his masterpiece.
>
> There is good reason for this failure. The evidence is scanty and consists almost entirely of recollections given many years after the event. Inference, speculation, and conjecture must be substituted, inadequately, for fact. The definitive story of Lincoln and the writing of the address has not been told, nor is it likely that it ever can be.

Robert E. Lee's Farewell Order[*]

Joseph E. Fields

One of the most revered names in American history is that of Gen. Robert E. Lee of Virginia. His military leadership, high sense of honor, and inflexible devotion to duty are well known. His definitive biography has been superbly written by Douglas Southall Freeman.[1] Few men have had such influence for good as has General Lee, and this influence was sorely needed at the close of the War Between the States and in the terrible days of Reconstruction that followed.

Many of Lee's letters and dispatches are in existence, owned by institutions, private collectors, and descendants of the original recipients. All are marked by the simplicity and sincerity that characterized the man. Among the most inspiring words of General Lee were those in his last order, General Order No. 9, which is also one of the most famous of military orders. No other words, spoken or written, had a more heartening effect on the veterans of the proud but weary Army of Northern Virginia. The attitude of these men toward their leader was akin to reverence. Gladly would they have followed him to their death; indeed, many expressed to him just such a wish. Lee's farewell to his comrades, from the lowest private to his highest-ranking staff officers, did much to alleviate the pain of defeat. To them it was plain that their great leader acted in their best interests, that he deeply appreciated their efforts to their common cause and their devotion to him. Certainly this message from a great leader deserves to take its place beside Washington's Farewell Address and Lincoln's Gettysburg Address. The substance of the order is well known and highly prized by those interested in the Confederacy.

On the night of April 9, 1865, following the surrender meeting between General Lee and General Grant, Col. Charles Marshall, Lee's chief of staff, was bidden to prepare an order to the troops that would express Lee's feelings toward his men.[2] Colonel Marshall was so busy that he was unable to write the message by the time General Lee had requested it. At ten o'clock the

---

*Originally published in 1949.

[1] Douglas Southall Freeman, **R. E. Lee: A Biography** (New York, 1935). 4 vols.

[2] Sir Frederick Maurice, ed., **An Aide-de-Camp of Lee: The Papers of Colonel Charles Marshall** (Boston, 1927), pp. 275-79.

following morning Lee sent Marshall into his ambulance and posted an orderly so that Marshall would not be disturbed in his writing. Colonel Marshall's first draft was in pencil. He took it to Lee, who struck out a paragraph that he thought would keep alive the feeling of animosity between the North and the South. General Lee made several other changes. Marshall then returned to the ambulance and wrote a revised draft, probably in pencil, which he gave to a clerk to copy in ink.[3] General Lee then signed this ink copy. Other copies were made by various clerks and signed by General Lee. These were sent to the corps commanders and chiefs of departments of the staff. Other individuals made their own copies and brought them to Lee, at various times, to be signed as souvenirs.

Freeman has pointed out that there is no original of Order No. 9.[4] It is possible that Colonel Marshall possessed two copies of the order. The first was the rough penciled draft that was corrected by General Lee. The other was the revised draft, probably written in pencil, given to the clerk to be used as a master copy. Neither of these copies was signed by Lee and their present location is unknown.[5] Marshall may have destroyed or misplaced them. Not even the substance of the deleted paragraph is known. In later years Colonel Marshall was of the opinion that he had loaned the first draft and that it had never been returned. After Colonel Marshall's death a copy signed by Lee was found among Marshall's papers. This was retouched in ink in 1909. Charles Marshall, the son of Colonel Marshall, does not remember if it was originally in ink or pencil, for it was so badly faded as to be difficult to read. This copy is reproduced in Maurice's **An Aide-de-Camp of Lee**. It can be definitely stated that this copy is not the first draft, corrected by Lee, or the second draft, the one given to the copying clerk, since it is not in Marshall's handwriting.[6] The origin of this traced copy is a mystery. It seems to be another souvenir copy.

There are a number of versions of Lee's General Order No. 9. All are dated Headquarters, Army of Northern Virginia, 10th April, 1865. Copies of the order signed by Lee, including one written entirely in Lee's handwriting, vary somewhat in paragraphing and textual details. There are minor variations in words. Nearly all these are souvenirs signed by Lee after April 10; they did not go through the regular military channels. These are of no value in ascertaining the exact original wording. No official printed copy of Order

---

[3] According to Marshall's account, there was no copy of the order made by Marshall and then signed by Lee. Marshall's family ignores his account and states that Lee signed the second Marshall draft. See Maurice.

[4] Freeman, vol. IV, p. 154.

[5] See note 3 above.

[6] Maurice, pp. 278-79, states that this facsimile is in Marshall's handwriting. Careful study reveals it is not in Marshall's hand.

No. 9 has been found, nor is it likely that one was ever made. For his biography of Lee, Freeman chose the text from Lee's letter book.[7] George Washington Custis Lee copied the order into the letter book some time after the surrender at Appomattox.

Below is a partial list of known copies of Order No. 9 signed by General Lee. They are identified by their present owners.

1.   Dr. Joseph E. Fields, Joliet, Illinois. This copy of the order is written on a folio sheet of blue paper of English manufacture. It is addressed to Gen. Walter Husted Stevens, chief engineer of the Army of Northern Virginia. It was found among Stevens's army papers.

2.   Foreman M. Lebold, Chicago. Written on a folio sheet of blue paper of English manufacture, this copy bears no address. It is accompanied by a contemporary manuscript copy of Grant's letter to Lee of April 9, 1865. The letter states the surrender terms, as well as the special Federal order under the terms of which paroled Confederate soldiers were to be allowed to pass through the Federal lines, and to travel on Federal transports and military roads so they might reach their homes more readily. The writer believes some officer entitled to receive the order may have come into headquarters while the several copies were being prepared and received his personally, uncorrected and unaddressed. Equally likely, it may have been an extra set of the papers.

3.   C. N. Owen, Chicago. This copy is written on a small octavo sheet. It bears no address and is uncorrected.

4.   R. L. Huttner, Chicago. Written on a large folio sheet, this copy bears no address and is uncorrected.

5.   Oliver R. Barrett, Chicago.[8] Written on a quarto sheet, this copy is uncorrected and unaddressed.

6.   Library of Congress. Written on a quarto sheet, this copy is likewise uncorrected and bears no address.

7 & 8.   Washington and Lee University, Lexington, Virginia. An uncorrected and unaddressed example is entirely in the handwriting of General Lee and signed by him. A second example was formerly owned by B. Bouldin and is supposedly in the handwriting of Bouldin's wife's brother, William J. Ward. Bouldin believed that Ward was the clerk to whom Colonel Marshall gave his original draft to have it copied in ink and signed by Lee. The copy is addressed to Ward. However, Ward was not an official member of the officer staff and was not entitled to receive a staff copy. Certainly it did not travel through the usual military channels.

----

[7]Freeman, vol. IV, p. 154.

[8]Carl Sandburg, **Abraham Lincoln: The War Years** (New York, 1939), vol. IV, p. 204.

Several other copies are known to have been in existence. A William P. Richardson of New Orleans had a copy that he offered for sale to the Library of Congress in 1908. Because of a difference of opinion on price, the library did not acquire it. We do know this copy was addressed to Maj. William Norborne Starke, who was adjutant general on Gen. Ambrose P. Hill's staff. Its present location is not known. [9]

Capt. A. R. H. Ranson, assistant chief of ordnance of the Army of Northern Virginia, was known to be in possession of a copy of the order as recently as 1911.[10] It was written on a folio sheet of paper and was addressed to Captain Ranson as assistant chief ordnance officer of the Army of Northern Virginia. This copy is corrected in its text. In the second and third lines from the bottom the word **constancy** has been crossed out. The text and handwriting of the Ward-Bouldin copy (8) are identical with those of the Ranson copy. The present whereabouts of the Ranson copy is unknown.

Thus we see that only three copies of General Order No. 9 that were addressed to men entitled to receive one signed by Lee and sent through military channels are known. The present location of only one of these, the copy sent to General Stevens (1), is known. The whereabouts of the other two, the Ranson copy and the Richardson copy, is unknown.

Careful examination of the Stevens copy shows that two corrections were made on it in two different handwritings. In the third paragraph, third line, the word **would** is overwritten by the better word for the context, **must.** In the next line the word **useless** has been inserted in a different hand, undoubtedly the same hand that addressed the copy to Stevens at the lower left. Let us reconstruct the scene at Confederate headquarters. The clerk who wrote the body of the order himself made the first mistake and wrote his correction over it. Perhaps Lee signed the order and pointed out the second error, which the addressing clerk corrected. Or, perhaps the error was noticed and corrected before General Lee signed the order and after it had been addressed to Stevens. Either way, this copy is twice corrected, carefully, and in the routine headquarters business of that day. The care with which this order was corrected and the fact that it went through the ordinary military channels indicate that its text is exact.

Sent with this Order No. 9 to General Stevens and present with it are (1) Grant's letter to Lee of April 9 giving the terms of surrender, in the handwriting of G. W. C. Lee and designated by him as a "true copy," and (2) Grant's special order of April 10 giving free transportation to the paroled officers and men of the Confederate Army, signed by "Official W. H. Taylor A. A. Gen'l." Stevens needed these two orders to parole his own men. Present

---

[9]Interoffice memorandum, Library of Congress, J. C. Fitzpatrick, assistant chief, Division of Manuscripts, to the Librarian of Congress, July 21, 1927.

[10]**Harper's Monthly Magazine,** pp. 122, 336.

also is General Stevens's parole, signed in Lee's name by Taylor, and Gen. John Gibbon's General Order No. 43 of April 11, signed by his adjutant, Colonel Moale. This order made the Confederate parole a free pass through Federal lines.

Among the other Stevens papers are his appointment to West Point, his recommendation to the Mexican government at the close of the war entirely in Lee's handwriting, a letter from Lee to Mrs. Stevens, and a letter from Mrs. Lee to Mrs. Stevens. Stevens's own penciled map of the first battle of Bull Run is also present.

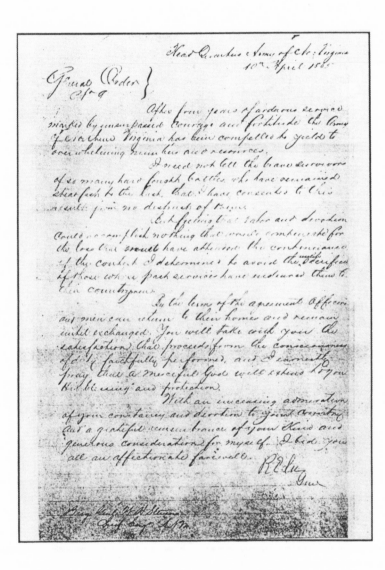

Illus. 1. The Stevens copy of General Lee's famous order.

Part 4.

PENMANSHIP AND WRITING SYSTEMS

B. Franklin and the Art of Writing *

William E. Lingelbach

Benjamin Franklin's handwriting has an interest very much broader than that of most of the great men whose autographs are of concern to historians and collectors. With Franklin, writing, penmanship, printing, and publication were intimately related, not by chance, but consciously and consistently. In a vigorous article protesting against the imposition of duties on foreign books, he wrote, "Art has furnished us with the astounding Invention of Printing which supplies the use of Speech both to the Dead and to the Distant, defying the Difficulties of Time and Space, and assembling together the Information of every human Being."

To Franklin, writing and printing were instruments for the conveyance of ideas; he practiced them with care, profoundly influencing the writing and penmanship of Americans for an entire century. Although the fact has been overlooked by his biographers, Franklin was responsible for the first American bestseller in a field that later brought fortunes to P. R. Spencer and others. It is therefore remarkable that so little has been written about Franklin's own writing, and almost nothing about his contribution to a subject that is of perennial concern to successive groups of young Americans as they begin their study of the three R's.

Fortunately the materials for the study of Franklin's calligraphy, and his art of writing in general, are unusually ample. The corpus of Franklin's extant writings in manuscript is very large. Moreover, his own comments and ideas on the subject are both numerous and pertinent. In other words, we have not only thousands of specimens illustrative of his style and his penmanship, but his own analysis and comments on both.

Pen, Presses, and Print

Much has been written about "Benjamin Franklin, Printer," relatively little on Franklin as a master of English prose, and still less on his role as America's earliest advocate of distinctive styles in penmanship and handwriting. Every American schoolchild should know Franklin's last will and testament, which opens with the words "I, **Benjamin Franklin** of Philadelphia, Printer, late Minister Plenipotentiary from the United States of America to the Court of France . . . ."

---

*Originally published in 1952.

Equally famous is Franklin's epitaph which he first wrote in 1728 at the age of twenty-two, and later rewrote with slight variations:

The Body of
B. Franklin,
Printer;
Like the Cover of an old Book,
Its Contents torn out,
And stript of its Lettering and Gilding,
Lies here, Food for Worms.
But the Work shall not be wholly lost:
For it will, as he believ'd appear once more
In a new & more perfect Edition,
Corrected and amended
By the Author

The unity of the pen, the press, and the printed page became a cardinal tenet in Franklin's thinking and writing on the subject. To this he added an understanding of the needs of the reader, whom he never forgot. From early boyhood, he was conscious of the successive steps of formulating his ideas, putting them into writing, and then putting them into print. Through constant association with manuscripts and printer's copy he developed a keen appreciation of the advantages of legibility, punctuation, emphasis, paragraphing, purity of language, precision in the use of words, and literary style. He was intimately acquainted with the instruments of writing, for he was also a shopkeeper; his shop and account books have many entries relating to quills, paper and regulations for its manufacture, and ink and its proper ingredients. Moreover, being a very practical man, he applied his knowledge of these things to his own needs. He was always partial to good quills, good ink, and good paper. Evident use of a poor quill, bad ink, or bad paper is rare.

Franklin's role as the master printer and publisher of the colonies necessitated the cultivation of a clear and forceful prose style. This is not the place to discuss the story of how the self-taught young printer and tradesman, through self-discipline and the study of classics like Addison's **Spectator,** developed a style that, in its simplicity and clarity, gives him a place with the foremost writers of English prose. Nonetheless, a thoughtful reading of the **Autobiography** and **Proposals relating to the Education of Youth in Pennsylvania** is recommended as a salutary exercise for both the youth and their mentors of our time.

"Correct Writing"

Franklin's active interest in writing continued to the end of his long life. Writing to an Italian correspondent, Bodoni, in 1787, to thank him for his manual on printer's type, he drew attention to three things writing and printing had in common: legibility, pleasing appearance, and economy. In a letter of December 26, 1789, to Noah Webster acknowledging the receipt of the **Dissertations on the English Language,** which he characterized as "an excellent Work . . . greatly useful in turning the Thoughts of our Countrymen to correct Writing," he humorously described certain current trends in writing and printing as "Improvements backwards." Among them he listed the abandonment of the initial capital letter in substantives, of italics for emphasis, and of the long s. He argued that this abandonment was like "paring all Men's Noses," which "might smooth and level their Faces, but would render their physiognomies less distinguishable." The conceit that "grey Printing"--gray ink and gray paper--is more beautiful than black he satirized as untrue and hard on "Old Eyes."

Pioneer in the Art of Writing

Franklin published, edited, and in part wrote what might be called a popular textbook on writing. Among the rare books in the American Philosophical Society's library is a small duodecimo volume of 378 pages entitled **The American Instructor or Young Man's Best Companion**, printed in 1748 by Franklin and Hall, Philadelphia. It is the "revised and corrected" ninth edition of one of those early eighteenth-century manuals on arithmetic, reading, writing, and other useful matters, and had already attained considerable vogue in England before its publication in America. In the colonies it soon attained a like popularity; new editions and printing followed quickly--one in Boston in 1749, another in Philadelphia in 1753, and, according to Karpinsky, sixteen in all before 1800.

The first American edition not only was published by Franklin and his partner, David Hall, but it was one of those books that Franklin had undertaken to publish before he set up the partnership with Hall and withdrew from active participation in printing. In a letter to Franklin of September 7, 1747, James Parker, his partner in the printing business in New York, wrote, "I received ye Pocket Companion safe, 'tis well enough:-may I ask if the Young Man's Companion be almost done?"

Obviously Parker, who was in frequent communication with Franklin, knew of the plans for the publication of the manual in the early autumn of 1747. Nearly two years before, in a letter of April 14, 1745, to his printer friend, William Strahan of London, he ordered "3 Doz. Mather's **Young Man's Companion** and 2 Doz. Fisher's **Ditto**," along with a considerable number of grammars, dictionaries, and vocabularies. Obviously, books of this character were much in demand; the colonists in this respect, as in so many others, still depended on the mother country. To a man of Franklin's initiative and business acumen, the publication of a manual like the **Young Man's Companion** must have looked like a simple and profitable venture quite apart from its contribution toward the education of Americans through their own efforts. At any rate, he decided to publish Fisher's manual.

More Than an Editor

Careful analysis of **The American Instructor** (the title Franklin adopted) affords unmistakable evidence that Franklin not only edited the book, but himself contributed certain sections of the volume. In a brief and thoroughly Franklinesque preface he wrote:

In the British Edition of this Book, there were many Things of little or no Use in these Parts of the World: In this Edition those Things are omitted, and in their Room many other Matters inserted, more immedeately useful to us Americans. And many **Errors** in the Arithmetical Part are here carefully corrected.

Apart from the Franklinian preface[1] and certain minor matters, two other features are significant. First, the models, or specimens, of handwriting are Franklin's own. Second, at the very end of the volume is the well-known **Advice to a Young Tradesman, written by an old One,** which begins with the characteristic sentence, "REMEMBER that Time is Money." Here Franklin develops his philosophy of thrift in the use of time, money, and credit. Although this letter was published by later editors of his works, none cites the original location. Yet, all give the date as 1748, which, along with other facts, would suggest that we may here have the first printing of this famous and oft-quoted letter. Hence **The American Instructor** is not just another Franklin imprint, but a Franklin publication of prime historical importance.

Franklin's Handwriting Models

Franklin contributed to the American edition of **The Instructor** four specimens of the letters of the alphabet. They are described as "Copies of the most usual, fashionable, and commendable Hands for Business." Morison[2] says, "The Round Hand is an individual creation of Franklin, owing little to his professional predecessors or contemporaries." It is, moreover, not just a specimen for the manual. A comparison with numerous examples of his writing of the period shows that it is to all intents and purposes Franklin's own familiar hand. There is a decided tendency to loop the downstrokes of **B, F, P, R,** and **S** and the small **f** and **s** when they descend below the line. Another feature is the weighting of the downstrokes of the lower-case letters **b, d, h, k, l, r,** and **t.** These in particular show the simple character of all Franklin's letters. They are made with the least possible effort. All unnecessary strokes are eliminated. There is no waste of effort, space, or time. It reminds one of Franklin's admonition in **Proposals relating to the Education of Youth in Pennsylvania,** written within a year of the appearance of **The Instructor:** "All should be taught to write a **fair** Hand, and swift, as that is useful to All."

Among the numerals, **4, 6, 7,** and **8** command attention. The heavy downstroke of the **4** and the **7,** the more erect stance of the former, and the combination of **1** and **7,** give them a conspicuous appearance among Franklin's numerals.

---

[1] In his excellent little book on **American Copybooks** (Philadelphia, 1951), Stanley Morison draws attention to this, but rather weakens his case by departing from Franklin characteristics in his quotation from the original.

[2] Ibid., p. 18.

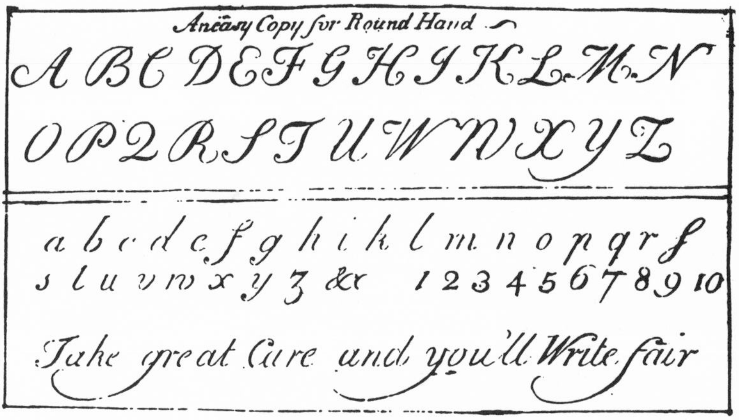

Illus. 1. The round hand as set forth in **The American Instructor.**

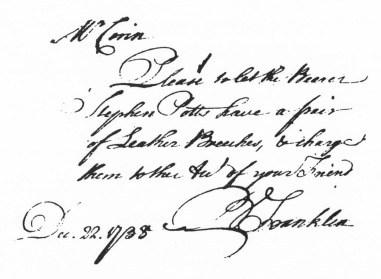

Illus. 2. Franklin's hand compares favorably with the copybook specimen shown in illustration 1.

Illus. 3. Inscription from Franklin's journal.

Capital Letters, Punctuation, and Paragraphing

Franklin consistently used initial capital letters for all substantives, a feature too often ignored by publishers of his writings. Most of his editors show a regrettable disregard for the original in this respect. Franklin regarded this use of capitals not only as a means of emphasis, but also as a feature enhancing the general appearance of the paragraph and page. Perhaps it was this meaningful use of capitals that kept him from using the medium-size letters that are so often the despair of conscientious editors of eighteenth-century texts.

Franklin's punctuation was reasonable and limited rather than profuse; it was used solely to bring out the meaning. Paragraph changes also were not overly frequent; they were used to indicate a shift to a distinctly new subject. Franklin used dashes in the text of his letters to introduce a new topic or line of thought not sufficiently important to call for a new paragraph. Also, dashes saved space and paper, and gave variety to the page. "A monotonous printed page," Franklin once wrote, "is like one of Whitefield's sermons delivered by a schoolboy."

The Autograph or Signature

Franklin's autograph is supposedly so well known that detailed consideration would seem unnecessary. This is, however, very far from being the case. More than any other part of his writing, the signature has given rise to misconceptions and enigmas that are difficult to explain. The signature with the ornate flourish, the paraph as the French call it, is often attributed to his early years as an expression of youthful exuberance and copybook influence, abandoned later in life as unbecoming a man of Franklin's robust character. This explanation seems plausible and has gained rather general acceptance. In all probability the unequivocal support of the idea by Franklin's close friend, Benjamin Rush, partly accounts for its currency even today. In a letter to his son in Philadelphia on June 22, 1803, Dr. Rush wrote:

. . . I observe likewise you subscribe your name in a different hand from that in which your letter is written. Avoid this in future. It looks like affectation. Dr. Franklin avoided it in all his letters. "Ex simplicitate decus" should govern our most trifling compositions. Dr. Franklin when a young man was in the habit of writing his name with a flourish. An old man who saw it by accident cried out,--"What fool's name is this?" Ever afterwards the Doctor wrote his name in a plain and simple manner . . . .

How Rush could make so erroneous a statement is hard to understand, for it was during the second period of his life, and not during the first, that Franklin added the flourish to his signature. The earliest example in the American Philosophical Society's collection of Frankliniana that has come to my attention occurs in a letter of November 28, 1747. If Rush had recalled the signature immediately below his own on the Declaration of Independence, he would have modified his statement for 1776 at least. Among the many letters in our Franklin collection of the later period, there are very few signed in "a plain and simple manner." When the plain signature occurs, it is usually because there is no room at the bottom of the paper for the flourish, or because the signature is followed immediately by another word indicative of Franklin's official role in relation to the particular communication.

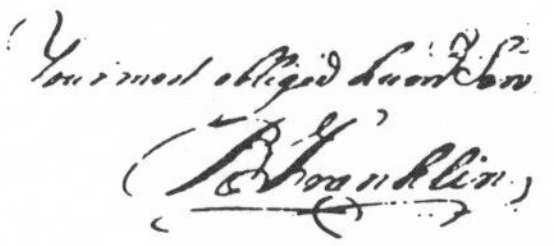

Illus. 4.   Early flourish--1747.

Illus. 5.   Paraph used by Franklin in the second half of his life.

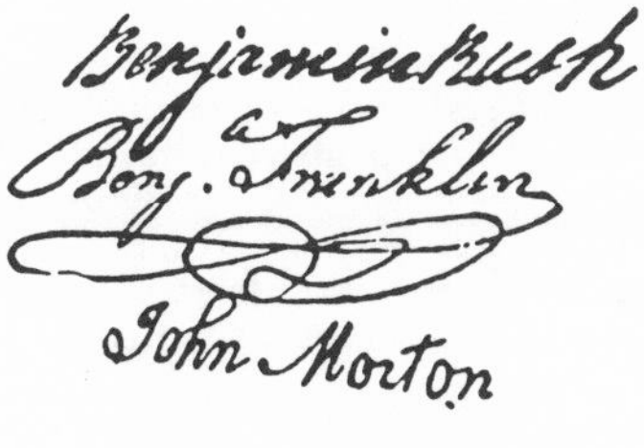

Illus. 6.   Declaration of Independence signature.

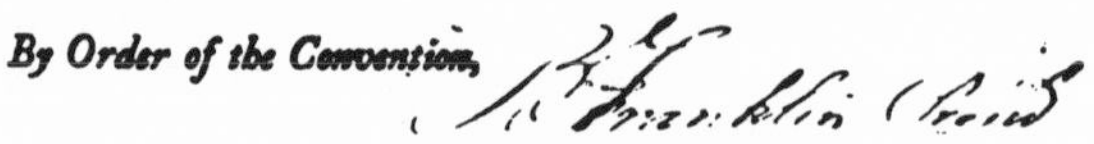

By Order of the Convention,

Illus. 7. Signature "in a plain and simple manner" only because of a lack of space and the additional word following.

Apart from the question of the presence or absence of the flourish, there are occasional departures from the usual "B. Franklin" signature. Foremost among these is "Benjamin Franklin," which is used in his wills and a few legal documents. There are "Benja Franklin," as in the Declaration, and "Benj" and "Benjn," especially in the account books. In later years, the period after the **B** is dropped and the liaison between the initials **B** and **F** more clearly established. Continuity is broken after the downstroke of the **F** for the cross-stroke, which is always placed low, affording a swift transition in the next downstroke to the small **r**, which, like the rest of Franklin's letters, is unusually simple and economical.

General Characteristics

In general, Franklin wrote in a clear, cursory hand with a distinct rhythm. The letters are round and the essential strokes well marked; words are evenly and generously spaced along a straight baseline from which there is very little deviation. As Franklin himself wrote in his "Idea of an English School," addressed to Dr. Samuel Johnson, "'Tis the Writing-Master's Business to take Care that the Boys make fair Characters, and place them strait and even in the Lines."

Space between the lines, like that between the words, is uniform. There is the printer's respect for generous margins coupled with the artist's instinct for the significance and appearance of the page as a whole.

Franklin developed good penmanship early in life, as is evident in **The Elegy** and in his shop and account books. It is the style of penmanship to which the other male members of the Franklin clan were also partial, and one might venture a guess that it goes back to a common original, even though the American edition of George Fisher's **Instructor** did not appear until 1748. Certainly Franklin's son and grandson, William Franklin and William Temple Franklin, adopted this style, as did so many others later, even down to the generation of Abraham Lincoln, who, as Albert D. Osborn says in his recent article on "Forged Autographs," "of course, learned to write before 1850 and learned the old round hand."

This style of penmanship involved a firm grasp of the pen, suggestive of wrist and forearm motion. Indeed, in Franklin's case, as in that of Jefferson, we have the physical evidence of a specially designed chair with a substantial arm rest for writing purposes. Hence, although we do not find any reference to the need of a firm base on which to rest the manuscript, Franklin took it for granted. As clerk of the Pennsylvania Assembly for fifteen years, he had all the conventional equipment for writing, so that even the doodling papers show firmness and clarity. Added to this is a rather unusual degree of consistency throughout the years. Apart from certain copybook characteristics in the early years, which were later eliminated, Franklin's calligraphy does not show any radical change except in the degree of pressure, the length of the letters, and, of course, the appearance of the flourish.

The 1789 letter reproduced in illustration 8 shows that the major characteristics of Franklin's handwriting did not change even in the last years of his life. There is very little wavering or other sign of decline. The writing continues firm and clear, consistent with the amazing activities and mental capacities of our great elder statesman up until his death at the age of eighty-four on April 17, 1790.

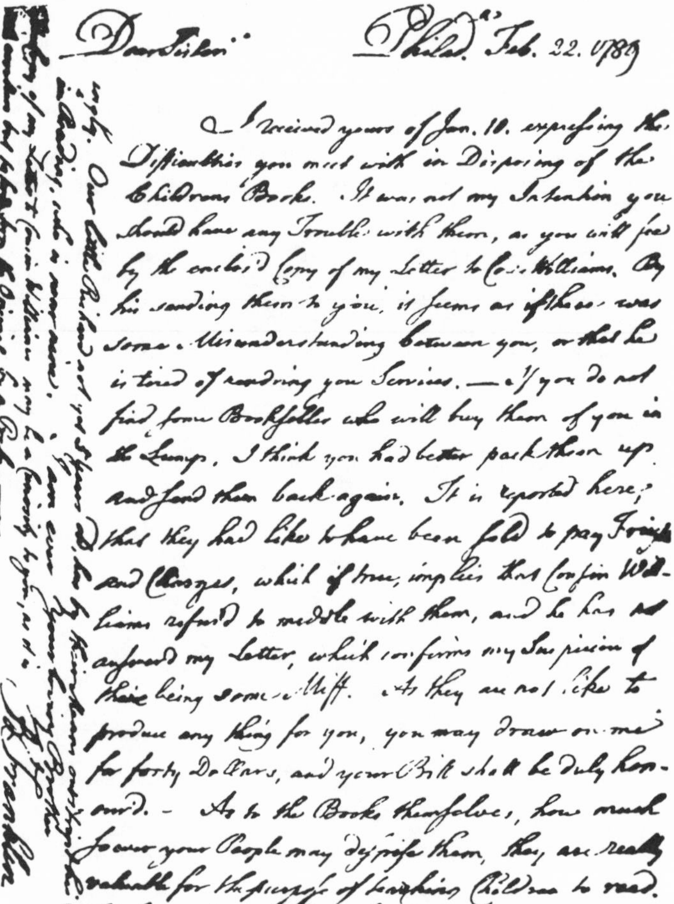
Dear Sister Philad.a Feb. 22. 1789

I received yours of Jan. 10. expressing the Difficulties you meet with in Disposing of the Childrens Books. It was not my Intention you should have any Trouble with them, as you will see by the enclos'd Copy of my Letter to Cousin Williams. By his sending them to you, it seems as if there was some Misunderstanding between you, or that he is tired of rendring you Services. — If you do not find some Bookseller who will buy them of you in the Lump, I think you had better pack them up and send them back again. It is reported here, that they had like to have been sold to pay Freight and Charges, which if true, implies that Cousin Williams refus'd to meddle with them, and he has not answer'd my Letter, which confirms my Suspicion of there being some Miff. As they are not like to produce any thing for you, you may draw on me for forty Dollars, and your Bill shall be duly honoured. — As to the Books themselves, how much soever your People may despise them, they are really valuable for the purpose of teaching Children to read. The largeness and plainness of the Character, and the little Sentences of common occurrence which they can understand when they read, makes them delight in reading them, so as to forward their Progress exceedingly

B Franklin

Illus. 8. Late Franklin letter shows little wavering or sign of decline.

George Washington's Handwriting*

Dorothy S. and Vincent L. Eaton

One of the "Rules of Civility" that George Washington painstakingly learned in his childhood was to "Think before you Speak pronounce not imperfectly nor bring out your Words too hastily but orderly and Distinctly."[1] He seems to have cultivated his handwriting with much the same precept in mind; if, as has been said of him, he seldom wrote a careless word, there also is much truth in the statement that he rarely wrote a word carelessly. His bold, regular penmanship is one of the handsomest and most legible of any American of his time.

It is customary to speak of Washington's "earlier" and "later" handwritings, for he practiced several styles before settling into a fairly fixed pattern. Let us first examine the later script, which evolved in the 1760s, since this is what characterizes the vast majority of Washington documents in public and private hands (see illus. 1).

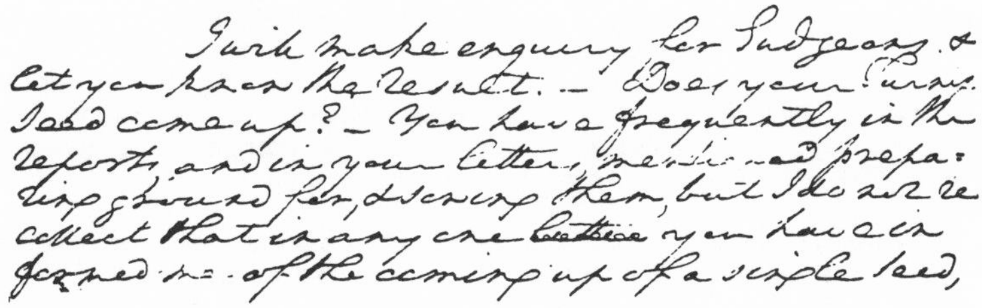

Illus. 1. From a letter to George Augustine Washington, August 12, 1787.

---

*Originally published in 1951.

[1]Quoted from the original manuscript in the Division of Manuscripts, Library of Congress. All examples cited in this paper are from the Washington papers in the same repository.

The Later Script

The later script is firm and flowing, and generally written with a fairly coarse stroke--what we might call a medium "stub" pen--for Washington did not cut his goose quills to such a fine, thin point as did his fellow Virginian Thomas Jefferson. The lines are closely and evenly spaced, averaging about three and one-half to the inch in autograph letters and documents, and they are generally straight and parallel--an effect that Washington practiced to achieve by placing heavily ruled guide sheets beneath the paper on which he was writing to keep his pen from going off the horizontal. The letters, formed with a pronounced left-to-right slant amounting in some cases to as much as forty-five degrees from the vertical, present a gracefully rounded appearance to the eye. They are seldom cramped; in fact, one finds that Washington ordinarily fitted an average of only nine words on a seven-inch line, and even fewer when he was writing in haste.   The letters are, moreover, formed efficiently, without wasted strokes of the pen, a necessary habit for a busy man who had to carry on a heavy correspondence.

Washington penned most of his individual consonants in several different ways, particularly the small **f, r, g, s,** and **t.** His very inconsistency in forming these letters is, in fact, so characteristic that if they are written in exactly the same manner throughout a document one may very well question its authenticity. He also was in the habit of lifting his pen before the letter **c** and after the letters **s, d,** and **v** in the course of a word; he would often do this, too, after the downstroke of a **q, g,** or **y.** Hence his words, if one looks at them closely, are seen to be considerably broken up.

In a number of respects Washington's handwriting bears the marks of eighteenth-century style. He capitalized words sporadically in the middle of sentences; he used ampersands liberally, writing them in various forms; and he often employed superior-letter abbreviations like "acct." for "account," "wch" for "which," or "wd" for "would." His spelling was on the whole good, but he lived in the days when a dictionary was a most uncommon household article and he had his difficulties, particularly with short words. [2]

Washington departed somewhat from contemporary fashion in certain habits of punctuation. When he had to break a word at the end of a line he would stop more or less at random, not necessarily at what we would regard as a conventional syllable ending. He seldom inserted a hyphen when he did this, but occasionally his pen would leave a double, not a single, hyphen in its wake. He employed parentheses frequently; in fact, the use of parenthetical words, phrases, or clauses is one of the signposts for identifying his style. And, most characteristic of all, he used dashes universally, with or without a comma or period, to indicate transitions from one thought to another.

----

[2] His spelling of French proper names is gratuitously phonetic; never try to find them in a biographical dictionary the way he writes them!

Variants

Students of handwriting variants will find a happy hunting ground in the documents of Washington's earlier years, prior to the 1760s.   In his school copybook, for example, practically every letter is individually formed, and in the surveys of 1749-50, Washington cultivated a close-knit, mannered script. Also, there is variation in the early diaries, the pages of which, written at different times, reflect conditions of calm and stress, and in the military papers of the 1750s, in which Washington's hand is fairly angular and without flourish. In general the script of this earlier period was less rounded than his later writing (as evidenced, for example, in his writing the letter **e** without a loop), the capital letters were more elaborate, and the left-to-right slant, though present, was less pronounced.   There are, however, certain individualisms that Washington carried with him throughout his life, and they show up even in the earliest documents (see illus. 2). These include the lifting of the pen before a **c** or after **s, d,** and **g** in the midst of a word; final **d** written with its upstroke curving back to the left; initial **r** formed with a round loop; and that commonest of all words, the definite article **the,** written with a straight, uncrossed **t.**

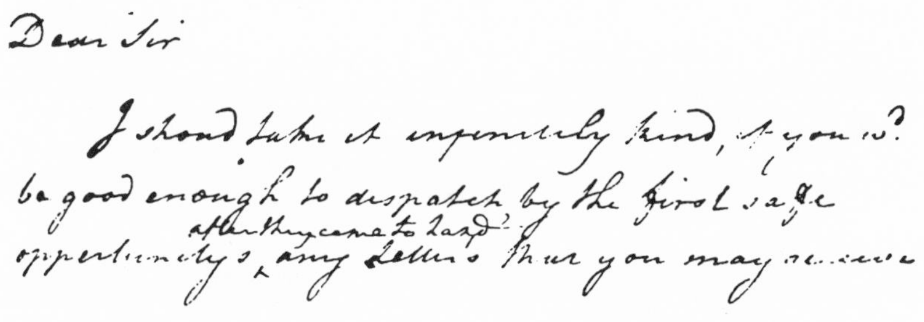

Illus. 2. From a letterbook copy of a letter written to Col. James Innes, July 2, 1775.

Signature Transformations

The progressive transformations of Washington's signature form an interesting study in themselves. Like Benjamin Franklin, Washington chose not to write out his first name in full, and even the earliest signed documents that have survived show him as just plain "G," not "George," Washington. Illustration 3 shows a sampling of signatures, beginning with his youth and continuing through the presidential period. It was in the 1750s that he began inserting a colon and a small superior **o** after his initial **G,** though for a while he was not wholly consistent in the practice. (It will always be a minor puzzle whether this was meant as a personal abbreviation for "Geo" or whether it was an individual flourish he adopted merely because he liked it.) In the course of time the small loop that he used as a dot for the **i** in his name became carried over and joined with the bar crossing his **t** to form a graceful figure that looks like an elongated letter **e**; his **s** changed its character, being formed with a downstroke rather than written on the level of the line; and he began crossing the inferior loop of his **g** with a horizontal line or a broad arc. By the 1770s Washington's signature had become solidified, and one finds few deviations in the way he wrote it, but the formations of the letters differ somewhat from those in his ordinary writing. An example is the elaborately looped capital **G** found only in his signature.

1749

1752

1757

1760

1767

1773

1787

1792

Illus. 3. Examples of Washington's signature, 1749-92.

John Morton, Changeable Signer *

Walter N. Eastburn

Some time ago I bought at auction some grab-bag lots of manuscripts, including Pennsylvania and New Jersey items, among which were four legal documents referring to property in Gloucester County, New Jersey, which had belonged to John Morton, father of John Morton, Signer of the Declaration of Independence from Pennsylvania. This property had been bequeathed by the elder John to the children (apparently eight in number) of his brothers and sisters. The name of the elder John was mentioned several times in the text of each of the documents, and the writing of the name looked so much like that of the Signer that I wondered if the four documents were not wholly in the Signer's hand. I decided to research this question.

I could not find any published biography of the Signer. Except for brief sketches in biographical dictionaries and various eulogies of him in pamphlets, there is not much known about him, and no authentic portrait has ever been found. The **Dictionary of American Biography** has this to say about him:

> Born after his father's death in Ridley, Chester County, Pennsylvania, son of John Morton and Mary Archer. His great grandfather, Morten Mortenson, emigrated from Sweden in 1654.

> He received only three months of public schooling, but was efficiently educated at home in all common branches of learning by his step-father John Sketchley, an Englishman, of excellent training and a surveyor by profession, who married his mother and took an affectionate interest in her son.

> Possessed of an alert mind, great industry and a fondness for precision, he soon was able to share the work of his teacher, so his early work consisted in surveying. Many tracts on Tinicum Island were surveyed by him. In 1754 (when thirty years old) he married Ann Justice (or Justis) a descendant of the Delaware Swedes; they had three sons and five daughters.

> He was early called into public life. Was made a Justice of the Peace in 1757. He served in the Provincial Assembly from 1756. He was High Sheriff of Chester County for three years from

---

*Originally published in 1960.

1766. In 1770 became judge for trial of negroes, and also Judge of Common Pleas Court of Chester County, and in 1774 Associate Justice of the Supreme Court of the Province. In 1765 he was a delegate to the Stamp Act Congress. He was a member of the Continental Congress from 1774 to 1777. He maintained an unrelenting stand for Colonial freedom.

The Signer died in 1777, less than a year after signing the Declaration of Independence, when he was fifty-three years of age. From the foregoing sketch of his life it is evident that his English tutor must have given him a good knowledge of mathematics and the classics. His surveying work doubtless became a part of his duties as justice of the peace in his rural community.

In preparing legal documents, a justice of the peace soon acquired proficiency in a plain, open-hand, legible writing, often very different from his everyday penmanship. My own collection contains a three-page ADS of John Morton, written in a beautiful script that contains many ceremonial symbols and flourishes, including the back-swept **d.** It is a deed dated April 6, 1764, and contains five of the Signer's signatures: two in the text referring to his having been an appraiser of the land conveyed, and three as witness and justice of the peace before whom the acknowledgment was taken (see illus. 1). I will call this document A.

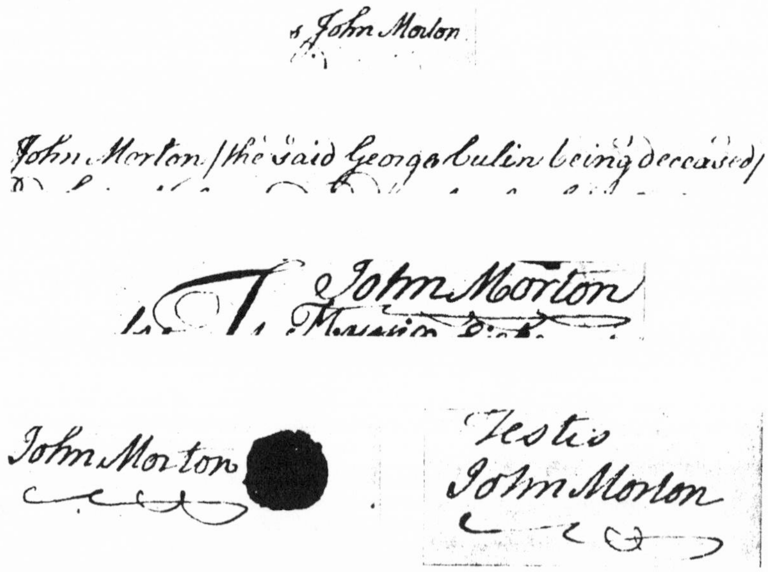

Illus. 1. From original 1764 ADS in the collection of the author.

I do not say, nor do I believe, that this specimen of Morton's writing is the hand he used for ordinary business or social correspondence. However, I will use this document A as my base for proving that the other documents I purchased at auction were written by Morton.

One of the four other documents is dated November 23, 1761. I will call this one document B. Another is dated December 9, 1763, and I will call that one document C. (The other two documents are duplicates of B and C and therefore need not be reviewed here.)

I decided first to study as many of Morton's letters and documents as I could locate. With permission of the owners, including the New York Public Library, the Pierpont Morgan Library, and the Historical Society of Pennsylvania, I have seen and studied forty-seven manuscripts, mostly written by, and all signed by, John Morton, Signer. Included in this lot were the four known ALSs of Morton, one dated in 1766, two in 1776, and one in 1769. If all the letters and documents I saw which were credited as being in his hand were laid face up on a table, I believe the average person on a hasty glance would say, "They look like the work of several different persons."

This study has convinced me that Morton, in the short period of his business and public life (1761 to 1776), shifted the style and type of his words, and the letters composing them, without losing that indefinable something that tied all of his pen work, especially his signatures, to himself without any doubt. In all of his pen work he used one or more of four very peculiar characteristics--I call them "pen prints"--which, like "finger prints," remain unchangeable. They are as follows:

1.   Bottom of capital **J** level with the bottom of other letters on the line

2.   Loop of **h** in **John** connected to **n** to look like an **m** following the **h** stem

3.   Lower-case **o** connected to following letter to look like **or** in **Morton**

4.   Use of virgule to enclose parenthetical remarks.

Morton also had two distinct habits in writing that he shared with others:

5.   Absence of punctuation

6.   Many misspelled words.

I made a thorough search among some hundred or more letters and documents of comparable period to see if any of the first four characteristics were used by other penmen of the period. Except for a capital **J** in one letter written above the line, though a style of letter different from the one used by Morton, I could not find these characteristics.

Characteristic No.	Document A Dated April 6, 1764	Document B Dated Nov. 23, 1761	Document C Dated Dec. 9, 1763
1	Lines 86, 93, & 98 (John)	Lines 2, 9, 18, 20, 23, 32, 39, 46, 50, 56, 63, & 64 (John)	Lines 1 & 5 (John)
2	Lines 22 & 30 (John) 86, 93, & 98 (John)	Same as above	Lines 1, 5, 10, & 19 (John)
3	Lines 5 (one), 4 (yeoman) 22 & 30 (Morton) 40 (tion), 46 (con) 50 (con), 66 (of), 68 (or), 92 (con) 93 (Morton)	Lines 2 (John), 12 (one) 13 (Elinor & Morton) 18 (doth) 63 (Elinor & Morton) 66 (one), 23 (Knowles)	Lines 2 (Morton) 11 (occupation) 19 (John), 28 (pounds)
4	Lines 30, 84, & 85	Lines 8-9 & 47-48	Lines 8-9
5	Total	Total	Total, except two commas in lines 15 & 19
6	Lines 35, 40, 96 (lawfull) 68 (premisses) 80 (Sett) 11 (Specefied) 25 (Valueation) 41, 96 (Pennsilvania) 70 (percal) 73 (accrewing) 80 (interchangably)	Lines 25 (lawfull) 6, 15, 19 (premisses) 16, 18 (Sett) 4, 6 (Seised) 51 (Yeild) 15, 28, 61 (intrest) 23 (Compleat) 58, 60 (Repairations)	Lines 5 (Bargined) 6 (Bargin) 9 (Mentons) 9 (haveing) 11 (Mentoned) 18 (intrest) 14 (untill) 15 (comeing) 20 (currancy) 21, 25 (dye) 28 (partyes)

(continued)

Illus. 2.   Comparison of John Morton's three documents A, B, and C showing the location of his characteristic "pen prints."

Similarity of letters		Document A Dated April 6, 1764	Document B Dated Nov. 23, 1761	Document C Dated Dec. 9, 1763
Capital **A**	(type 1)	Lines 7, 9, 11, 14 18, 20, 22	Lines 3, 7, 8, 40, 58	Lines 1, 3, & throughout
	(type 2)	Lines 2, 7, 10, 14, 19, 42, 46, 61, 81, 96	Line 7	Lines 1, 5, & 6
" **B**		Line 6	None in	Lines 2, 7, 16, 25, 26
" C	(type 1)	Lines 3, 4, 7, 10, 39, 59	Lines 1, 2, 4, 7, 9, 58	None
	(type 2)	Lines 10, 12, 13, 28, 33	Lines 6, 8, 9, 66	Line 3
" **D**		Lines 5, 23, 30, 48, 71, 72, 76	Lines 2, 5	Lines 2, 16, 23
" **G**				
" **M**	(type 1)	Line 6 & throughout	None	None
	(type 2)	None	Lines 2, 12, 19, 61, 63	Lines 2, 3, 5, 9, 10, & throughout
" **T**	(type 1)	Lines 3, 5, 6, 10, 11 13, 17, &c.	Lines 5, 9, 11, 26, 30, 35 45, 49, &c.	Lines 12, 15, 20, 22
	(type 2)	Lines 26, 28, 37	None	Lines 3, 14, 16, 21
Small z	(type 1)	None	Lines 10, 12, 14, 33, 41, &c.	None
	(type 2)	Line 48	Lines 1, 18, 30, 36, 62	None
Word **All**		Lines 14, 31, 63, 65 70, 92	Line 60	Lines 7, 17, 19, 28
Ampersands (3 varieties)		Lines 35, 68, 89		

Illus. 2. (continued) Comparison of John Morton's three documents A, B, and C showing the location of his characteristic "pen prints."

One or more of these characteristics shows up in nearly all the letters and documents Morton wrote among the forty-seven items I studied. So the fact that they also appear in documents B (first two pages) and C seems to prove that those two documents are also in his hand.

Illustration 2 shows where the aforementioned characteristics appear in each of documents A, B, and C. Also shown are where certain letter formations are carried forward from year to year in Morton's writing. There were too many examples in the text to list all of them, so a representative sample is given.

I was puzzled why in documents B and C Morton used the round-top style capital **M** until I saw in one New York collector's Morton items an undated document evidently written when Morton was quite young. It is a survey description written and signed by him, in which he used the same formation of capital **M.**

In documents B and C John Knowles, party to both documents, is referred to as "Yeoman." Webster defines a yeoman as "an attendant, a man of the commonalty." A genealogy of the Knowles family shows that Knowles's grandfather John Knowles emigrated from Wales to America. His son John married a Quaker maid near Philadelphia and died in 1743. Their son John married Elizabeth, daughter of Thomas Tatnall of Chester County, Pennsylvania, and he is mentioned in his mother's will dated 1777 as one of her executors. She died in 1778. There is no evidence that this John Knowles, evidently the party to B and C, had much of an education, and he was a bad speller, as was John Morton.

John Knowles evidently wrote pages 3 and 4 of document B, and while he did fashion certain letters very much as Morton did, a close study shows evidence of haste and poor formation of letters, of which John Morton was not guilty.

In document A, written in 1764, Morton used double flourishes at the end of his **d's,** and the ALS of Morton in the New York Public Library, written in 1769, also has many of these double flourishes in its **d's.**

Two other things seem to prove that Morton wrote pages 1 and 2 of B and all of C. In line 11 of B is the word "Intituled," a rare word derived from the French **"intituler"** and the Latin **"intitulo,"** meaning "to give a valid right to, or entitle." Then in line 12 of C is the word "Videlicet," from the Latin **"videre licet,"** meaning "to wit; namely, and our modern 'viz'." I doubt very much if John Knowles ever heard of either of those two words, though Signer John Morton's classical education and his work as a justice of the peace and deed scrivener doubtless made him familiar with them.

John Knowles made two insertions of the word **April** in the first page of B and spelled it with two **l's** while Morton in A spelled it with one **l.**

John Morton was familiar with the three types of ampersand shown in modern dictionaries, and used all three of them, with perhaps one or two inventions of his own. Except for the capital **M** (as noted above) the words **Morton** in documents A, B, and C are strikingly alike.

The Magee Chart on "Watermarked Paper used by the Signers of the D. I." omits mention of Morton, but the paper used in these three documents has a large Crown watermark. The 1776 ALS I saw among the Morton items of a New York collector has the same watermark.

It is anybody's guess as to what caused Morton to change his style of writing between 1761 and 1764. He may have had access to the two books listed by Professor Nash of Dartmouth (see **Manuscripts** vol. VII, no. 4, p. 208): Mather, published in 1727, and Franklin and Hall, in 1748. Or perhaps the influence of his stepfather Sketchley brought out in Morton the need for a change such as is mentioned in **The Psychology of Handwriting,** by Robert Saudex (London, 1925):

> English teachers of Calligraphy for more than a century and a half have sought exclusively to attain as "beautiful" and at the same time as rapid a writing as possible. Beyond this they have no pretensions . . . . We shall see in modern English types of writing how individual copies vary considerably according to the professions for which the pupils are being prepared . . . . Where the character of a person changes his writing is subject to change; moods and speed of writing also affect handwriting.

Simon Gratz, the noted Philadelphia collector, in **A Book About Autographs** (Philadelphia, 1920), quotes Samuel L. Sotheby:

> Comparatively few persons adopt any other than the ordinary handwriting they use in their daily transactions. Their writing does not vary throughout their lives more than by its failure in precision and boldness as their physical powers decay. On the other hand, many examples might be given of the handwriting of eminent persons, the character of which is totally different at various periods of their lives.

Gratz then continues:

> The pen, the posture of the hand, the space at command for the writing, even the condition of the health, have a positive influence upon the formation of the written words.

A later authority, and even more to the point, is **Autographs: A Key to Collecting,** by Mary A. Benjamin (New York, 1946):

> The variations in methods of signing his name by one writer present problems which are companioned by other variations in the script itself. Generally speaking, it is not unusual for a man's handwriting to undergo changes in the course of his life. This

normally is to be expected, but after the age of twenty-five, when certain **characteristics** have more or less become imbedded in penmanship style, differences are apt to be slight.   It is the exception when an individual's script "suffers a strange sea change," and it is the rule that at least **some recognizable similarities are present in both the slant and type of handwriting no matter how many years have elapsed.** [Emphasis mine.]

In **The Collector** no. 754, page 33, Mary Benjamin tells of the difficult research required for her to prove the authenticity of certain varying signatures of John Hart (Signer of the Declaration of Independence from New Jersey).   Hart in one portion of a document used a crossed **t** and in another place the German **t**.   She could find no precedent or reason for his having done it--he just did it!

Illustration 2 shows that Morton twice used two types of the same letter in one document, namely, the capitals **A** and **C** in document A.   Also, there is no valid explanation for why Morton wrote his name in the text of document A (see the first two signatures in illustration 1) with capital **J**'s extending below the line--he just did it!

I believe experts agree that only four ALSs of John Morton, Signer, are known to exist and all four were among the forty-seven items I studied.   One of them (1776) is at present unavailable, but with permission of the owners, it is my pleasure to reproduce in illustrations 3, 4, and 5 the few last lines and the Morton signatures of the other three ALSs, written in 1766, 1769, and 1776.   Many differences in the writing in these letters will be noticed.

It might be of interest to note here that my research brought to light two other John Mortons of comparative period: one, whose signature is shown in illustration 6, was a Philadelphia merchant and third president of the Bank of North America in that city; the other was a merchant who lived in New York City and later in Basking Ridge, New Jersey. I have been unable to find a sample of the latter's writing.

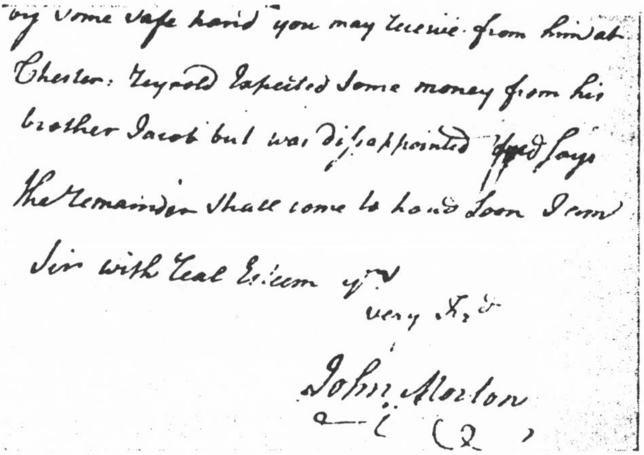

Illus. 3. From original 1766 ALS in Pierpont Morgan Library.

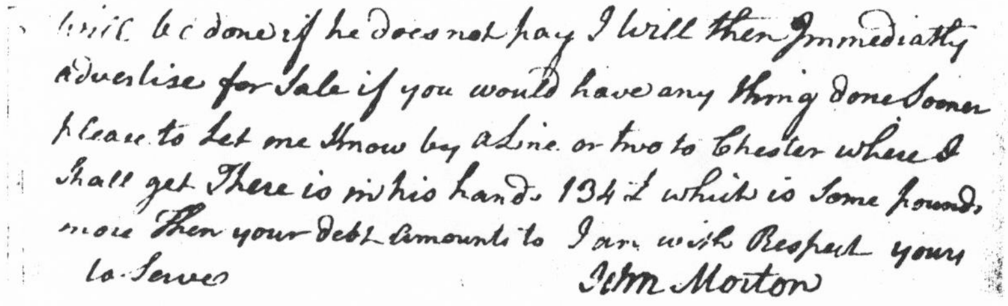

Illus. 4. From original 1769 ALS in the Emmet Collection (no. 1601), Rare Books and Manuscripts Division, The New York Public Library, Astor, Lenox, and Tilden Foundations.

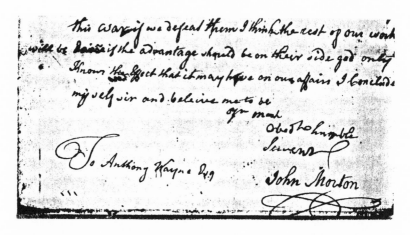

Illus. 5. From original 1776 ALS in collection of Dr. Joseph E. Fields.

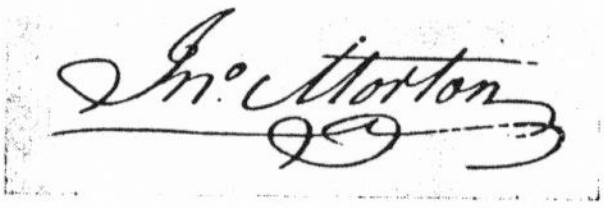

Illus. 6. The signature shown above is of the president of the Bank of North America, 1809-22.

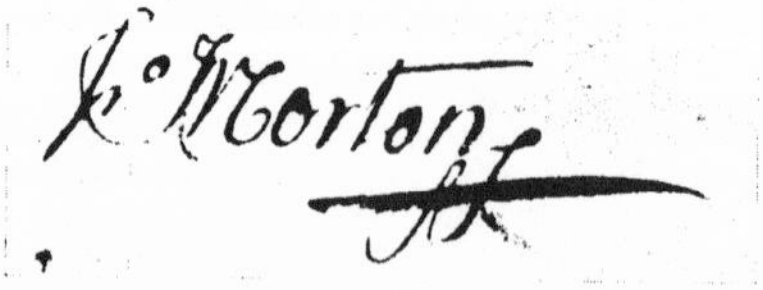

Illus. 7. In just one of the forty-seven items of the Signer that I have seen did he write his first name "Jno." From original 1756 ADS, Historical Society of Pennsylvania.

Thomas Lynch, Jr., and His Autograph*

Joseph E. Fields

From the historical perspective, Thomas Lynch, Jr., a Signer of the Declaration of Independence, cannot compare in importance with most of his fellow Signers or with many other Revolutionary contemporaries. Even his father, Thomas Lynch, Sr., was a far more important person, and one whose contribution to American freedom was infinitely greater. From the autographic perspective, however, Thomas Lynch, Jr., is extremely important, for examples of his handwriting are among the rarest in the entire field of Americana.[1]

Early Life

Lynch the Signer was born in 1749 in Prince George Winyah Parish, South Carolina. Little is known of his early years except that he attended school at the Winyah Indigo Society School in Georgetown. In 1764 he enrolled at Eton, where he remained for three years. On March 6, 1767, he was admitted to the Middle Temple of the Inns of Court. On May 18 of that year he matriculated at Gonville and Caius College, Cambridge, although it is doubtful that he ever took up residence there. In 1771 he arrived back in South Carolina, fully trained in the legal profession. But despite this, he became a planter.

Public Service

Lynch was a member of the Charles Town Convention of July 6, 1774, which condemned the Boston Port Bill and set forth "The Rights of Americans." He was elected to both the first and second Provincial Congresses and served throughout all the sessions. On June 17, 1775, he was

---

*Originally published in 1951.

[1]In 1951, clipped signatures brought about $750. As of that date, the highest price paid for a Lynch autograph had been in 1929, when the Rosenbach Company paid $9,500 for a DS at an Anderson Galleries sale. Additional information on Lynch's autograph appeared earlier in this volume (see part 2).

commissioned a captain in the First Regiment being raised in the province and served in and around Charles Town. On February 11, 1776, he was named one of a committee of eleven to prepare a constitution for the state, which was adopted on March 26. On March 23, 1776, the Provincial Congress resolved to send an additional delegate to serve in the Continental Congress and Lynch was named as a delegate, probably in order to be near his father, who had suffered a stroke on February 18. He resigned his commission, departed for Philadelphia, and presented his credentials to the Congress on April 24. In his six months of service in Congress he served on seven committees, most of them of considerable importance. He was present when the resolution for independence was adopted on July 2 and signed the document on August 2.

End of Two Careers

By December 1776 Thomas Lynch, Sr., was believed well enough to make the journey back to South Carolina. The son and father began the trip south by carriage, but at Annapolis the father had a fatal attack. The son arrived back in South Carolina early in January. His health, which had also been declining for about a year, continued to fail until as a last resort he and his wife resolved to sail for the south of France in the hope that the sea voyage and the warm, dry climate would restore him to health. They sailed from Charleston in December 1779 and were lost at sea.

Thus, Lynch had a very short public career of two and one-half years and he died a young man, aged thirty. He was the second-youngest Signer, being three months older than Edward Rutledge. Not until fifty years after his death was there any incentive to collect or preserve specimens of his handwriting. By that time much of his correspondence had been discarded by the recipients and their families as worthless or of little consequence. Numerous fires and two wars have also destroyed much of the remainder of his handwriting.

Only Sixty-Four Autographs Extant

There are sixty-four Lynch autographs known to be extant: two ALSs, one AMsS, eight DSs, and fifty-three signatures. Of the signatures, thirty-five have been clipped from books, six still remain unclipped although the title pages upon which they were written have been removed from the binding, and twelve still remain within eleven intact books. Lynch exceeds Button Gwinnett, whose signature is the rarest among the Signers, by fifteen examples.[2] Yet, there are far fewer "grade A" Lynch autographs available. Disregarding signatures, there are about four times as many Gwinnett autographs as there are Lynch autographs, yet Gwinnett autographs have brought prices five times as great as those of Lynch. There are several reasons for

---

[2]Joseph E. Fields, "The Known Signatures of Button Gwinnett," **The New Colophon,** 1950, pp. 132-45.

this. First, the Gwinnett autographs have been of better quality. Second, Gwinnett has had excellent publicity in newspapers, magazines, and auction catalogues. Third, the Gwinnett name is unusual and, in itself, excites interest and curiosity. Certainly Lynch is much more a man of mystery and had it not been for his proclivity for signing his name in the books in his library there would be but nine or ten known Lynch autographs.

Good Provenance

I do not wish to leave the impression that I am belittling the Lynch signatures. Serious collectors prefer not to collect mere signatures and would rather have better examples for their collections. However, in the case of Lynch this preference must be waived if one is to complete a set of Signers, for there are not enough autographs to go around. However, the lack of confidence one may have in a poor lonesome signature may be somewhat allayed in the case of the Lynch signatures. Fortunately, their provenance is good, being supported by reliable documentary evidence. It is most unfortunate that these signatures were clipped from the books, for the books, in themselves, were of little value and the signatures would be far more conclusive and of greater intrinsic value had they not been separated from their original habitat.

Classification of Signatures

From an examination of the Lynch autographs it is apparent that there are rather wide variations in the signatures. These variations may be considered to illustrate a normal transition from the immature handwriting of the adolescent to the more mature and stable handwriting of the adult.

I have classified the Lynch signatures as follows:

1.   The early period, circa 1766. This date is established by the fact that most of the signatures of this group had their origin from the 1766 edition of **The Works of Dr. Jonathan Swift** (illus. 1). A signature cut from Lynch's Latin exercise book is also dated 1766 (illus. 2). All the signatures of this group are derived from books once a part of the Signer's library. With only a few exceptions they consist of merely the word **Lynch.** The signatures are bold, heavy, almost perpendicular in position, and uniform in size. These signatures have three distinguishing qualities. In about two-thirds of the instances the top of the **L** is reversed, the letter being begun with a hook from right to left (illus. 1). In the remaining instances the **L** is begun in the usual manner with a loop from left to right (illus. 2). The second characteristic is the downward hook on the terminal **h** (illus. 1). Only in rare instances is the tail of the **h** carried upward (illus. 2). The third characteristic is the dismemberment of the word **Lynch.** Lyman C. Draper attempted to point out a consistency in the

way in which Lynch broke up the word.   Actually there is no
such consistency. In almost all instances the **c** and **h** are
joined, but the other letters are separated according to the
whim and fancy of the writer. The principal characteristic of
this period is the diagrammatic and calligraphic appearance
of the signatures.

Illus. 1. An early signature,
from the author's
collection.

Illus. 2. An early signature,
reproduced through
the courtesy of the
Pierpont   Morgan
Library.

2.   The middle period, circa 1770. Most of the signatures of this
period take the form of **T Lynch Junr.** The handwriting is
more delicate and the pen pressure is lighter. The **L** takes off
on an upstroke from left to right in the conventional manner
in all instances. There is no downward hook on the terminal **h**
in any instance (illus. 3 and 4). In a few instances the initial
T seems abnormally large in proportion to the **L** (illus. 4).
This form marks a transition between the early and middle
periods.   The **J** and **u** of **Junr** are seldom joined and in all
instances the terminal **r** is placed high above the baseline.
With few exceptions it is joined to the **n.**

Illus. 3 and 4.   Two signatures from the middle period. The one on the left is
reproduced courtesy of the Pennsylvania Historical Society;
the one on the right, courtesy of the State Historical Society
of Wisconsin.

---

[3]"An Essay on the Autographic Collections of the Signers of the
Declaration of Independence and of the Constitution," New York, 1889, p. 26.

3.   The late period, 1773-79. These are the signatures that appear in the two known letters, the eight known signed documents, and several clipped signatures. These signatures were written when Lynch was between twenty-three and thirty years old and represent the mature handwriting of the adult years. They are gracefully written, have a free-flowing character to them, and seem more mature in form. They have lost the stiff and diagrammatic form so characteristic of the early and middle period. There is an even greater tendency for the handwriting to slant to the right. As in the previous groups we find the letters in the signature unjoined and there is perhaps a greater degree of consistency in this group, for we find the terminal **ch** joined in all instances and in all but one or two instances the first name is broken up as **T-h-om-as.** The **Junr** also takes on a somewhat different form in this period. The **J** is larger and the terminal **r** is larger and not so far above the baseline as in those signatures from the middle period (see illus. 5).

Illus. 5. A late signature.

It was once claimed that Lynch always used the **Junr** as part of his signature until after the death of his father, but we now have a number of examples in which he omitted the **Junr** while his father was still alive. There are two consistencies that may help in identifying the signatures of the Signer. The initial **T** (when used) is always begun with a curled upstroke and the first hump on the letter **n** is always noticeably higher than the second hump.

Father and Son

Probably the greatest single obstacle to be overcome in authenticating the handwriting and signatures of the Signer would be in differentiating the handwriting and signatures of the Signer's father. We are fortunate indeed in having available letters and signatures of the father written at the same period as those of the son. Essentially there are no changes in the signatures and handwriting of Lynch, Sr., from 1770 until his death in 1776. Illustration 6 outlines the main differences in the handwritings of the father and son.

Additional and previously unknown signatures of the Signer may yet be discovered. For the past seventy-five years many collectors and dealers have believed that no further Lynch autographs would be forthcoming, but, inevitably, additional examples have appeared from time to time. For example, within the past three years the writer has brought to light six previously unknown examples, owned by descendants of the sisters of Thomas Lynch, Jr. It is hoped that in the future these examples will make their way into the hands of collectors who need them to complete their sets of Signers.

The foregoing study was based upon an examination of all the known signatures of both the Signer and his father. The writer has photostats of sixty-two of the sixty-four Lynch, Jr., examples. More than three-fourths of the known Lynch, Jr., autographs were examined in their original form.

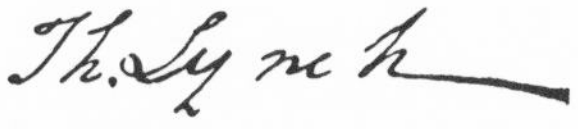

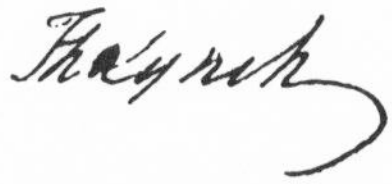

Thomas Lynch, Sr.

Thomas Lynch, Jr.

1. Handwriting and signatures are large.

1. Handwriting and signatures are smaller.

2. Terminal **h** has a long, heavy tail sweeping off to the right and then downward below the baseline.

2. Terminal **h** ends in a short downward loop in the early period and a short upward swing in the middle and late periods.

3. First name is abbreviated **Th, Tho,** or **Thos** and never spelled out in full.

3. First name is either abbreviated to **T** or written in full.

4. Initial **L** always begins in a gentle upswing from left to right.

4. Initial **L** may begin in conventional manner from left to right or in a short hook from right to left.

5. Abbreviated form of **Thomas** is almost always joined to **Lynch.** From 1770 the **L** is always superimposed upon the terminal **o** of the **Tho.**

5. The **T** or **Thomas** is never joined to the **Lynch.**

6. The **y** and **n** in the signature are always joined. In the ALS there are breaks present between the letters but they are relatively infrequent.

6. The method of joining letters is inconsistent. The **c** and **h** are usually joined. Breaks between letters in ALS are very frequent.

7. Pen pressure is very irregular to light.

7. Pen pressure is heavy in the early period and lighter in the later periods, but always even and regular.

8. Handwriting is hesitant and irregular, inconsistent and erratic. The lines are crooked and the writing is scrawled. This seems to denote the lack of a formal education. There is a noticeable lack of punctuation.

8. Handwriting is smooth, regular, and even in contour. The lines are straight and neat. The handwriting seems to denote a high degree of formal training and education.

Illus. 6. Comparison of the handwriting of Lynch, Sr. (1769) and Lynch, Jr. (1773). Signatures reproduced through the courtesy of the New York Public Library. The 1769 signature is in the library's Emmet Collection (no. 219), Rare Books and Manuscripts Division.

Abraham Lincoln: His Hand and Pen

Vincent L. Eaton

It has been estimated that nearly 1,100,000 words that Abraham Lincoln set down on paper have survived. In his sesquicentennial year, we turn back to them with reverence, finding in them a range of utterance and a diversity of speech tones that no other American statesman has commanded.

A fitting and proper tribute to Lincoln would be to take a fresh look at his papers and to try to single out some of the signposts by which his handwriting can be identified. Although Lincoln has been the most written about of all American presidents, there is no succinct statement of the principal elements for which one should look in attempting to determine the genuineness of a Lincoln document. This study is in no sense definitive, but it attempts to record some of these elements with the hope that others will join in further mapping the chirography of Lincoln.

If there is one general observation that can be made about Abraham Lincoln's handwriting, it is that although his pen might move rapidly, it was guided by a mind that acted with practiced forethought. The late William E. Barton well expressed this point some years ago:

> Lincoln wrote slowly and carefully. He did everything else in the same way. His mind and body both moved slowly. His partner Herndon said that Lincoln's nerves had to run a long way through dry soil to establish a connection between brain and hand. He did not act on impulse; he thought and wrote and acted deliberately. Yet his handwriting has a free, fluent quality, such as is usually associated with rapid writing. His pen wrought rhythmically; his thought though not rapid flowed with precision, and so did his pen . . . . He knew what he wanted to say before he wrote it and while he corrected carefully, it is surprising to discover how little of change his corrections involve.
>
> As he wrote, he pronounced his words aloud, or at least shaped them with his lips. He had learned to read and write in "blab-schools," where the pupils were required to study aloud, and he never learned either to read or write in any other way. His

---

*Originally published in 1959.

partners in the law-office were sometimes disturbed by this habit of his, but it was incurable; and it had for him this value, that he weighed his words as he uttered them.

In analyzing the specific points of Lincoln's handwriting, one comes to a realization of the dangers of excessively free generalization. Lincoln's letter formations cannot be sorted out into a Procrustean classification, and individual exceptions can be found to all general statements made about them. To say this is not to accuse Lincoln of inconsistency, but to recognize his profound individuality. The observations that follow must be taken to apply to a majority, but not all, of the cases.

First, let us consider Lincoln's signature. Throughout his life he was consistent in not signing letters with his first name alone; he was never "Abe" or "Abram" or "Abraham," even in his proposal of marriage to Mary Owens in 1837, and while he addressed letters to Mary Todd Lincoln as "My dear wife," he concluded them with the formal "A. Lincoln." In his sum book of the 1820s he penned the full "Abraham Lincoln" a number of times, but by 1830, as soon as he had launched into the business of making a living, he showed himself to his correspondents as "A. Lincoln," and this was his most frequent signature throughout his life. There were, however, certain variations: in communications to some of his close friends, such as the handful of letters to Mary Owens, he signed himself merely as "Lincoln"; this signature also is appended to legal pleadings, followed by "p.q." or "p.d." to indicate his acting as counsel for the plaintiff or defendant. In legal pleadings "Abm Lincoln" with the m underlined also occurs, and there are signatures indicating his law partnerships, such as "Logan & Lincoln," "Harlan & Lincoln," or "Logan & Lincoln & Herndon." In letters of the presidential period, "A. Lincoln" is most common, but he signed formal documents of state with the full "Abraham Lincoln"; and in transactions of business--notes to his secretaries and to members of his official family, or endorsements on documents--he frequently merely used the "A.L." initials (sometimes writing them as "A--L--").

In the group of Lincoln signatures shown in illustration 1, one can see both consistency and inconsistency. Despite the gulf of nearly forty years between the early sum book signature at the top and the one from the Emancipation Proclamation at the bottom, there is a striking resemblance in general appearance, particularly in the formation of the capital A and capital L. From the very beginning, Lincoln wrote the large A of his name in much the same way, starting it nearly level on the line, usually with a slight loop, then slanting his pen diagonally upward from left to right, bringing it down slightly from right to left, then up again to make the center loop. In the course of time, in his "A. Lincoln" signatures, he generally continued into the capital L without lifting his pen, and the center loop of the A might then become a small flourish starting the stroke of the L. Most familiar in these signatures, too, is the way the loop in the second l of Lincoln swings over to the right so that it projects over the final, flattened-out n.

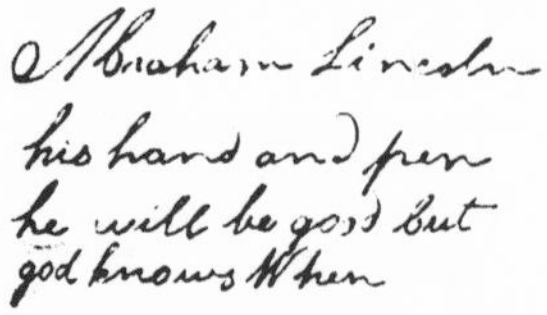

One of the earliest signatures, from Lincoln's youthful sum book (probably about 1826).

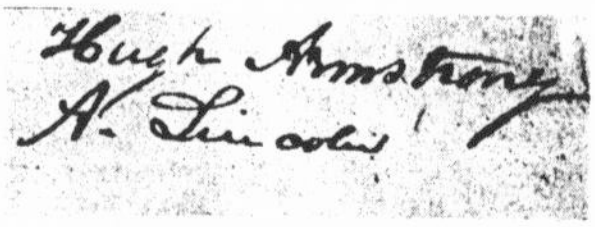

From an 1834 survey.

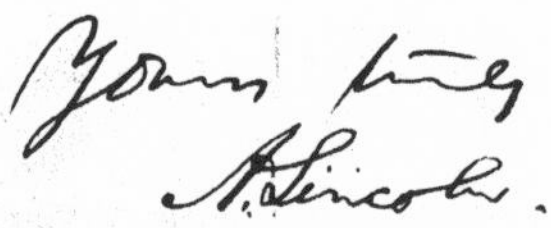

An 1858 signature.

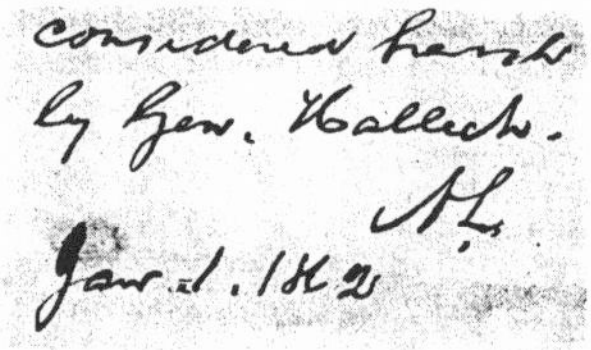

An endorsement in initials, 1862.

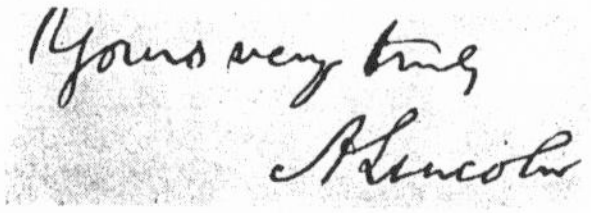

A typical presidential signature on an 1863 letter.

A formal presidential signature (from the Emancipation Proclamation, January 1, 1863).

Illus. 1. Some Lincoln signatures.

In dotting the i of his last name and in placing the period after his initial A, Lincoln's practice varied. In many cases the period is not actually a period, but two small dots or tiny diagonal slashes at the level of the line--reminiscent of the double dot or colon George Washington placed after the G in his own signature. Sometimes, too, the dot and period are omitted; sometimes one occurs and the other does not. In twenty-five of Lincoln's presidential signatures selected at random, dots for the i were found in only eight, and in these it mostly appeared over the c or the o, where a hurrying pen had deposited it; the dot and period were omitted entirely in twelve. Another variation, not shown in illustration 1, is "A. Lincoln" followed by a small dash, which occurs not uncommonly in signatures of the 1850s.

In writing the **Abraham** for a formal presidential signature, Lincoln would frequently employ one continuous stroke of the pen, then lift it and begin **Lincoln** almost at the level of the line, producing a capital **L** somewhat similar in appearance to a thin capital **S.** He then usually finished the name without lifting his pen. This characteristic of forming words or other units of writing without breaks may be said to be his fairly uniform practice--always qualified, of course, by individual exceptions--and directs our attention to the elements of his handwriting in general.

We need not concern ourselves too greatly with the writing of Lincoln's early youth for the purposes of this paper, since so few examples have survived. The reader who wishes to make a study of it will find the known surviving leaves from his sum book of the 1820s conveniently brought together in facsimile in the first volume of **The Collected Works of Abraham Lincoln,** edited by Roy P. Basler and others (New Brunswick, N.J., 1953). The example reproduced in illustration 1 shows a few of its characteristics: studied formation of individual letters, an apparently conscious attempt to keep the writing to a level horizontal line, and--a feature noticeable in Lincoln's later handwriting--a tendency not to close the loop of the letter **p.** The generally neat appearance of the writing bears out the testimony gathered by Herndon from an Indiana contemporary that "Abe Lincoln was the best penman in the neighborhood."

Lincoln's handwriting of the 1830s shows the typical slant toward the right, particularly in the formation of tall letters such as **f, g, p, q,** and **y,** that it was to retain to the end of his life. Especially noticeable is a tendency to add small flourishes in making capital letters, as may be seen in the loop on the left of the **L** of **Lincoln** in the signature reproduced in illustration 1. As time went on, and the young lawyer matured and took on added responsibilities, such flourishes were discarded, giving way to basically simple letter formations lacking in ornamental strokes or wasted motion. Noticeable, too, in the handwriting of the 1830s is the levelness of the lines, seldom deviating from the strict horizontal, and the even spacings between words--characteristics that Lincoln maintained all the days that he wrote with a pen. A tendency to make long downstrokes in the letters **f, g, p, q,** and **y** is likewise observable; sometimes their lower loops are enmeshed in words on the line immediately below them. With the passage of time, the downstrokes became shorter and this difficulty, of which Lincoln was doubtless never very conscious, was overcome.

By 1842, as can be seen in illustration 2, Lincoln's handwriting had taken on its new character. One finds that much of the flourishing has disappeared; he has come to write with few excess pen strokes. In its altered form, except in documents purposely written out with great care for some particular purpose, his penmanship has become less easy to read than before. He has acquired a tendency to flatten out his small letters, so that often an **e, o, i, c,** or **r** is barely more than a small peak above the level of the line, and the arcs in an **m** or an **n** are hardly distinguished from one another. By this time, too, Lincoln had adopted the frequent practice of using dashes rather than periods to separate sentences and end paragraphs, placing them usually on the level of or almost on the level of the line. Dashes continue to appear in his writings up to the last year of his life.

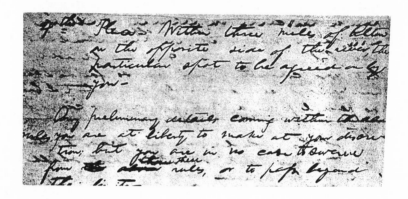

Illus. 2. From Lincoln's memorandum of September 19, 1842, to Elias H.
Merryman, stating the terms for his duel with James Shields.

By 1848 Lincoln's writing had evolved into the general pattern that it
retained for the rest of his years. Because it falls into such a pattern and
because, taking **The Collected Works of Abraham Lincoln** as a reliable
yardstick, approximately seven-eighths of the known Lincoln manuscripts date
from these last seventeen years, let us select four examples, dating from 1848
(illus. 3), 1858 (illus. 4), 1860 (illus. 5), and 1863 (illus. 6), and note in detail
some of the salient features.

Lincoln's typical **A,** starting level with a line or with a small curve from
just above it, has already been mentioned in the discussion of his signatures;
this occurs in the words **As, Almighty,** and **And** in illustration 3. (An alternate
A, oval and slanting, occurs much less commonly.)   The **B** begins with a
downstroke, then continues upward and around, forming the required central
recess, but ends openly, without meeting the downstroke, as in the
Blackstone's of illustration 4, **But** in illustration 5, and **Burnside** in illustration
6.   The **G** spreads above and below the line, with a pronounced down loop,
shown by **Greenleaf's** in illustration 4, **Gov** inserted interlinearly in illustration
5, and **Gen** and **Grand** in illustration 6.   The **H** of **Halleck** in illustration 6 is
characteristically formed with its right half looking like a capital **C**--the type
of capital that appears in the words **Commentaries** and **Chitty's** in
illustration 4.

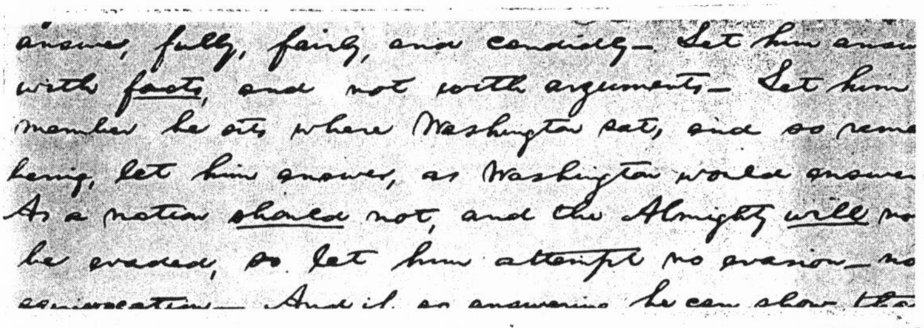
answer, fully, fairly, and candidly— Let him answ
with facts, and not with arguments— Let him
member he sits where Washington sat, and so reme
bering, let him answer, as Washington would answer.
As a nation should not, and the Almighty will no
be evaded, so let him attempt no evasion—no
equivocation— And if, so answering he can show tha

Illus. 3. From Lincoln's speech of January 12, 1848, on the war with Mexico.

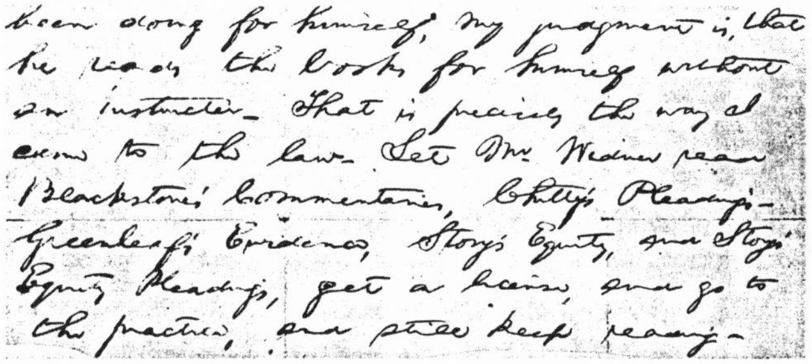
been doing for himself, my judgment is, that
he reads the books for himself without
an instructor— That is precisely the way I
came to the law. Let Mr. Widmer read
Blackstone's Commentaries, Chitty's Pleadings—
Greenleaf's Evidence, Story's Equity, and Story's
Equity Pleadings, get a license, and go to
the practice, and still keep reading—

Illus. 4. From an 1858 letter.

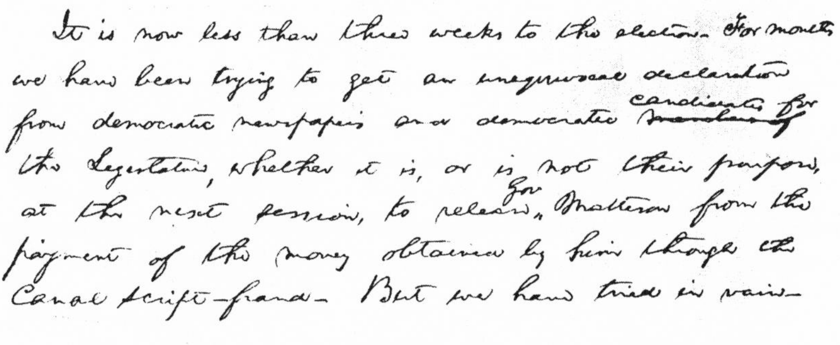
It is now less than three weeks to the election— For months
we have been trying to get an unequivocal declaration
from democratic newspapers and democratic ~~members of~~ candidates for
the Legislature, whether it is, or is not their purpose,
at the next session, to release Gov. Matteson from the
payment of the money obtained by him through the
Canal Scrip-fraud— But we have tried in vain—

Illus. 5. From a group of notes, probably written in October 1860.

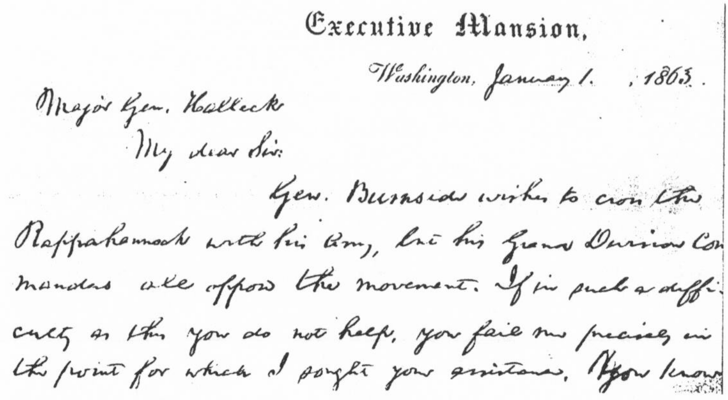

Executive Mansion,

Washington, January 1. , 1863.

Major Gen. Halleck

My dear Sir:

Gen. Burnside wishes to cross the Rappahannock with his Army, but his Grand Division Commanders all oppose the movement. If in such a difficulty as this you do not help, you fail me precisely in the point for which I sought your assistance. You know

Illus. 6. From Lincoln's letter to Halleck of January 1, 1863.

The **I**, befitting its writer, is modestly shaped, consisting of an upstroke from the approximate center of the line to form a sharply pointed loop and continuing into a small loop to the left, as in the **I** of illustration 4, the **It** of illustration 5, and the **If** and **I** of illustration 6. The **L**, in its frequent appearance as a kind of slanted capital **S**, can be seen in the word **Let** in illustrations 3 and 4. The **M** very consistently begins with a high arc, and then its mounds diminish progressively in size, as in **Mr** in illustration 4, **Matteson** in illustration 5, and **Major** in illustration 6. Not illustrated here but also worth mention are Lincoln's **Q**, which generally resembles a large Arabic **2** finished with an upstroke, and his **N**, formed with the same starting penstrokes as the capital **A**, but with the final stroke made diagonally upward to the right instead of crossing to form the loop in the center.

Among the lower-case letters, the **m** or **n** at the beginning of a word or of part of a word is noteworthy. It begins boldly and then trails off into virtual nothingness, as shown by **member** in illustration 3, **my** in illustration 4, **months** and **next** in illustration 5, and **manders** in illustration 6. Within a word or at the end of a word, **m** and **n** are often so flattened out as to be almost indistinguishable, as are **a**, **c**, **e**, **i**, **r**, and **s**. Because of the pronounced slant to the right of Lincoln's ordinary handwriting, the upper loop of a **b**, **f**, or **l** often leaned over the next letter, if it was a low one. This is particularly noticeable in his **h**, for which one may see instances in such words as **him** in illustration 3, **himself** in illustration 4, **have** in illustration 5, and **his** in illustration 6.

Other features recurring so often as to be called characteristics are **p** made without a closed loop, as in **attempt** in illustration 3, **practice** in illustration 4, **payment** in illustration 5, and **oppose**, **point**, and others in illustration 6; and the haphazard crossing of a **t** when it is followed by an **h,** as in the words **that** in illustration 4, **three, the, whether,** and others in illustration 5, and **the** and **this** in illustration 6. In a word containing the letter **t** twice with other letters intervening between them, Lincoln often would write out the entire word without lifting his pen, then cross or make an attempt to cross both **t**'s with a single long line. For illustration, see **attempt** in illustration 3 and **that** and **without** in illustration 4. For the letter **r** he used two forms rather indiscriminately, shown in illustration 3 by the words **answer** and **Answering** and in illustration 6, to cite only two of many other examples, by **Burnside** and **cross.**

Starting his writing career when the goose-quill pen was still a fairly common household article (and in his boyhood years also using charcoal and chalk), Lincoln progressed to the penholder with steel nib. In general, he appears to have preferred a fairly fine point and a medium or dark brown ink. But there is considerable variance in the thickness of his letters, and he could lay his pen down very boldly on a line when he wished to be emphatic. He occasionally underlined words to make his meaning particularly clear to the reader. In doing this he carefully avoided running the underlining across any letters, such as **f, g,** or **y,** that dipped below the level of the line. An example is the word **facts** in illustration 3. If a letter with such a downstroke occurred inside a word, he would cut the underlining in two to avoid crossing it. This is a point that seems to have been overlooked by the most successful forger of Lincoln's handwriting, Martin Coneely ("Joseph Cosey").

Lincoln's use of the dash as a substitute for a period is visible in illustrations 3, 4, and 5--though illustration 6 demonstrates that this usage was not invariable. His commas and apostrophes generally had little or no curve to them, but were formed as short, straight slashes. He often employed a double hyphen in breaking a word at the end of a line. A double period, short double dash, or two short diagonal slashes might be used under superior letters, as, for example, when he wrote the **th** of **4th,** the **l** of **Genl,** the **t** of **obt,** or the small **c** of **McClellan** above the level of the line.

Finally, Lincoln's orthography is also an individual characteristic of the products of his pen. His vocabulary was impressively large for a man who, at the time he came of age, by his own account, "could read, write, and cipher to the Rule of Three, but that was all." Throughout the entire range of his writings one finds occasional misspellings: forms like "vigilence," "streching," "immaginary," "Hazzard," "wizzard," "inconsistant," "trancended," "gover-ment," "litteral," and the like. He had well mastered their meaning, and could use them powerfully, but he was not always able to spell them as did Noah Webster, whose **American Dictionary of the English Language** had come out while he was still in the backwoods. Who would take to task the author of the Gettysburg Address and the Second Inaugural for such small slips of "his hand and pen"?

My friends.
No one, not in my situation, can appre-
my feeling of sadness at this parting. To this
place, and the kindness of these people,
I owe every thing. Here I have lived
a quarter of a century, and have
passed from a young to an old

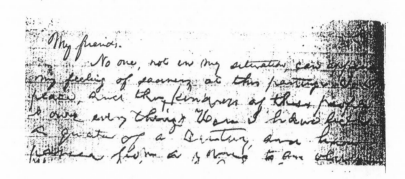

Illus. 7. An example of writing under extreme duress. Leaving Springfield for his inauguration in 1861, Lincoln attempted to write while the train was moving.

Executive Mansion
Washington, Aug. 23, 1864.
This morning, as for some days past,
it seems exceedingly probable that
this Administration will not be reelected. Then it will be my duty

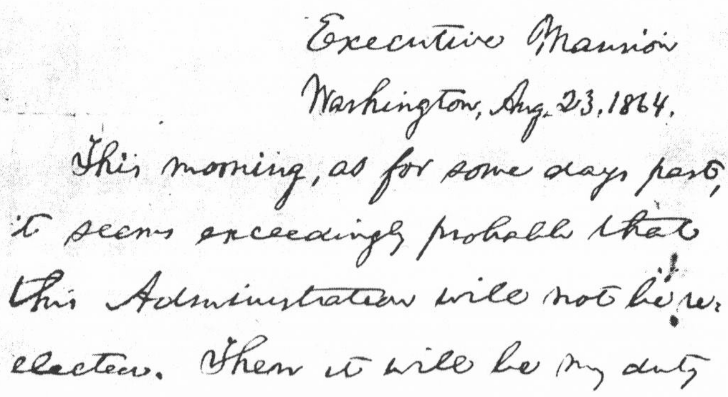

Illus. 8. Lincoln's 1864 memorandum for his cabinet is characteristic of the more formal and deliberate handwriting with which he penned important documents.

This paper was based on study of the Lincoln documents in the Robert Todd Lincoln and Herndon-Welk collections in the Library of Congress. Secondary sources which have been helpful, and which the reader may wish to investigate, are Paul M. Angle, "The Minor Collection: A Criticism," **The Atlantic Monthly**, vol. 143, no. 4 (April 1929), pp. 516-25; William E. Barton, essay on Lincoln autographs, in Thomas F. Madigan, **A Catalogue of Lincolniana** (New York, n.d.); and Manfred E. Henderson, **The Handwriting of Lincoln: A Study in Identification** (Los Angeles, 1931).

Angle's essay deals with a celebrated instance of Lincoln forgery. The career of the most notorious forger of Lincoln documents, "Joseph Cosey," was entertainingly described in an article by John Kobler entitled "Yrs. Truly, A. Lincoln," which appeared in **The New Yorker**, vol. 32, no. 1 (February 25, 1956), pp. 38-39. The writer is indebted to Robert W. Hill, keeper of manuscripts at the New York Public Library, for checking the point about "Cosey's" forgeries in that library's special collection of spurious documents.

The Literature of Concealment*

Walter Hart Blumenthal

During the American Revolution several of the leaders, including Franklin, sought secrecy in confidential correspondence by means of code and cipher. In the published writings and unpublished letters of Jefferson, Madison, and Monroe there are various undeciphered passages.

The dictionary cipher was quite common, and merely required that each correspondent possess the same edition, together with an agreed scheme. Richard Henry and William Lee, between 1777 and 1779, used Entick's **New Spelling Dictionary:** an arabic numeral indicated the page, an **a** or **b** the column, and a roman numeral the line. Other, less simple, schemes had the book paged backwards, transposed the alphabet, or adopted more intricate forms of concealment.

The notorious "millinery letters," which indicated that Peggy Shippen shared responsibility for the treason of her husband, Benedict Arnold, helped to bring about his downfall. The letters formed part of a secret code and their name was derived from the fact that Major Andre had commenced a correspondence with his wife in 1779 under pretence of supplying her with millinery. The apprehended letter of August 16, 1779, was an offer of Andre to purchase materials such as cap-wire, needles, and gauze for Peggy (each term having a code significance). This, as well as subsequent correspondence, disclosed troop movements and furthered the conspiracy of Arnold to secure command of West Point and then surrender it to the British.

Invisible ink also was used in espionage in this country as far back as the American Revolution, and earlier abroad. An extant letter dated September 15, 1776, from John Jay to Robert Morris describes how military and political information was sent to the colonies by means of invisible ink. It concerns letters written by Silas Deane, in France, to Jay, and by Sir James Jay, a physician in England, and brother to John Jay. Sir James invented the ink whereby secret data reached the Continental Congress. The preparation was supplied to General Washington, who used it and wrote for more. The method was to send what appeared to be family letters from abroad in a few casual lines, and to fill the remaining blank paper with invisible communication.

Rich Library Cipher Holdings

In the Huntington Library is a contemporary copy of a letter from Robert Morris to George Washington, from the Office of Finance, Philadelphia, August 17, 1782. It is in cipher (decoded), in the handwriting of Gouverneur Morris. Likewise, there are three original missives, partly in cipher, dated Berlin, 1798, from John Quincy Adams to Rufus King; a lengthy telegram in cipher (decoded) from Robert E. Lee to Gen. Joseph E. Johnston, dated Richmond, February 24, 1865; and a telegram from Jefferson Davis to Johnston, dated Richmond, July 11, 1864.

Also at the Huntington Library are letters in cipher appearing throughout the 314-page folio manuscript volume of John Jay, 1779-82, appointed minister plenipotentiary to the court of Spain, September 27, 1779. He had been president of the Continental Congress and a member of the secret committee of the Second Congress for corresponding with foreign powers. The Spanish ministry gave some secret assistance in munitions and money. In the spring of 1782, Jay was summoned to Paris by Franklin to act as joint commissioner for negotiating a peace with Great Britain.

In the voluminous Franklin papers at the American Philosophical Society's rich holdings in Philadelphia are documents in cipher code used by Franklin and his associates during the War for Independence. Others of that period and later are at the Historical Society of Pennsylvania in the same city. The Clements Library at Ann Arbor has specimens, but the New York Public Library notes that "the bulk of this material" in possession of its Manuscript Division precludes detailed description in response to inquiry.

Original cipher letters of the Aaron Burr conspiracy are in the Newberry Library, Chicago. One that figured in Burr's trial was written by Burr and dated July 22, 1806. It states, as deciphered, that he now has funds and "the best blood of the country" to support him, and that from Natchez the forces will march to seize Baton Rouge. General Wilkinson betrayed Burr by sending the letter and a decoded transcript to Jefferson.

These were lucid communications when decoded, and wholly unlike those eighteenth-century esoteric works on occult subjects prevalent abroad and written in curious devices, such as the eighteenth-century manuscript in Rosicrucian characters, **Le Livre des Pantacles,** or the work on magic, alchemy, and other arcana by the Count de Saint Germain.

English and French Cipher Diaries

In the eighteenth century there was another famous figure who regularly used concealed writing. John Wesley not only wrote voluminous letters, but daily he committed to paper a cryptogrammatic diary. He supposed the cipher was confidential to himself, but it has been decoded and we have an almost constant record of his activities and thoughts.

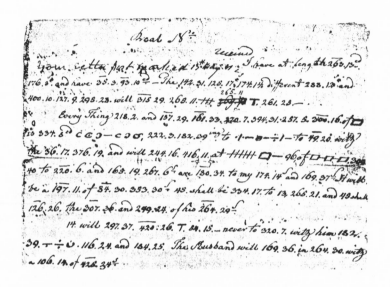

Illus. 1.   Part of the first page of a letter in cipher from Aaron Burr to Gen.
James Wilkinson, detailing Burr's plans to move with his companions
on New Orleans.

And in France, M. Thibot, bookseller of the Quai Voltaire, in 1878 came
into possession of a cipher manuscript diary in forty-five volumes, written in
what appeared to be oriental characters.   Not until years later were the
contents unraveled.   It was then found that the diary had been kept by one
Henri Legrand.   M. Pierre Louis declared that it outdid Pepys's classic diary
(discussed later) in three respects: length, intricacy, and impropriety.

Legrand, born in 1814, was an architect.   He began to set down his cipher
annals in 1835 and continued for thirty years.   He married an illegitimate
daughter of the earl of Clarendon.   Dissolute, he was popular in the
aristocratic circles of his day, dabbled in occultism, and was a replica of
Casanova.   Legrand transcribed hundreds of letters from a patrician
demoiselle with whom he had enjoyed a rhapsodic affair.   Even the letters of
her friends, which she had forwarded, are included, in cipher.   It is a **chronique
scandaleuse** of Tuileries twaddle and gossip of the court of Louis Philippe.   But
it is more than this.   Legrand included facts and names, documents and
commentary.   Those who should know say the material is authentic and bears
notably on the secret history of the period, the original records of which were
destroyed by fire during the Paris Commune in 1871.   It would seem that none
of this material--a medley of autobiography, liaisons, and intrigue--has been
printed since the find was first described in 1878 in an article in **Intermediare
des Chercheurs et des Curieux.**

Da Vinci's Enigmatic Manuscripts

On the peculiarity of Leonardo da Vinci's writing and the difficulty of deciphering his manuscripts, much can be written. He wrote from right to left, as in Hebrew, adopting from his twentieth year onward a reversed or "mirror" handwriting such as would be seen by looking at a reflection of normal script. Moreover, he neglected punctuation (nothing unusual in his day), and he further confounded future probers with an elaborate system of abbreviation. What is more important, this most gifted figure of his age was adept, a century before Galileo, as an experimentalist in mechanics.

Illus. 2. In a page from his notes on "The Practice of Painting," da Vinci treats the depiction of natural phenomena such as rain and wind. This particular sampling bears both his conventional writing (above) and "mirror writing" (below).

Da Vinci, who died in 1519, bequeathed his manuscripts to his friend Melzi. After the death of the latter, the precious, enigmatic notebooks were virtually lost to the world of nascent science for two centuries, when most of those still extant were acquired by the famous Ambrosian Library at Milan. In addition to twelve volumes of notes, there was a bulky miscellaneous collection bound into a large tome known as the **Codex Atlanticus.** The dozen notebooks were commandeered by Napoleon (who had an unerring eye for such things) in 1796, and by his orders were sent to Paris to be kept in the **Institut de France,** where they remain.

Much has been done to decipher these amazing da Vinci notebooks. From the principles of art to the laws of dynamics in physics, the range and profundity of da Vinci's knowledge and conjectures were, for their period, staggering. Thus, unlike others of his time, he had little patience with seekers after perpetual motion, or the dreams of the alchemists. "Oh speculators on perpetual motion," he wrote, "how many vain projects of the like character you have created. Go and be the companions of the searchers after gold." The motives that led him to conceal his speculations in so elaborate a disguise may be readily surmised. Probing of nature was heretical, and many minds from Roger Bacon onward felt the necessity of obscuring their speculations and prognostications in the veil of cryptography.

The Decoding of Roger Bacon's Cipher

What might well have been termed the most mysterious manuscript in the world, the work of the medieval churchman Roger Bacon, English scholar and groping scientist, held its secret for six hundred years. Written during his imprisonment, when Bacon was forbidden by his superiors to make further research into the mysteries of the unknown, the treatise concealed perhaps the most abstruse metaphysical arcana known to man. In it were hidden--in addition to biological formulas and discoveries--astronomical findings and prognostications.

In 1928, **The Cipher of Roger Bacon** partially elucidated this most cryptic of works, a triumph for the researches of William Romaine Newbold of the University of Pennsylvania. Newbold was entrusted with the manuscript by the bibliophile Wilfred M. Voynich, who had discovered it and brought it to America. The work consists of intricate elaborations concealed in apparent delineations by Bacon, some having biological, others astronomical import. Newbold, with the most persevering and painstaking effort, succeeded in deciphering these involved arabesques by scrutinizing them under a powerful lens. His elucidation appeared posthumously and recorded step by step his untangling of the cryptogram. The story of his mastery of the key, and his analysis of the intricate cipher devised by the earlier Bacon, is without parallel in the literature of cryptography.

The disclosures of this hermetic manual show Bacon to have been one of the most extraordinary solitary geniuses in pioneer experimental science. His cipher was written with unprecedented intricacy by means of an enlarging lens, so that only through a magnifying glass can some of the elements be resolved into their significance. As a Franciscan brother he was not permitted to experiment or to record his discoveries, but was kept busy with tasks that so galled his proud nature that he eagerly found deliverance for his questing spirit through means of the code. Of the millions of people who lived between the downfall of classical cultures and the dawn of modern science, he alone stood exalted by his intellectual caliber as a pioneer in the vanguard of the modern age. Sentenced to prison in 1277, he was not liberated until about 1290, and then still suffered from repressive measures.

His unique manuscript probably remained in an English monastery until the dissolution of the religious houses in Britain in the sixteenth century. Then it came into the possession of the alchemist John Dee, who presented it to Emperor Rudolph II at Prague, from whose possession it passed into the hands of others, until it was discovered by Voynich in 1912, in a chest in an ancient castle in southern Europe. The facts are told in the Newbold study. That the author was Roger Bacon is established by the fact that the alphabets worked out from the key on the last page of the manuscript, when properly applied, spell the name **R Baconi.**

Newbold, in a paper read before the American Philosophical Society in 1921, announced that he had partially unraveled the six-cipher code under which Roger Bacon hid his meaning when he wrote his cipher manuscript. Newbold stated:

> The text of the manuscript looks like writing of ordinary size. But each word, as it appears to the ordinary observer, is composed of a large number of microscopic shorthand symbols. Each letter is a sentence. Each word is a paragraph. What appears to be an ordinary "O," for instance, is an aggregation of seventeen shorthand signs. When the shorthand has been read it has to be decoded five times.

The Ancient Appeal and Danger of Concealment

The inquisitive human mind takes to the baffling and is intrigued by the scope for ingenuity afforded through concealing the true meaning of writing. This was expressed in a fluent sentence by a student of the subject who wrote:

> As soon as man discovered that words could be made visible as well as audible, one can imagine that they must have been exercised by the problem of how to secure for the written word the secrecy of private talk, without abandoning the advantages of transmission by any hand and to any distance or of retention for future reference. (**Bibliographical Society Transactions,** vol. 6, p. 127)

There was risk attached to the study of cryptography in the days when alchemy was still in the air. The covert symbols concealed hermetic lore. It was perilous to incur suspicion of practicing the occult arts. Hence the earliest two authorities on cryptography saw fit to let their works be printed posthumously. The **Polygraphia** of Trithemius saw the light in 1518, two years after his death, while the treatise **Steganographia,** ascribed to him, first

Illus. 3. Left, Roger Bacon's writing in actual size. Right, an enlargement
reveals tiny shorthand strokes concealed within the normal letters.
Newbold has repeated and clarified these below each letter.

appeared in 1551.   J. B. Porta's **De Furtivis Literarum Notis,** which describes
181 systems, had the first of its several editions in 1563.   Ludwig Hiller's
Mysterium Artis Steganographicae, of 1682, may have been known to Poe, for
the latter in "The Gold Bug" sets forth similar rules for deciphering.

Hieroglyphic Bibles and Parchment Rolls

Cryptography, also called steganography (from the Greek for "a
covering"), may be regarded as part of the study of esoteric literature, with
the baffling factor in the medium of presentation rather than in the intrinsic
context. But it includes the simple hieroglyphic Bibles that provided rebus
pictorial entertainment for the children of past generations.

Beginning with the first hieroglyphic Bible published in Augsburg in 1687,
these entertaining rebus puzzles remained popular through several centuries.
In 1745 appeared the French **Sentences from the Bible,** a passage from which is
shown in illustration 5. Also shown in illustration 5 is a page from Frederick
A. Laing's **New Hieroglyphic Bible Told in Stories,** which appeared in Glasgow
as late as 1894.

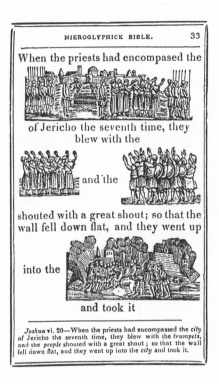

Illus. 4. A page from a book published by S. Andrus & Son, Hartford,
Connecticut, in 1855: **The Hieroglyphick Bible; / or / Select Passages
/in the / Old and New Testaments, /Represented with /Emblematical
Figures, / for the / Amusement of Youth: / Designed Chiefly / To
familiarize tender age, in a pleasing and diverting manner, / with early
ideas of the Holy Scriptures.**

The ancients had a method of concealment called the **scytale,** from the
staff employed in making and decoding the message. A ribbon of parchment
was wound slantwise around a staff, the characters being written across the
edges, so as to be divided when the spiral strip was unrolled. The message was
deciphered after having been rewound by the recipient on a staff of
corresponding size.

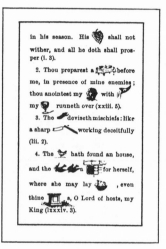

Illus. 5.   This French selection from the "Song of Solomon" reads, "I am the rose of Sharon, and the lily of the valleys.   As the lily among thorns, so is my love among the daughters."

Selected verses from familiar Psalms.

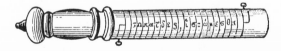

Illus. 6.   The **scytale** of the Lacedaemonians.   This example, when properly wound, reveals a quotation from Sophocles's **Oedipus Rex:**   "Let us arise, children."

The Lure of Interpretation

The extent to which cryptography was used in early correspondence is seldom appreciated nowadays, just as its futility was not apprehended at the time. A modest literature of interpretation has arisen. Thus a brochure, **Le Masque de Fer** (Paris, 1893), reveals the cipher correspondence of Louis XIV. It is known that Charles I had a penchant for ciphers and that many of his letters and state papers were in code. One such document, entirely in numbers, was deciphered in 1858 by Prof. Charles Wheatstone, who invented a crypto-machine, and the elucidation was printed by the Philobiblon Society (London, 1862-63).

The penchant, on the one hand, to conceal the purport of a work by secret writing and the inclination, on the other hand, to fathom such baffling media are always alluring. The old saying that conversation is a form of concealing one's thoughts may be applied also to the urge of authorship that resorts to writing of hidden purport.

Although there is less use of secret writing today, there are still people who seek to elucidate past works. Some decode cipher writings unintelligible without a key; others allege that readily readable works have a secondary and concealed meaning within their context. The Scriptures and the various plays ascribed to Shakespeare have been sources of this latter kind of imputed inner significance. The allegations regarding Shakespeare are empty, except for obscure allusions and puns.

Some Roots of Prejudice Against Cryptograms

Spurious attempts to discover cryptograms where they do not really exist have resulted in bringing this whole fascinating field into disrepute. Today some people believe that cryptograms are trivial and that authors of importance should not pursue such methods of concealment. Perhaps Ignatius Donnelly's **Great Cryptogram** (1888) did much to bring about this common prejudice against purported ciphers; and the stale Bacon-Shakespeare controversy as a whole lessened, rather than enhanced, the regard in which secret writing and its elucidation are held. Such arbitrary readings as those that Donnelly imposed on the text through excessive zeal brought the whole subject into something approaching contempt in his day, and excluded the Baconian hypothesis as a topic of serious academic investigation. Indeed, it was wholly baseless.

The endeavors of mystics to read ciphers into the Scriptures still persist, with self-anointed efforts at dowering "divine truth" on mankind. Some of the books that purport to be startling cipher elucidations belong rather in the alcove for alienists. Perversions of history and distortions of the Scriptures through alleged ciphers have not received the attention that has been lavished on the Bacon-Shakespeare contention.

The veils of time are lifted and prehistory emerges (in disguise) in the works of James Churchward, whose **Sacred Symbols of Mu** (1933) and two previous volumes assume to interpret the alleged symbols of "Mu the

Motherland before it sank and the First Great Civilization was wiped out" (capitals are believed by this author to give added weight to his maunderings). The prehistoric world is wrapped in the cipher symbols of a submerged continent, which he readily unravels.

Churchward states:

> Jesus understood the language of Mu. His acquaintance with it is proved by his last words when nailed to the cross: "Eli, Eli, lama sabac tha ni." This is not Hebrew nor any tongue that was spoken in Asia Minor during the life of Jesus. It is the pure tongue of "Mu the Motherland."

Churchward cites in corroboration the late Don Antonio Batres Jaurequi, who in his book **History of Central America** says, "The last words of Jesus on the Cross were in Maya, the oldest known language." And the latter gives the same translation as Churchward, who explains that there were two divergent lines of colonization from Mu--to ancient Asia and to old America.

In **The Cryptography of Dante** by William Arensberg, the **Divina Commedia** is made to yield "acrostics, telestics (acrostics with letters at the ends of the lines), interior sequences, anagrams, irregular letter clusters, string ciphers, and cabalistic spelling devices," as we are assured at the outset of this five-hundred-page book, published in 1921. The Dante classic teems with cryptograms, so we are told, and with symbolism beneath the allegory. But although the volume has every appearance of scholarship, it leaves the reader stranded.

Practical Uses of Cryptography

Yet cryptography was commonly used for centuries in a variety of forms and from varied motives. Thus, in manuscripts preceding the era of title pages, hidden signatures or acrostics served as a means of establishing authorship. Where there was a need for anonymity for religious or political reasons, such secret identification served a valid purpose. Where manuscripts had title pages, these might be lost and the work appropriated by another less scrupulous scribe by supplying a new title page or colophon. Thus the motives for concealment were not trivial, and above all, in many esoteric works there was symbolism in addition to the outward semblance of the text.

Code concealment has long been put to practical use in the marketplace. Cipher entries in the bookkeeping of that anarch of finance of the 1920s, Ivar Kreuger of Sweden, had precedents. The ninety-six account books of the fifteenth-century Medici family, acquired by the Baker Library of Boston in 1928, have many entries in cipher, in addition to accounts and memorandums in Latin, Italian, and Spanish. The Medici had sixteen banking houses in different cities, with headquarters in Florence.

The Pepys Diary

Most noted of all shorthand bibliographic items is, of course, the famous diary of Samuel Pepys, in which the Shelton system of abbreviated writing was used. Begun just before Pepys's twenty-seventh birthday, it was written during the decade from 1660 to 1669 and lay for 153 years unknown and undeciphered until a young Cambridge scholar applied himself for three years, "usually twelve and fourteen hours a day," to the task of decoding it. Pepys gives us a cross section of the period, and his graphic and gossipy pen bares the soul of Restoration England. His six thick volumes of closely written shorthand mirror the times, and there was the stuff of history in his 3,012 pages of pothooks, dots, and dashes, conveying some 1,300,000 words. Pepys ended his journals because of failing eyesight when he was thirty-six years old.

Deciphering the Pepysian journals was a laborious job, begun in 1819 by the Cambridge undergraduate John Smith, later a clergyman. The code was intricate, and had it been disclosed during the diarist's lifetime, the political babble and revelations would doubtless have cost him his ears. Parts were published in two volumes in 1825, for a posterity which, in the belief of Robert Louis Stevenson, Pepys had in mind. In 1828 appeared a second edition in five volumes, followed by others, of which that of H. B. Wheatley, 1892-99, transcribed all but thirty pages of the six manuscript volumes. Thus we have virtually all of the piquant satire and sparkling wit of that virtuoso of gossip. Still, we miss the thirty pages!

The National Maritime Museum of Greenwich, England, in 1931 acquired from the estate of the late Pepys Cockerell a large volume written in cipher by his famous collateral ancestor. It contained three letter books, all inscribed in cipher: **Secret Acts of the Admiralty--1660-1673--With Comment by S.P.** The work of deciphering these has revealed that they are highly confidential commentaries by the diarist, who between 1660 and 1688 held two posts in the Admiralty.

The William Byrd Diaries and Some Other Shorthand Publications

Concealment rather than speed was the major motive for most of those early figures of fame who employed shorthand for diaries and the like. William Byrd, the younger, son of one of the land-rich planters of old Virginia, at his death in 1744 left voluminous journals in his cryptic script. Two of the younger Byrd's diaries have been deciphered and published, but portions remain still unprinted. Louis B. Wright, editor of one of the diaries, covering the years 1709-12 (Richmond, 1941), wrote of its revealing tenor and occasional sly humor:

> The Virginia Historical Society, which owns a section covering the years 1717-21, has declined to permit its publication. In this suppressed part, Byrd describes with Pepysian frankness his amatory adventures in London when he pursued without discrimination whores, chambermaids, and great ladies.

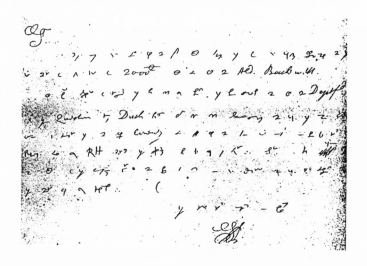

Sir

 I doubt not mine is come to hand which told you of my giving compliance to your last desire of a bill of £2,000 which is sent to Alderman Blackwell.

 What small parcel of ropes you shall hereafter collect you will please to send to Deptford.

 For your Question about Dutch ships we are here unempowered to give you any advice thereon, but refer you to Mr. Coventry who came to town last night and will be ready to signify how His Royal Highness directs your proceedings shall be in that matter. Sir, I have given him an account of your continued care to serve the King and my endeavors to give due respect to your desires in his absence.

I am

Your very ready friend and servant

S.P.

Illus. 7. This shorthand letter of Samuel Pepys was directed to Mr. Johnson, Admiralty agent at Yarmouth, December 6, 1664.

Except for this interlude, however, most of the diary concerns his numerous contacts and responsibilities, his reading, and the management of his Westover estates. However, the portion covering Byrd's middle years, 1717-21, was finally published in 1958.

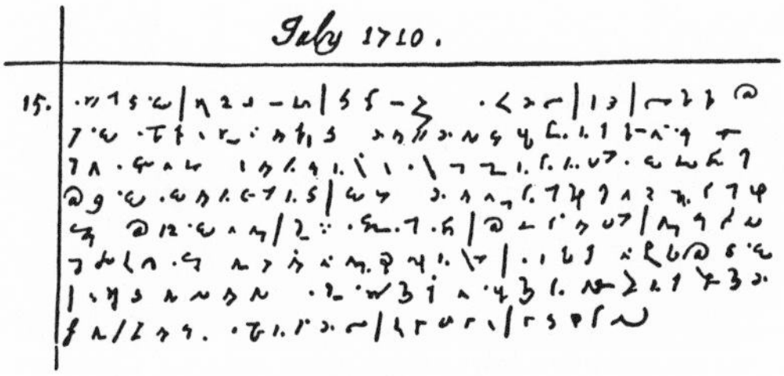

Illus. 8. An entry from the shorthand diary of William Byrd of Westover, now in the Huntington Library. It is based on a system developed by Jeremiah Rich, perfected by William Mason and set forth in **La Plume Volante (The Flying Pen)**, published in 1707.

As for other shorthand publications, **Pickwick Papers** in shorthand may be no more than a literary curiosity. It was published in two volumes by F. Pitman at London in 1897. One of the earliest bibliographies of works in and about shorthand, **Geschwind-Schreibkunst,** was published in German in 1863 and listed some 1,500 titles.

A Miscellany of Cryptographic Anecdotes

In the history of concealed writing there are curious anecdotes. For example, there is the letter written by Cardinal Richelieu to the French ambassador at Rome, introducing a friar. Read across, the letter prays for courteous reception to be accorded; folded through the middle vertically so that only the left half is read, it urges caution and impugns the character of the friar.

"Lewis Carroll" (the delectable Dodgson) delighted in whimsies as an escape from higher mathematics and logic. His lighter letters indulged in acrostics, anagrams, and riddles. He was proud of his word-game invention, "Syzygies." Sometimes the creator of **Alice** wrote in cipher or completely reversed the order of his words.

Ronald Knox, in **Essays in Satire** (1928), "proved" by an ingenious concocted cryptogram that Tennyson's **In Memoriam** was "really written" by Queen Victoria! Casanova on occasion used a cipher signature to conceal his name in printed pamphlets and articles in gazettes. Among imaginary books there is the one on cryptography Sherlock Holmes is supposed to have written.

William Blair's article "Cipher" in Abraham Rees's **American Cyclopedia** (1809) at the time was the most exhaustive encyclopedic treatment of the topic that had appeared. It concealed a model cipher in his presentation. It was discovered by Michael Gage, who disclosed it in a pamphlet now rarely encountered. Another curiosity was the series of cipher advertisements appearing in the agony column of **The** [London] **Times,** 1852-54, which resulted in an eventual disclosure in a book entitled **A. B. Has Returned; or the Romance of Advertising** (London, 1856).

All pseudonymous writings are in a sense designed for coverture, even though lacking cipher or code. They do not fall within the scope of this paper, however, which focuses on texts having hidden significance.

The literature of concealment has another category calling for mention. There have been real books--many in the eighteenth century--masked by false or imaginary places of publication. Indeed, a two-volume German bibliography of these, compiled by Emil Weller, was published in 1864, and a French listing by Gustav Brunet in 1866.

Just as the Rosetta Stone was an enigma until decoded, so at the present time Mayan hieroglyphics in Yucatan and Aztec codices remain for the most part sealed in their significance. Hence they are, to all intents, virtual ciphers, though not so intended. Perhaps it would be more accurate to say that they are for the most part undeciphered.

World War I revived the study of all types of cryptic writing. The secret intelligence departments of the various armies carried forward the science of cryptography to a marked degree. A popular description of this was found in Herbert C. Yardley's **The American Black Chamber** (1931). As a result of its revelations the manuscript of Major Yardley's second book was officially impounded, and Congress passed the Secrets Bill. Yardley, who died in 1958, had headed the World War I secret bureau of the American Intelligence Service, known as the Black Chamber.

A reasonably accurate survey of cryptic writing appeared in Fletcher Pratt's **Secret and Urgent** (1939), a story of ciphers and codes from old Egyptian inscriptions to modern times. The narrative covers data from Lysander of ancient Sparta to World War II. Casually written, it discusses both tragic and amusing events.

Cipher writing includes grill, numerical, diagrammatic, sliding-card, double circle, biliteral, phonetic, dictionary, checkerboard, and other techniques. Another medium remains to be again mentioned--secret inks. During World War I, a German woman spy known as Madame de Victorica was sent by Wilhelmstrasse to the United States to transmit data. According to E. Alexander Powell in his **Slanting Lines of Steel** (1933), she memorized a code before leaving Berlin. "The secret ink in which her letters were written was given her at the Chemical Institute and was obtained by saturating in cold water the two silk mufflers which she carried, and wringing them. Writing in this ink could be developed with iodine tablets dissolved in vinegar." Other messages were sent by pricking certain code letters in newspapers with a pin.

In World War II cryptography was brought to new complexity and wider use in military transmission and in diplomatic communication.   The top American cryptanalyst was William F. Friedman, who served the government from 1921 to 1955 as coding and decoding expert.   He devised new methods and cracked the machine cipher of the Japanese Foreign Office.   In 1956 Congress appropriated $100,000 for him as part compensation for the inventions he could not exploit because they were held secret by government orders.

No end of cryptograms and codes have been used in mystery stories. Jules Verne used cryptograms in several of his romances, notably **A Journey to the Center of the Earth** (1874) and **800 Leagues on the Amazon** (1881).   In 1870 James De Mille published his novel **The Cryptogram.**   Conan Doyle used several ciphers in his Sherlock Holmes stories.   Mention may also be made of **The Moabite Cipher** and **The Blue Scarab** by R. Austin Freeman.   Then there is a brainteaser in Melville D. Post's **Monsieur Jonquelle.**   James Branch Cabell mystified the reader with a talisman in **The Cream of the Jest.**   Charts in the hunt for treasure are inevitable.   Kenneth S. Cooper's **A Cipher Stories Puzzle Book,** consisting of twenty-five original little stories each containing at least two cipher puzzles, appeared in 1928.   **The Ravenelle Riddle** by E. Best Black is a story of the London underworld with ingenious cryptograms.   Another engaging volume for the relaxation of analytic minds was **The Cryptogram Book** (1927) by Prosper Buranelli and others, commended to those who are bored with misspent evenings.   The latest such mystery story is **The Cipher** by Alexander Gordon (1961).

But diversion was not the intent of the literature of concealment.   Its primary purpose was to hide secret information from prying eyes.   As codes are indispensable to warfare, so does the callow youth in the missives of his calf love inscribe crosses for kisses!   The basic lesson we learn from cryptography is that any system that the human mind can evolve can be elucidated.

Part 5.

MANUSCRIPTS AS A KEY TO BIOGRAPHY AND HISTORY

Manuscripts Tell Most*

Broadus Mitchell

How can we resurrect the dead, the long dead whom nobody living has seen or heard? Of course there is the embalmed body of Lenin lying in state for the millions, or--for that matter--there are the physical remains of pharaohs. But these corpses are far removed from their former reality. Contemporary portraits or sculptures are better, for the cunning of the artist has caught the glance, the posture. Folklorists, visiting those whom Walter Page called "our contemporary ancestors" in our southern highlands, have recorded what they believe to be the speech and songs of Elizabethans. Armor furnishes us the bodily dimensions of knights of old. Greenland graves, preserved in deep freeze, yield the clothing of Scandinavian exiles of the fourteenth century, down to the very patches. Gifted actors, by meticulous study of every source of information, are able to recreate Dickens and Mark Twain in their public readings. The biographer and historian try to do as much in bringing back a personality or an age.

Everyone who searches the past is constantly reminded of how much one may discover through diligence. The most precious evidence--of thoughts--is recorded in writings. The printed version fixes the ideas and the emotions. But the manuscript often offers what would seem to be beyond the possibility of recapture, the instant process of mind and purpose. Corrections, deletions, interlineations, and additions bring us the writer as he communed with himself. This must be the closest to the living truth of the person who held the pen. Of course, drafts are more revealing than fair copies. Practiced writers, able to frame their final meaning in the beginning, left us less of themselves. Unfortunately, many whom we would like to know more intimately were so adept in composition that they needed no second thoughts. But, though their holographs may be too nearly perfect, we may study their amendments of the manuscripts of amanuenses. It is an experience to scan the lines of an anonymous clerk and come upon corrections by his principal. The alterations in a well-known hand leap at you from the page. A word substituted for more vigor, an expression tactfully softened, a transposition improved, a crossing-out that sacrifices nothing and gains much in terseness--these bespeak decision or courtesy as though they were declared in our presence.

A manuscript practically without alteration may be eloquent of the mood of the writer beyond the testimony of the words set down. If memory serves,

---

*Originally published in 1963.

Alexander Hamilton, in addressing a petition to Congress to be signed by Steuben, became so imbued with his plea and so identified himself with the general that he first appended his own name!

All who examine original historical documents, especially reports, speeches, and essays, are familiar with how much may be determined of the circumstances of their composition. That a manuscript is not a first draft may be proved by the sudden appearance of another hand, manifestly that of a copyist. Whether a paper was written at a sitting or put together over a period of time may be shown by change of pen, ink, or character of the hand-- easy and flowing when the author was fresh, careless or cramped when the author was fatigued. A household may be reflected in such papers: here is the wife's hand running on for several pages until she was called to other duties, turning the task over to a young son or daughter whose uncertain script contrasts with the ease and point of the composition. In many instances only the manuscript offers a clue to accurate dating; the paper, the ink, the sealing wax may tell a tale.

A scrap of paper supplies visible evidence of the close collaboration of two men who did the most to secure ratification of the Constitution by New York. The first resolution offered at Poughkeepsie committed the convention to take no vote on the Constitution until all articles of it had been discussed. This meant that the Clinton forces, in heavy majority against the new plan of government, would not be able to dismiss the proposed reform after a few days of general debate. The motion that gained time for the then minority to explain and persuade, through arduous weeks, to final success is in the writing of Hamilton and Robert R. Livingston.

Printed works frequently acknowledge an author's indebtedness to other books. Celebrities' letters will be searched for more evidence of their reading, and every volume known to have been in their libraries will be described. But little-suspected manuscript sources may add to our knowledge of their intellectual interests. For example, the University of Edinburgh has preserved the ledgers in which borrowers from the library signed opposite the titles of books they withdrew. In a year when **The Wealth of Nations** was nearing completion, and amidst hundreds of names unknown to fame, occurs the plain script of Adam Smith, with the shillings and pence he paid for the loan of a work of history, philosophy, or poetry.

William Kidd*

Nathaniel E. Stein

Webster's dictionary defines pirate as "a robber or freebooter on the high seas." In the long history of piracy during the past three centuries, no other name has so fired the world's imagination as that of William Kidd. His deeds and exploits have been romanticized to a prodigious degree, and it is a paradox of history that his name has become synonymous with piracy and treachery. So large does he loom on the stage of picturesque piracy and highly colored marine blackguardism, that no sooner does someone speak of the exploits of some golden-earringed, hairy-jowled, tattooed, blustering scoundrel of a "beastlie pyrate," with dewlaps dripping gore, than someone else is sure to mention Captain Kidd. One would think that there had never been a pirate worth the name before him--and none after him.

William Kidd was born in Greenock, Scotland, in 1645, the son of a Calvinist minister. Migrating to the colonies as a young man, he arduously built up his fortune, first as a seaman, then merchant, and later shipowner. When, in 1690, the colonies were harassed by French privateers who preyed upon the small trade vessels along the coast of New England, William Kidd brought his ship into the service of the Crown. He fought two successful engagements against the French and on May 14, 1691, the Provincial Council awarded Kidd 150 pounds for "Meritorious Services Rendered To His Majestie The King."

The twice-widowed Sarah Oort entered Kidd's life at this time, and at the advanced age of forty-five Kidd and she were married. The union brought added fortune to Kidd, as his wife was both the widow of two prosperous sea captains and the only daughter of Samuel Bradley, a man of considerable property. The couple had two daughters and subsequently acquired a townhouse at what is now Hanover Square in the city of New York and a country seat in Harlem.

An Agreement in Good Company

In 1695 the great East India Company was embarrassed by the financial inroads that the Red Sea pirates and brigands were making against helpless British merchantmen. They petitioned King William III to dispatch an armed

---

*Originally published in 1952.

ship-of-the-line on a punitive expedition, but because of the war with France none was available. A possible alternative was to fit out an armed privateer for the purpose, and King William appointed Richard Coote, the earl of Bellomont, to carry out his plans. The latter sought out his good friend Richard Livingstone, prominent in New York affairs, and after protracted conferences the two-man committee decided to approach Capt. William Kidd, who by chance was in London giving evidence before the Lords of Trade in a colonial elections dispute.

Kidd was cool to the proposition at first but altered his opinion after Bellomont threatened retaliation and restraint. Articles of Agreement were drawn up on October 10, 1695. The syndicate behind Bellomont consented to raise four-fifths of the necessary six thousand pounds, and to receive four-fifths of the prize-money profits; barring profits, it was to be reimbursed for the original investment. As commander of the expedition, Kidd held a one-fifth share.

The syndicate consisted of the earl of Bellomont, Sir Edmund Harrison, Sir John Somers, the earl of Orford, the earl of Romney, and the duke of Shrewsbury. Bellomont was an Irish nobleman of Whig sympathies. He was appointed governor of New York in 1695 but did not assume his duties until 1698. Somers was one of the most distinguished jurists in England and trustee of the realm during the king's absence in the Netherlands. Romney was the intriguing and licentious uncle of the second earl of Sunderland. Orford was a distinguished admiral during the reign of Charles II. Shrewsbury was also one of the Lord Justices, and although only thirty-five years of age, he was regarded as one of the greatest noblemen of England, and dubbed by the king as the "King of Hearts." Harrison was a prosperous merchant and director of the East India Company. Shrewd, calculating, and ambitious, Harrison supervised the selection of Kidd's crew, rejecting all Scotsmen and colonists on the ground that their sympathies would probably be with smugglers and pirates. These men were all virtually Kidd's employers, and it is not surprising that the names were carefully concealed from public knowledge.

Doubts Arise

The closing of the year saw the successful launching of the **Adventure Galley**, weighing 237 tons and mounting thirty guns. On April 23, 1696, after several delays, she set sail from Plymouth bound for American shores. The exciting three-page letter that came into my possession, via Goodspeed's Book Store in Boston, now enters the story. There must certainly have been some doubt in the minds of Kidd's backers regarding their commander's integrity. Addressed to Isaac Addington, John Foster, and Andrew Belcher, all of Boston, the letter reads in part,

> ... here inclosed is a letter for you from the Earle of Bellomont who wth. several greate Lordes of ye highest quality are concerned in the Ship Adventure Galley Captn. Wm. Kidd (of New York) commandg. I am a considerable Owner wth those greate Men in sd ship & have had the managmnt of her outsett. The Earle of

Bellomont gives you some account of the Matter. What Prizes &c said Galley takes ye Captn is to carry to Boston & deliver up to sd Earle or his order.

In his Absence his Lordshp desires you to receive ye same; & to take an exact account of all goods, merchandizes, Treasure and othr things whatsoever which the sd Captn Kidd shall send or carry in to yor Port, in ordr, to make a division thereof according to the Earles agreement with the sd Captn, wch, is one fifth part to the Captn & his men for their share in full of all pay for the Service they shall have done. the other four fifths are to remain with you for ye Account of the Owners, of whch, ye Captn had one tenth part but he sold one third of his interest to a person here, yt I know off. Wt els he may have sold I cannot tell. Coll Robert Livingston of New York has also one tenth part but I am of opinion he sold most of all his interest . . . .

I hve not a line from ye Captn since he went from Plymouth, but hears he tooke one or two Ships, with Wine Brandy & salt; that he hath sent the Prize or Prizes to New York. I pray you will please to write to some trusty friend there, to Enquire if any such Prizes be there careyd in, what was done wth them, if sold wt was their amount & how disposed, & wt information may bee hadd off this Ship & Captn; the Galley has 30 guns & should have 100 men.

Mr. Wellen who was Mastr of a Ship & whose fathr is a minister in Boston, is one of the Volontiers, yt went wth Capn Kidd, whose friends may perhaps hve some Accont of him, & give you some information.

The Earle of Bellomont is in Ireland. I saw Old Winthrope yesterday but have not sd anything to him of ye mattr the Present Ordrs relating only to those of you that are at Boston . . . .

Edmund Harrison
67133096

The numerals under Harrison's signature were an intriguing puzzle. Robert Nesmith supplied the possible solution. The digits must be broken down into five separate parts:

   6 -- the file number
   7 -- the seventh month of the year (July)
 13 -- the sum of the first two digits (obviously to baffle people)
 30 -- day of the month
 96 -- the year (1696).

Thus, the meaning is "file no. 6, July 30, 1696." This seems like an obvious solution to the numerals, but there may be others.

From Protector to Pirate

History relates that Kidd, on this maiden leg of his odyssey, captured a small French vessel and from the prize received 850 pounds used for additional supplies in New York. Augmenting the adventurous crew was comparatively simple, for numerous able-bodied seamen were attracted to the enterprise by the roseate prospects of vast hordes of treasure to be taken from the enemy pirates. The **Adventure Galley** sailed from New York on September 6 and proceeded down through the Cape of Good Hope. Here, Kidd's actions seemed to take on a strange twist, because instead of heading for the east coast of Madagascar and the pirate-infested waters of the Indian Ocean, he ran for the west coast and the Cormoro Islands. Meanwhile tragedy struck. Half of the crew died of cholera, and the other half were in open mutiny. Kidd killed one member of the crew with a bucket.

At this point the captain crossed the line of demarcation between privateer and pirate. He decided to plunder the very ships he had sworn to protect. What were his motives? Were these "orders from the syndicate"? Or did Kidd suddenly realize that here was a shortcut to success and riches? On January 30, 1698, he captured his richest prize, an Armenian ship named the **Quedagh Merchant** of over four hundred tons. Scuttling his disease-infested ship after dividing the booty among the joyous crew, he joined hands with the notorious pirates Kelley and Culliford. The union was enormously profitable, and, after months of ranging the eastern seas, he sailed away from Madagascar in September 1698, loaded to the gunwales with treasure and headed for the Tortugas and the West Indies.

Meanwhile, England awoke to the news of Kidd's treacherous actions. There followed a wave of protests calling for "explanations" and the names of the sponsors of the "bloody pirate." The nervous Admiralty sent a ship in pursuit of Kidd, who, upon being apprised of the price on his head, sailed for New England in another small vessel. Anchoring off Oyster Bay, he negotiated with Bellomont (now governor general) through an intermediary. Kidd later testified that he was "wheedled" into terms of promised amnesty, but after appearing before the Colonial Council in Boston, he was clapped into jail for "not rendering a satisfactory account of his voyages and actions." Perhaps Bellomont was not satisfied with the amount of prize money that the captain turned over to him.

The colonies delivered their famous prisoner up to the king, and he languished in Newgate prison until May 1701. The House of Lords deliberately passed his trial to the House of Commons. Had he given evidence against the "Greate Lordes" of the syndicate, he might have been pardoned; but he stubbornly proclaimed his innocence, vainly hoping that his backers would come to his rescue. He was finally condemned and sentenced to be hanged for the "brutal murther of John Moore, gunner." When sentence was pronounced on May 9, Kidd replied, "My Lords it is a very hard sentence indeed. For my part I am the innocentest man of them all . . . ."

On May 23, the stoic adventurer was led to the execution dock on the Thames in the company of a common felon who was to share his fate. After his partner's execution, he was made ready to meet his maker. Still he did not "talk," and when the trap was sprung, both scaffold and rope broke under the weight of the captain. The grim practitioner once more pursued his duty from the limb of a nearby tree, and William Kidd joined the immortals, having left a legacy of strange and confusing maps of buried gold.

Caesar Rodney's Ride*

Justin G. Turner

Poetry has often brought immortality to individuals and historical incidents by dramatically focusing attention on them. Longfellow's "Ride of Paul Revere" is a good example. Revere's friend Rufus Dawes accompanied him on this famous ride, yet Dawes is not mentioned in the poem and is therefore known to relatively few Americans. Revere's contribution to the history of the Revolutionary period as a silversmith and engraver is also comparatively unknown. The Battle of Balaklava was immortalized by Tennyson's familiar ballad "The Charge of the Light Brigade," and its dramatic verses are known to every schoolchild. The story of the expulsion of the Acadians is known to the general public only through Longfellow's "Evangeline."

If the little state of Delaware had had a Longfellow, the story of Caesar Rodney's ride to save the day for independence would doubtless have become as famous as Revere's ride.

One of the many historical treasures in the Estelle Doheney Collection at St. John's Seminary, Camarillo, California, is a letter written by Caesar Rodney dated July 4, 1776, from Philadelphia to his brother Capt. Thomas Rodney. It reads as follows:

> I have enclosed you a summons directed to the Sheriff to Summon the member for our County to meet in Assembly in Newcastle on the 22nd day of this Instant which I hope you will have put into his hands as soon as possible after it comes to yours. I arrived in Congress tho detained by thunder and rain/time enough to give my voice in the matter of Independence--It is now determined by the thirteen United Colonies without even one dissenting Colony--We have now got through with the whole of the Declaration and ordered it to be printed so that you will soon have the pleasure of seeing it--Hand bills of it will be printed and sent to the Armies, Cities, County Towns, etc.--to be published or rather proclaimed in form--Don't neglect to attend closely and carefully to my Harvest and you'l oblige, Yours, etc.

---

*Originally published in 1957.

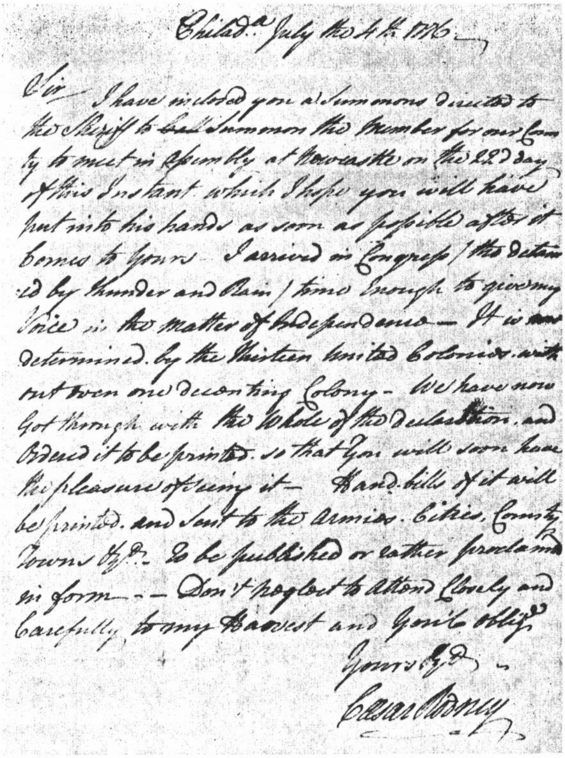

Illus. 1. A Signer's letter bearing the date that was remembered. (Doheny Memorial Library, St. John's Seminary, Camarillo, California.)

I believe this is one of the few known letters written by a Signer bearing the magic date of July 4, 1776.

One must understand the existing political situation in Delaware as well as know what had transpired in the Continental Congress to appreciate the full import of Rodney's letter. Richard Henry Lee's resolution for separation was first introduced on June 7. Independence was declared on July 2, 1776, and the resolution was adopted on July 4. The period between the introduction of the resolution and its adoption was tense and critical. Independence hung in the balance and one could only guess at the outcome. The Tories had ably presented the advantages of connection with the mother country. The question was argued heatedly and vigorously in Philadelphia as well as in the colonial assemblies. There were powerful Tory political figures in the middle colonies of Pennsylvania, New York, New Jersey, and Delaware. New England and Virginia were in the forefront in the struggle for independence.

Only the determination and aggressiveness of the radical minority in Congress made possible the adoption of the resolution. Early in 1776, the outspoken advocates of independence in Congress were Wythe of Virginia; Gadsden of South Carolina; McKean of Delaware; Franklin of Pennsylvania; Ward of Rhode Island; Deane of Connecticut; Samuel Adams, John Adams, and Elbridge Gerry of Massachusetts; and Samuel Chase of Maryland. Gadsden returned home and Ward died, but these losses were offset by the arrival of Richard Henry Lee. These patriots relentlessly persisted in prosecuting the cause of independence. That they ultimately succeeded was due to the skill and resourcefulness with which they adroitly maneuvered in Congress during the few months prior to the Declaration.

Delaware's three representatives to the Continental Congress were Caesar Rodney, Thomas McKean, and George Read. The entire day of July 1 was spent debating the question of separation from England. It was necessary to have the unanimous vote of all the colonies, but some of the delegates were divided among themselves. Although McKean favored independence, Read opposed it, and, as Rodney was in Delaware attempting to influence the public in its favor, Delaware's delegation was divided. McKean sent a mounted messenger in haste to search for Rodney and have him return to Philadelphia immediately.

The messenger located Rodney eighty miles from Philadelphia and Rodney set out on a mad ride, for the message stated that the decision would come sooner than had been anticipated. Rodney rode all day through the midsummer heat and on the evening of July 2, just as the vote was approaching, he strode dusty and exhausted into Independence Hall to cast Delaware's vote for freedom.

John Adams wrote his wife, "The second day of July, 1776, will be the most memorable Epoch in the History of America--I am apt to believe that it will be celebrated by succeeding generations as the great anniversary Festival." Instead, the celebration of the Fourth commemorates the adoption of the Declaration, which gave written form to the resolution of July 2, when the decisive step had been taken. Rodney's ride and vote stand out as the most dramatic, and perhaps the most decisive, incidents of July 2, 1776.

The Personal Side of History:
Rebels and Redcoats

George F. Scheer

Rebels and Redcoats differs somewhat from similar books in the field of Revolutionary War history because it does not narrate the war solely in terms of command, strategy, and accomplishment. These elements, of course, are dramatic enough in themselves to make a good book. But an account, however dramatic, of that war, or of any war, exclusively in these terms somehow fails to touch intimate responses in a reader for the simple reason that these elements are impersonal and suprahuman. But the reader can relate to the commonplace, to hunger and thirst and fatigue, to humor and disappointment, to fright and relief and danger--even to individual determination and courage. These are the terms in which Hugh Rankin and I chose to relate the story of the war of the Revolution, terms spelled out only in the contemporary writings of participants. That is the kind of book **Rebels and Redcoats** is. Call it, if you will, a supplement to the more formal histories, for it focuses more upon the trivial, the humdrum, the intimate in the lives of ordinary men and women of 1776, more upon their daily sacrifices, dangers, and sufferings--and splendid triumphs--than it does upon the professional or scientific elements of military history.

To establish a feeling of intimacy and to maintain it for the duration of a long book, it is not enough only to read and study the written documents. The writer also must know literally the texture of the things the men and women of the time handled every day. For example, I recall how much more immediate a scrawled battlefield note became after I had handled a Revolutionary lead pencil. It was not, of course, the lead pencil of today, which is not lead at all but graphite encased in cedar. It was a little bar of soft lead fabricated from a bullet and may have been used by a soldier to mark a piece of tenting, to cast up his accounts, or to keep tally in games of chance. The writer should think about that pencil when he thinks about a soldier writing a note. One gains something significant by handling the **things** as well as the manuscripts, by feeling the coarseness of cloth, the weight and balance of a musket, the feel of a canteen or a powder horn.

One thinks of women in camp, for we know about laundresses, wives, and followers. The letters and diaries are full of references to them. But another world opens when one looks at the toys found in a Revolutionary campsite.

---

*Originally published in 1957.

These are the things, in addition to the written words, that the writer tries to keep in mind, to keep in the front of his senses, as he writes. And there are others, too: how hard the ground can feel after you have been lying on it seven or eight hours, how cold some summer nights can get, how in battle the earth moves and folds and breaks and deceives the foot and the eye. These are the things the letters of the soldiers constantly remind one of.

Soldiering has a timelessness, just as human character seems to have a timelessness. And an evocation of this continuity, it seems to me, can be achieved only through the physical things and the personal documents. Soldiering has not changed much and soldiers less, but when we turn away from the first-hand letters and documents, we tend to forget how many emotions and experiences familiar to us were also familiar to the soldiers of 1776.

For example, there is the waiting, dry-mouthed, for the business to start. Hemingway never forgot how it was in Italy in 1917, but a letter describes it in 1780, too. It was on a rainy morning at King's Mountain on the border between North and South Carolina. The rebels were forming in the woods at the foot of the mountain, determined to charge up the rough wooded slopes to destroy Patrick Ferguson's Tories. An American officer told his men that cowards would be quietly excused. James Collins, who was sixteen, was there. Later he admitted,

> Here I confess I would willingly have been excused, for my feelings were not the most pleasant. They may be attributed to my youth, not being quite seventeen, but I could not swallow the appellation of coward. We were soon in motion, every man throwing four or five balls in his mouth to prevent thirst . . . .

For a variety of considerations it seemed logical to open **Rebels and Redcoats** with Paul Revere and the night it all began, April 18, 1775. Although Revere said "rid" for "rode" and sometimes "come" for "came," he had a sense of the valuable, a sense of the poetic, a feeling for the image-building word or phrase that one finds so often in an intelligent, perceptive man who has not been neatly schooled or over-civilized. Here is a sampling of his direct but colorful letter:

> At ten o'clock Dr. Warren sent for me. Dr. Warren begged that I would immediately set off for Lexington, where Messrs. Hancock and Adams were, and acquaint them of the movement of the regulars and that it was thought they were the objects . . . . I left Dr. Warren, called upon a friend and desired him to make the signals [in the North Church tower]. I then went home, took my boots and surtout, went to the north part of the town where I had kept a boat. Two friends rowed me across Charles River, a little to the eastward where the **Somerset** man-of-war lay. It was then young flood, the ship was winding, and the moon was rising. They landed me on the Charlestown side. When I got into town I met Colonel Conant and several others. They said they had seen our signals. I told them what was acting and went to get me a horse. I got a horse of Deacon Larkin . . . .

After the battle of Concord, an American army encamped around Boston overnight. Typical American responses began to exert themselves. And again the commonness of experience is apparent. There is an hilarious scene in the World War II production of **Mr. Roberts** in which the ship's crew, cleaning binoculars, accidently discovered that by using them they could spy on nurses in barracks across the harbor. And here is what an American lieutenant wrote in his diary outside Boston in 1775:

> I mentioned among the officers Mr. Beckwith's observation that before he left home he made a covenant with his eyes, concerning women, when Colonel Huntington replied that there was no need of that here, for he and Mr. Trumbull were yesterday obliged to use a spy glass to get a sight at one.

With its army, America got its general, George Washington, a splendid human being despite his violent temper, his closeness with a shilling, his shyness on the one hand, his austerity on the other. Again it is in the personal documents that he comes alive. After reading the thirty-seven volumes of his writings and numerous accounts of him by other people, I am at a loss to explain how he acquired the reputation as a stuffed shirt. Although he was not a back-slapper or a particularly jovial man, he was affable enough. A visitor to his headquarters during the war describes how he sat about the table after dinner each evening with his officers, sipping wine, making serious and frivolous toasts, and cracking nuts in his teeth and munching them with relish. And there is evidence of an occasional waggish humor. In a series of letters to Lafayette he writes airily about laying siege to the heart of the marquis's wife; his bantering is just the kind of nonsense two devoted friends might be expected to exchange over a lovely young wife whose husband reports she is positively in love with his older friend.

No doubt about it, the general enjoyed the ladies. There was the time he danced with the winsome wife of General Greene for three hours, according to General Greene, without once sitting down. Greene called it a "pretty little frisk." And again it is from documents that we learn he had his troubles with the fair sex. It was Kitty Greene who started the rumor that at one of Colonel Biddle's parties Mrs. Olney was heard to tell the general angrily that "if he did not let go her hand, she would tear out his eyes, or the hair from his head. Though he was a general, he was but a man."

Usually the ladies enjoyed him. There is a letter from Martha Bland to his sister-in-law, describing a visit with the Washingtons at Morristown, in which she says, "He can be downright impudent sometimes, such impudence, Fanny, as you and I like, and I have wished for you often."

And this human man had a temper. There are plenty of letters showing that; if he did not swear until the leaves shook on the trees, his own letters and those of others reveal he often wrote and spoke with passion.

From the manuscripts and nowhere else also comes a picture of Washington's soldiers. Again, to take examples, their letters reveal a strong spirit of sectionalism. Washington himself, shortly after taking command, was calling New Englanders "an exceedingly dirty and nasty people," and it took him some time to get over this attitude. He had an aristocrat's sense of caste with its privileges and its responsibilities, but the idea of "leveling," so prevalent in New England, was just as appalling to the ordinary "low-caste" man of the southern colonies as to him. Democracy in the "leveling" sense was strictly a New England institution. It was a Pennsylvanian who was horrified to find a captain who had been a civilian barber shaving one of his privates on company parade. Worse than that, he lamented, the barber did not seem to see anything wrong in it! Sectionalism was not merely a matter of region against region, but often of state against state. New Yorkers were suspicious of Connecticut men, and the latter often warned in their letters never to trust a New Yorker! And a Pennsylvanian deplored Negroes' serving in a Massachusetts outfit.

The documents upset many cherished myths, among them that of the riflemen, who turn out to have been more of a nuisance than a value to the army in the long run. The documents attest to the trouble that both sides had in maintaining discipline; on both sides daily courts martial sat on a multitude of crimes. Sometimes these problems led to amusing orders, witness General Greene's order on rural Long Island in the summer of 1776:

> Complaint having been made by the inhabitants situated near the Mill Pond that some of the soldiers come there to go swimming in the open view of the women and that they come out of the water and run to the houses naked with a design to insult and wound the modesty of female decency, 'tis with concern that the general finds himself under the disagreeable necessity of expressing his disapprobation of such a beastly conduct.

I think it is to be expected that, with the shift of the war to the South, personal accounts diminish in quantity. Probably many more New Englanders than southerners were literate. But the campaigns in the South, it must be remembered, consisted in great part of smaller, frequently spontaneous actions by relatively local forces in places that were often obscure. The men sometimes slept at night in their own homes or served for brief periods and then went home, so they did not write many letters or keep long-term diaries. They fought, but a large percentage of them did not go to war in the sense that many New Englanders and Middle Staters did. The men from the various regions, of course, were essentially the same. At Guilford Court House, while Greene's Continentals and militia waited for Cornwallis's advance to come through a defile and into the field, Maj. Richard Harrison, a militiaman, hunched against a rail fence and thought longingly of his wife. This day she was supposed to give birth to a child. Pulling pencil and paper from his pocket, he wrote her:

> It is scarcely possible to paint the agitations of my mind struggling with two of the greatest events that are in nature at the same time: the fate of my Nancy and my country. Oh, my God, I trust them with thee: do with them for the best. The day seems nearly at hand that will render North Carolina perfectly happy or completely miserable . . . . This is the very day that I hope will be given me a creature capable of enjoying what his father hopes to deserve and earn--the sweets of Liberty and grace.

This brief report of some eyewitness accounts of the Revolution has been confined more to the soldier than to the citizen; as much as anything this is because accounts concerning the civil side of the war would have required more background discussion. Perhaps that is as it should be, for in the end the business of that war was accomplished by the fighting men. In the early American soldier's own words one finds his portrait; for all his cynicism, rowdiness, meanness, his real and pretended toughness, his disillusion, cowardice, profaneness, he was usually at heart typified by Pvt. Josiah Atkins, who did not live to see the end at Yorktown in 1781. A Connecticut man, he lay dying of fever in alien Virginia, October 4, 1781, when he wrote a last letter to his wife which underscores precisely what I have tried to express about the force of the personal document.

> I thought I could not be contented to take my last little portion of land--though but my length and breadth--and leave my lifeless lump on this barren soil. However, when I reflected that this barren soil of Virginia must be enriched with the rich manure of Connecticut; that our cause is just and must be supported, and that God will raise the dead here as well as in Connecticut--these thoughts put me to silence and I become (I hope) in some measure resigned to God's will.

The Correspondence of the
First First Lady*

Joseph E. Fields

In comparison with her illustrious husband, who carried on one of the most extensive correspondences of any of our great national figures, Martha Washington wrote few letters. This is not to be wondered at, for the age was one in which the affairs of the world belonged to men, and women, like children, were to be seen and not heard. Ladies carried on a polite correspondence dictated by the social amenities of the day. Their only regular correspondents were close relatives. While the correspondence of colonial gentlemen sheds considerable light on the political and economic questions of the day, it is the letters of their ladies that give us an insight into the colonial household and its problems.

George Washington's letters are noted for their smooth-flowing but somewhat stiff style, the truly majestic handwriting, and the uniformity of the spelling. There is no handwriting that surpasses it in distinction. In contrast, Mrs. Washington's handwriting is laborious and difficult to read, and shows frequent mistakes in punctuation, capitalization, and spelling. This is not to be considered unusual, for the well-bred colonial woman received little education beyond the rudiments of reading, writing, and arithmetic. On the plantation where Martha was raised, she probably had the advantage of a tutor for only a few months each year; beyond that, her education was limited to what could be learned from her mother. Undoubtedly she acquired some appreciation for reading from her two husbands, both of whom possessed large libraries.

With all their eccentricities, her letters have a down-to-earth sincerity and friendliness in them that are not present in her husband's correspondence. She displays compassion, kindness, and benevolence--a genuine interest in the welfare of her friends, relatives, neighbors, and mankind in general that her husband seldom put on paper but nevertheless felt keenly in his heart.

Martha's correspondence, while never extensive, also has been considerably depleted by destruction. It has been hinted that after her death, members of the family destroyed portions of her correspondence, believing that her poor spelling was a reflection of a poor education. There are no known letters from Mrs. Washington to the general, and only two letters of the general to her are now known to have survived. It is extremely unlikely that additional letters will turn up.

---

*Originally published in 1956.

It now appears quite certain that Mrs. Washington undertook a systematic destruction of all the correspondence between her husband and herself. Undoubtedly she knew of the efforts of many people to penetrate the official correspondence of the general for the purpose of historical writings and biography. It is possible that the general himself may have had a hand in the destruction of the correspondence, having agreed to make his papers available for publication, by several persons, following his death.

The two surviving letters from the general to Martha are those that for sentimental reasons she could scarcely have brought herself to sacrifice. The first is the letter informing her of his selection as commander in chief of the Continental Army, together with his reasons for acceptance. The other letter tells of his departure for Boston, his trust in Divine Providence, and the prospects for their early meeting at the camp near Boston.

By far the majority of the extant letters of Martha Washington were written to her niece, Frances Bassett Washington, although it is likely that not all of them have been discovered. Fanny, as she was affectionately called by the Washingtons, was the daughter of Martha's sister, Anna Maria, and her husband, Burwell Bassett of Eltham in New Kent County. For several years she had lived with the Washingtons at Mount Vernon. In October 1786 Fanny and Maj. George Augustine Washington were married. The major was a son of Charles, youngest brother of the general, and he had been an aide to Lafayette.

The marriage received the active encouragement of the Mount Vernon Washingtons, and the newlyweds were invited to live at Mount Vernon, where the major continued his duties as manager. During the early presidential years the major acted as financial agent for the president under a general power of attorney. During 1792 George Augustine's health began to fail rapidly. Visits to the mountains, to Barbados, and then to Eltham were of no avail, and he died in the spring of 1793, probably of tuberculosis. Fanny was left a widow with three small children. Always solicitous of her welfare, the Washingtons allowed Fanny the use of the house owned by them in Alexandria.

Martha and Fanny carried on a frequent correspondence during the presidential years. Fanny was relied upon to see that the plantation house was well cared for, as well as to act as hostess in the owners' absence. It was Fanny who supplied Martha with news of the rest of the family, as well as of the black members of the household. Fanny also had the responsibility of seeing that the Negroes of the mansion were kept busy and that the house was kept clean and fresh. It was to Fanny that Martha turned when she became anxious over the health of George, her grandchildren, or other members of the family. It is the letters to Fanny that shed so much light on the character of Mrs. Washington and reveal so many intimate details of life at Mount Vernon.

For a number of years, Tobias Lear served as one of the general's secretaries and lived at Mount Vernon. There he had ample time to become acquainted with the beautiful Fanny Washington. By coincidence Lear became a widower at the same time that Fanny became a widow, and in the summer of 1795 they were married. It was a short marriage, for the following March Fanny died suddenly. Martha was crushed with grief.

This letter, written at Philadelphia, November 30, 1794, is typical of Martha Washington's letters to Fanny:

My Dear Fanny

Not having received any letter from you since my letter to you by Mr. Lear--I have only to tell you that we are all well--and hope when I next hear from you, that I shall have the pleasure to hear that your children are quite well,--I am my dear Fanny, glad you brought the keys of our House home with you and desire you will keep them,--the President seemed a good deal surprised--at the quantity of wine that you have given out, as it never was his intention to give wine or goe to any Expence to entertain people that came to Mount Vernon out of curiosity to see the place; if it is continued--we shall have but very little for our selves if we should come home--rum may always be had--and I beg you will not give out another Bottle out of the vault--I make not the least doubt but Frank drinks as much wine as he gives to the visitors--and rum boath,--and wish you not to give more out unless the President should order it--my love and good wishes for you and the children in which the President joins me I am my dear Fanny your ever effectionate

M Washington

Mr & Mrs West arrived hear last week--by them I hope to get the shoes for maria--

The only other significant quantity of letters to a single recipient are those written to Mrs. Elizabeth Powel, wife of Samuel Powel, mayor of Philadelphia. The acquaintance with the Powels dated back to the Revolution and was renewed when the Washingtons took up residence in Philadelphia during the general's presidency. Through the years the two ladies carried on a fairly regular correspondence.

While very few of Martha's letters to Fanny bear any signs of having been drafted by her husband, it is quite evident that a number of those to Mrs. Powel and others were drafted by him. In fact, a number of his original drafts still exist and are identical with letters received by Mrs. Powel. Martha leaned heavily on George for help with business letters as well as with letters to any but her closest friends. This was especially true after the presidential period. Following George's death, when she went into virtual seclusion, she relied upon Tobias Lear for almost all of her correspondence, particularly for the replies to the many letters of condolence that she received.

The Mount Vernon Ladies' Association owns the largest collection of Martha Washington correspondence. Other notable collections are at the Henry E. Huntington Library, the Pierpont Morgan Library, the Historical Society of Pennsylvania, and Harvard University, and in the hands of descendants.

The Second First Lady*

Nathaniel E. Stein

The election of John Adams was a bitter and stormy contest, involving the destruction of the Federalist party and the break between its founder, Alexander Hamilton, and John Adams. Hamilton politically schemed in such a way that, had his conspiracy not backfired, Pinckney would have carried the electoral majority for the presidency. Thus, the aborted political coup failed to rob Adams of the office, and the resulting split in the Federalist vote made Thomas Jefferson instead of Charles Pinckney vice president. This was a rare instance of a presidential election in which the president and vice president were chosen from opposite tickets.

Beautifully and succinctly the eminent historian Douglas Southall Freeman wrote about Abigail Adams:

It was to her husband's welfare and interests that she consistently devoted her fullest efforts. Surely, whatever John Adams accomplished, he did the better because of his admiring and admired Abigail--his chief informant, wise counsellor, defender. If she assumed command in many matters of home and state, she commanded at the same time the respect of all. Her right to "be seated high" never, never was seriously disputed, but it was herself, not her position, that won universal esteem. Being most of her life "in delicate health", her activities and accomplishments contradict this background of physical fraility. She wore affliction with grace as readily as she wore the becoming garments of a lady of station and charm. Of high native intelligence, blessed with endurance and determination, she seemed fitted for the "bravest or most delicate duties". Mastering the demanding details of the exacting assignment as wife of the first American envoy to Great Britain, a certain masculinity of mind gave force and direction to her thinking, and an unusual perception of the people and politics around her. The dangers and difficulties in the struggle to establish a new government were as understandable to her as were those of earlier years in the great struggle for independence. Whether, as in 1776, the roar in her ears was that of nearby Revolutionary cannon in Dorchester Heights, or, as in the '90's that

---

*Originally published in 1963.

of the fervent and rabid Federalists Haters on the streets of Philadelphia, she always reacted with courage. She was quick to praise and extol the virtues of others, but she did not spare, in spoken or written words, those who incurred her disapproval. Brilliant in conversation, this remarkable woman was apt of phrase, and happily for posterity she was facile and picturesque of pen. The flavor and vitality of her letters were monumental then; they are her best monument today.

Abigail Adams was blessed with a keen sense of values and as an observer of the political scene had very few peers. The brilliant letters she left to posterity are indeed her "monument to fame." This one to Elbridge Gerry makes the task of the historian a delightful chore; for this reason, I keep it among my presidential letters:

Quincy, December 31, 1796

Dear Sir;

Your obliging favour of December 28th I received by the hand of Dr. Welch. I thank you Sir for your congratulations, which received their value from the sincerity with which I believe them fraught. The elevated station in which the suffrages of our country have placed our friend [John Adams], is encompassed with so many dangers and difficulties, that it appears to me a slippery precipice, surrounded on all sides with rocks and shoals and quicksand. There is not any man in whom again can be united such an assemblage of fortunate circumstances to combine all hearts in his favour--and every voice in unison, as has been the lot of the President of the United States. Yet, even he with the full tide of favour and affection, has tasted the bitter cup of calumny and abuse, an imported cup, a foreign mixture, a poison so subtle, as to have affected even native Americans. What must a successor expect who has near half the country opposed to his election, as well as all the friends of the rival candidates mortified at their defeat?

You, Sir, have been too long conversant in Publick life, and full well know the pangs and heartaches to which it is subject; not personally to risk commiseration with your congratulations. At my time of life the desire to wish to shine in publick life is wholly extinguished.

The Retirement to Peace Field (the name Mr. Adams has given to his estate) is much more eligible to me, particularly since my health has severely suffered by my residence in Philadelphia. But personally, I shall consider myself the small dust of the balance, when compared with the interests of the nation. To preserve peace, to support order, and to continue to the country that system of government under which it has become prosperous and happy, the sacrifices of an individual life, important only to its near connections, ought not to be taken into consideration.

I fully agree with you in sentiment as it respects the election of Mr. Jefferson. I have long known him, and entertain for him a personal friendship, and though I cannot accord with him in some of his politicks, I do not believe him culpable to the extent he had been represented. Placed at the head of the Senate, I trust his conduct will be wise and prudent, and hope it will be a means of softening the animosity of the party, and of cementing and strengthening the bond of the union.

There never was any publick or private animosity between Mr. Adams and Mr. Jefferson. Upon the subject of Paine's Rights of Man there was a disagreement in sentiment. Mr. Jefferson does not look quite through the deeds of men. Time has fully disclosed whose opinion was well founded.

The Gentleman [Alexander Hamilton] you alluded to as an active agent in the election has no doubts in his views and designs. There are some characters more supple than others, more easily wrought upon, more accommodating, more complying. Such a person might be considered as the ostensible engine which a master hand could work. To what other motive can be ascribed the Machiavelian policy of placing at the head of a government a gentleman [Pinckney], not particularly distinguished for any important service to his country, and scarcely heard of beyond the state which gave him birth, until sent upon a publick embassy.

"Corruption wins not more than honesty."

I feel, Sir, when addressing you, the confidence of an old friend, and that an apology is not necessary for the freedom of the communication.

Be pleased to send my compliments to Mrs. Gerry. It would give me great pleasure to receive a friendly visit from you and from her. I am dear Sir, with sentiments of Respect and Esteem

Your Friend and Humble Servant
ABIGAIL ADAMS

The Case of the Missing Whaler*

Leon Howard

When I read about manuscript hunters in a book like Richard D. Altick's **The Scholar Adventurers,** I feel that I am reading about a different race. I am no adventurer, and I am afraid of people. I have never sought out a relative of any literary figure, and I have never asked to look at the possessions of a private collector. Even librarians make me so nervous that I will hesitate for hours before making out a call slip for a manuscript I know is readily available to the public. In short, I am one of those timid souls who would never dream of charging off on a bicycle in search of treasures buried in Welsh attics, of staging a campaign to gain admission to a forbidden library, or of insinuating myself into the good graces of an old lady who had invited me to tea.

Yet the most timid of professional scholars sometimes finds that one particular manuscript is necessary to the completion of a job he has undertaken. In all probability, it might be a manuscript that does not exist or that has no significance for anybody except himself. He may hypothesize its existence and attempt to locate it by a variety of inferences. And then he has to beat the bushes until he either flushes it into the open or else proves all his inferences wrong and his hypothesis unproductive. Herman Melville created such a situation for me by getting lost in the South Pacific during the winter of 1842-43. He was probably on a whaling vessel of some sort, but the whaler itself was missing from all known records.

Melville, in fact, was a discouraged young man who had decided to get lost for a longer period than a single winter when he shipped out of New Bedford on a freezing January day in 1841. Nothing except what he chose to tell was known about his experiences from that time until he returned home in the autumn of 1844. What he chose to tell was a mixture of fact and fancy, and most of it was incorporated in the three autobiographical romances that dealt with his Pacific adventures: **Typee,** in which he deserted from his first whaling ship and took refuge among the cannibals of the Marquesas; **Omoo,** in which he mutinied off the coast of Tahiti, was imprisoned, and escaped to the neighboring island of Eimeo or Moorea; and **White Jacket,** in which he came home as a sailor in the United States Navy. Some bits from the early chapters of **Mardi** and substantial portions of **Moby Dick** might have been based on personal experiences, but no one knew. His earliest biographers and critics

---

*Originally published in 1960.

could draw only upon these sources of information, and the degree to which they misrepresented his life or misinterpreted his books was determined by their impressionistic guesses as to what were the facts and what were the fancies.

Scholars' Earlier Discoveries

The scholarly effort toward a more complete knowledge of Melville's life and a better understanding of his books has been long and active. It was known from the beginning that he had sailed on the **Acushnet** and returned on the **United States,** and Lt. Henry A. Wise made an early identification of the Australian whaler in **Omoo** as the **Lucy Ann** out of Sydney. From a careful study of the books, Robert S. Forsythe made an elaborate chronology of Melville's South Sea wanderings, which Charles Anderson corrected and improved after discovering the official log of the **United States** and gathering together many contemporary allusions to Melville for his own painstaking work on **Melville in the South Seas.** It became known that the court records of the **Lucy Ann** mutiny were extant, though not immediately available, and that the true story of the Tahitian adventure could one day be told. Although the log of the **Acushnet** still remains for scholars the object of vain search, Wilson Heflin discovered, in the National Archives of the Department of Agriculture, an abstract of it that had been prepared for the researches of Matthew Fontaine Maury.

By the time I was browbeaten into undertaking a new biography of Melville, the full story of his South Sea adventures seemed almost within grasp. Both Jay Leyda and Harrison Hayford, my principal browbeaters, had made important discoveries. Leyda, in the early stages of preparing his own monumental **Melville Log,** had independently turned up the abstract record of the **Acushnet** and was eager to make it available to me. Since it gave the daily location of the ship, the state of the weather, and the number of whales sighted or captured during each twenty-four-hour period, it could be supplemented by various bits of information from printed sources to enable one to draw fairly sound inferences about the changing circumstances of the voyage and the conditions that led Melville to desert. Hayford had at last located the records of the **Lucy Ann** mutiny and was in the process of obtaining copies from Australia. From this material, from the log of the **United States,** and from a substantial amount of new incidental information, it would be possible to locate Melville's physical presence almost every day from the beginning of 1841 to the autumn of 1842 and from the summer of 1843 to the autumn of 1844. It would also be possible to make some well-grounded guesses concerning his thoughts and feelings at crucial periods during these months. The gap that needed to be filled by systematic effort was the ten-month interval between October 1842, when the Tahitian authorities lost interest in him, and August 17, 1843, when he gave up his job with a Honolulu merchant and enlisted in the U.S. Navy.

Our Hypothesis and Approach

By this time the imaginative process by which Melville created his autobiographical romances had become sufficiently evident to give us a practical hypothesis on which to base our effort. In **Typee** and the first half of **Omoo** (though not in **White Jacket**), the basic pattern of his narrative had been that of real personal experience. But he was obviously less inclined to write about what had happened to him in actuality than about what might have happened if circumstances had been somewhat different. In short, he made a good story out of his real experiences. Consequently, we might assume (as **Omoo** and circumstantial probability both indicated) that he had left Eimeo on a whaling vessel that was short of men and willing to pick up a runaway who was not too disreputable. Furthermore, since the somewhat different circumstances that controlled the invention in **Typee** had been an exaggeration of his stay in the Marquesas from four weeks to four months, it was possible that he had left Eimeo after about two weeks instead of staying for the two months he claimed in his book. This was guesswork, of course, but it impelled us to allow Melville only a short period of the beachcomber's indisputable privacy before trying to pick up his trail at sea.

We were looking, then, for some record of a common sailor on an unidentified fly-by-night whaling vessel that had left the Tahitian islands in the late fall (probably about the first of November) of 1842 and arrived at the Hawaiian islands in the spring or early summer of 1843--in time, that is, for the sailor to find himself on his uppers in Honolulu, sign a year's contract to clerk in a drygoods store, write to his family about his decision, and then get homesick enough to change his mind and join the Navy for the voyage home. The obvious place to begin looking was in the American consular records for Honolulu, but Leyda had already examined them and found no record of Melville except Captain Pease's certification of his desertion from the **Acushnet**. There was no way to start from Tahiti, because there was no American consulate there, and the British and French records provided no clue to the time and means of Melville's departure from Eimeo. The only thing left to do was to find all the possible ships that Melville might have taken and use them as a means of directing our search for some specific document that would reveal his presence among the crew.

For that purpose, near the end of a long and busy summer, Leyda, Hayford, and I converged from the North, West, and South upon the center of the nineteenth-century whaling industry. We wanted the local newspapers that printed weekly summaries of the news from all the whaling vessels sighted or spoken of throughout the world. Hayford and I began at New Bedford, where we enlisted the help of Sam Bogorad, who was on vacation from the University of Vermont and somewhat intrigued by the discovery that his native town had become a center of scholarly research. Leyda went directly to Nantucket, where he was to consult the columns of the **Enquirer** and exercise his peculiar genius for moseying around. Later we would all meet on the island, pool our information, discuss its significance, and, if necessary, spread out again from there on some particular pursuit.

Frustration in Nantucket

After working through the newspapers in the New Bedford Public Library and making use of the compendium of information in the **Whalemen's Shipping List,** Hayford and I arrived in Nantucket with the names of some eight or nine whalers (several of which were real possibilities) reported near Tahiti in the autumn of 1842 and near Hawaii the following spring. Leyda had a similar list and the intuitive conviction that one ship which had interested us all--the **Charles and Henry,** out of Nantucket, John B. Coleman master, and Charles and Henry Coffin owners--was the vessel we wanted. Much of his intuition, I suspected, was wishful thinking. He had already discovered in the private collection of M. M. Armstrong of Darien, Connecticut, a letter from Coleman to the owners describing conditions on the whaling grounds and saying that he was expecting to ship a new boat steerer or harpooner from Eimeo on the following day. The date, November 2, 1842, was perfect. The captain sounded like the well-balanced, competent character Melville described in **Omoo,** and he displayed a similar selectivity in his crew when he wrote of his hesitancy about signing two reckless runaways from the **John Adams.** Furthermore, if Melville had been the new crewman, this would explain his later and otherwise mysterious references to himself as a "harponeer." And Coleman's declared intention to go to Japan, in the event that luck was bad during the coming season on the line, was relevant to what had always seemed to be the most personal passages in the opening chapter of **Mardi.** It was all too apt to be true. It was more like a scholar's dream.

It remained a dream. Leyda's enthusiasm had already led him to search for the owners' records and discover that the log of the **Charles and Henry** had probably been patriotically disposed of in a scrap-paper drive during the Civil War. The local customhouse records, which might have contained a certification that Melville, an American citizen, had been discharged in a foreign port, had all been destroyed by a flood in the basement a generation before. The information we had gleaned from the newspapers showed that the **Charles and Henry** had been sighted sailing away from Tahiti on November 7 and enabled us to make a rough chart of her course to Lahaina on April 26 and Honolulu on May 4 before she actually set sail for Japan. But there was nothing to show that Herman Melville had ever set foot upon her decks.

Nor was there anything in Nantucket to indicate that he had ever set foot on the **Peruvian** or any of the other vessels we considered possible. As we dispersed to our own devices rather than to any particular pursuits, I decided, in a final gesture of futility, to go to Washington and take another look at the Hawaiian records that Leyda and Heflin had already exhaustively explored.

The Search in Washington

In the National Archives I was as unsuccessful as I had expected to be. The records of the Honolulu consulate contained nothing that Leyda had not already told me about. There was no American consulate at Lahaina and, from all I could see in the catalogue or hear from the archivist, no report to the Honolulu consulate from any vice consul or agent there. And I was getting into a state.

There are two kinds of minds that rarely meet. One is that of the scholar who is hell-bent in his search for a particular fact, who has exhausted all the conventional means of searching, but who is not yet wholly convinced that the fact is unobtainable. The other is that of the guardian of a collection who hopes that it will be used or fears that it may be exploited according to the categories by which it is assembled. The archivist was obviously convinced that I was another incompetent crackpot who either did not know what he wanted or did not know how to find it. At the moment, she was wrong. But I was about ready to crack from the frustration of having some unimaginable classification or call number stand between me and that last unidentified volume which alone would convince me that I had done all I could. The bureaucracy forbade me the stacks. But the noon hour was approaching and the scales of inertia were tipping in my favor. Not even the most suspicious of librarians employed by the federal government, I figured, would exercise her suspicions on her own time or sacrifice the sacred cup of coffee for them.

I waited for the clock and the civil service reaction and then persuaded a more humble and sympathetic subattendant to get rid of me by escorting me into the stacks and showing me that there was nothing left for me to see. There was nothing among the consular records, but next to them was a single volume of records of the U.S. Commercial Agency at Lahaina for 1842-55. I seized it without benefit of call slip and almost immediately found myself reading a letter of May 18, 1843, which said that, in addition to the "cases of relief," three men had been in the agency office and had been sent to Honolulu by the schooner **Star**: "Herman Mellvil, Jos. Whiting & Francis Scarsfield dis. from Barque Damon."

This, surely, had to be our long-lost Herman, turning up in the right place at the right time, however he might have got there and however the agent might have spelled his name. But the bark **Damon** was a new mystery. For of the scores of ships I had spotted throughout the Pacific it was one that had never before sailed into my ken. The last train that would get me to the first meeting of my fall classes was leaving Washington in less than five hours, so I had little time left for mysteries. After assuring myself that there were no more references to Melville in the volume, I hurried to the Treasury section of the Archives to see whether there were any surviving Customs records of the **Damon** that might verify Melville's discharge from her crew. According to the records, there were; but they were in a certain specified packing box in the basement of the customhouse in the **Damon**'s home port in Rhode Island.

The Last Phase of the Search

By this time I was literally on the run because I wanted to satisfy my curiosity enough to sleep that night, and I grabbed a cab for the Library of Congress to check the **Damon** through the **Whalemen's Shipping List**. But the **Whalemen's Shipping List** was not catalogued, it was in neither the **Union List of Serials** nor of **Newspapers**, and the library's bibliographers had never heard of it. Apparently the copy I had been so casually using in the New Bedford Public Library was unique. I used my last moments of time to sit at a desk and write a special delivery note to Sam Bogorad, begging him to send me the

Whalemen's word on the **Damon** before he went back to Vermont, and a longer letter to Jay Leyda, exhorting him to beat his way into the Newport Customhouse and break open the box in the basement. I had shot my bolt, my last two arrows were in the air, and I had nothing left to do but catch my train.

A prompt reply came from Bogorad. Information on the **Damon** was scanty, but it was no wonder that its name had failed to catch my eye: it had sailed eastward, around the Cape of Good Hope, and arrived at Lahaina from the Sea of Japan without having passed anywhere near Tahiti. I could not believe it. If Melville the author had really been discharged from the **Damon**, he would have had to leave the **Charles and Henry** or some other ship coming from Tahiti in mid-ocean--perhaps in the manner so meticulously described in the opening section of **Mardi**--in order to get on board. If the opening pages of **Mardi** were autobiographical, then my whole conception of Melville's personality and creative imagination had to be changed. If he had been on board a vessel that had come around Good Hope, then there was more vicarious experience than anyone had suspected in his account of the voyage of the **Pequod** in **Moby Dick**. My lectures suffered as I questioned my own critical sensitivity and biographical perceptiveness and anxiously awaited news from Leyda.

When it came, it was what I was used to. He had got the packing box open by a technique that only he knows, and he had found nothing. But, characteristically, he had kept opening boxes until he found the **Damon's** records and no mention of Melville. But this negative evidence really meant little, for the ship was obliged to account only for the men who had sailed or returned on it. Leyda had told the whole story to Wilson Heflin, whose position at the United States Naval Academy gave him ready access to the National Archives and would enable him to follow up any other clues that might develop. Heflin could sniff through the Archives, I was convinced, and identify hidden documents from the South Seas by a faint odor of sandalwood. But I was also convinced that the Melville trail had petered out--that the scent was too cold to be followed by anyone.

My first conviction was right, and my second wrong. A few weeks later Heflin extracted from an uncatalogued box of loose papers the original letter of which I had seen only a careless copy. Its concluding words were "Herman Mellvil, Joseph Whiting, dischd from Ship Chs & Henry & Francis Sarsfield dischd from Barque Damon."

The hypothetical, improbable manuscript had existed and survived. The mystery of the missing whaler was solved. And it was at last possible to write a complete biography of one of America's greatest authors.

A Man Out of Manuscripts:
Edwin M. Stanton at the
McCormick Reaper Trial*

Harold M. Hyman

An attempt to write a new biography of Edwin McMasters Stanton would have been all but useless had there been no fresh letters available. So many facts of this man's life are obscured by the accumulations of a century of partisan controversy that only the insights offered by informative manuscripts promised an approach to the truth.

The late Benjamin P. Thomas began a biography of Stanton which I am carrying on. We were fortunate in obtaining the cooperation of several autograph collectors who made their materials available. Stanton descendants, now scattered from Alexandria, Virginia, to New Orleans, and to Belvedere, California, opened their family holdings. Archival depositories at many universities and historical societies proffered endless cooperation. From these sources, there emerges a picture of Stanton which, I believe, requires another look at him as a public figure and as a man.

In 1865, Francis Lieber, the German-born scholar and friend to Stanton, described him as a character worthy of a Plutarch.[1] Without presuming to fill that bill, I agree with Lieber that Stanton deserves the most diligent biographical research. In no existing treatment in print is Stanton considered as a human being. He is either a saint or a devil. The latter opinion stems from the conclusion of James Gordon Bennett, the publicist, who claimed he had investigated Stanton's life thoroughly, and that "his whole characteristics were exhibited in this, that when a youngster going to school he kissed the ___ of the big boys and kicked those of the little ones."[2]

To approach Stanton either as an unstinting defender of his reputation or as an unsparing critic of his actions is unfair to him, and to an understanding of the events in which he participated and of his significant achievements.

---

*Originally published in 1960.

[1] Lieber to "My Dear Sir," probably Benson J. Lossing, December 2, 1865, Lieber Papers, Library of Congress.

[2] Bennett's undated memorandum in John W. Schuckers Papers, Library of Congress.

Like Seward and others of the Civil War cabinet, Stanton has stood in Lincoln's shadow. The acrimonious events of the Johnson impeachment and the bitterness stemming from Reconstruction issues have played a larger part in the writings on Stanton than has his role as Lincoln's war secretary. I hope that Thomas and I have followed a middle way.

Stanton's humanity is only now becoming apparent through the fresh manuscript sources I mentioned earlier. This can be illustrated by recounting Stanton's and Lincoln's first meeting, which has received an inordinate amount of scholarly and popular attention. The occasion was the famed McCormick Reaper case.

By the early 1850s, the inventiveness of Cyrus McCormick and other entrepreneurs of his genius was taming the prairie frontier. The virgin midwestern soil was being fructified in the implacable advance of mechanical agricultural machinery. Every year the demand for McCormick's and other reapers swelled. It was inevitable that competitors should arise to contest McCormick's claims to prior patent rights.

During the preceding two decades, Stanton and Lincoln, unknown to each other, were achieving different kinds of success as aspiring young lawyers. In Illinois, Lincoln followed the pleasant pace of the rural circuit courts. An able lawyer, his reputation was largely local. He loved the snug male jokefests of these informally conducted tribunals. Traveling at a deliberate pace, Lincoln mixed his legal practice with political ambitions and a wide range of other interests. As a raconteur, Lincoln stored up a fund of stories and entertained colleagues, jurors, and judges with the charm and appropriateness of his anecdotes.

On the surface, Stanton appeared to be a very different kind of man. Ohio-born and college-educated, he reflected a greater degree of sophistication. Stanton's goals as a young man were almost wholly materialistic. He wanted a share in the great wealth he saw being created around him. Moving eastward, Stanton successively made Columbus, Pittsburgh, and Washington, D.C., his residences and bases of operations for the legal work that carried him throughout the Northeast. By the early 1850s, he had a far higher standing in law circles than Lincoln did. Stanton was a driving, unresting, "modern" man-in-a-hurry. He had no patience with humor in the courtroom. Once, while an opposition lawyer amused the courtroom with a humorous address, Stanton fidgeted impatiently. When the opposing lawyer had finished, Stanton rose and said, "Now that this extraordinary flow of wit has ceased, I will begin," to which the other lawyer retorted, "Wit always ceases when you begin." Ignoring the ensuing laughter, Stanton bored ahead with his sober and convincing array of facts, and won the case. [3]

By 1854, Stanton's reputation was such that he was chosen as the junior of three lawyers defending the John H. Manny Company against a patent

---

[3] William Stanton to Mrs. O. S. Picher, October 12, 1907, owned by William Stanton Picher.

infringement suit brought by the McCormick interests. This was going to be a legal battle for very high stakes and the best talent was employed on both sides. For Manny, Stanton's seniors were George H. Harding, rated at the top of the aristocratic Philadelphia bar, and Peter Watson of Washington, the country's best patent attorney. McCormick was represented by Marylander Reverdy Johnson and Edward N. Dickerson. Stanton knew that this was to be a great opportunity for him.

The trial was originally scheduled for the Chicago courts. As was the practice at this time, Manny's counsel decided to employ an Illinois lawyer to guide them through the peculiarities of local law. Since better-known men were unavailable, Watson took on Abe Lincoln of Springfield with a $400 retainer. But before the case came to trial, it was transferred to Cincinnati. Harding, Watson, and Stanton forgot about Lincoln.

They were reminded when, in Cincinnati, as they were on their way to court, they beheld a lanky, ungainly backwoodsman, bearing a furled umbrella and a sheaf of legal papers. This creature presumed to approach them and appeared to consider himself their professional and social equal. Everyone snubbed him, Stanton included. No one among the lawyers on either side gave him any attention or invited him to share the social meals and pleasant walks with which they indulged themselves. To be sure, it was impolite to snub Mr. Lincoln, but this was Lincoln the country lawyer, not the great man of a decade later.

Such snobbery was then common in urban American law courts. Lincoln's country practice had not prepared him for the kind of etiquette Stanton and his peers practiced. Stanton's admiring nephew remembered a similar occasion when Stanton's opponents were "country lawyers." The younger Stanton remembered,

> It was hard to tell which was the most "haughty, severe, domineering, and rude" in his treatment of those lawyers--Stanton, or the Judge of the Court, Grier. I thought that if anybody should treat me so I would want very much to shoot him--and both Judge Grier and Edwin Stanton deserved it.[4]

At Cincinnati, everyone assumed that Lincoln no longer had any business in the Reaper case. To be sure, Harding had paid him a retainer (which Lincoln had accepted), but had then thrown away the brief Lincoln had laboriously prepared. Stanton was one among the many who made Lincoln's inferior position clear to him. Donn Piatt, Stanton's journalist friend, reported Stanton's reaction to Lincoln's presence, but though long accepted as truth, the anecdote is probably apocryphal. Piatt said Stanton described Lincoln in most uncomplimentary terms, which is believable enough, but then Piatt added that Stanton decided, "If that giraffe appeared in the case, I would throw up my brief and leave."

---

[4] Ibid.

This is completely out of character and lacks the substantiation of other witnesses or even of necessity. Lincoln was out of the case once it was moved from Chicago. There was no need for Stanton to make such a drastic professional threat. It should be remembered that, according to one contemporary, Piatt was two of the three greatest liars extant. [5]

But there is positive proof that Stanton never contemplated giving up the case because of Lincoln's presence or for any other reason. Stanton's letters to the young woman who was soon to become his second wife are now available. In his minute descriptions to her of every person and event at Cincinnati of any significance, there is no mention at all of the Illinois interloper. And there is not even the slightest intimation of his intention to throw up the case.

These letters, too, correct a serious distortion of Stanton's contribution to the case that has arisen from the overly credulous zeal of his biographer, Frank A. Flower. Flower accepted without qualification a description of Stanton's courtroom performance at Cincinnati that attributed charismatic qualities to the lawyer, and made it appear that Stanton did the whole job of pleading the case for his client.

Stanton, to be sure, did a good job. Harding assigned him the task of researching the intricacies of patent precedents, work for which Stanton was particularly fitted. But Stanton's letters to his fiancee indicate that his scholarly and secondary role was his major contribution. They also show that, behind the smug exterior, Stanton was a frightened young man who worried that Harding's frequent illnesses during the trial might throw too heavy a load on his relatively inexperienced shoulders. He wrote of Harding and Watson as lawyers better than himself, as they were at this stage. In later years, Stanton was to surpass them and to become the highest-paid lawyer in the land. [6]

The only reason that Lincoln enters this story at all is that he was present in Cincinnati on a retainer from the defendant. The work he had done on the case was discarded. Stanton, on the other hand, performed his work well. But the two men were not then closely allied. Their association did not begin at the Reaper trial in 1855, but five years later in Washington, D.C.

----

[5]Piatt, **Memories of Men Who Saved the Union** (New York, 1887), p. 56; S. B. Pillsbury to Horace White, October 14, 1913, Illinois State Historical Society.

[6]Stanton to Ellen Hutchison, September 25/26, 1855, owned by Mrs. E. K. Van Swearingen. The traditional accounts in Frank A. Flower, **Edwin McMasters Stanton** (New York, 1906), pp. 62-63; Albert J. Beveridge, **Abraham Lincoln**, (Boston, 1928) vol. 1, pp. 575-83; and Otto Eisenschiml, **Why Was Lincoln Murdered?** (Boston, 1937), p. 191, should be compared with the new light shed by these Stanton manuscripts. See, too, E. Hinschliff, "Lincoln and the 'Reaper Case,' " **Illinois State Historical Journal**, vol. 33, pp. 361-65; and R. H. Parkinson, "The Patent Case that Lifted Lincoln into a Presidential Candidate," **Abraham Lincoln Quarterly**, vol. 4, pp. 105-20.

Stanton may yet emerge as a man, with all the limitations and imperfections that a man can have. If this goal is realized, it will be because only out of manuscripts may the biographer make a man, for only from them can a sense of intimate truth be gained.

Military Dispatches from Yellow Tavern*

David Herr Coblentz

How often the lesson must be relearned that one cannot ring down the curtain on any life or event until all the facts are in. Unless one stands by a deathbed and watches the occupant sign his name for the last time to a will or other document, one cannot honestly say what final writing closed that earthly career. Year after year archaeologists, doctors, historians, scientists, and Biblical scholars bring to light new evidence that modifies or dispels altogether the facts currently accepted.

Years ago my parents presented me on my birthday with a book entitled **Jeb Stuart,** by the late John Thomason, Jr. It is an excellent biography and one of my favorite volumes. Through the years I have read and reread this book, and so was delighted a few years ago when I acquired two military dispatches written by Stuart in 1864.

Union cavalry, twelve thousand strong, under the leadership of General Sheridan are reported advancing south of the Rappahannock River below Fredericksburg one morning in May 1864. Sheridan's column is thirteen miles long; his objective is to fight Stuart, whip him if he can, and march to Butler on the James River, where he will get fresh supplies, and then return to Meade's headquarters.

Jeb Stuart has hastily assembled between four and five thousand men, and we find his troops harassing the enemy's rear guard at Jerrald's Mill, about forty-five miles north of Richmond on what was then known as the Telegraph Road. Sheridan manages to hold him off and, pushing south on the Groundsquirrel Road, pauses at Beaver Dam long enough to liberate a few hundred Federal prisoners and set the torch to a railroad yard and to a depot of medical supplies and food before heading his column on towards Richmond, only thirty miles away.

Stuart, in hot pursuit, stops in Beaver Dam a moment to note the damage inflicted and to visit his wife and two children, who are staying nearby with a Dr. Edmund Fontaine; then leaving a brigade under Gordon to follow Sheridan's rear, he abruptly leaves the road he has been following and heads with the rest of his forces for Hanover Junction, twelve miles to the southeast, where the

---

*Originally published in 1956.

Virginia Central Railroad crosses the Richmond, Fredericksburg & Potomac. After a brief pause there we find him early on the morning of May 11 at Ashland, about sixteen miles from Richmond. A little farther south two roads converge and become the Brook Turnpike at a place called Turner's. Half a mile south of Turner's and east of the turnpike is an old inn called Yellow Tavern. No one seems to know how it got its name. It was an empty shell in 1864, a forlorn spectacle, situated on a ridge not far from the Chickahominy in a region of overgrown fields and dotted timberland.

There is a line of small hills that can be seen at Yellow Tavern, which Stuart must have noted on his map--a map now in the Confederate Museum at Richmond--a position where one can make a stand, facing north and west, and repulse an attack. With only 3,200 men he then takes position, his line extending along the Telegraph Road to the north and along the Brook Turnpike to the south.

Maj. Henry McClellan is having a rough time of it this week. As Jeb Stuart's aide, he has the responsibility of carrying dispatches back and forth from the general's headquarters to Gen. Braxton Bragg in Richmond. Stuart sends his aide off with a dispatch dated "Headquarters, Ashland, May 11, 6:30 AM," notifying Bragg that his troops have encountered the enemy at Ashland and that he now lies astride the road on which the enemy is marching toward Yellow Tavern, six miles from Richmond. His men and horses are "tired, hungry, and jaded . . . but all right." The dispatch rider returns with news that Bragg believes he can stave off the attack if it comes.

Of this dispatch to Bragg, John Thomason, Jr., asserts in his biography of Stuart that it was "the last he ever sent." Apparently a well-known, esteemed firm in New York agreed a few years ago when it advertised this same military dispatch for sale, listing it as "General 'Jeb' Stuart's Last Letter, Scrawled from the Battlefield at Yellow Tavern the Day He Was Mortally Wounded." Yet, according to the two dispatches I have, this is not the last written message we have from General Stuart. No doubt the one sent from Ashland is similar to these in my possession, 4" x 5-5/8" pieces of paper, written in pencil, with the words "Military Dispatch" printed at the top. I wonder if the Ashland dispatch is numbered? These two are, which may help clarify the issue. One might assume that the one written from Ashland at 6:30 a.m. is no. 1. A second one was probably written from the position indicated in dispatch no. 3, which gives us the following information:

Headquarters Near Kelby's Mill, 1864, 9:40 o'clock AM
To General Bragg   No. 3

Gen'l.

Since writing a dispatch to you ten minutes ago I have received another report that the enemy is moving down the same route of march already indicated--that is by a road leading into the head of the Brooke [sic] Turnpike. It is not improbable that both may be true. I desire to keep in their rear and flank. They may push down to Richmond on either of the roads but if they can be kept in check we hope to punish them severely. Enemy at R.F.& P. RR bridge over Chickahominy.

> Most Respt,
> J E B Stuart
> Major Genl

Over
I will not move across from Yellow Tavern till I ascertain the route of the enemy more definitely.

> Most Respt,
> J E B Stuart
> Major Genl

From this dispatch, together with other information available to us, we may surmise that Stuart reaches Yellow Tavern about 8 a.m. At 9:30 a.m. a courier is dispatched to General Bragg in which Stuart describes his present situation. Rumors have it that the enemy has gone westward toward the James. "Repeat this to General Lee, Guiney's Station," he concludes. Then at 9:40 a.m., ten minutes later, off goes another courier with the foregoing dispatch to Richmond. The rapidly approaching enemy is already at the R.F. & P. Railroad bridge a few miles distant. About 10:30 the dispatch below, which is the second one I possess, may conceivably have been written and sent hastily down to Bragg.

Head Quarters: Yellow Tavern, May 11
To Gen'l Bragg   No. 4

The enemy seems to be making demonstrations here only--but we cannot exactly tell yet--I think his attack more likely to be made somewhere between Brook Turnpike and James River--Please caution our troops not to let any body of cavalry advance on any road without being halted a sufficient distance and its real character, whether friends or foes investigated.

> Most Respt,
> J E B Stuart
> Major Genl.

There is no time given on this dispatch, nor is the year specified, but it seems obvious that the place and number dispel any suggestion that the year is other than 1864.

By eleven o'clock that morning the two forces meet and the fighting begins in earnest, Sheridan attacking steadily. For over an hour charge is met with countercharge; then comes a lull as both sides draw breath. Around four o'clock the Federal troops renew the attack. In a short time the Confederates give ground, falling back about five-hundred yards. Stuart on his horse rounds

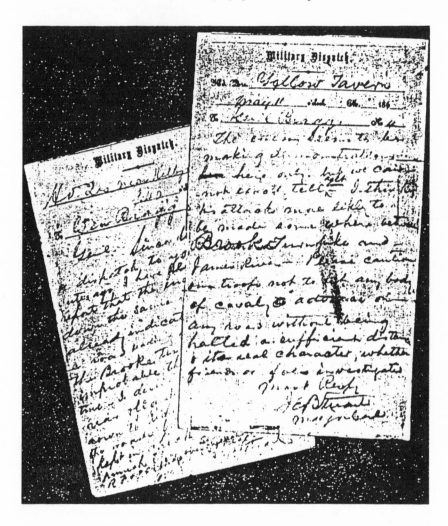

Illus. 1. Is dispatch no. 4 (top) the last letter written by the incomparable Jeb Stuart?

up about eighty men and they charge into the line. Michigan cavalrymen collide with the First Virginia mounted, and again charge is met with countercharge. As the Michigan troops fall back, one of their number, Pvt. John A. Huff, running back on foot toward his own lines, pauses in flight long enough to point his pistol and fire one shot at a mounted officer wearing a plumed hat.

(Thomason says it was "a sergeant in dusty blue" who fired the fatal shot. Dr. Joseph E. Fields tells me that he met a man in Pennsylvania years ago, a Sergeant Brown, who reportedly shot Stuart. Huff is given recognition for it in the **Official Records of the Union & Confederate Armies,** vol. 36, part 1, pp. 828-29.)

The hat falls off the head of the rider as he sways in the saddle. Strong, loving hands support him back out of the thick of battle. Fitz Lee comes up and takes command. A courier is sent off post haste to General Lee and to Dr. Fontaine. An ambulance is brought onto the field, and Stuart is gently lifted into it, his body wracked with pain. They loosen his yellow sash and discover that he is shot through the abdomen. A long, tiresome trip is made over hazardous roads to Richmond and some time after dark they arrive at a house on East Grace Street, the home of Stuart's brother-in-law, Dr. Charles Brewer. There, on the evening of the 12th, while friends and staff members gather round the bedside to voice a prayer and hymn ("Rock of Ages, Cleft for Me"), they hear him repeat the words, "God's will be done." When Mrs. Stuart arrives at the house at 11:30 p.m. she finds that he has passed away nearly four hours before.

They buried Jeb Stuart the following day in Hollywood Cemetery in Richmond. His commander in chief said of him, "He never brought me a piece of false information." "Endeavor," wrote Stuart to J. R. Chambliss a month before he died, "to secure accurate information," and this directive he sought to apply to himself. The dispatch riders rode long and often for this officer of the Confederacy. With fast-moving troops, a force not one-third as great as the enemy's, Stuart forced Sheridan to give up the game without ever reaching the inner fortifications about Richmond.

Just off the old Telegraph Road, a few miles above Richmond at Yellow Tavern, one comes upon the Stuart Monument, a tall granite obelisk "erected by some of his comrades to commemorate his virtues." Whenever I visit this area I wonder if my two Stuart dispatches are really the final written words we have of this gallant soldier.

References

Blackford, W. W. **War Years with Jeb Stuart.** New York: Scribner's, 1945.

Freeman, Douglas Southall. **Lee's Lieutenants,** vol. III. New York: Scribner's, 1944.

Thomason, John W., Jr. **Jeb Stuart.** New York: Scribner's, 1930.

The History of America in Documents, part 3. Philadelphia: The Rosenbach Company, 1951, pp. 50-51.

Virginia, A Guide to the Old Dominion. New York: Oxford University Press, 1947, pp. 355-56.

The Wartime Papers of
Gen. Robert E. Lee*

Louis H. Manarin

In the late 1950s the Virginia Civil War Commission undertook to compile Gen. Robert E. Lee's wartime papers, with a view to publishing a one-volume edition of his important papers. The collection to date contains more than six thousand letters, dispatches, telegrams, special and general orders, and endorsements, and it is easily divisible into two major categories--official correspondence and personal correspondence. Although Lee's correspondence reveals an awesome consistency, a product of his upbringing and his military career, there is a noticeable difference between the man revealed in his official correspondence and the man presented to his family and friends.

Lee's Military Correspondence

The character of Lee's military letters varied as the war progressed. Early in the war Lee wrote diplomatically, carefully stating his desires, needs, and ideas. He was a master of the technique of leading his correspondent by questions or suggestions, leaving it up to his recipient to interpret the facts. Later he became more outspoken in describing the situation and presenting his proposals to correct it. Throughout the last year and a half of the war, when he realized that time was not on the Confederacy's side, this type of letter predominated.

The character of Lee's letters also changed as his position changed. When he commanded the Virginia forces, he was an organizer. In western Virginia he was a coordinator. In South Carolina, as commander of coast defenses, he was a little of everything, from quartermaster and commissary officer to recruiting officer. At the same time he had to organize and coordinate. This was also his baptism of fire concerning coordination between the Confederate government and state governments. Here also Lee was given his first opportunity to display his military talents. His letters reveal quite vividly his strategy: to abolish isolated indefensible positions and to concentrate at points of probable attack, keeping forces mobile. When he became presidential adviser, we see how he suggested to General Jackson the movements we now know as Jackson's Valley Campaign. His suggestions had to be written in such a way as not to offend Gen. Joseph E. Johnston, who jealously guarded his position as commander of the army.

---

*Originally published in 1961.

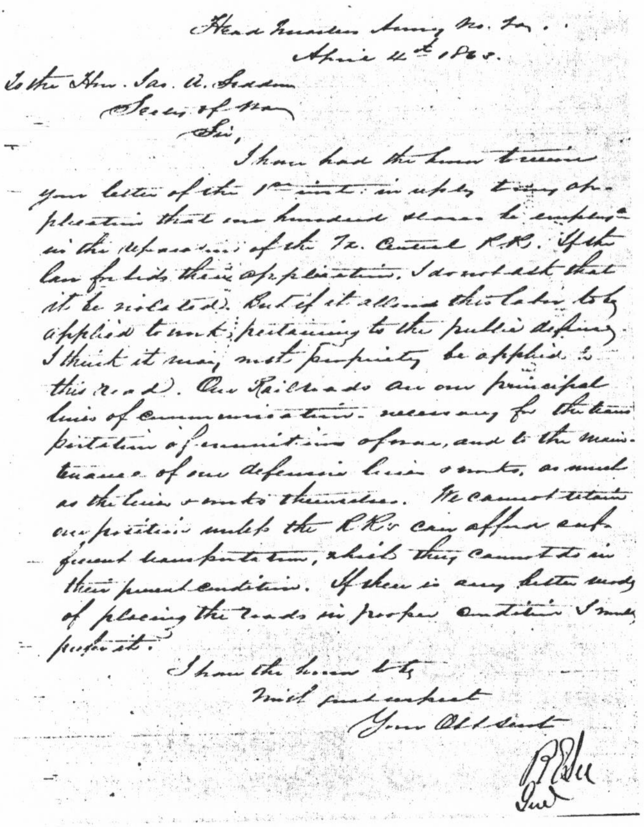

Head Quarters Army No. Va.
April 14th 1863.

To the Hon. Jas. A. Seddon
Secy of War
Sir,

I have had the honor to receive your letter of the 1st inst. in reply to my application that one hundred slaves be employd in the reparation of the Ga. Central R.R. If the law forbids their application, I do not ask that it be violated. But if it allows this labor to be applied to works pertaining to the public defense I think it may with propriety be applied to this road. Our Railroads are our principal lines of communication—necessary for the transportation of munitions of war, and to the maintenance of our defensive lines & works, as much as the lines & works themselves. We cannot retain our position unless the RR's can afford sufficient transportation, which they cannot do in their present condition. If there is any better mode of placing the roads in proper condition I would prefer it.

I have the honor to be,
with great respect
Your Obt Servt
R E Lee
Genl

Illus. 1. A signed letter to Secretary of War James Seddon, dated April 14, 1863. "I have had the honor to receive your letter of the 1st inst. in reply to my application that one hundred slaves be employd in the reparation of the Ga. Central R.R. If the law forbids their application, I do not ask that it be violated. But if it allows this labor to be applied to works pertaining to the public defense I think it may with propriety be applied to this road. Our Railroads are our principal lines of communication--necessary for the transportation of munitions of war, and to the maintenance of our defensive lines & works, as much as the lines & works themselves. We cannot retain our position unless the RR's can afford sufficient transportation, which they cannot do in their present condition. If there is any better mode of placing the roads in proper condition I would prefer it." (National Archives, War Department Collection of Confederate Records)

When Lee became commander of the Army of Northern Virginia in June 1862, his correspondence dealt mostly with strategy and the needs of his army. After Second Manassas his army needed food, so a series of letters to commanders in the Shenandoah Valley requested livestock, and long letters to Richmond requested supplies. One of the reasons he went into Maryland was to get those needed supplies. After the affair at Bristoe Station in late 1863, when Meade had withdrawn the Army of the Potomac to Centreville, Lee wrote to Jefferson Davis, saying that if he had fresh supplies he would invade Maryland again while he had Meade backed up to the Potomac River. His plan was to invade Maryland and move north of the capital, but Lee's men were without shoes and blankets, and his horses, Lee said, would not last three days under campaign conditions. From his letters it is quite evident that Lee was fighting a losing battle with attrition long before Grant moved east.

Many of the dispatches, reports, and general and special orders sent with Lee's signature were not actually written by him. An example of an order not written by Lee is this general order to the army:

> Soldiers! You tread with no unequal step the road by which your fathers marched through sufferings, privations, and blood to independence. Continue to emulate, in the future, as you have in the past, their high resolve to be free, which no trial could shake, no bribe seduce, no danger appall, and be assured the just God who crowned their efforts with success will, in His own good time, send down his blessing upon yours.

This eloquent piece was written by a member of Lee's staff, Lt. Col. Robert H. Chilton, for Lee's signature. Except in special cases, Lee's military correspondence on administrative matters was usually either written by or dictated to a member of his staff. Lee would often dictate the essence of what he wanted to say and let one of his aides write it for his signature. Of the six thousand items collected, approximately one-sixth are special and general orders and paperwork passed on by his subordinates for his signature. They reveal nothing of Lee as soldier or individual. It is interesting to note that there was a noticeable change in the style of the congratulatory orders once Chilton had left his staff.

Many of Lee's letters and dispatches were repetitious, as he often wrote on the same subjects to different people and, with passing time, added only some new detail or nuance. Of Lee's total military correspondence while commander of the Army of Northern Virginia, approximately one-half was devoted to maintaining his army physically in the field and coordinating the actions of other forces not immediately under his control. This correspondence dealing with subsistence and strategy could be divided into separate categories: organization of the army, maintenance of its numerical strength, conscription and desertion, and supplies for men and animals. A special category would include the shortage of animals, the poor condition of those on hand, and the remedies necessary to prevent their collapse. Under strategy, besides the obvious letters to Davis and the War Department, there is correspondence dealing with the disposition of troops throughout the Confederacy, with particular emphasis on Virginia and surrounding states. Lee

Illus. 2. Telegram from Lee to Secretary of War Seddon. "10.30--Advance of
enemy to Falmouth was to break up party removing iron. I wish a
telegraphic operator placed at Hamiltons Crossing to communicate
with me." The telegram is dated November 5, 1863, and carries
endorsements by Seddon ("Dr. Morris will please attend to this at
once.") and Morris ("An operator is now at Hamiltons Crossing . . . .").
(National Archives, War Department Collection of Confederate
Records)

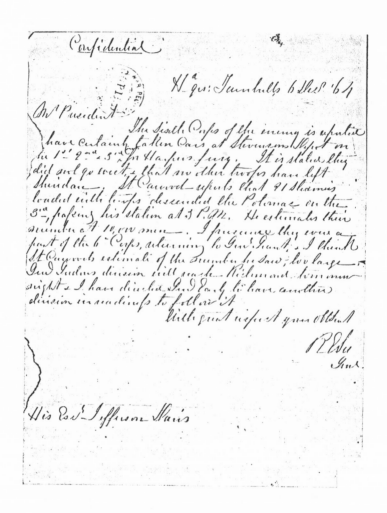

Illus. 3. Lee ALS to Jefferson Davis, December 6, 1864, begins, "Mr. President--The Sixth Corps of the enemy is reported to have certainly taken cars at Stevensons Depot on the 1st 2d & 3rd inst for Harpers ferry. It is stated they did not go west, & that no other troops have left Sheridan . . . ." (National Archives, War Department Collection of Confederate Records)

frequently urged Davis to abolish unnecessary positions and to allow the garrisons to concentrate at the most likely point of attack. His main emphasis was to keep the force mobile, so as to retain the initiative.

Some of the commanders in peripheral areas were, in one way or another, unsatisfactory, and it can be observed that Lee wrote more often and more at length to persons whose lack of ability he recognized. The thorn in Lee's side in Virginia consisted of various units in the Shenandoah Valley which did not coordinate their operations in order to carry out his orders. Lee wrote numerous letters to various commanders urging united action, outlining what had to be done and how it should be carried out. Frequently, he would send the commanders on special missions to find new sources of meat and grain. As their failures mounted, his letters to them became more detailed. In 1864, when Gen. R. H. Anderson was placed in command of Longstreet's Corps after the Battle of the Wilderness, Lee recognized Anderson's lack of experience as a corps commander and wrote him frequently on matters such as camp sites, order of march, and the disposition of troops when halted for the night.

The greatest gap in General Lee's papers occurred during battle, when most of his orders were verbal. His battle reports usually describe facts and events fully, but not reasoning or concepts. These battle reports were usually written many months after the battle. For example, the report for Second Manassas, August 29-30, 1862, is dated April 18, 1863. Some of the originals were written by a member of his staff, Col. Charles Marshall, for Lee's signature. Even the battle reports do not cover the entire war. Reports for 1864 and 1865 were burned in Lee's wagon on the retreat from Petersburg. The closest to a battle report that we have after Mine Run in 1863 is a letter to Davis on April 12, 1865, in which Lee gave a detailed account of the retreat and surrender. Along with the battle reports and papers burned in his wagon we know that he burned some of his incoming correspondence and the copies of his replies while he was at Petersburg. This fact was uncovered in a letter from Lee to William Porcher Miles of South Carolina, a member of the Confederate Congress.

In summary, Lee's official correspondence reveals careful composition but no sign of any attempt at eloquence. His dispatches were usually terse and clear, stating only what was necessary. As the war wore on, his letters became shorter statements of the condition of the army, its needs, and capabilities. These were not the only subjects discussed, but a detailed analysis would carry us beyond the limit set for this article.

Lee's Personal Correspondence

Whereas the official correspondence reveals Lee the soldier, the personal correspondence reveals Lee the husband, father, and friend. There is a casual acknowledgment of the larger events and the course of their fortunes in the intimate, homey exchanges.

Lee's letters to his wife demonstrate his anxiety for her health and safety. They seldom contain anything revealing on the military situation. Lee discussed his physical condition, clothing, and camp life; frequently he would enclose letters received from relatives and friends. As the war progressed he wrote more about the needs of the army. In the latter part of 1864 and early 1865, many of his letters to his wife were short notes acknowledging receipt of socks she had sent.

As for Lee's letters to his children, those to Custis, his oldest son, differ in tone and subject matter from those to his other children. Lee placed on Custis's shoulders the responsibility of looking after the family estates and manumitting the slaves inherited from Mrs. Lee's father. Very few letters exist to his other sons, Rooney and Robert, Jr., who were in the Army of Northern Virginia. Letters to his daughters are in a lighter vein. He seemed to enjoy writing to them and would often tease them about their male companions and marriage. Most of his letters discuss the terrain, social life in camp, and news about other members of the family and friends. Frequently he would inject a note of humor. Only in his correspondence to his daughters and to Charlotte, Rooney's wife, do we see this side of Lee.

Lee's personal correspondence is not always correct in grammar and syntax. Many letters were written in haste and consequently contain errors in spelling and verb tense. Throughout his correspondence he spelled **agreeable** with one **e.** The only place name that gave him trouble was New Bern, North Carolina; he spelled it Newberne, Newbern, New Berne, and New Bern. It should be noted, however, that even today the exact spelling in use at the time of the Civil War is unclear. Following a common practice of the time, Lee used capitals frequently; however, he always began a sentence with a capital and ended it with a period or a dash. In his official correspondence the salutation and complimentary close were formal; for example, to Davis he would write "Mr. President," and close with "Your obedient servant," frequently abbreviated. When writing to members of his family, he would often leave off the salutation and mention the recipient's name in the first sentence: for example, "I received your letter of the 20th, dearest Mary . . . ." His closing would be simply, "Your devoted husband" or "Your affectionate father." Lee always signed his letters, both official and personal correspondence, "R. E. Lee." In all the documents collected for the project there was only one exception. A letter to his wife, who was behind the Union lines, is signed "R. E. L." Interestingly, he mentioned all members of the family in the letter simply by using their first initials.

The letters Lee wrote are records that help us to more fully understand the general who commanded the Army of Northern Virginia, and at the same time, help us to see the army through the eyes of its commander. As Lee himself stated, "Our letters . . . certainly present a good criterion for judging of the character of the individual."

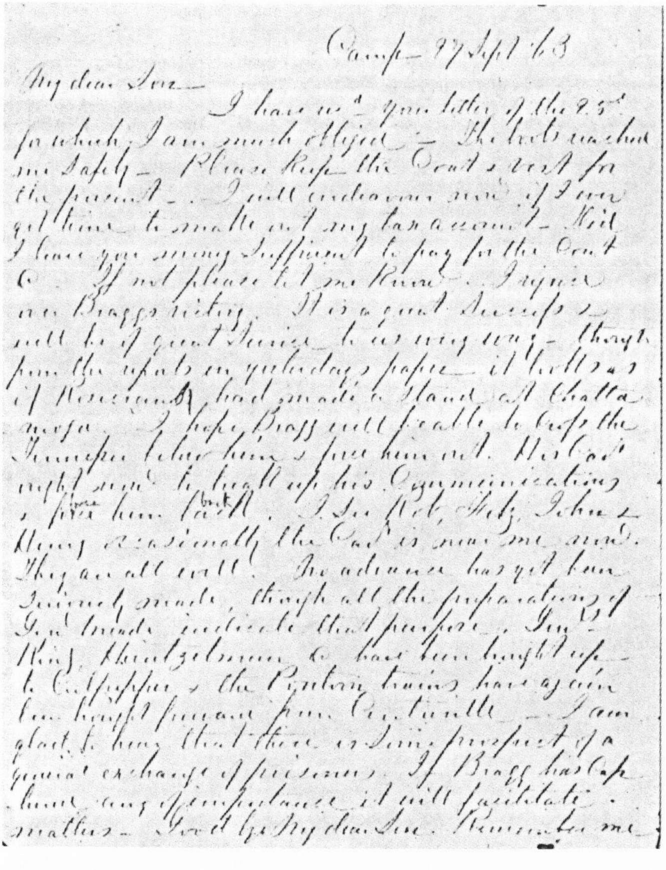

Illus. 4. The first page of a two-page ALS from Lee to his son, G. W. Custis Lee, dated "Camp. 27 Sept. '63." "...The boots arrived safely. Please keep the coat & vest for the present.... I rejoice over Bragg's victory.... I am glad to hear that there is some prospect of a general exchange of prisoners. If Bragg has captured any of importance it will facilitate matters. Good bye my dear Son...." (Robert E. Lee Papers, Duke University)

A Blockade Runner Who Never Returned*

Lawrence B. Romaine

Somewhere along the banks of the Altamaha River, hidden behind Saint Simons Island on the coast of Georgia, there was a grave. Perhaps, through the courtesy of the folks in the "big white mansion," it is still there, carefully marked, in the family burying ground. More likely, the storm tides of the old Atlantic have long since washed away the marker and the last human bone.

If it had not been for a loyal captain, a sentimental family, a faithful caretaker, and a bookman of Halifax, Nova Scotia, there would not be even a memory of James Dickson or his grave. Through this cooperative company I can present an unknown chapter in our Civil War. Perhaps it will seem short and insignificant, but to me it is a challenge to again champion "the little guys" who have contributed much to American history.

What little I know about James Dickson came to me from my friend, a bookman, through his friend, the caretaker of the Dickson estate. There are no members of the Dickson family living. The old homestead still stands about ten miles from Halifax, where the diary-logbook has been reverently handed down through the years. The story of the return of the **Standard** to Hantsport, short one of its crew, has come down in family memory only. The captain's tale of the accidental shooting in the excitement of trying to escape up the river and the return of the hand-tooled calf-bound book to Dickson's mother were impressed on the mind of the last survivor long ago.

Get-Rich-Quick Scheme

Dickson's diary starts in New York City. Dickson and his mother had come from Canada to New York before the war to "make good" in the "big boiling pot of success." They hoped to retire to Nova Scotia wealthy, but success had not come so easily as they had been told it would. Then came the idea of quick profit from one good voyage through the blockade. Under a plan developed with the help of Confederate sympathizers, Dickson arranged by correspondence with the master of the brigantine **Standard** for the voyage.

---

*Originally published in 1955.

It is history that President Lincoln's blockade was not very well planned and equipped until the end of 1862, yet here is manuscript evidence that, among those who planned to break through to the southern markets, the blockade was a handicap even in 1861. Some may say that it was only a mental hazard even in 1862 but, from the incidents in Dickson's account, it would seem that the blockade was then a fact--at least in spots.

The Trip Begins

Jim Dickson described the start of his trip this way:

On Monday evening December 16th, 1861, arranged with the skipper of the British Brigantine "Lilly-Dale" to take us to Hantsport, up the Bay of Fundy, we to sail the next morning at 7 .... The moon was throwing its lengthened shadows down Washington Place, the stately old elms in the park stood out like grim spectres in the silent ghost-like scene and the frosty air of a December morning caused us to quicken our pace .... On board the Brig at 7, hauling into the stream off the Jersey City Ferry house, awaiting our pilot; weighed anchor and stood down with the ebb to the Battery, pilot on board .... At 10 anchored a few hundred yards from the revenue cutter, her beautiful low black piratical looking hull, her fine tapering masts, well braced yards and taut rigging a perfect picture on the bespangled horizon, lit as bright as day by the silvery rays of the moon. We would not go to sea without our papers being examined and found correct and all vessels bound in or out after sundown, were compelled to anchor until daylight under her guns.

Dickson had to hide below deck during the government's inspection of the ship. Later he was freed:

After some little time our skipper, a huge specimen from Nova Scotia, half potato, half codfish kind of a fellow, put his bullet head, encased in a huge seal skin cap, down the companion way and roared out "All right now."

The **Lilly Dale** sailed safely out of the sound, on up around Nantucket Shoals and then ran into bad weather in which the crew lost their bearings completely. All had planned to have Christmas dinner at home in Nova Scotia, but on December 23 the skipper gave up his charts as a conglomeration of Admiralty hieroglyphics, threw his dead reckoning overboard, and decided that no one knew where they were. On Christmas Day the mate aloft thought he sighted Long Island, to the dismay of all hands. Dickson merrily described the holiday meal as "A fine dish indeed for a party of Esquimaux consisting of fat salt pork and salt codfish minced and then fried in a sea of hog oil." He continued, "Poor old cook has been rather imprudent in eating too freely of his 'duff,' imitating no doubt the Royal Beef-Eaters of Old, by way of restoring the confidence of all hands in the sanitary qualities of his bread." Poor cook indeed--they fed him the whole medicine chest!

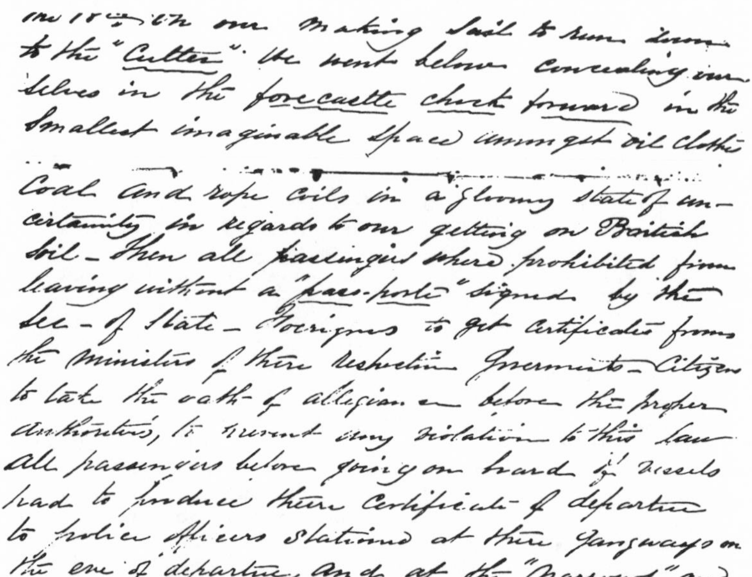

on 18th on our making Sail to run down
to the "Cutter". We went below concealing our
selves in the forecastle check forward in the
smallest imaginable space amongst oil clothes
Coal and rope coils in a gloomy state of un-
certainty in regards to our getting on British
soil - Then all passengers where prohibited from
leaving without a "pass-porte" signed by the
Sec - of State - Foreigners to get certificates from
the Minister of there respective Governments - Citizens
to take the oath of allegiance before the proper
authorities, to prevent any violation to this law
all passengers before going on board of vessels
had to produce there certificate of departure
to police officers stationed at there gangways on
the eve of departure, and at the "Narrows" and
below "Hell-Gate" each had its respective
Cutter on the alert to overhaul every craft
bound in or out, examine papers question the
Captain if desirable to the officers and detain
her and make a thorough search if necessary - As we ran down to the Cutter
we could hear the noise above on deck
as the top-sail was hauled aback our
dark subterranean hiding place redolent
with tar, bilge water, and murderous volumes of black and sulphurous vapours from the
bituminous compound on fire in a small cracked
stove which at variance to all scientific law

Illus. 1. Page from the diary in which James Dickson tells of his adventures.

At last they sighted Baker Island Light and ran in for Mount Desert Rock, where they managed to land and purchased eight geese to vary the diet. Riding out a gale in Frenchman's Bay, they were blown ashore and almost "kicked" to splinters by the sea. On January 4 the **Lilly Dale** finally dropped anchor in Windsor River off Hantsport.

In a severe blizzard, Dickson and his friends traveled by sleigh to Halifax, where brilliant holiday activities presented a jolly scene. The Sleighing Carnival was in full swing, and the streets were lined with "the now fast arriving regiments, brilliant with dashing uniforms of the Guards, Rifles and Artillery of the British Army." Teas, dinners, and dances were the order of the day. Collins Inn presented a delightful frolic and the goose hung high. But the time soon came for the business at hand:

> I bid Uncle Peter goodbye and once again we are afloat, this time on the Brigantine "Standard" of Windsor, N.S., ten all told on board, drawing 9 feet, 110 tonnage--assorted cargo of groceries, medicines, boots, dry goods, lead & gun caps etc. and cleared for Matamoras, Mexico--which none of us expect to see, but know we are to run the blockade on the Georgia coast unless wrecked or captured.

A Little the Worse for Rum and Foul Weather

Leaving the harbor, Dickson wrote, "We have a first rate cook and plenty of everything on board--our crew are just the lads and all good sailors but a little the worse for rum today." On the twenty-fifth the good ship **Standard** ran into foul weather, with the barometer dropping fast, and the galley was staved in, stores soaked, and the stove smashed for the rest of the voyage. This proved to be only the beginning of their troubles, as they soon-lost all bearings and were driven off course some four hundred miles out into the broad Atlantic. Not knowing where the Federal blockaders might be stationed, they were afraid to sail west until they could ascertain their position. At this rather disheartening moment, the cabin remained merry, and Dickson recorded an amusing incident:

> Charley, our 2nd mate, a rough looking specimen of salt water from New Foundland, his feet hid by a huge pair of cow skin boots, his body enveloped in oil clothes, a long white night cap surmounting his head, a tassel of rope yarn hanging from and falling on the side and resting on a most piratical beard, as he braces himself to meet the next roll of the Brig, his face lost in a cloud of blue smoke from an outrageous pipe filled with the most villaneous quality of pigtail, asks with a knowing smile, "Well, Boys, who the hell wouldn't sell the farm and go to sea."

With every possible means of cooking broken or washed overboard, the cook built a fire on the chain cable forward and fried flapjacks on an old iron coal shovel. These flapjacks seem to have been the crew's entire diet for about three weeks, sometimes hot, more often cold! Dickson, like so many diarists, is careless about setting down the date each day. I am not sure just when they sighted the schooner from New Brunswick bound for Jamaica, but from her they managed to get their bearings and to borrow an old coffee pot and some dry rations. They then set a course for Florida, deciding that capture by the enemy would be preferable to starvation if worst came to worst. Morale improved with a dry biscuit and a definite course of action, and our friend recorded a rather amusing bedtime story:

> We turned in to fight the vermin, hungry, half-famished with cold and half starved for want of a decent meal. These vermin have been increasing since we got in warmer latitudes and now swarmed from every seam in the ship and as our bunk seemed to be their rendezvous before starting on their foraging expeditions, everything that Lyons, the bug-exterminator ever saw or dreamed of, tortured us--bedbugs like snapping turtles, "grey-backs" that would walk away with your shirt, fleas running and jumping the Zouave drill in battallions over us, cockroaches charging in squadrons to the right and to the left with a noise almost equal to the tramp of cavalry; their name was legion and as savage as though they all had hydrophobia. We set to work burning oakum to smoke them out but nearly smothered ourselves--after scratching and killing to very little advantage, we finally fell asleep on our wet couches--only to be awakened by the skylight and half of the Atlantic coming down on us and the roars of the entire crew as skipper James shouted through the gale "I'll be damned if that sea left many bedbugs on you chaps."

Secondhand Tobacco and Ship Repairs

Luck and the weather changed after St. Enoch's Fire appeared on the mast (see **Moby Dick**), just as it is supposed to, and Dickson remarks, "If we can hold on for several days at this rate we will be in the Gulf, after which a few hours will decide whether we shall arrive on the coast of the Confederate States or be taken by the Yankees as a prize." Encouraging signs of gulfweed appeared in the water and the enterprising cook managed to catch a porpoise for a change of meat, though there is still no mention of any stove but the old coal shovel and the fire on deck. The tobacco shortage reached its peak and coffee and oakum were smoked, while chewed tea was found to be almost equal to the real thing. This caused an amusing row. First-mate Hutch had been chewing a cud for some days and after meals hiding it in the binnacle. Charlie, the alert second mate, followed him and discovered the veteran chew, adopted it, chewed it, dried it out, and then smoked it in his pipe. Hutch smelled real tobacco--and I leave the rest to your imagination.

As the warmer waters of Florida's coast drew nearer, all hands were busy caulking holes, mending sails, and trimming ship in every possible way so as to be able "to run in or run away from the blockaders. If everything is properly overhauled, and we get the wind, the entire Yankee fleet will have their hands full to catch us." The log clearly showed a shell and sandy bottom and with position off the northernmost tip of Florida in mind, it was decided to run in to about fifteen fathoms under cover of night. Then at dawn, with no enemy in sight, they planned to run into the first sound with the flood tide for

Fernandina. Plans were changed abruptly, however, by the roar of cannon and the realization that Confederate batteries were firing on blockaders too close for comfort "in some part of the bloody drama that would make future history." Dickson described one of the large steamers as "no doubt of the Crowell Line converted into a gunboat for the blockade." They put all sail on the **Standard** and she "scudded over the waves westward, a perfect cloud of canvass" until the enemy was lost in the mist on the horizon.

Grounded

Whether the appearance of the blockaders rattled the captain it is hard to say, but at any rate, from the Dickson comments it appears that they were far from knowing their exact position. On one page they were about to run into Fernandina, on the next they were aground on the tip of Cumberland Island, and on the next they were about to land on Sapelo Island off Darien, Georgia. From further developments it would seem that they grounded on Cumberland Island and decided to prepare for capture at any moment. As much as possible of the most valuable cargo was loaded into the rebuilt boat and rowed some four and a half miles from the shoal to shore, with an old shirt and the English flag held aloft to prevent the Confederate pickets from firing upon them.

A hasty check on the island proved it to be "as uninhabited and forbidding as the Great African Desert, with thickets of bayonet and scrub palmetto." They concluded that "our forces" had evacuated and that "we must be on our guard against runaway negroes who undoubtedly swarmed these islands and whom we might have more occasion to dread than Yankees." Another boatload of cargo landed, and it was decided to divide the crew, half to land and the others to get the **Standard** off the reef. If the blockaders should appear, the **Standard** would be set on fire at once, the entire crew meeting on the island for a council of war. If the ship got free in deep water again, she would reconnoiter and find out the lay of the sea, then return for the rest of the crew and the cargo.

The description of that night on land is detailed and fascinating. The diary tells of the men's despair when the brig shook herself loose and sailed away; they wondered if she would fall into the hands of the Yankees, leaving them stranded in enemy territory without provisions or protection from surrounding unknown dangers. About 9:00 the next morning, however, the **Standard** appeared inside the reef and the old lifeboat, raising the Union Jack, started for the shore. Never in all the manuscripts I have read have happier men appeared. The men loaded the cargo and returned to the ship. They were greeted by a large stack of flapjacks, and Ben the cook threw down the shovel, with which he was still working, to greet them heartily.

End of the Voyage

With the full complement reunited, another council of war was held and Tom Hernandez, a former Savannah pilot, decided they were off Saint Simons Island, about thirty-five to forty miles from Darien. Jim Dickson's voyage was about over. It was decided to take the boat and send an expedition up the Altamaha River to find a pilot to bring the **Standard** in to a safe anchorage and to contact the Confederates. These are the last lines Dickson penned:

> A white flag was placed in the bow, and the English flag a sevenpence, halfpenny Union Jack handkerchief in the stern, a tin pan of flapjacks, a valise and carpet bag of mine [with the diary?] and a small trunk of Tom's stowed in our leaky old boat. John Day, Fraser, Ben, Dugan, Tom and myself again left the old Brig with a cheer and good wishes for a speedy and safe return. Like all the streams on the Georgia coast it was very circuitous; marsh, marsh, marsh--not a house nor a brat or anything betokening an inhabited country could be seen--but we kept on. Coming around one of the bends in the river a large white painted house partly hid in dense foliage opened upon our eyes, apparently inland about a mile. About dusk we came up to a wharf opposite this mansion--making fast, we jumped ashore taking our two flags with us, I going ahead with Dugan next. A few hundred yards across a kind of causeway we came to a stream and a small bridge----.

If I could make these notes into a short novel in which the hero escaped as the **Yankee** steamed into the Altamaha River and destroyed the poor old **Standard,** appearing again in history at Lee's surrender, covered with Confederate glory, it would undoubtedly make better reading. However, I prefer what I believe to be a true story of blockade running in 1862, with the hero buried in a Georgia swamp on the banks of the Altamaha River. I would rather think of that burly Windsor captain as a loyal friend who did what he thought right and made amends as best he could to Dickson's mother. I am rather glad that the **Standard** and her crew again reached home, whether they accomplished their mission or not.

In Support of Maximilian*

John M. Taylor

There have been lobbyists in Washington for over a century, and the legal agent of a foreign power can today operate with relative freedom once he has registered with the United States government. Few attempts at lobbying, however, have been so bold, or have involved such high stakes, as one attempted at the close of the Civil War.

This article is based on some hitherto unpublished correspondence of Clarence A. Seward, nephew of the secretary of state. It relates to an imaginative effort by agents of the Maximilian government in Mexico to discredit and thereby neutralize Secretary Seward, one of their most forceful opponents. The correspondence in question--property of the author--comprises several letters relative to the episode preserved by an associate of Clarence Seward, together with a long letter in which Clarence Seward gives his side of the story.

With the conclusion of the Civil War, the Andrew Johnson administration faced monumental problems, not only in reconstructing the Union but in handling foreign affairs. While North America was absorbed in its own struggle, the emperor of France had launched a venture of his own. South of the border, France's sponsorship of a puppet state in Mexico gave rise to the first clear-cut challenge to the Monroe Doctrine.

The election of Lincoln in 1860 had coincided with the rise in Mexico of a reform-minded leader, Benito Juarez, who, like Lincoln, had humble origins. Juarez sought to unite the squabbling political factions of his country and to set the bankrupt nation on a firm economic footing. While the fate of the American Union was being decided to the north, Juarez sought to subdue Mexico's feudal chieftains and to satisfy its European creditors, notably France, England, and Spain. It was a large task. With the Lincoln government preoccupied, the European monarchies did not disguise their disposition to intervene in Mexico, ostensibly to protect their financial interests there.

Ultimately France took the plunge, when Napoleon III persuaded Archduke Maximilian of Austria to assume the "throne" of Mexico. At first Maximilian demurred; he was not unliberal in his own outlook, and he knew of

---

*Originally published in 1965.

no popular groundswell for his services as sovereign in Mexico.   He was susceptible to flattery, however, and a referendum that gave the impression of widespread Mexican support for the archduke was arranged.

Secretary Seward's Warning to France

The installation of Maximilian, supported by the French army, could hardly have been more poorly timed.   In America the tide of war had turned in favor of the North, and the Lincoln administration warned France that it regarded the existence of Maximilian's regime as incompatible with the Monroe Doctrine.   As the strength of the Confederacy ebbed, the tone of Secretary of State Seward's notes to the French court became more admonitory.

Thus, a primary task for Napoleon III came to be the neutralization of American hostility toward his Mexican venture.   The United States, with its superbly equipped and battle-tested army, could no longer be lightly regarded by the European powers.

The key to the American position was Secretary Seward, on whose experience and sagacity President Johnson came increasingly to rely. Seward felt strongly on the Mexican issue, and in the aftermath of a series of personal misfortunes* he instilled a proud man's eloquence into his communication to the French court:

> The United States have at no time left it doubtful that they wish to see a domestic and republican system prevail in Mexico rather than any other system . . . .

> It is hardly necessary for me to indicate where the present attitude and proceedings of the French government in regard to Mexico seem to be variant from the policy and sentiments of the United States which I have thus described . . . . France appears to be lending her great influence, with a considerable military force, to destroy the domestic republican government in Mexico, and to establish there an imperial system under the sovereignty of an European prince, who until he assumed the crown, was a stranger to that country.

No great perception was required to see that Secretary Seward was not susceptible to French blandishments. Where, then, was Napoleon III to turn?

---

*Seward and his son Frederick both narrowly escaped death when each was assaulted and knifed by a member of the group that successfully assassinated President Lincoln. Seward's wife, an invalid, died two months later. His only daughter, who witnessed the assault, died within the year.

Clarence Seward's Venture into Diplomacy

Clarence A. Seward was the secretary's nephew. He had been reared by the William H. Sewards after the death of his own parents in 1835, when Clarence was seven. In time Clarence Seward graduated from Hobart College and became the law partner of a close associate of Secretary Seward. By 1865 he was on his way to becoming a recognized legal specialist in New York City.

Although diplomacy was not his forte, circumstances conspired to place the secretary's nephew in a position of seeming influence in the Department of State. When Frederick Seward was incapacitated by his wounds in April 1865, it was Clarence who--in the casual fashion of the day--came down from New York to serve for three months as "acting under secretary" to his uncle. Probably at this time young Seward attracted the attention of the Maximilian interests. In any case, the pressures gathering to the South were shortly to involve him over his depth.

In May 1865, Maximilian granted one Eugene De Courcillon an exclusive franchise for a sea-rail carrier for all freight entering Mexico. De Courcillon promptly sought American financial backing for his venture, in part, perhaps, to commit American interests on behalf of Maximilian. He scored an early coup by signing up Clarence Seward as attorney for his Mexican Express Company. Although young Seward was in fact a specialist in the law of common carriers, one suspects that extralegal factors were involved.

Pleasantly surprised by Clarence's willingness to associate his name with the Mexican Express, pro-Maximilian agents tried again. According to Clarence, in late September "two gentlemen" called on him at his office in connection with a confidential matter. One of them produced a letter, "written in French," which closed with the sentence, "Monsieur M____ sails by the next Steamer, with the proper authentications." According to Seward's respondents, the word "authentications" referred to a sum of $100,000.

The visitors went on: The amount in question had been provided to create a "favorable press" in America toward the Maximilian government. They wished for Clarence Seward to accept the money and use it as he saw fit, with no accounting required. Clarence later stated that he had demurred, observing that the American people supported the Monroe Doctrine, and, besides, he knew of only one editor who might be "purchased." By his own admission, however, Clarence left the door open for further discussions.

Clarence Seward was obliged to go to Texas on some legal business, and his conversation with the two strangers troubled him. One evening, at a gathering that included his uncle, he sought the advice of Secretary Seward's political mentor, Thurlow Weed. Young Seward could hardly have made a less fortunate choice. Although Weed's personal estimate of Clarence is unrecorded, Weed combined the cynicism of the professional politician with an almost paternal solicitude for his protege, the secretary. One can only imagine his reaction to Clarence's explanation that he had left open the matter of the $100,000, since it would be better for him to have this money than for it to fall into irresponsible hands! Subsequent events demonstrated that Weed may not have fully comprehended Clarence's tale; he understood enough, however, to urge Clarence to secrecy and to express regret that dispatch of the money could not be stopped.

Matters Come to a Head

Shortly after Clarence Seward left for Texas, matters came to a head. On November 1, General Grant called on Secretary Seward to express concern over Clarence's public connection with the Mexican Express Company. Moreover, Grant contended, Clarence's trip to Texas was actually a cover for a trip into Mexico on some devious business. Thurlow Weed lent no comfort to the harassed secretary of state. He repeated his conversation with Clarence, indicating, however, that Clarence had already received the $100,000 and had offered half of it to Weed.

Secretary Seward was aghast. To Weed he spoke of being "ruined" by the incident; to Clarence's law partner the secretary stated that the firm's connection with the Maximilian lobby would force the State Department to withdraw its offer of a place on a Civil War claims commission.

Not until mid-November did word of the furor reach young Seward in Galveston, Texas. Replying to a letter from his partner, Clarence gave a detailed account of his meetings with the "two strangers." Insisting that Weed had endorsed his plan of action, Clarence denied ever having offered to split the $100,000. He went on:

> I saw the gentleman who produced the letter in French, and for the purpose of keeping matters unchanged said to him very much as Hamlet says to his two friends "perhaps--it may be--it may so fall out" and left him, he repeating his assurance that Mr. M____ was on his way, which assurance I repeated on a subsequent occasion to Mr. W[eed]. Here the matter rested until some short time thereafter and after the arrival of the Steamer, among whose list of passengers I did not find the name of Mr. ____. I said to the gentleman who produced the letter in French, "How about the $100,000. I do not see that your friend M____ has arrived." He answered, "No he has not come, he may have been delayed for family reasons."

Clarence Seward said that he had seen this contact on several occasions subsequent to the meeting described, and the subject of the money had never been mentioned. He flatly denied ever having received the money, and on this point his word must carry as much weight as that of Weed, whose information was derived from what Clarence had allegedly told him.

Assessment of the Venture

How deep was Clarence Seward's involvement with the Maximilian lobby? Undoubtedly he appeared as a ripe target to French agents, whose projects already included a pro-Maximilian newspaper in New York and at least one commercial venture, the Mexican Express Company. His family connection, together with his willingness to serve as counsel to the Mexican Express, marked him as an intelligence target.

It appears doubtful, however, whether anyone planned to turn $100,000 over to young Seward. The amount is not peanuts today; in 1865 it was a staggering sum. Inasmuch as the approach to Clarence was a singularly "cold approach," and his response apparently hesitant, one may ask whether "M___" was ever expected on the steamer in question.

A number of questions remain unresolved after a study of the letters describing this episode. The nationality of the "two gentlemen" is presumed to be French, but this fact is never clearly stated. The motives of Thurlow Weed, whose description of his talk with Seward is so at variance with Clarence's version, remain unclear.

The approach to Seward appears to have been exploratory in design. But the rewards might have been considerable. Had Clarence Seward accepted this money and had this fact become known, the end result might have been Secretary Seward's resignation. The secretary had, after all, spoken of being "ruined" by the public mention of Clarence's relatively innocuous connection with the Mexican Express Company.

Clarence Seward wisely passed up a career in diplomacy and went on to become a prominent New York attorney. When he died in 1897 the obituaries spoke of his "short but notable career in Washington" following the assault on his uncle, and cited his eminence in the fields of patent law and the law of common carriers. There was no mention of the Mexican Express Company.

Mark Twain, Edited and Bowdlerized*

Herbert E. Klingelhofer

When reading Mark Twain's autobiography one day, I came upon a chapter that made me hasten to my filing cabinet and get out a Mark Twain letter that had baffled me for many years. And sure enough, here was the answer to the problem I had been unable to solve. One more find in a different book, one more apparently unprinted manuscript source, and the picture had become coherent enough to present here as a whole.

To tell the complete story I must go back to the year of my buying the ALS. At the time I was intrigued by Mark Twain's rather strong language. The letter, dated London, August 27, 1900, was addressed to a Mr. Murray, apparently an editor, and Mark Twain took him to task--severely, I thought-- for having changed his (Twain's) manuscript. To my amusement the letter closed in a most cordial manner, contrasting strangely with the body of the communication.

Other interests prevailed at the time, and the letter was laid aside. Years later, I chanced to mention it to a friend. He suggested that the "Mr. Murray" was John Murray of London, the famous publisher. I wrote to Sir John Murray, the current head of the firm, but he denied that his father, T. Douglas Murray, had been the addressee. "Our firm never published for him and I cannot find any trace of letters to, or from, him here, though as the letter is addressed to Mr. Murray it looks as if it might have been; but if it really was sent to my father, I cannot imagine how it got away from here. There are vague rumors of Mark Twain having called on my father at one time, and their having had some disagreement on a point of history, but I cannot confirm this in any way."

Mark Twain had two books published in London not long after 1900, **A Double-barreled Detective Story** in 1902 and **A Dog's Tale** in 1903. Thinking that his publishers in England, Chatto and Windus, might know the answer, I wrote to them, but the reply was negative again. At this point I solicited help from Cyril Clemens, the editor of **The Mark Twain Journal,** again without results.

---

*Originally published in 1959. The previously unpublished letter of Mark Twain to which Dr. Klingelhofer refers in this article was copyrighted 1959 by Edward J. Willi and Manufacturers Hanover Trust Company as trustees of the Mark Twain Foundation, which reserves all reproduction or dramatization rights in every medium. It is published here with the permission of the University of California Press and Robert H. Hirst, general editor of the Mark Twain Project at Berkeley.

When I found no hint whatever in the published **Letters** of 1900, 1901, and 1902, I more or less gave up hope, conjecturing that the book had not been published and that, in fact, Clemens had been most secretive about it. Possibly the manuscript dealt with a subject that his regular publishers would not touch, and he had, for that reason or another, submitted it to some other man. Perchance it was published under a pseudonym. He had done this before, and "Mark Twain" was not his only alias. So I mused, and here matters stood when, after quite an interval, the answer came most unexpectedly. I became convinced that the "Mr. X" whom Mark Twain talks about and whom Paine also mentions in his biography was in fact my Mr. Murray. And going back to his **Letters,** but this time to the ones written in 1899 (which I had not done when I first consulted them--the index did not mention any Murray), there, in a letter to W. D. Howells, came the introduction to the whole episode, and Mr. Murray was indeed mentioned.

Finally turning to the Mark Twain Papers (University of California), I found Professor Henry N. Smith, editor, and Frederick Anderson, assistant editor, able and willing to help. There were letters from Murray to Mark Twain; there was also the manuscript emended by Murray. All the missing pieces were dropping into place and the astonishing "incident" now made sense indeed. The amusing story can now be told in some detail.

The Two Protagonists

T. Douglas Murray, born in 1841, was educated at Rugby and Exeter College, Oxford; was barrister-at-law at Lincoln's Inn; and led the life of a well-to-do Englishman of the time. In keeping with our present image of this type of man, he showed what may be called slight traits of eccentricity. In his younger days he traveled all over the world, spent many winters in Egypt, and was a decided sports addict. He created the present breed of Pekingese spaniels in England by importing some from the palace at Peking. He started the first permanent band in Hyde Park. His contribution to literature consisted of a book about Sir Samuel Baker, whose helper he had been. The publication convinced him that he was endowed with certain literary gifts; aside from that, he was a bit pompous and smug, but well-meaning and generous.

In contrast, there was Mark Twain, one of the most talented of writers, a personality genuine and true, a man not unaware of his tremendous reputation in Europe as well as America, immensely gifted yet very human, not without a touch of vanity, and rather sensitive about criticism of his writing. It is evident that he was not the type of man who enjoys being patted on the back and being called "my dear fellow."

The Joint Enterprise

These two men met, and in the summer of 1899 they became associated in an enterprise possible only because of their common devotion to a female knight in shining armor, Joan of Arc. Twain had been in love with the young heroine ever since he had read about her on a printed page, picked up off the street. It was the beginning of a reverent, lifelong friendship. This charming and ardent worship resulted in a masterpiece of delicate artistry, his **Personal Recollections of Joan of Arc,** and was to have a second fruition during the very months with which this paper is concerned.

Murray had come across a French source, the official record of the Trials and Tribulations of Joan of Arc, which he thought worthy of translation into English. Having produced his first opus, he considered himself a writer of decided ability and planned to edit the record himself. He asked Mark Twain to write an introduction to the book. Twain was flattered, pleased, and quite willing to comply. He started to compose the essay while in Sweden and finished it in London in October 1899. Murray, as editor, planned to write a preface, briefly defining the scope and contents of the book and evaluating the documentary evidence. This preface was to be followed by Mark Twain's introduction, an "historical survey by an expert (if possible); and Strategy and Tactics of the maid, by an expert (if possible)." [1]

Mark Twain suggested a certain lady for "writing Joan's Voices and Prophecies, the Lord Chief Justice of England on the legal prodigies which she performed before her judges, Lord Roberts for her military genius, and Kipling for her patriotism." [2]

Murray went into action, capturing the lady and getting Roberts and Kipling to "take hold and see if they could do monographs worthy of the book." The notemaking was to be undertaken by the translators. So far everything had gone very well. Mark Twain spoke of Murray, in a letter to Howells, as "my excellent friend, a rich Englishman who **edits** the translation." He himself had set out to "treat the subject with the reverence and dignity due it, and would use plain, simple English words, and a phrasing undefiled by meretricious artificialities and affectations." [3] Accordingly, he had taken great pains with the introduction and admitted that it "was no slouch of a performance." [4]

"Little Pencil Marks Here and There"

Twain handed the completed manuscript to Murray and waited for the deserved acclaim. Murray had it "type-copied" and wrote him, on October 14, "I think the Introduction full of beauty and pathos. You may find little pencil

---

[1] ALS by T. Douglas Murray to S. L. Clemens, October 14, 1899. The original is in Mark Twain Papers, University of California Library, Berkeley.

[2] ALS by S. L. Clemens to William Dean Howells, October 15, 1899, published in **Mark Twain's Letters,** Albert Bigelow Paine, ed. (New York: Harper and Brothers, 1917), vol. 2, p. 686.

[3] **Mark Twain's Autobiography,** Albert Paine, ed. (New York: Harper and Brothers, 1912), p. 176.

[4] **Mark Twain's Letters,** p. 686.

marks here and there." [5] This last sentence discomfited Twain a little, but it was in no way an indication of the jolt he suffered when Murray brought by the typewritten copy, assuring him that the introduction had met with his approval and was "really quite good--quite, I assure you." Murray mentioned on his way out that he had made a few corrections, suggestions, "oh, nothing of consequence, I assure you," and would like Twain to send the introduction back to him as soon as possible so that he could get it to the printer. [6]

Little did Murray suspect that this marked the end of their literary cooperation. Mark Twain, rather incensed but still not quite prepared for the shock to follow, glanced at the edited pages. Now his eyes did pop, his adrenals did start secreting their powerful brew, and a great many wild thoughts bubbled upward. He had been edited indeed, for the first time in thirty-two years. Every page bore witness to that. "The idea! That this long-eared animal--this literary kangaroo--this illiterate hustler, with his skull full of axle grease--this ... ! But I stopped here, for this was not the right Christian spirit." [7]

Mark Twain's Letter to Murray

Twain sat down again and composed a long and spirited letter to Murray, starting off rather quietly by proposing to comment upon Murray's corrections and to point out why the changes did not seem to be improvements. He hoped in this way to be as helpful to Murray, he wrote, as Murray had desired to profit him. Space does not permit, unfortunately, the reproduction and the amended texts in their entirety, with Mark Twain's cutting comments, but a few examples will give some idea of the suggested changes and of the reaction induced. (Twain's comments are in parentheses.)

Mark Twain's original: **Joan of Arc**

Murray's version: **Jeanne d'Arc**

(This is rather cheaply pedantic, and is not in very good taste. Joan is not known by that name among plain people of our race and tongue. I notice that the name of the Deity occurs several times in the brief installment of the **Trials** which you have favored me with; to be consistent, it will be necessary that you strike out "God" and put in "Dieu." Do not neglect this.)

---

[5]ALS by T. Douglas Murray, see note no. 1.

[6]**Autobiography,** p. 178.

[7]Ibid., p. 179.

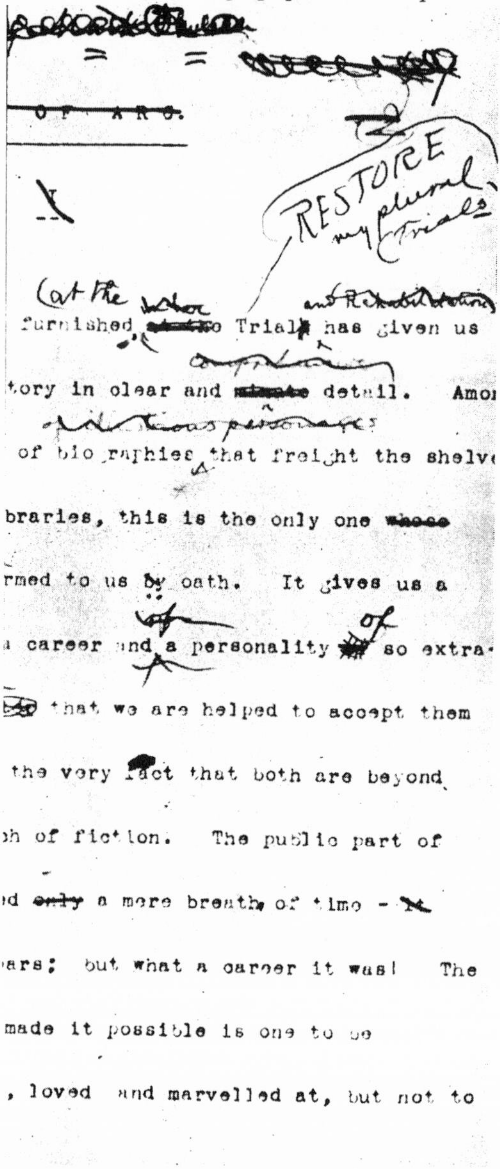

OF ARC.

I

RESTORE my plural Trials

furnished Trial has given us
tory in clear and detail. Amo
of biographies that freight the shelv
braries, this is the only one
rmed to us by oath. It gives us a
a career and a personality of so extra-
that we are helped to accept them
the very fact that both are beyond
h of fiction. The public part of
d only a mere breath of time -
ears; but what a career it was! The
made it possible is one to be
, loved and marvelled at, but not to

Illus. 1. The original Twain handwritten manuscript for the introduction to T. Douglas Murray's book on Joan of Arc was typed by Murray and corrected, much to the chagrin of Twain, whose angry objection was inked on the page reproduced above.

Twain: The evidence furnished at the Trials has given us Joan of Arc's history in clear and minute detail. Among all the multitude of biographies that freight the shelves of the world's libraries, this is the only one whose validity is confirmed to us by oath.

Murray: The evidence furnished in her Trial and rehabilitation has given us Jeanne d'Arc's history in clear and comprehensive detail. Amongst the multitude of biographies of illustrious personages that freight the shelves of the world's libraries, this is the only one the validity of which is confirmed to us by oath. 8

(What is the trouble with "at the"? And why "Trial"? Has some uninstructed person deceived you into the notion that there was but one, instead of half a dozen? "Amongst." Wasn't "among" good enough? Have you failed to perceive that by taking the word "both" out of its proper place you have made foolishness of the sentence? And don't you see that your smug "of which" has turned **that** sentence into reporter's English?) 9

Twain: Joan asked one other favor: that now that her mission was fulfilled she might be allowed to go back to her village . . . .

Murray: Joan asked one other favor: that now that her mission was fulfilled she might be allowed to return to her village 10

(You have a singularly fine and aristocratic disrespect for homely and unpretending English. Every time I use "go back" you get out your polisher and slick it up to "return." "Return" is suited only to the drawing-room--it is ducal, and says itself with a simper and a smirk.) 11

Twain: In accordance with a beautiful old military custom, Joan devoted her silver armour and hung it up in the Cathedral of St. Denis. Its great days were over. Then, by command, she followed the King and his frivolous Court, and endured a gilded captivity for a time, as well as her free spirit could; and whenever inaction became unbearable, she gathered some men together and rode away and assaulted a stronghold and captured it . . . . Thus ended the briefest epoch-making military career in history.

Twain: In accordance with a beautiful old military custom, Jeanne devoted her silver armour and hung it up in the Cathedral of St. Denis. Her

---

8Saint Joan of Arc, by S. L. Clemens, **Harper's Magazine**, 1904, this is substantially identical with Mark Twain's Introduction of 1899 manuscript, emended by T. Douglas Murray, among Mark Twain Papers, University of California Library, Berkeley, p. 1.

9Autobiography, p. 181.

10Saint Joan of Arc, p. 6.

11Autobiography, p. 182.

392 Manuscripts as a Key to Biography and History

great days were over. Then, by command, she followed the King and his frivolous Court, and endured a gilded captivity for a time, as well as her free spirit could; but whenever inaction became unbearable, she gathered some men together and rode away to assault and capture a stronghold .... Thus ended the briefest epoch-making military career known in history. [12]

("Her" great days were **not** "over"; they were only half over. Didn't you know that? Haven't you read anything at all about Joan of Arc? The truth is, you do not pay any attention; I told you on my very first page that the public part of her career lasted two years, and you have forgotten it already. You really must get your mind out and have it repaired; you see, yourself, that it is all caked together. She "rode away **to** assault and capture a stronghold." Very well; but you do not tell us whether she succeeded or not. You should not worry the reader with uncertainties like that. I will remind you once more that clarity is a good thing in literature. An apprentice cannot do better than keep this useful rule in mind. "Known" history. That work is a polish which is too delicate for me; there does not seem to be any sense in it.)[13]

Twain: Joan was fated to spend the rest of her life behind bolts and bars .... By the rules of war she must be held to ransom, and a fair price could not be refused, if offered. John of Luxemburg paid her the just compliment of requiring a prince's ransom for her. In that day that phrase represented a definite sum--61,125 francs. It was of course supposable that either the King or grateful France or both would fly with the money and set their fair young benefactor free. But this did not happen. In five and a half months neither King nor country stirred a hand nor offered a penny. Twice Joan tried to escape. Once by a trick she succeeded for a moment, and locked her jailor in behind her: but she was discovered and caught; in the other case she let herself down from a tower sixty feet high, but her rope was too short and she got a fall that disabled her and she could not get away.

Murray: Jeanne was fated to spend the remainder of her short life behind bolts and bars. By the rules of war she should have been held to ransom, and a fair price could not have been refused, if it had been offered. John of Luxembourg paid her the just compliment of demanding a prince's ransom for her. In those days, that phrase represented a definite sum--61,125 francs. It was of course supposable that either the King, or grateful France, or both, would fly with the money and set their fair young benefactress free. But this did not happen. In five-and-a-half months neither King nor country stirred a hand nor offered a centime. Twice Joan tried to escape. Once, by a trick, she succeeded for a moment, and locked her jailor in behind her: but she was discovered and caught. In the other case, she let herself down from a tower sixty feet high: but her rope was too short, she sustained a fall that wholly disabled her, and so prevented her escape. [14]

---

[12] Saint Joan of Arc, p. 8.

[13] Autobiography, p. 182.

[14] Saint Joan of Arc, p. 10.

("Remainder." It is curious and interesting to notice what an attraction a fussy, mincing, nickel-plated artificial word has for you. This is not well. But she **was** held to ransom; it wasn't a case of "should have been" and it wasn't a case of "**if** it had been offered"; it **was** offered, and also accepted, as the second paragraph shows. You ought never to edit except when awake. Why do you wish to change the fourth sentence? It was more than "demanded"; it was **required.** Have you no sense of shades of meaning in words? Changing it to "benefactress" takes the dignity out of it. If I had called her a braggart, I suppose you would have polished her into a braggartress, with your curious and random notions about the English tongue. "Sustained" is sufficiently nickel-plated to meet the requirements of your disease, I trust. "Wholly" adds nothing; the sentence means just what it meant before. In the rest of the sentence you sacrifice simplicity to airy fussiness.) [15]

Twain: **Finally, Cauchon, Bishop of Beauvais, paid the money and bought Joan--ostensibly for the Church, to be tried for wearing male attire and for other impieties, but really for the English, the enemy into whose hands the poor girl was so piteously anxious not to fall. She was now shut up in the dungeons of the Castle of Rouen . . . .**

Murray: **Finally Cauchon, Bishop of Beauvais, paid the bloodmoney and bought Jeanne, ostensibly for the Church, to be tried for wearing male attire and for other impieties, but in reality for the English, the enemy into whose hands the poor girl was so piteously anxious never to fall. She was now shut up in the dungeons of the Castle of Rouen . . . .** [16]

(It was not blood money, unteachable ass, any more than is the money that buys a house or a horse; it was an ordinary business transaction of the time, and it was not dishonorable.) [17]

Twain: **When the fires rose about her and she begged for a cross for her dying lips to kiss . . . .**

Murray: **When the flames leapt up and enveloped her frail form and she begged for a cross for her parched lips to kiss . . . .** [18]

("When the flames leapt up and enveloped her frail form" is handsome, very handsome, even elegant, but it isn't yours; you hooked it out of "The Costermonger's Bride; or The Fire Fiend's Foe." To take other people's things is not right, and God will punish you. "Parched" lips? How do you know they

---

[15] Autobiography, p. 183.

[16] Saint Joan of Arc, p. 11.

[17] Autobiography, p. 184.

[18] Saint Joan of Arc, p. 15.

were? Why do you make statements which you cannot verify, when you have no motive for it but to work in a word which you think is nobby?) [19]

The Denouement

This pithy letter was never sent, and the one Mark Twain actually sent must have been rather different. It is likely that it contained no counter-proposals, no insults, no sarcasm. This assumption is justified by the friendly tone of Murray's letters to Twain written during the following summer; they do not in the least sound like those of a man who has been grievously offended. Mark Twain, it is likely, wrote a polite but decidedly cool letter pointing out that he could not accept any emendations of his manuscript and that the deal was off. Murray, one can imagine, must have been taken aback, but did not feel this as a direct rebuff. His confidence in himself remained unshaken. He had done Clemens a service by suggesting certain ameliorations, by rendering his somewhat straightforward wording more graceful and even bringing out the hidden meaning in some spots. Twain was a first-rate chap, a humorist of the first water, and it was a fortunate happenstance that he had some genuine interest in Jeanne d'Arc, had, indeed, written a book about her; but in matters of phrasing and rendering the whole more attractive, a true stylist was indispensible. An Englishman like himself was not likely to err here.

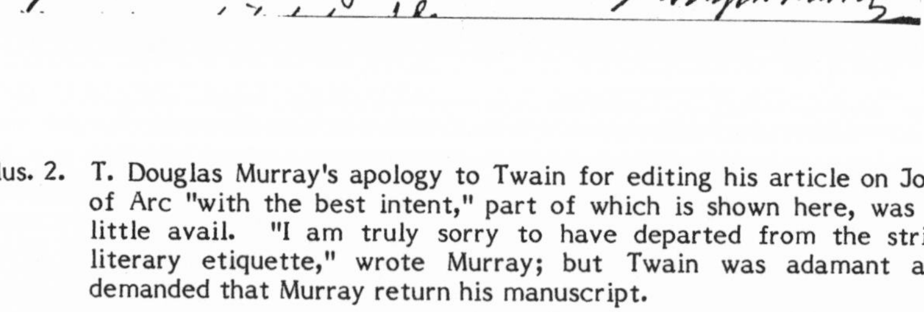

Illus. 2. T. Douglas Murray's apology to Twain for editing his article on Joan of Arc "with the best intent," part of which is shown here, was to little avail. "I am truly sorry to have departed from the strict literary etiquette," wrote Murray; but Twain was adamant and demanded that Murray return his manuscript.

---

[19] **Autobiography**, p. 185.

At any rate, it is doubtful that Murray realized what he had done. He continued to try to get Twain's introduction for his book. Relations between the men remained friendly. When Murray heard of Twain's new interest in a health food called Plasmon, he wrote to Sir William Crookes, the eminent chemist, to get some information about it and relayed the news to Twain. Several times he promised to send him partridges and grouse, and his letters, to the last, written shortly before Mark Twain's return to America, remained amicable and cheerful.

On August 5, 1900, Murray, obviously in answer to a renewed request for a return of various manuscripts and copies, promised to send first the "lecture MS"* and a copy he had made because the original was difficult to read, and Twain's autograph manuscript as soon as he could find it.

"Please note," he goes on, "that I have only altered copies I had made for myself, as I felt some sort of revision was required, and I knew that every moment of your time was occupied with anxious literary work, and so I hoped to save you time by these suggestions for your approval or the reverse. I am truly sorry to have departed from the strict literary etiquette: but I erred with the best interest. I do really think that if you will take the trouble to read through the clear copy you will feel, as I do, that it has need of some revision, anyhow my mind is at rest on the matter and your decision satisfies me, as it would had it been otherwise--though I should have preferred the 'otherwise.'   All I want is that you should be happy and content in the matter." [20]

To this Mark Twain wrote the letter that was the main reason for this article:

Dollis Hill House, London, N.W.
August 27/00

Dear Mr. Murray:

I am afraid you did not quite clearly understand me. The time-honored etiquette of the situation is this: An author's MS. is not open to any editor's emendations. It must be accepted as it stands, or it must be declined; there is no middle course. Any alteration of it--even to a word--closes the incident, and that author and that editor can have no further literary dealings with each other. It was your right to say that the Introduction was not satisfactory to you, but it was not within your rights to contribute your pencil's assistance toward making it satisfactory.

---

*Apparently Mark Twain used this lecture manuscript when giving lectures on Joan of Arc. He had been approached on October 19, 1899, by Canon Wilberforce to give a lecture on Joan of Arc in his drawing room. Twain had let Murray explain to Wilberforce his (Twain's) reasons for postponing the lecture.

[20] ALS by T. Douglas Murray to S. L. Clemens, August 5, 1900, Mark Twain Papers, University of California Library, Berkeley.

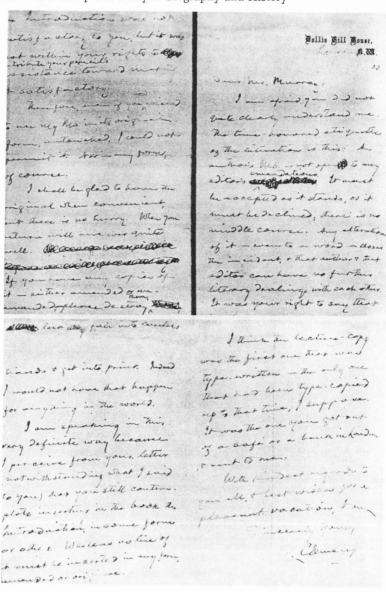

Illus. 3. Politely but firmly, Twain declined to allow Murray to change his manuscript, and in the letter reproduced here insisted the manuscript be returned and all copies destroyed.

Therefore, even if you now wished to use my MS. in its original form, untouched, I could not permit it. Nor in any form, of course.

I shall be glad to have the original when convenient, but there is no hurry. When you return will answer quite well. If you have any copies of it--either amended or unamended--please destroy them, lest they fall into careless hands and get into print. Indeed I would not have that happen for anything in the world.

I am speaking in this very definite way because I perceive from your letter (notwithstanding what I said to you) that you still contemplate inserting in the book the Introduction, in some form or other. Whereas no line of it must be inserted in any form, amended or original.

I think the lecture-copy was the first one that was type-written--the only one that had been type-copied up to that time, I suppose. It was the one you got out of a safe or a bank in London and sent to me.

With kindest regards to you all, and best wishes for a pleasant vacation, I am

Sincerely yours,
S. L. Clemens.[21]

On August 30, T. Douglas Murray answered, "I am altogether in harmony with you and quite endorse your views as regards the Introduction. I admire it immensely--and it would form a most valuable paper for publication later on." He again promised to send him the original and all existing copies and to see to it that not a word of it would be published. He thought that while the world was in such a disturbed condition (the Boer War), his own plans for publication would have to wait. [22]

His book, called **Jeanne d'Arc, Maid of Orleans, Deliverer of France,** was published in 1902. His grand project for various monographs by famous personages, designed to serve as introductions, came to naught. Instead he

---

[21] ALS by S. L. Clemens to T. Douglas Murray, August 27, 1900, in possession of the author, reproduced here by permission of the Mark Twain Estate.

[22] ALS by T. Douglas Murray to S. L. Clemens, August 30, 1900, Mark Twain Papers, University of California Library, Berkeley.

wrote the introduction himself. It is altogether different from Mark Twain's, except in a few minor similarities such as "a career and a personality of so extraordinary a character" (Twain) and "her extraordinary career" (Murray). Murray cannot be accused of having borrowed ideas, sentences, or words from Mark Twain. Murray's introduction is about the trial itself, while Twain gives us a brief biography dealing with events in Joan's life, as well as with her beliefs.

The contrast in styles is marked. Twain used rather plain and unadorned sentences, whereas Murray's style is much more florid, ostentatious, and often a bit stiff, marked by expressions like, "She held by the belief that her own unworthiness in the world's eye was the cause of her being chosen as a single instrument in the hands of the Lord."   Or, "After all that can be done by the rationalizing process, the mystery remains of an untutored and unlettered girl of eighteen years old, not only imposing her will upon captains and courtiers, but showing a skill and judgment worthy, as Gen. Dragomiroff says, of the greatest commanders, indeed of Napoleon himself." [24]

Murray sometimes used awkward grammar: "God and His angels were as real to her, more real indeed, than the men and women of her native village." [25] Several times he is guilty of a crime of which he accused Twain, such as repeating a word, "Nor did she **ever** become a law unto herself, as the 'illuminated' are apt to be, rather she was more than **ever** observant of all the duties and claims and observances of ordinary religious obligation, being **ever** in heart the simple maid, whom the Lord for his own mysterious purpose, and without any merit of hers, had chosen for a mighty task." [26]

While Murray suffered disappointment in losing the contributions of Mark Twain, Kipling, and others, he did have the satisfaction of recognition in high quarters: Pope Pius X thanked him in private audience for his praiseworthy effort in behalf of the Maid of Orleans. Murray died not long after Samuel Clemens, on November 20, 1911. His prediction that Clemens's introduction would be published by itself came true in 1904 when it appeared in **Harper's Magazine** as "Saint Joan of Arc." It was published without Murray's emendations--except one: Mark Twain did change "the angels counselled her, advised and heartened her" (page 27) to "counselled her, comforted and heartened her," as Murray had suggested.

Thus ends the strange story of T. Douglas Murray's attempt to amend, revise, and improve Mark Twain. It cannot be denied that he succeeded: but his triumph was confined to one solitary word.

---

[23] **Jeanne d'Arc, Maid of Orleans, Deliverer of France,** T. Douglas Murray, ed. (New York: McClure, Phillips and Co., 1902), p. xii.

[24] Ibid., p. vii.

[25] Ibid., p. x.

[26] Ibid., p. xiv.

Algernon Charles Swinburne to Paul Hamilton Hayne*

John S. Mayfield

Algernon Charles Swinburne, the pugnacious, sometimes rambunctious little Englishman, and Paul Hamilton Hayne, the mild-mannered, beloved American, never met each other face to face, and so far as I have been able to determine there exists no account of the manner in which they became correspondents. Both men were poets and therefore it might be said that they were kindred souls, and as such required nó introduction. A common interest was sufficient, particularly when that interest was poetry.

It is a guess that Hayne initiated the correspondence, probably expressing his admiration for some of Swinburne's verses which he might have seen published in this country. Swinburne was by far the brighter light in the literary world, and Hayne was hardly known outside the states which had at one time formed the Confederacy and of which he had been proclaimed the poet laureate. The first American editions of some of Swinburne's works (**The Queen-Mother and Rosamond, Atalanta in Calydon, Chastelard, A Song of Italy,** and **Laus Veneris**) had begun to appear in 1866 and 1867, after they had brought popularity and fame to their author in England, and it is certain that Hayne was familiar with them and others that closely followed from the publishing houses in Boston, New York, and Philadelphia.

Few Published Letters

Of the letters from Swinburne to Hayne a few, pleasant and temperate in tone, have been published in whole or in part in such books as **The Letters of Algernon Charles Swinburne,** edited by Edmund Gosse and Thomas James Wise (London, 1918, and later editions) and **Swinburne: A Literary Biography,** by Georges Lafourcade (London, 1932). The letter in my collection, however, exudes a red-hot intensity, and for sheer invective and abuse it takes some kind of a prize--perhaps a bag of gall and brimstone. It has never been included in any collected edition, but about thirty-four years ago it enjoyed the limited circulation of the now defunct Boston **Evening Transcript** in the issue for October 16, 1918. There it appeared, incorrectly transcribed, introduced by journalist George H. Sargent with four meager preliminary paragraphs, two of which were garbled by the printer.

---

*Originally published in 1952.

According to Sargent, the letter was then in the possession of Patrick F. Madigan, an autograph dealer of New York City, who had acquired it following its discovery among the southern poet's papers some years after his death. It is presumed that the letter then floated around from dealer to collector and from collector to dealer until finally it came into the stock of an autograph and book shop, also in New York City, from the proprietors of which it was my pleasure in 1944 to purchase it. The proprietors had described it as being "without parallel the finest and most sensational Swinburne letter ever offered for sale in the United States."

The Letter

In March 1877, when the letter was written, forty-seven-year-old Hayne, in genteel poverty and ill health, enduring the rigors of postwar reconstruction, was eking out a slim existence for his family and himself by his literary output and living in a shanty on a place he called Copse Hill, near what is now Grovetown, in the vicinity of Augusta, Georgia. Swinburne was approaching his fortieth birthday when his father died during the first week of March. The loss of this parent, coupled with other problems, caused his spirits to sink and his temper to become short and sharp. Following the funeral, he was at the family seat, Holmwood, in the neighborhood of Henley-on-Thames, not far from London, and it was there he wrote on mourning stationery to Hayne:

Holmwood*
Henley on Thames
March 20th 1877

*As this address may not find me much longer, I will ask you to write to me next time to the 'care of Messrs. Chatto & Windus 74 Piccadilly London W.'

My dear Sir

It is a genuine pleasure to me to see your handwriting again, & to acknowledge with thanks your interesting & cordial letter received this morning. I am not aware that I have ever by inadvertence failed to acknowledge any former missive; but it strikes me as just possible that owing to a protracted & at one time dangerous illness from which I suffered thro' [a] great part of last summer & autumn, I may have to apologize to you as well as to other friendly correspondents for the seeming negligence of a very involuntary intermission or suspension from writing of any kind for a month or two.

The said illness began in a fashion which would just have suited & delighted Poe as a subject--though not enviable as an experience; from sleeping in a room with great flowering Indian lilies in it, & waking in an hour or two literally poisoned by the perfume, in such agony of brain & stomach as I hope never to feel again.   However no <u>very</u> permanent damage was done to my general health in the long run either as regards mind or body, tho' both alike were wellnigh prostrated for many wretched & unprofitable weeks. It is rather amusing to remember that in my first boyish book written at college I had introduced a case of poisoning by perfume. I little knew what the actual symptoms would be. Dante's Hell was a child's playground to that fragrant & delicate bedroom.

I have been following with great interest the political struggle in your country--& I suppose I need not assure you that I was grieved & disappointed by the upshot which certainly--as far as a foreigner (however candidly & anxiously desirous to see the truth without prejudice) can judge from the report of foreign journals-- would seem, & did to me seem at once, the result of such injustice & treacherous or violent immorality as you describe. Time, as in France, can (I suppose) alone be looked to for help. Some of our papers say that Mr. Lowell is about to come hither--I will not say as your ambassador, but as envoy of the 'Yankees'; who must in that case intend a gross insult (possibly not undeserved) to this country by the mission as ambassador to England of one among the most rancorous & virulent of its revilers. It should be enough that one of our two universities has already (as I told its most distinguished living member at the time or shortly after) disgraced itself by lowering the former standard & degrading the previous recipients of its honours in order to inflict on them the unsavoury society of a vulgar & indecent buffoon. Till then the distinction conferred on Mr. Lowell had been held throughout Europe as an honour from which the most eminent of European statesmen, generals, writers--men of highest note in any public capacity-- might naturally & reasonably derive a fresh source of just & honourable pride. Since then, I must say, the man who is not too proud to be ambitious of a share in honours which may be bestowed on a mountebank of letters in a cash suit of threadbare motley,-- one who chooses such subjects as the blindness of Milton for the mark of his professional jests--jests for which, in the days when persons of his kind filled only their proper places (among which the post of ambassador between two great nations was never reckoned till now), he would assuredly & deservedly have been liable to the just correction of a sound whipping by the order of his royal (or other) master--a man of such humble ambition may certainly claim credit at least for the Christian virtue of modesty.   The distinguished person to whom I made this remark (intended of course to imply a mild remonstrance with himself for having allowed such a thing to pass without protest or expostulation-- which might naturally have been expected, & must necessarily have been effective--on his part) replied with real earnestness, 'I wish I had known of this' (an especially offensive passage in one of Mr. Lowell's books, to which I had referred him) 'in time to prevent the conferring of his honorary degree. I could have prevented it--<u>and I would</u>.' In that case, as I told him, he would in my humble opinion

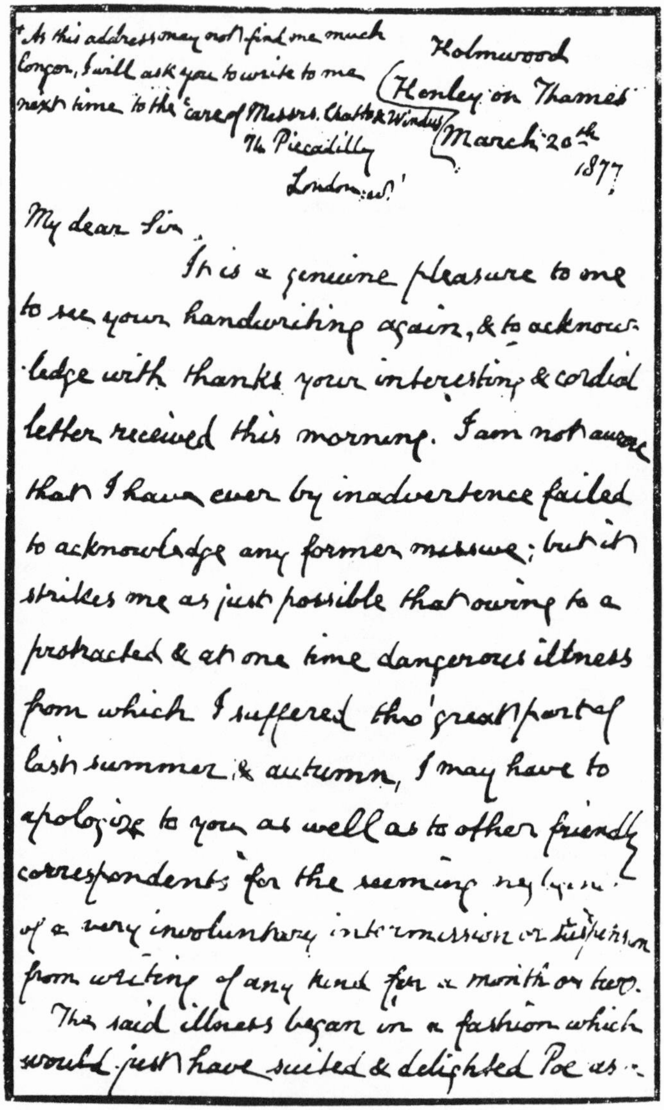

Illus. 1. Portion of a letter from Swinburne to Hayne in the author's collection.

have saved his University from a disgrace--& consequently (in some degree) the whole country from just discredit. But if this end had happily been effected through my humble agency, I presume my unfortunate name would have been in still worse odour than ever among the good citizens of Massachussetts [sic]. And certainly (as you say) an assault with a copy of Emerson's 'Poems' would be a danger liable to quell the hardiest courage. Though I must in common honesty & candour--as I cannot be suspected of any personal tenderness or respect for a man who has indecently exposed himself as (with reference to <u>myself</u>) a foul-minded & foul-mouthed old driveller--make so much reserve in his favour as to admit that I think one or two of those poems exceptionally beautiful & powerful; portions, for instance, if not all, of the poem on a son who died in boyhood--& most especially the noble, manly, & pathetic Threnody on his brothers. I always think that to ignore or to deny whatever there may be of genuine merit in the work of an enemy or backbiter, however virulent or abject in his filthy malignity, is to lower one's own self for the moment to the base level of even such a currish & venemous dastard as the calumniator. And I always wish to make this known as my opinion by the simple process of trying to act up to it.

Pardon this egotism, & allow me to express my sincere sympathy with your own verses--& to assure you how very cordially & sorrowfully I feel the weight & force of their plaintive & patriotic protest. It is still, not unnaturally, difficult in England to express sympathy with the Southern States & escape the charge or at least the suspicion of jealous & vicious malevolence towards the Republic in general. And it is, I fear, undeniable that a great part of what passed for English sympathy with the South was mere hatred or prejudice against democratic institutions--if not mere malice & rancour against America. Then, as now on the eastern question, I found myself (an Englishman of the same class by birth & of the same opinions by instinct as Shelley & Landor & Byron) utterly opposed to the current of English Radicalism--& yet unable to deny, or to disguise from myself, that the mass of Englishmen on my side had adopted the same view for reasons opposite to mine & on principles which I detested & despised. In such a case, it seems to me, the only thing for a loyal & honourable man to do is to hold fast to his own instincts & principles in spite of friend or foe, regardless of the reluctance & regret he must naturally feel to find himself arrayed (it may be) against men whom he respects, in the company of men whom he assuredly does not.

However ill the matter of the Poe Memorial may have been managed, it can hardly have ended in such an outrageous burlesque of failure as the Byron Memorial in London--in which enterprise I am thankful to remember that I had the good sense (knowing the capacity of my countrymen in such matters) to decline taking any part beyond the payment of a necessary subscription.--I have barely room or time left to say how much pleased I am by what you say of my unfinished Tristram & Iseult--& that it wd. be a great addition to your kindness & my pleasure if you were to send me anything you may ever see said of it in print.

Yours sincerely
A. C. Swinburne.

This remarkable letter could, I imagine, be of interest to psychologists, character analysts, and such, but the concern here will be only with a few details of some of the things to which Swinburne referred.

Poison by Perfume

The "protracted & at one time dangerous illness" is mentioned in Sir Edmund Gosse's brief record of **The Life of Swinburne** (written for the **Dictionary of National Biography,** but first privately printed, London, 1912), where it is stated, "In July [1876] he was poisoned by lilies with which a too-enthusiastic hostess had filled his bedroom, and he did not completely recover until November." In his "much fuller" volume, **The Life of Algernon Charles Swinburne** (London, 1917), Gosse amplified this to read,

> He attributed his loss of health and spirits [in August 1876] to having been "poisoned by perfumes." A lady, at whose house he had spent the night, had, he said, sought to do him honour by filling his bedroom with great Japanese [sic] lilies in blossom, and the poet had waked in the middle of the night in a delirium, rousing the household with his shrieks.

Gosse had first learned of the incident, of course, from Swinburne's letter to him, written at Holmwood, October 17, 1876 (published in the Gosse and Wise volumes of collected letters, London, 1918), in which the poet wrote,

> I am very sorry to hear that Mrs. Gosse has been so ill. It seems to have been a bad season for health. I have been very ill myself for some time. (I don't know whether you heard from any quarter of my being accidentally poisoned some months since by the perfume of Indian lilies in a close bedroom--which sounds romantic, but was horrible in experience, and I have not yet wholly recovered the results, or regained my strength.)

Lafourcade mentioned this illness also, but declared that it happened in October 1876, "under somewhat obscure circumstances." Lafourcade continued,

> During the months that followed, Swinburne was fond of referring to and describing this incident which, had it been fatal, would have been a fitting close to the career of the author of .... **Lesbia Brandon** ....

Lafourcade's footnote explains, "In the last chapter . . . the heroine poisons herself slowly with flowers and Eau de Cologne."

In a letter written at Holmwood on October 28, 1876 (the Bonchurch edition of **The Complete Works of Algernon Charles Swinburne,** edited by Gosse and Wise, vol. 18: **Letters,** London and New York, 1927), Swinburne gave an account of the incident to his friend John Nichol:

> Since I last wrote or heard from you I have been so ill and am still so seedy and weak or uncertain as to memory of details that I cannot be sure when I did write last . . . . Ever since I most involuntarily solved the question I have heard debated (and denied for example by our old friend W. B. Scott, 16 or more years since, à propos of an incident in my first book, **The Queen Mother** [published in 1860]) whether a man could be actually poisoned by perfumes--as I was sleeping in a room with a large India lily in full flower near the bed, recalling Hawthorne's story, of which you expressed such admiration to me once at Oxford in the years before the Flood, **Rappuccini's** [sic] **Daughter,** to whom the lady at whose house I was then a visitor must assuredly have been akin ever since this possibly romantic but certainly unpleasant experience of a literally flower-strewn approach to the door of delirium if not of death, I have been but a rag of unmanned manhood, barely able to read or write or think consecutively.

Swinburne's reference to Nathaniel Hawthorne's narrative is to **Rappaccini's Daughter,** which first appeared in the **Democratic Review,** 1844, and was reprinted in **Mosses from an Old Manse,** 1846. It is the story of a scientist who feeds his daughter poison so that her breath will be fatal to her lover.

Several years ago I supplied a copy of Swinburne's letter to Hayne to Randolph Hughes, whose edition of **Lesbia Brandon** was recently issued in London. I am indebted to him for pointing out to me this passage in the letter to Nichol when I queried him about the poet's "first boyish book written at college" in which had been introduced a case of poisoning by perfume. The phrase, declared Hughes, "does not (and, by the way, could not) refer to **Lesbia Brandon,** but to **The Queen Mother.**" "It is curious," he noted, "that the single (or--in a double sense--singular) lily in this letter [to Nichol] should be multiplied to a plural in the one written [to Hayne] less than half a year later."

Scandals

The "political struggle" and Swinburne's grief and disappointment at "the upshot" undoubtedly refer to the rampant fraud and graft and unprecedented corruption and scandals prevalent in Grant's administration: the president's recent show of military strength in the South during the presidential campaign and the riots, massacres, and intimidations brought on by the carpetbaggers, political tricksters, and dishonest men present in the southern states throughout the Reconstruction era and particularly violent during the general election in November 1876 and the weeks following, when the presidency was stolen from the rightful winner. Hayne and his fellow southerners were suffering, and Swinburne was sympathetic.

"Mr. Lowell is about to come hither" was only a rumor that did not materialize until later. In 1877 James Russell Lowell was appointed minister to Madrid (he was a staunch Republican and had been a presidential elector in 1876), and three years later minister to London, where he remained until 1885. He had trenchantly criticized England's part in the War Between the States and contributed a powerful influence on the patriotic sentiments of Northerners. Hughes explained Swinburne's comments as follows:

> Lowell had not only shown himself a hater of England, and been guilty of the other crimes Swinburne mentions, but he had also virulently attacked the poet's work, so that the latter's feelings regarding him are quite easy to understand. When Lowell came to England, and really got to know it, he quickly (and somewhat funnily) made a complete volte-face, and among other things sought an introduction to the poet, who magnanimously received him.

At this meeting in 1882, according to Gosse's 1917 biography, Swinburne "made himself 'very pleasant,' and the old quarrel was healed." In a letter to the American banker-poet E. C. Stedman, Swinburne wrote on April 4, 1882 (Gosse-Wise 1918 edition of collected letters), "I shall look out for your article on Mr. Lowell, whose acquaintance I had the pleasure of making not long since (a very real pleasure it was to me) . . . ."

The University

The university that "disgraced" itself was Oxford, and "the distinction conferred on Mr. Lowell" was the honorary degree of D.C.L., given to him in the spring of 1873. Hughes explained that by the "most distinguished living member" Swinburne meant

> . . . unquestionably [Benjamin] Jowett, the then Master of Balliol (Swinburne's college), and Professor of Greek, with whom the poet remained on very friendly terms in spite of the fact that his academic career ended in what the authorities could only look on as a debacle.

Hughes continued,

> As an Oxonian I have more than once since I came down felt an indignation no less strong than Swinburne's at the granting of honorary degrees to persons utterly unworthy to receive that distinction, and whose adoption by that University could do nothing but cheapen it . . . .

Swinburne's phrase "cash suit" puzzled Hughes. "And what is a 'cash suit'...?" he asked. "To me this makes no sense," he later wrote. "Perhaps it should be 'cast (i.e., cast off, discarded) suit': Swinburne's **t** often looks like **ts,** and sometimes like **h.**" I prefer, however, to think that the word is **cash,** for I find it, as a derivative of **cashmere,** defined in one of my dictionaries as "a fine and soft woolen dress-fabric, usually made in plain colors, also, a cotton-and-wool imitation of it."

When Swinburne wrote of Lowell's jest about Milton's blindness, he undoubtedly had in mind the sentence in the section on "Italy" in **Fireside Travels,** 1864, which reads, "But Milton is the only man who has got much poetry out of a cataract,--and that was a cataract in his eye."

The Emerson Case

The reference to Ralph Waldo Emerson as a "foul-minded & foul-mouthed old driveller" stems from the unsigned account of an interview with the philosopher of Concord which appeared in **Frank Leslie's Illustrated Newspaper** for January 3, 1874. Men have killed other men for much less than that which Emerson is quoted as having said about Swinburne. The story is that Swinburne gave Emerson a few direct opportunities to declare that he had been misquoted, but no reply was forthcoming. The second and last letter from Swinburne to Emerson, dated January 30, 1874, with a few variations and omissions, found its way into the New York **Daily Tribune** for February 25, 1874. It is interesting to note that Hayne, after having read it, on March 19 following wrote to John Greenleaf Whittier (**Whittier Correspondence,** etc., edited by John Albree, Salem, Massachusetts, 1911):

By the way, in regard to the latter [Emerson], did you read the foul abuse of him, published in the "N.Y. World" or "Tribune," this abuse being the substance of a communication from Swinburne? Please tell Mr. Emerson, that but one feeling of intense disgust, has greeted the appearance of that infamous letter, South, no less than North. Was ever such mean arrogance, such maudlin impudence, such colossal conceit obtruded before, upon the public view? The miserable scamp! Why his name ought to be spelt Swineburn! Were I a young man, a relative of Emerson's and near to this dog--I'm afraid I should be tempted to thrash him within an inch of his filthy life.

This letter might indicate that it was not until after March 1874 that the correspondence was commenced between Hayne and Swinburne.

The two Emerson poems that found favor with Swinburne as being exceptionally beautiful and powerful were "Threnody," written upon the death in 1842 of Emerson's five-year-old son, Waldo, and "Dirge," which commemorated the deaths of his brothers, Edward in 1834 and Charles in 1836.

The Poe Memorial

In July 1873, Hayne visited Poe's grave in Baltimore and found it unmarked and overgrown with weeds; when he returned to Copse Hill he wrote some lines "To Edgar Allan Poe" which were presently rejected by the editor of a publication to whom he sent them. He evidently wrote about Poe to Swinburne, for in the latter's letter dated at Holmwood, July 22, 1875 (Gosse-Wise edition, 1918), Swinburne thanked Hayne for the offer of an autograph of Poe, and congratulated him "on the honour of having been the first to set on foot the project of a monument to that wonderful, exquisite poet." It was time, Swinburne continued, "that America should do something to show public reverence for the only one (as yet) among her men of genius who has won not merely English but European fame."

On November 17, 1875, Poe's new grave was dedicated and Hugh Sisson's monument was unveiled. The occasion was rather a school-board-controlled affair and had been preceded by several years of uncertainties, misunderstandings, and financial difficulties. Among the speakers was Prof. Henry E. Shepherd, and it is significant that he referred to Swinburne as "one of the master-spirits of the new poetic school" who had accorded to Poe the preeminence among American poets. Hayne must have complained to Swinburne about the manner in which the ceremonies were conducted, and for that reason the English poet commented in the manner he did in his letter.

The late Hervey Allen, author of **Israfel, the Life and Times of Edgar Allan Poe,** when he read Swinburne's communication to Hayne, verified to me that there were

> ... curious fatalities, difficulties, and ineptitudes which led up to the carving of the figures on Poe's tomb before the memorial was finally placed in November 1875 in Westminster Churchyard, Baltimore. Maybe it was that Swinburne also had in mind the curious difficulties of moving Virginia Poe's bones to rest beside her husband. As I recollect, the exercises themselves at the Churchyard were dignified enough, but all of the tradition and difficulty that pursued Poe seemed to be inherited by those who tried to raise money and get the marble in place in the Churchyard.

Prof. Thomas Ollive Mabbott, one of the foremost literary scholars in this country, gave me his opinion regarding Swinburne's reference to the Poe ceremonies:

> All special students of Poe, even my humble self, tend to admire him. When we come to that memorial in Baltimore in 1875, we approach it with the idea it was a very lovely and deserved tribute to a great poet. We picture ourselves helping to carry a wreath. And when it comes to me, I have taken it very seriously that I have twice been permitted to deliver the annual oration at Westminster Church .... But when it comes to a purely historical question about the ceremonies of 1875, historical candour is necessary. Hayne and Swinburne were entirely justified in thinking the thing a

failure from a contemporary point of view, because no author then recognized as of first rank attended. Seventy years later [1946 is the date of Prof. Mabbott's comments], time has altered the whole thing--one prominent author did come; good old Walt Whitman; the modern tendency is to regard him and Poe as the two chief American poets--and the presence of Walt makes the ceremonies seem to us a perfect triumph of the Muses. What more can you ask? In 1877, however, the position of Walt was highly debatable; and the most intelligent contemporary, who admired Poe, was justified in the idea: "A memorial has been held for a great poet, to which no other real poet has come, except an eccentric fellow whose position is debated." Time has removed the debatable part, but Hayne could not know that.

Whitman had not been invited, but on his own initiative he went to Baltimore, though ill from paralysis, and consented to hobble up and sit silently on the platform.

Hayne was not present at the ceremonies and his name was not even mentioned among those responsible for the success of the project. But a couple of years later **Edgar Allan Poe: A Memorial Volume,** compiled by Sara Sigourney Rice (Baltimore, Maryland, 1877), was published and it contained a record of the ceremony proceedings; included among the three poetic tributes were the lines Hayne had written in 1873. Of the nineteen prose pieces, six were reproduced in facsimile--those by Tennyson, Whittier, Bryant, Longfellow, Holmes, and Swinburne, whose four-page, exquisitely written composition was placed immediately after the poet laureate's six-line contribution, which was the first in the section.

Swinburne's allusion to the Byron Memorial is explained in Gosse's biography:

In April 1874 he was greatly, and justly, incensed by being put on the Byron Memorial Committee without his consent having been asked.   This was particularly unfortunate in face of the excruciating prejudice against Byron in which he now indulged. The leader of this rather unlucky movement was Trelawney [sic], Shelley's friend, now in his eightieth year.   This picturesque buccaneer called on Swinburne to apologise, and was perfectly successful in soothing his outraged feelings.

The poet let his name remain as a member. The committee was not successful in unveiling a monument to Byron until 1880.

There is no comment on record by any of Swinburne's biographers regarding this letter written to Hayne seventy-five years ago, but when Sir Edmund Gosse, in his 1912 sketch, declared that the poet was "fierce in the defence of his prejudices" and that "the extravagance of his language was often beyond the reach of apology," he accurately described the only man who could have penned such a communication.

All the principals who were involved are dead, and in all likelihood they are enjoying their various degrees of immortality. It is enough for us who are still mortal to muse on the greatness and littleness of men, and to wonder whether tomorrow morning we should mail that letter we wrote tonight.

Postscript

Shortly after this piece was published in 1952, I learned that the original of Swinburne's envelope for this letter to Hayne was in a special collection preserved by a private institutional library. After seven years of honest negotiation and libidinous cajoling, I was finally able to get the empty envelope decatalogued, and I joyously acquired it. It is now with the letter where it belongs.

Manuscripts and the Biographer*

Ray Allen Billington

Biographers will always disagree on the value to their craft of personal manuscripts. "Personal papers are unessential," say some. "The importance of public people lies in the image that they project to the world, and this is revealed in their speeches and published writings." "Nonsense," answer others. "Public utterances can be explained only by understanding the psychology of the individuals, and this becomes clear only through a study of their letters and diaries."

During most of a lifetime as teacher and writer, I now confess shamefully, I adhered to the "manuscripts are unessential" school. During those years I wrote my share of books about history, contenting myself with the public documents and printed narratives, and avoiding the time-squandering task of digging through mountains of manuscripts to unearth a few new scraps of evidence. Fortunately I attempted no biographical studies while thus deluded, or the result would have been a sorry failure. For I am now convinced that any biography prepared without access to the private papers of the subject would be as empty as **Hamlet** without the prince of Denmark and as unsubstantial as Banquo's ghost.

This conviction was brought home to me by two unrelated experiences. One was reading a doctoral dissertation prepared by one of my students at Northwestern University last year. This able young candidate had chosen as his subject a minor Chicago politician and ward boss of the late-nineteenth century, knowing full well that the man's papers had been deliberately destroyed, and for very good reasons. The result was an excellent case study of a ward politician, as it was supposed to be, but so many questions were left unanswered that the reader was more tantalized than satisfied. Why had this man, a devoted father and husband possessing a captivating personality and a fine mind, resorted to such immoral tactics? How could a politician from a working-class background ruthlessly cheat working men, fleece the taxpayers, sell out his own Republican party, and sacrifice his most intimate friends without any apparent twinges of conscience? To read of such a man without the character clues that his personal papers would contain was to have the cake without the plum.

---

*Originally published in 1964.

A second opportunity to learn the error of my ways came when the manuscripts of Frederick Jackson Turner at the Henry E. Huntington Library were opened to scholars in January 1960. This was an event worth a few months at the Huntington, even though I honestly believed that I knew all that could be known about Turner. I had read all his published works and the larger quantity of books and articles written about him. I knew that he was an eminent historian, whose paper on "The Significance of the Frontier in American History," read at Chicago in 1893, had launched the whole frontier school of historical studies. I knew that he had taught at the University of Wisconsin until 1910, and at Harvard until his retirement allowed him to spend his last years at the Huntington Library. I knew that his conception of the frontier and the section had revitalized the study of United States history, stirred usually placid historians into a generation of bitter controversy, and influenced statesmen and politicians from the days of LaFollette Progressivism to those of the New Frontier. What more could be learned about his ideas?

Moreover, I believed myself well acquainted with the man. Sprinkled through the voluminous printed literature about Frederick Jackson Turner were reminiscences by friends and former students that pictured him as he appeared to his own generation. These formed a clear image: a man of medium height with penetrating eyes and a resonant voice; a man bursting with robust health whose love for the out-of-doors was reflected in a ruddy complexion and iron constitution; a retiringly modest man who was always ill at ease in the spotlight and eager to advance his friends at his own expense; a scholar so intrigued with frontier and sectional studies that other aspects of history were neglected; a product of the nineteenth century who was totally unaware of such modern approaches to the past as urban history, social history, and the history of ideas. This image, the one that Turner presented to the world, was unquestioningly accepted by his own generation and by all later students of historiography.

The Huntington Library Trove of Turner Manuscripts

The extent to which this image was a distortion slowly became clear as I spent happy months among the Turner papers at the Huntington Library. What a treasure trove I found there: nearly sixty boxes of correspondence, all properly arranged and indexed; a dozen manuscript volumes containing tributes to Turner or the records of some sustained effort such as the launching of the **Dictionary of American Biography**; thirty-four letter-size file drawers crammed with reading notes, clippings, and drafts of books, articles, and speeches; a battery of three-by-five drawers overflowing with reading notes and the cryptic notations that he used as a basis for dictation; and a welter of newspaper clippings, hand-drawn maps, photographs, lantern slides, and enough odds and ends to delight any magpie.

No merely quantitative description could reveal the riches in this great collection. It could not make clear, for example, the importance of the hundreds of letters Turner wrote to his fiancee, Caroline Mae Sherwood, during their two years of courtship. Young Fred was an ardent swain, and this series is virtually a day-by-day record of his life and thought during his most formative period.   Neither could a quantitative description reveal the significance of the half-dozen boxes of correspondence with Mrs. William Hooper, a trusted confidant after Turner's move to Harvard in 1910, with whom he discussed his friends, his politics, his students, and his professional ideas. Nor could any description convey an impression of the hours of tedious research that he lavished on the most trivial problems; for example, one whole file drawer is jammed with notes for a single article on "The Children of the Pioneers" that occupied twenty-five pages in the **Yale Review.**

Contradictions in the Public and Private Turner

These were exciting finds, but even more startling was the gradual realization, as I worked my way through his papers, that the public image of Frederick Jackson Turner was largely false. His friends, obviously, never knew the real man; indeed, Turner did not really know himself.   Only those thousands and thousands of pages of letters and manuscripts revealed him in all his strength and weakness; without them no true portrait was possible.

Turner's friends thought of him as a model of robust health; they never tired of commenting on his ruddy cheeks and his passion for out-of-door living. Yet his letters reveal that he was often unwell, and that he was plagued with a succession of illnesses that seriously handicapped his scholarly efforts.   An appendectomy in 1903 and a liver complaint in 1907 slowed his research, as did a painful bout with erysipelas in 1915. After 1917 he was seldom well, and his letters tell a tragic story of recurring bouts with illness: bronchitis, high blood pressure, repeated colds and influenza, a tonsilectomy, a disturbance of the middle ear, frequent attacks of vertigo, two excruciating bladder operations, and a deterioration of the heart that finally caused his death in 1932. What agonies that facade of good health concealed.

Turner's friends believed that he was shy and retiring, uncomfortable in the public eye, and modestly ready to aid others at the expense of his own ambitions. Actually, he was cursed with an over-developed ego that made him thirst for public acclaim and the plaudits of those about him.   His papers contain ample evidence of this need. Every favorable review of his books or articles was carefully saved with the name most favorable comments heavily underlined in red. He loved to sign his name; his clear signature, "Frederick J. Turner," appears helter-skelter on envelopes, manuscripts, filing boxes, everywhere. One cardboard filing box has been signed at least a dozen times. And he had sufficient self-assurance to believe that a biographer would someday rummage through his papers.   All manner of guideposts were carefully left to aid him: notes on the background of this episode or that, comments to explain certain events, diplomas and other honors tidily arranged for convenient use. This thirst for acclaim helps explain Turner's scholarship as well as his character, but it would never be suspected from his published works.

Turner's colleagues knew him as a dedicated teacher, so interested in his students that he neglected his own scholarly career to further theirs. That he was a capable teacher there can be no doubt, but his letters reveal that every hour in the classroom was distasteful to him, that he left each lecture in a state of near-exhaustion, and that he longed to retire long before such a step was financially feasible. Had Turner spent the time on writing that he did ciphering to determine when his income would let him retire so that he could write, he would have produced some of the books that he planned but never completed.

Most important of all, Turner was known by his friends and attacked by his critics for his professional narrowness. He has been branded a "monocausationist" who believed that American history could be understood solely by the study of frontier and sectional forces. Nothing could be further from the truth. His letters and notes reveal an amazing catholicity of interest; thirty-four file drawers of reading notes and manuscripts testify to his concern with every aspect of American history from Christopher Columbus to Herbert Hoover. Rather than being a monocausationist, Turner was so aware of the multiplicity of forces shaping human behavior that he could be more properly acclaimed as one of the pioneers in popularizing the concept of multiple causation.

"I do not," he once wrote his friend Carl Becker, "think of myself as primarily either a western historian, or a human geographer. I have stressed those two factors, because it seemed to me that they had been neglected." He explored every phase of the past for no other reason than to appease his own insatiable curiosity. Immigration history, which became popular only after his death, was a subject in which he encouraged his students to pioneer. "One cannot," he once wrote, "understand 'Anglo-Am[erican] Civilization' apart from the immigrant stocks." He saw social and intellectual history as "the new line of work for the future," and confessed that "if I were giving a general course in American history I should find time for some of the best in the literary, religious, and idealistic aspects, and enjoy them the most, too." The history of urbanization, a subject even now gaining popularity, intrigued him no less than frontier history; he once prepared notes for a paper on "The Significance of the City in American History," and he confessed to a friend that he anticipated an "urban reinterpretation of our history" in years to come. Turner would have felt as much at home at a meeting of the American Historical Association today as in 1910, when he served as president of that prestigious body.

Conclusion

Examples could be multiplied, but I hope that I have made my point. The image of Frederick Jackson Turner that emerges from his manuscripts differs markedly from that projected to the world: we can know him as a scholar of catholic interests who pioneered in the most modern aspects of historical investigation, as a frustrated individual plagued by illness and haunted by the desire for praise, as a writer racked by the inability to perpetuate on paper the brilliant concepts that stirred in his mind. This truer picture of one of America's great historians could never have been drawn had not the Henry E. Huntington Library made his manuscripts available to investigators.

The Value of the Manuscript to the Playwright*

Dore Schary

A writer who concerns himself with an historical or biographical enterprise is either foolhardy or without conscience if he attempts what he hopes will be a definitive work without fully consulting the record.

As a screenwriter I have been involved with three biographical subjects: first, the life and work of Father Flanagan, the founder of Boys Town; second, the life and accomplishments of Thomas Alva Edison; and third, the life of the South American liberator, Simon Bolivar. In all three instances I dug into the histories and records available in newspapers, files, and books--and with the first two scripts I had the advantage of sharing the personal reminiscences of people who knew Father Flanagan and Thomas Edison. I have also written a play about Franklin D. Roosevelt, which will be discussed later in some detail.

Someone has told us that people live their lives until they are forty and from that point on the rest of their work is a commentary on what they believe and stand for. It has also been said that an individual is composed of three people: what he thinks he is, what others believe him to be, and what he actually is.

The problem, then, is for the writer to determine how the character with whom he is involved lived his life and what he truly believed and stood for. Then he must sift through all the information available to him and reach a clear conclusion as to the kind of person he is dealing with, based on what his subject thought he was and what others believed him to be.

Some Problems With Personal Records

In many instances the writer will find personal records, perhaps in the form of autobiographies. I am a little suspicious of autobiographies. After studying the lives of many men, I am fairly well convinced that most conclusions successful people make about their lives are a result of hindsight. I am skeptical of sentences and paragraphs that begin with words such as "I have always believed that . . ." or "Never in my life have I . . ." or "I have always been guided by the fact that . . ." or "An early lesson which I have never forgotten is . . . ."

---

*Originally published in 1958.

It is closer to the truth to assume that the life of a vigorous, active person is full of emotions and drives of disparate coloration, and this disparity can be found in the various decisions that punctuate that person's life's work. There will be decisions made out of compassion or animus, decisions made out of careful reflection or out of temper, decisions made on a broad general plane and others on a highly personal level, decisions of selflessness and selfishness.

Some people leave behind them full records that enable the biographer or historian to place a close and correct evaluation on what they did and why. But no matter how full the record, there is an area we can never probe: it is the area of information that a person will never reveal to anyone and no one will ever be able to discover. We can guess at it, and reach opinions about it, but we will never know. We will never know of the ingrained fears, hidden ambitions, slights, and insecurities. Some of the facts we will know will be superficial and others may be significant. But the stream of consciousness and unconsciousness will, in most instances, never be probed or determined.

The complexities of a person's nature can never truly be analyzed. What we usually do is catch some facets and assume that this is the clear and hard matrix of that person. The conscientious worker must read avidly and digest thoroughly all manuscripts that pertain to the person on whose biography he is engaged. Often what appears to be a tangential piece of information can turn out to be an illuminating specific. For example, information that I read while doing the background work on my play about Franklin D. Roosevelt led me to the reasons why he so quickly learned to crawl after his illness.

Perspective Colors a Writer's View

It is true that most of us form our opinions about people based on some of our own personal drives, ambitions, and convictions. Woodrow Wilson is a saint to many and a stubborn charlatan to others. Harry Truman has already, in the minds of many, assumed the stature of a great president. To others he is a haberdasher who wound up in the wrong job. While he is still in office, Eisenhower, in the minds of some, has already been committed to the group of our weakest presidents, while to others he is a shining example of steadfastness, courage, and accomplishment. Many books have already been written about these three presidents. The newspaper files are full of accounts, columns, and editorials. You can find documentation for almost any point of view. This, of course, is particularly true in the field of politics. Students of Lincolniana know this to be so, and it is true that almost every great American has had somebody rake his back with the sharp prongs of distrust and harsh criticism. All our presidents have had the treatment--and that includes Washington, Jefferson (whose library, which he had offered to Congress in 1815, was viewed as a possible rabbit warren of subversion), Andrew Jackson, Grover Cleveland, Theodore Roosevelt, Calvin Coolidge, Hoover, and the others already mentioned.

It is the job of the thoroughly objective biographer or historian to search out the record and to ascertain the truth--but inevitably he, too, will be accused of finding only that truth for which he searches.

Truth, like beauty, is in the eyes of the beholder. In most cases everyone will agree on where a man was born, who his parents were (though in some instances there is even an argument about **that**), where he lived, and when he died (**how** he died may again be a source of discussion, as witness the case of President Harding).

Flanagan, Edison, and Bolivar

When I worked on the film **Boys Town,** I was more concerned with Boys Town as an institution than with the life of Father Flanagan, though I did have to learn something of his personality and his ambitions. The records were full of incidents at Boys Town that made for good cinema. It was a matter of selection and dramatic focus. Everybody agreed about the good instincts and morality of Father Flanagan, though I did run across some criticism of his early methods. But even these objectors agreed that what he did accomplish with Boys Town was something of credit to the human heart.

In the case of Thomas Alva Edison I was dealing with a rather uncomplicated personality. The man was an indefatigable worker and the long list of his efforts was staggering. There were few dramatic ebb tides and flood tides in his life. He made a great deal of money with one of his first gadgets, which was an improvement of the ticker tape, and from that time on, money was hardly a problem. But again there are detractors and critics who claim Edison was more of an innovator than inventor--more of a technician than a creator. I personally think that he was an incredible man with incredible skills. I leave the muckraking for someone else. Certainly he was a complete man, with moods and temper and salt and spice.

Simon Bolivar, too, was a man of extraordinary gifts. Volatile and energetic, a man obviously gifted, he was an expert horseman and one of the best fencers of his time. He had inexhaustible energy on the battlefield and in the bedroom. As a matter of fact, it is said that he could combine both of these latter talents in remarkable fashion. He was tempestuous and impetuous. He dreamed of a South American union modeled much after the United States of America, and it was the failure of this dream that lay bitter in his mind as he died in Santa Marguerita, rejected and almost forgotten by the countrymen whom he had released from bondage. It is granted by most that Bolivar was an epileptic, but this illness did not prevent him from winning stunning victories over trained Spanish armies. Defeated by the wild Llaneros during one war for independence, he later sought out their new leader and won them over to his side, using them to ensure final victory.

The historians of many South American republics have written and rewritten Bolivar's record. Numerous embarrassments must be accommodated. How can Colombia account for the fact that its first president, Santandar, once participated in an attempt to assassinate Bolivar? And while we call Bolivar "The Liberator of South America," Argentina recognizes as its liberator San Martin, who, however, gave up his medals and titles and retreated to Europe for reasons not completely clear to most historians. And there is O'Higgins of Chile.

It is true, too, that Bolivar stole the wife of a dentist named Saenz. Everybody knows this, but this, too, provides embarrassment. In some instances, pride of a dubious nature was expressed by ladies who proudly called their children Bolivar in the happy claim that the liberator was their father.

When I worked on the story of Bolivar's life I read and reread, but generally had to content myself with records that only verified the same old story. My conclusions had to be based finally on what I personally felt, which was that he was an exceptional man. Incidentally, there is in his life a wonderful mystery--the mystery of a meeting held at Guayaquil between Bolivar and San Martin. Each was proceeding with an army of liberation into the area now known as Peru. One of the two armies had to withdraw or the two forces might fight over which one had the right to do the liberating. The leaders spent some hours together in Guayaquil unattended by anyone. What was said, no one knows; neither man ever referred to what was said at this meeting. We only know that following it San Martin withdrew, ordered his forces to fall back, and then returned to Argentina, later to resign his post and travel to Europe. What happened in that room at Guayaquil is a good scene for a dramatist, but he had better not pretend to be a historian.

Sunrise at Campobello

My most difficult work as a biographer was an assignment I proposed to myself in February 1957. I determined to do a play on one phase of the life of a man whom I had never seen or met, but a man whose work I admired and whose personality I loved--Franklin Delano Roosevelt. The first time I voted for a presidential candidate, I voted for FDR. Ever since that time in 1932, I had admired him and supported him in every possible way. After his death I continued my interest in him and in his life by collecting everything written about him.

But it was not until last January, when I began to buckle down to the actual research for my play, **Sunrise at Campobello**, that I realized how much I was to learn by careful, intense study. Much had eluded me because of hurried reading.

I read everything I could find about the man. I pored through papers and memorabilia at the Hyde Park Library. I spent hours in conversations with his friends, his associates, members of his family.

Not all of what I learned could be included in **Sunrise at Campobello.** I had not known, for example, that in 1912, when Roosevelt was a member of the New York State Legislature, an Albany newspaperman had written him a letter which began, "My dear future Mr. President." The newspaperman was Louis Howe, who had been moved to write the letter by a thumping victory he had seen Roosevelt win over the Tammany forces in Albany.

Afterward, Howe served Roosevelt as a public relations counsel and went on to become his closest confidant. Only Harry Hopkins, who came along after Howe's death, was to come as close to FDR. Howe was a man of extraordinary perception, and to him Roosevelt's greatness and his potential destiny were clear even then, twenty years before he went to the White House.

The Onset of Roosevelt's Illness

I had not known, either, that Roosevelt's illness was not correctly diagnosed as polio for ten days after it struck him down. I think almost everyone is familiar with the circumstances: Roosevelt and his family had been sailing near Campobello Island, the family summer home in New Brunswick, Canada, when they saw a brushfire on shore. They went in and fought the fire. It was a tremendous exertion. After that, they went for a swim to cool off and then dogtrotted across a spit of land and finished their exercises with a plunge into the ice cold water of the Bay of Fundy. Then they all dogtrotted home.

When FDR arrived at the house, his bathing suit was still damp and he was beginning to feel chilly. However, instead of changing into dry clothing at once, he sat and talked with Eleanor, read through some mail that had just arrived, and glanced at some newspapers that had come in. He was uncomfortable and mentioned this fact to his wife. He said that he could not recall another swim that had not refreshed him. That night, paralysis came. The year was 1921, and he was thirty-nine.

The first diagnosis was a simple one: a heavy cold. Then a local doctor decided that a blood clot had formed on the spinal cord. Not until ten days later, when the family had called a Boston internist, Dr. Lovett, did FDR learn that he had what was then called "infantile paralysis" and what we know now as poliomyelitis.

During those ten days, of course, he had no treatment that might have mitigated the attack--except that Eleanor Roosevelt and Louis Howe had taken turns massaging his legs. They could think of nothing else to do. They worked tirelessly, but their efforts were futile. These events went into the play.

Roosevelt's Reactions to Polio

Polio is a brutal disease. At Warm Springs in Georgia, the great polio center FDR set up with his own funds and helped to support all his life, the kids say that polio will either make you or break you. It is particularly cruel to adults. (The tough little Warm Springs kids have a saying about that, too: "If you have to get polio, get it in the legs and get it before you're five.") Polio can take almost everything from an adult; it is easier if you get it young, so that, in a sense, you will not know what you are missing.

Polio **made** Franklin Roosevelt, though. He fought back. Later in life, when someone commented on his apparently bottomless reservoir of patience, he said, "If you'd spent a year trying to move your big toe, you'd be patient, too." His fabulous sense of timing, the envy of many an actor, derived from polio, too: when he made a move, it had to count. This was good material for the stage.

Basil O'Connor, the attorney who was to become Roosevelt's lieutenant in the fight against polio, first saw him flat on his back in the lobby of a Wall

Street office building. Coming to call on a friend, Roosevelt had tried to walk into the building on crutches. One of them had slipped and he had fallen, hard, as a polio victim nearly always does, his legs locked stiff in their braces. O'Connor happened to be the nearest of the people passing by and FDR looked up at him and said cheerfully, "Give us a hand, will you?" O'Connor helped him up and thus their friendship began.

Roosevelt had a sturdy build, but the tremendous musculature he knew in his prime, the wrestler's arms hanging from a fabulous span of shoulder, all this he built after the polio attack. He was proud of his strength. It was natural to depict this strength in the play, and I did.

Roosevelt never thought of himself as sick, and no one ever heard him use the term. He considered that his trouble was strictly mechanical, a sort of physical short circuit, and it was in that way that he explained it to his children. He did not want them to think of him as sick, and they have told me that they never did.

Everyone who has known a polio victim has learned to watch for two things: periods of apparently inexplicable irritation or depression, and obvious fear. Even the best-adjusted victims, the hardiest and the most courageous, show these two things, and Roosevelt was no exception.

When Roosevelt was depressed, he showed it, but he never allowed his self-discipline to relax to the point of conceding why he was depressed. He would make a fuss over a mistake that someone on the staff had made, an appointment overlooked or an error in a typed letter. He would blow off steam over some trifle that actually did not concern him at all. He was, just for a few seconds, shaking the iron bars that bound him. That gave me the opening for the second act.

One thing seemed to bring Roosevelt quickest to this state: he hated to have someone who was talking to him move about. Most people, bemused by the astounding force of FDR's personality, speedily forgot that he was chair-bound, and sometimes a visitor, in the enthusiasm of presenting an idea or a plan, would stride up and down the room. This always irritated Roosevelt, and he nearly always showed it. Again, he would never betray the real source of his annoyance. He would fasten on something else. This made for an effective theater scene.

As a child Franklin Roosevelt had not led quite so active a life as some of his cousins. He grew up a healthy, cheerful child, nonetheless. He did have a slight fear of fire, perhaps a little more than was normal, and after he was paralyzed it naturally increased. He sometimes practiced crawling on the floor to see how quickly he could reach a door or a window, and no one who has not seen a big man propelling himself across a room with his arms alone, his legs dragging and flopping behind him, can know how piteous and moving a sight it is. Mrs. Roosevelt told me that one of the first things the president did, the first night he was in the White House, was to work out a fire drill with Gus Gennerich. It involved FDR's crawling across his bedroom floor to a window, through which he could crawl out and drop himself to the ground through a canvas chute.

For the most part, though, Roosevelt ignored polio. Frances Perkins, who became his secretary of labor, said that it was not until 1932 that she heard him refer to his sickness in any but a light-hearted way. He told Miss Perkins that the days at Campobello, immediately after onset of the disease, had been for him "days of deep despair." I backdated that confession to 1923 in my play.

In 1924, when Roosevelt had had polio for three years, he resigned from his golf club, saying that he did not think he would be able to play again "for some time." When a man wrote an ill-tempered letter criticizing him for having remained seated at a banquet when the national anthem was being played, Roosevelt returned a calm and polite reply; he would have preferred to stand, he said, but unfortunately he could not.

Roosevelt might have been president before 1932. He could certainly have had the nomination before that time. He probably could have had it in 1924, when he was Al Smith's campaign manager. That was, of course, the year he made the famous "Happy Warrior" nominating speech for Smith. He walked to the rostrum that day, ten steps on crutches, a feat roughly equivalent to covering the same distance hand-over-hand hanging from parallel bars, but much harder, because in addition to moving his entire weight with his hands, he had to balance. I knew that had to be in the play.

The Family's Reaction to the Play

My first reading of the completed play was for Mrs. Roosevelt. I hardly need suggest the trepidation I felt as I approached this meeting in her New York home. My audience included, besides Mrs. Roosevelt, two of her sons (Franklin, Jr., and Jimmy), Jimmy's wife, and a friend of Mrs. Roosevelt, Lady Reading. Mrs. Roosevelt asked if she might make notes while I read. Naturally I agreed. Then I took a deep breath and began: "Act One, Scene One. The curtain rises . . . ."

As I was reading the opening description, I saw Mrs. Roosevelt make her first note. Scarcely a sentence later she made another. I could feel my throat going dry but I continued, drawing on some hidden well of strength. As I read on through the first act, there were no more notes. At the end of the act, I suggested a normal intermission, but Mrs. Roosevelt declined, and I went on through the remaining two acts to the end.

When I had finished, the room was quiet. No one said anything. We seemed to sit suspended in a vacuum. Then Mrs. Roosevelt spoke, "I don't presume to tell you anything about the play itself," she said, "because I know little or nothing about playwriting." A second's pause seemed like five minutes. "But," she went on, "this I do presume to tell you because on this I am an authority." She paused again. The vacuum was now inside me. But then she smiled, "It's quite remarkable. It sounds exactly like Franklin."

A dam seemed suddenly to break in my mind, a dam that had been holding back the cumulative anxiety through all those weeks of wondering how he sounded.

"It sounds exactly like Franklin."

I had caught the sound of the president's mother, she continued, and of Louis Howe. "And," she added, "I think it sounds like me, though I'm inclined to believe you flatter me." (I assured her I had not.)

Pleased and relieved, I asked Mrs. Roosevelt about the two notes she had made as I started reading. Mrs. Roosevelt had caught a mistake in stage setting in the first scene, set at Campobello. "We didn't have electric lights at Campobello," she told me. The second note was a matter of emphasis. In my reading, I had Roosevelt address his mother as **"Ma**-ma," placing the accent on the first syllable. "Franklin called his mother 'Ma-**ma,**'" she explained, stressing the final syllable much as the English do.

Jimmy suggested, "I don't think Pa wore crutches when he appeared at Madison Square Garden in 1924 to nominate Al Smith." I know what tricks memory can play and I had had the foresight to bring along some pictures and accounts, which proved that Roosevelt had used crutches at the Garden in 1924. Jimmy admitted that he must have confused this instance with 1928, when his father walked with two canes instead of crutches. They made a few other corrections and suggestions and gave me some useful additional information. But so far as the construction of the story and the attitudes of the characters were concerned, they offered no objections whatever.

A Fabricated Fairy Tale

In all the biographies of Franklin Roosevelt and in the autobiography of Mrs. Roosevelt, there comes a moment, several months after his illness, when Mrs. Roosevelt is reading a fairy tale to the children. In the midst of the story she suddenly begins to cry. She had endured everything with outward calm until then, but on this day the imposition of constant strain finally took its toll. When I first discussed the projected play with Mrs. Roosevelt at Hyde Park, I asked her what fairy tale she had been reading that night. She could not remember. I forgot to do anything more about this detail until I found myself writing the scene. I was in a hotel in London and I suddenly realized that I had not yet selected a fairy tale to use. I had no book of fairy tales with me. It was late at night and I could not buy or borrow one. So I made up a story to fill the gap, assuming that I would swap it later for one of the standard fairy tales. In this scene Mrs. Roosevelt picks up the tale from wherever she had left off the night before. All I wrote was a couple of paragraphs about a shoemaker and a pair of blue shoes. It had no beginning, no ending. But when I read it to Mrs. Roosevelt, she was so moved by it that she suggested I leave it in. So many people have liked it, too, that it has never been replaced.

This is the only thing in the play that is made up. All of the events are true, although many times I was tempted to invent a situation. I rejected these temptations. Time and events are constricted--the dialogue is invented--but the events are as they happened. The characters themselves rarely tempted me to improvisation, for they were superb dramatic characters to begin with. You could not invent a better character than Louis Howe, for instance, a short, homely man, a chain smoker, a sardonic, warm, smart, wry man who had had an absolute conviction that Roosevelt would be president since he had first seen him. Howe had a real flair for the theater, too. He wrote little birthday shows for Roosevelt and entertained him with improvisations in Dutch and Irish dialects.

As we came closer and closer to production of **Sunrise at Campobello,** I became impressed by one fact about the development of the play. For good or for bad, its construction had remained constant since it began to take shape in my mind. The last image in the play is the very first image I had when I first thought of doing it--Franklin D. Roosevelt, standing with his crutches in Madison Square Garden and facing his first large audience since his illness, as he places the name of the man he called "The Happy Warrior" in nomination for the presidency.

The play could not have been written without the large documentation that was available to me. To all the men and women who have recorded the life and times of FDR, I am eternally grateful. I know how valuable the manuscript is to the playwright, because I have been there and traveled the rich terrain.

Mrs. FRANKLIN D. ROOSEVELT
211 EAST 62nd STREET
NEW YORK 21, N. Y.

March 13, 1958

Dear Mr. Schary:

I have had many, many enthusiastic comments on "Sunrise at Campobello" but I thought it might interest you to read the following from Mr. Anthony Cucolo of Suffern, NY.

"It would be wonderful if this play were made into a move and you could see your way to continue from where the play ends until the end of the President's journey through life. By showing his entire life the movie would help many people, not only those who are handicapped, but also the younger generation, who could learn a great deal from his courage and determination to continue his achievements even after he was struck by infantile paralysis".

With my warm good wishes,

Very sincerely yours,

Eleanor Roosevelt

Illus. 1. Letter from Eleanor Roosevelt to the author concerning his play.

Notes About Contributors

THOMAS J. ACHESON, a charter member of the Manuscript Society, has completed several important sets of autographs.

FREDERICK B. ADAMS, JR., was for more than two decades director of the Pierpont Morgan Library in New York City.

THOMAS R. ADAMS was curator of rare books at the University of Pennsylvania Library when he participated in the panel discussion that is summarized here.

REGINALD ALLEN, a Life Fellow of the Pierpont Morgan Library, was business manager of the Metropolitan Opera Company at the time he wrote this article for **Manuscripts.** Previously he had been manager of the Philadelphia Orchestra.

GORDON T. BANKS was for many years head of the autographs department of Goodspeed's Bookshop, Boston. He was active in the affairs of the Manuscript Society for many years and once served as its president. He died in 1981.

MARY A. BENJAMIN is proprietor of the well-known dealership Walter R. Benjamin Autographs, Inc. She is author of **Autographs: A Key to Collecting** and **The Presidents: A Survey of Autograph Values,** as well as of numerous articles and monographs.

RAY ALLEN BILLINGTON, a distinguished author and lecturer in American history, has specialized in the history of America's westward expansion. He is the author of a number of historical textbooks; his biography of Frederick Jackson Turner won the Bancroft Prize in 1974.

WALTER HART BLUMENTHAL of Philadelphia was a collector of curiosa, including Lilliputian books and books with odd bindings. A popular lecturer on book and autograph collecting, he also wrote a number of books about books. He died in 1969.

CECIL K. BYRD served as librarian of Indiana University, Bloomington, from 1964 to 1972; he was president of the American University of Cairo from 1973 to 1977. In addition to having an interest in autographic material concerning Indiana, he is an authority on early printing in Southeast Asia.

GERALD CARSON is a prominent chronicler of American social history and a former director of the Manuscript Society. Among his many books are **The Social History of Bourbon, Cornflake Crusade,** and **The Dentist and the Empress** (Houghton Mifflin Co., forthcoming).

DAVID HERR COBLENZ, who died in 1981, was a Presbyterian minister who served as a director and president of the Manuscript Society. His collecting interests were chiefly in American history and he contributed many articles to **Manuscripts.**

WALTER N. EASTBURN was long active in the Manuscript Society, serving as both secretary and treasurer, and making frequent contributions to **Manuscripts.**

DOROTHY S. EATON, a charter member of the Manuscript Society, now lives in South Hadley, Massachusetts.   For many years she worked as a specialist on the Revolutionary and early presidential periods in the Division of Manuscripts, Library of Congress.

VINCENT L. EATON, a charter member of the Manuscript Society, was assistant chief of the Rare Books Division at the Library of Congress at the time his article was first published.   Later he was the Library's publications officer.   Singly and in collaboration with his wife, Dorothy, he wrote many historical articles. He died in 1962.

DR. JOSEPH E. FIELDS, a physician and noted collector, was a founder and the first president of the Manuscript Society. His special interests have been the Revolutionary period and the Signers of the Declaration of Independence. He has been a frequent contributor to **Manuscripts** and is the editor of **The Papers of Martha Washington** (forthcoming).

HARLEY L. FREEMAN was the dean of currency collectors at the time he wrote this article. A retired Cleveland, Ohio, business executive, he lived in Ormond Beach, Florida.

HERMAN HERST, JR., is one of the early members of the Manuscript Society. A professional philatelist, he is one of the increasing number of stamp people who, while following their own hobby, have shown considerable interest in collecting autographs.

DR. LEON HOWARD, the author of a number of literary biographies, was professor of English at the University of California at Los Angeles from 1950 to 1971. Among his published works is **Herman Melville: A Biography,** published in 1951.

DR. HAROLD M. HYMAN is the author of several volumes in American history, including **To Try Men's Souls: Loyalty Tests in American History** and **Stanton: The Life and Times of Lincoln's Secretary of War.** Dr. Hyman was for several years chairman of the history department at Rice University.

VICTOR JACOBS, a practicing lawyer for more than fifty years, has been collecting autographs and first editions for sixty years.

DR. HERBERT L. KLINGELHOFER, a Fellow of the Manuscript Society and a past president, was a coeditor of the Society's book, **Autographs and Manuscripts.** A private collector specializing in historical autographs, he has lectured on various aspects of autograph collecting and is the author of numerous articles.

ALFRED J. LIEBMANN was president of Schenley Research Institute when he wrote this article. A life-long student and collector, he presented his extensive collection of American historical documents related to distillation and alcoholic beverages to the New York Public Library. He has contributed a number of articles to **Manuscripts.**

DR. WILLIAM E. LINGELBACH, historian and student of Benjamin Franklin, was librarian in charge of the American Philosophical Society's great collection of Franklin's writings at the time this article was first published.

DR. LOUIS H. MANARIN, now the state archivist of Virginia, has written on a variety of Civil War topics. He is now researching Robert E. Lee's strategy and other aspects of the Civil War and Virginia history.

JOHN S. MAYFIELD, who started collecting books and autographs in 1923, was the author or editor of numerous publications on Mark Twain, Sidney Lanier, Lord Byron, Algernon Charles Swinburne, Vachel Lindsay, and others. A founding member of the Manuscript Society, he received the Society's Award of Distinction in 1982 for his efforts to promote appreciation and preservation of manuscripts. He died in 1983.

ROBERT F. METZDORF was curator of manuscripts at the Yale University Library at the time he participated in the panel discussion summarized here. For a number of years he was in charge of manuscripts and books at Parke Bernet. At the time of his death, he was a private appraiser.

BROADUS MITCHELL was a distinguished economist by profession, an historian by avocation. Among the books of which he was author or coauthor are **Postscripts to Economic History** and **Alexander Hamilton: The Revolutionary Years.**

PHILIP G. NORDELL was working on a history and checklist of American lotteries at the time he wrote this article.

VICTOR HUGO PALSITS was for a number of years the keeper of manuscripts and chief of the American History Division of the New York Public Library. Called the "dean of autograph collectors," he wrote on many historical subjects. He died in the 1950s.

DR. LAWRENCE CLARK POWELL was for many years chief librarian of the University of California, Los Angeles. He wrote a large number of books on literary subjects and topics of California interest, including **Robinson Jeffers: The Man and His Work, Islands of Books,** and **A Southwestern Century.**

RAY RAWLINS collected autographs for nearly fifty years. At the time of his death in 1980, he owned some 17,000 items. He was the author of **The Stein and Day Book of World Autographs.**

JOHN F. REED, a Fellow of the Manuscript Society, has collected historical manuscripts for more than thirty years. Director of the Valley Forge Historical Society, and trustee and historian of Freedoms Foundation at Valley Forge, he has written two books: **Campaign to Valley Forge** and **Valley Forge, Crucible of Victory.**

LAWRENCE B. ROMAINE was a dealer and expert in trade catalogues and business Americana when he wrote this article.

VIRGIL Y. RUSSELL was head of the social science department of Natrona County High School in Casper, Wyoming, when he wrote this article.

DORE SCHARY was a prominent motion picture producer and playwright. Among his many film credits are **Sunrise at Campobello** and **The Unsinkable Molly Brown.**

GEORGE F. SCHEER, a professional historian in North Carolina, first developed an interest in history as a schoolboy. He is the author of **Rebels and Redcoats,** a full-length portrait of the Revolutionary War soldier.

WILLIAM MARVIN SPENCER was chairman of the board of directors of the North American Car Corporation at the time he wrote this article. A student of Napoleon and his era, he has one of the finest private manuscript collections in this country.

NATHANIEL E. STEIN was a founder and subsequently a president of the Manuscript Society. He was active in promoting the use of manuscripts in scholarship and during his lifetime assembled a distinguished collection of autographs and Americana.

MADELEINE B. STERN, partner in the rare-books firm of Leona Rostenberg and Madeleine Stern, is the author of numerous books and articles on nineteenth-century Americana, biography, feminism, and publishing history, and coauthor with Leona Rostenberg of three books including **Old & Rare: Thirty Years in the Book Business.**

BOYD B. STUTLER, a former director of the Manuscript Society and managing editor of the **American Legion Magazine,** retired to his home in West Virginia in the 1950s to write a book on John Brown.

FOREST H. SWEET, a long-time dealer in Battle Creek, Michigan, was one of the foremost autograph authorities of his day. He died in the 1960s.

JOHN M. TAYLOR, a past president of the Manuscript Society, is a prominent collector and the author of several books, including one on presidential autographs, **From the White House Inkwell.** He has been a frequent contributor to **Manuscripts** and other periodicals.

DR. LAWRENCE S. THOMPSON was for many years director of libraries at the University of Kentucky, Lexington. In addition, he is the author of a number of books and articles relating to literature, the South, and the civil rights movement.   Among his books are **Folklore of the Chapel** and **The Kentucky Novel.**

JUSTIN G. TURNER, a renowned Lincoln scholar, was active in the Manuscript Society for many years. He was the author of **Mary Lincoln: Her Life and Letters,** as well as of numerous articles on the Civil War period.

A. W. YEATS, long a scholar of Kipling, was a member of the department of English at the University of Texas, Austin, at the time he wrote this article.